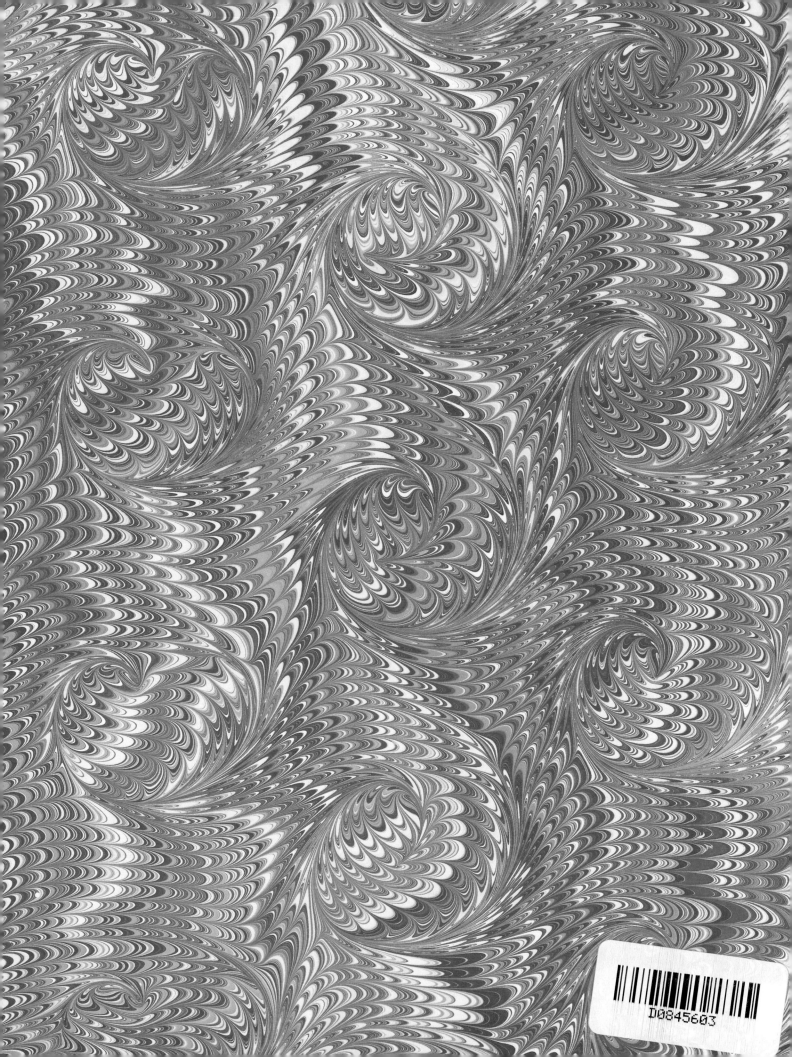

The Debden Warbirds
The Fourth Fighter Group in World War II

Frank E. Speer

Schiffer Military History
Atglen, PA

Colonel Donald J. M. Blakeslee

As Commanding Officer of the 4th Fighter Group in World War II, I was associated with many top scoring pilots. We had an aggressive Group which destroyed over 1,000 enemy aircraft, more than any other Fighter Group during the War. However, the top Aces could not have done this job alone. Their work was made possible by the combined effort of a team. A team of dedicated wingmen, crewmen, homer operators, radiomen, armorers, weathermen, intelligence personnel, clerks and others whose every working moment was committed to making each mission an unqualified success.

These auxiliary forces worked around the clock to keep our pilots flying and to make sure that they had every possible advantage when facing the Nazi pilots. The number of enemy planes destroyed speaks well for this team effort. Our pilots had the training, the skill and the daring. And they were supported by the best crews in the Air Force. This, combined with the P-51 Mustang, created a winning combination that was a scourge to the Luftwaffe.

The Debden Warbirds recalls the story as it happened. It describes in vivid detail the true experiences of a unified Fighter Group as it seeks out the enemy to protect the Bombers, and engages and fights the best the Luftwaffe has to offer. You can literally feel the danger as the Fighters attack the enemy Airdromes when the Luftwaffe chooses not to fight. The cost was high but the end was unconditional victory.

Frank Speer has done a remarkable job of detailing the essence of this great Fighter Group's dangerous operations and recording the innermost feelings of the men as they gnawed away at the Luftwaffe's best aerial defenses over Germany's heartland. The story is told as it happened by one who was there and participated. If you would like to feel how it was to be a part of this great team, this authentic book is a must for you!

Jeffrey L. Ethell

Across the more than 50 years since the end of World War II, the 4th Fighter Group has remained a subject of historical fascination for anyone with even a passing interest in the fighter battles over Europe. Though many books have been written about the 4th, including my own *Escort to Berlin* with Garry Fry, it seems the appetite for every possible bit of information on the Group has not abated.

Fortunately, Frank Speer has taken the next step in appeasing that appetite by documenting the 4th's history in this monumental work from an entirely new perspective. Using official records, some only recently uncovered, Frank takes the reader through life at Debden and the skies of Europe on a day by day basis. Personal accounts fill out the human side of the statistics and within a few pages the reader is lost among the men who made history. The reason the account comes alive is quite simple...Frank was there, flying his own P-51 Mustang. That makes it pretty easy to sort out fiction about the Debden Eagles in need of eliminating...besides, the fact is far more fascinating.

Rarely does a former fighter pilot develop a passion for historical accuracy, though those of us who write aviation history professionally continually look for such a person. With this book that passion takes flower, giving the generation that fought the most cataclysmic war of all time their due. The 4th Fighter Group was something special from the start and Frank Speer has added much to its luster. I heartily endorse this effort and can only hope that other men in other groups will take the same pains to uncover the real story of their rousing past when boys quickly lost their adolescence and won a war as men. *—Jeffrey L. Ethell, Aviation Writer*

Acknowledgments

Thanks to the many friends and members of the 4th Fighter Group who sent me dozens of personal accounts, combat records, documents, and photographs. Most of these contributors are acknowledged with their associated contributions throughout *The Debden Warbirds*.

I also extend my gratitude to those who helped in the compilation, assembly, and printing of *The Debden Warbirds*. Special thanks is indicated for:

James Doddy, whose magnificent painting, *Mission No. 14: The Edge of Compressibility*, inspired the cover design.

Natalie Golden, who drove me "up the wall" with her editing of my mistakes, grammar, and general abuse of the English language.

Don Allen for photos of his "Nose Art" reproductions, which were recently dedicated to the Air Force Museum in Dayton, Ohio.

Bruce Zigler for his hundreds of photos copied from various collections.

Jeffrey Ethell for his help, encouragement, and advice.

Don Blakeslee, not only for his insight and encouragement, but for his wartime leadership.

Bob Tullius for his inspiration and insistence on completion of *The Debden Warbirds*.

To Anne Kramer for her insistence of my use of *proper* English and attention to details.

To all, many thanks.

In addtion, there are four men who deserve special recognition for their hitherto unrecognized part in the preservation of the historical aspect of this and many other similar works.

Sgt Isadore Swerdel, who as base photographer captured the wartime feel of the members of the 4th Fighter Group and their Debden base in hundreds of candid photos, which have since been copied and recopied to such an extent that their origin has long since been lost.

Captain Ray Pool who, as Assistant Station Adjutant and Officers' Mess Officer, had the foresight to cull through and save many of the original photographs, and who has willingly offered them to me for use in this book.

Sgt Pinckney Lackey, for his rescue and preservation of the *Tower Diary*, which he has shared with me along with copies of the Squadron Diaries, letters, pictures, and personal accounts.

Lt. Robert Spencer, for saving and sharing with me the 334 and 336 Squadron Diaries.

Book Design by Ian Robertson.

Copyright © 1999 by Frank E. Speer.
Library of Congress Catalog Number: 98-87843

Printed in China.
ISBN: 0-7643-0725-8

We are interested in hearing from authors with book ideas on related topics.

Published by Schiffer Publishing Ltd.
4880 Lower Valley Road
Atglen, PA 19310
Phone: (610) 593-1777
FAX: (610) 593-2002
E-mail: Schifferbk@aol.com.
Visit our web site at: www.schifferbooks.com
Please write for a free catalog.
This book may be purchased from the publisher.
Please include $3.95 postage.
Try your bookstore first.

In Europe, Schiffer books are distributed by:
Bushwood Books
6 Marksbury Road
Kew Gardens
Surrey TW9 4JF
England
Phone: 44 (0)181 392-8585
FAX: 44 (0)181 392-9876
E-mail: Bushwd@aol.com.

Try your bookstore first.

CONTENTS

FOREWORD

This book details the lives of the Pilots and Enlisted Men of the Fourth Fighter Group, Eighth Air Force, in the European Theatre during WWII.

The chronology of the book is a compilation from the legible parts of the separate diaries of the three Squadrons—334, 335, and 336. In addition to the Squadron Diaries, I have used available parts of the Debden Tower Diary, and Official Combat Reports. All were previously classified "Secret."

The language of the diaries is often cryptic and written in present tense. In order to retain the urgency and "now" feeling of the work, this language is used as much as possible where it does not tend to confuse the reader.

Dozens of personal narratives and letters have been included in appropriate instances to present the unofficial nature of individual feelings and insights regarding the day-to-day operations.

There are thousands of pages involved in the background research and the diary entries, as well as the personal accounts. They, therefore, were edited to delete much of the extraneous information included therein.

INTRODUCTION

Brave men are not fearless. Brave men are ordinary men with normal fears who accomplish their dangerous duties or missions in spite of their fears. This is a story of such men.

They came in twos and threes, before the United States was officially involved in WWII. They came because of principle; they came because of alluring adventure; they came to help in a cause in which they believed; they came. One thing they all had in common was that they wanted to fly. They wanted to fly in spite of the fearsome odds stacked against them.

They left the safety of a seemingly peaceful country with no immediate fear of direct involvement in the war to go to the aid of a country that they believed to be desperately in need of any help they could give.

They came in spite of the possibility of dire consequences which they might face from their own country due to its policy of strict neutrality. They left homes and families and jobs; and they struck out to help where they knew they were needed. They went to a land where they spoke the same language—almost—but where many customs and practices were often quite different. They learned their vocation well and became Fighter Pilots in the Royal Canadian Air Force and the Royal Air Force.

They came together in what was to become known as the Eagle Squadrons. They flew Hurricanes and Spitfires. They flew in British Squadrons, in planes that were crewed by British and Canadian men and women. They wore British uniforms with British insignia; they ate British food and slept in British quarters. They were paid British allowances, and they earned British Decorations for their part in the Battle of Britain. To all intents they were British, but they came from Chicago, Duluth, Phoenix, and Queens, and they lived in Debden.

Then, on that fateful day, 7 December 1941, the attack on Pearl Harbor thrust the United States into the war.

This, then, is the continuing story of these valiant men and the crews that soon joined them.

1

Birth of the 4th Fighter Group

"On the occasion of the merging of the Eagle Squadrons with the U.S.A.A.C., I would like to thank them, through you, for all that they have done for the past two years. The RAF will never forget how the members of the Eagle Squadrons came spontaneously to this country, eager to help us in the critical weeks and months during and after the Battle of Britain."

Air Chief Marshal Sir Charles Portal in a message
to Major General Carl Spaatz, D.F.C., and D.S.C.

12 September 1942 -"Pursuant to the provisions of 320.2 Hq Eighth AF 8 Sept 1942, subject: Constitution and Activation of the Fourth Fighter Group, the following units having been constituted, are hereby activated with station at Bushey Hall, England. Personnel from the units indicated are assigned thereto."

With this terse statement of General Order No. 5, Headquarters VIII Fighter Command, dated 12 September 1942, the Fourth Fighter Group was born.

The Fourth, sired by the Eagle Squadrons of the RAF, commenced operations with five Officers and four Enlisted Men from the 1st Fighter Group of the Hq and Hq Sq 8th Fighter Command with a unit of Hq 4th Fighter Group and three Fighter Squadrons: 334, 335, and 336.

On that day, Col. Edward Wharton Anderson, a husky six-foot Floridian who began his flying career in 1928, was appointed Commanding Officer. He assumed command the same day. "With him came 2nd Lt. Eugene E. Grunow, Group Adjutant, and Pvt. Guzzard with D.S. Ibsley en route to join."

21 Sept - Lts. Kelley and Slater, 335 Squadron, on a Shipping Reconnaissance, encountered a large convoy escorted by flak ships. "Wild Bill" Kelley decided to make a pass on it. Lt. Slater was hit during the pass and called Lt. Kelley on the "R/T" (radio) to inform him that he was bailing out. As Slater attempted to climb, his kite nosed down and plunged into the sea. Lt. Slater became the first 4th Group Pilot killed in action.

24 Sept - The 335 Squadron received a contingent of flying Officers on "DS" (Detached Service) from the British Air Ministry, which included Major James Daley, from Amarillo, Texas, who assumed command of the 335 Squadron.

26 Sept - Eleven pilots of 336 Squadron were lost. They were KIA (killed in action) or became POWs (prisoners of war) in a tragic combination of bad weather, navigational error, German Fighters, and lack of fuel.

Twelve aircraft had become airborne. Lt. Beaty returned early due to a shortage of fuel and crash-landed in a field in Devon. From what he heard on the R/T (radio), he assumed the rest of the Squadron had landed in occupied territory. Later it was discovered that three, Ryerson, Neiville, and D.R. Smith, were buried at Brest. Jackson, Cook, Sperry, and Middleton were POWs. R.E. Smith was later returned to allied hands. Brettell, Baker, and Wright were listed as MIA (missing in action).

28 Sept - Major John F. Malone was assigned to the Group. The next day, the three famous Eagle Squadrons, 71st, 121st and 133rd were officially handed over to the USAAC with appropriate ceremony.

At 1200 hours, the Air Chief Marshal Sir W. Sholto Douglas, KCB, MC, DFC, who was accompanied by Major General Carl Spaatz, DFC, DSC, Air Marshal Edwards, RCAF, and Brigadier General Hunter, DFC, DSC, arrived at Debden. They were met at

Colonel Edward Wharton Anderson

Wing Commander R.M.B. Duke Wooley (*left*) and Colonel Chesley Peterson. Charles Konsler collection.

the Main gate by Group Captain J.R.A. Peel, DSO, and DFC, the station commander.

The guard of honor was supplied by the 2798th Squadron, RAF Regiment and was "beautifully" turned out. The Squadrons were assembled on the parade ground in review formation in this order:

71st Squadron	Major G.A. Daymond, DFC
121st Squadron	S/Ldr W.A. Williams, DFC
133rd Squadron	Major C.W. Mc Colpin

The Wing was under the command of W/C Flying R.M.B. Duke Woolley, DFC, and BAR. The band was from RAF Duxford. Echelon personnel, Station Headquarters, and WAAF personnel paraded.

Brigadier General Frank "Monk" Hunter and Air Chief Marshal Sir W. Sholto Douglas as the General Salute was played when the three Eagle Squadrons were handed over to the USAAC. Bruce Zigler collection.

The Wing Commander brought all to attention as the General Salute was played. The Squadrons were then inspected and an address was delivered by Air Chief Marshal Sir Douglas. In part, he said:

"We of Fighter Command deeply regret this parting. For in the course of the past 18 months, we have seen the stuff of which you are made, and we could not ask for better companions with whom to see this fight through to the finish.

It is with great personal regret that I today say 'Goodbye' to you whom it has been my privilege to command. You joined us readily and of your own free will when our need was greatest.

There are those of your number who are not here today—those sons of the United States who were first to give their lives for their country. We of the RAF, no less than yourselves, will always remember them with pride."

General Spaatz and General Hunter gave brief talks. At their conclusion, the Wing Commander gave the command: "Wing General Salute, Attention." The Stars and Stripes were hoisted by two U.S. Army Corporals and the band played, "The Star Spangled Banner." The three Squadrons then marched past the reviewing stand.

Lunch was served in the dining room for the three Squadrons. Seventy some members of the press were served a standing buffet in the billiard room, and the station staff was accommodated in the "Ladies' Room."

After lunch, the party proceeded to the vicinity of the watch office where three Spitfires with RAF markings and three with USAAF markings were drawn up. General Hunter then presented wings to the three Squadrons' Commanding Officers, signifying that their commands were now part of the USAAF.

In the transfer, the 71st Squadron, the first and most famous Eagle Squadron, became the 334th Fighter Squadron. The 71st had been sponsored by Col. Charles Sweeny, an American who founded the famous Lafayette Squadron of the Americans who flew with the French in the last war. The 71st was formed 8 August 1940. The Squadron's first CO (Commanding Officer) was Squadron Leader W.E.G. Taylor of Kansas, a U.S. Naval Air Service Officer who transferred to the RAF. Early personnel of the unit were pilots who had already volunteered with the RAF for service in British Squadrons. New volunteers crossed the border into Canada, and they were drafted to Britain as pilot officers. Immediately after the Squadron was formed, the King approved the design of the special Eagle badge. After a few months of training, the 71st became operational in March 1941. For several weeks, the Squadron did convoy patrol. On their first offensive flight over Calais, the unit claimed a "Probably Destroyed."

It was not until July 1941 that the Squadron saw its first major action. While escorting bombers attacking targets at Lille, the Squadron Leader got his first "kill," destroying a Me 109. Two other U.S. Pilots each destroyed one e/a (enemy aircraft). One of these pilots was G.A. Daymond, then a Pilot Officer, who later became Commanding Officer of the Squadron. Youngest of the Eagles, Daymond was 22 years old. He held the DFC and the BAR. In civilian life, he flew freight in Brazil, and he was once a Hollywood make-up expert. While leading the Squadron for its first time in August he destroyed an FW 190.

All the Eagles began flying Hurricanes, but they subsequently transferred to Spitfires.

On the date of transfer, the 334th Squadron had the following officer complement:

1 Major	G.A. Daymond
3 Captains	O.H. Coen
	R.S. Sprague
	S.A. Mauriello
4 1st Lieutenants	
21 2nd Lieutenants	

Among the early Pilots of the 4th Group were two Officers with unusual backgrounds, Mike Sobanski and Jim Goodson.

Mike Sobanski was a university student when Germany attacked Poland. He tried to join the Polish Air Force, which was practically non-existent and therefore had no need for pilots. He then joined the Polish Infantry, where he was seriously injured in a bombing raid. In the hospital, he nursed an overwhelming hatred for the Germans.

Still not recovered from his wounds, Mike made it to his father's home in Warsaw, arriving as the city was crumbling under German attack. He acquired a photocopy of his American birth certificate. By a circuitous route, he used this American birth certificate to make it to New York City. His aunt's husband, Harry Bruno, arranged to have Mike inducted into the Royal Canadian Air Force. He graduated as a Fighter Pilot, fought in the Battle of Britain, and transferred into the newly formed 4th Fighter Group.

James Goodson was in Paris as a student. He sensed that war was about to be declared on England by Germany, so he headed for home to the States aboard the *Athenia*. Shortly after departure from England, the *Athenia* became the first British ship to be sunk by a

Major Winslow M. "Mike" Sobanski, 334 Squadron C.O. Mike was seriously injured while serving in the Polish Infantry. He made his way to Canada where he was inducted into the Royal Canadian Air Force and then into the USAAC. Air Force Museum collection.

Major James A. Goodson - one of the top scoring "Aces" with 30 victories to his credit prior to becoming a German POW. George Anderson collection.

German "U" boat. Jim survived, and his rescuers returned him to England. Having had some flying experience, he immediately joined the RAF and became a Fighter Pilot. He probably was the first American to do so. He fought in the Battle of Britain and subsequently transferred into the 4th Fighter Group.

2 Oct 1942 - The three new Squadrons took part in their first major mission as the 4th Fighter Group. It was Circus (bomber escort mission) 221, to the Calais/Dunkirk area, led by W/C Duke Woolley. The 334th and 335th engaged a group of e/a at 24,000 feet. Captain Coen attacked a FW 190, which he destroyed. Lt. Anderson and Lt. Gene Fetrow each sent a FW 190 spinning earthward, while W/C Woolley and Lt. Clark shared in the destruction of another FW 190.

9 Oct - The three Squadrons, led by W/C Woolley, flew a Diversion to Lille/Fives locomotive works accompanied by three Flying Fortresses. Eight 190s were seen, but were too distant to be engaged. There were no casualties.

10 Oct - Major Daley led a Close Escort for 12 Boston bombers to Le Havre. No e/a were sighted.

17 Oct - The newly organized Ground staff and the Squadron staffs numbered 96 Officers and 11 Enlisted men.

20 Oct - Major Arthur S. Osborne joined the Group as Flight Surgeon.

Two Spitfires of 334 were on convoy patrol when Lt. Seaman, #2, experienced engine trouble. His plane was seen to explode, and he was killed as it crashed into the sea.

25 Oct - An Escort mission for 12 Boston bombers was aborted due to unfavorable weather.

26 Oct - 2nd Lts. Blanding, Boyles, Carpenter, Fetrow, and Halsey were commissioned 1st Lts.

4 Nov 1942 - The A.O.C., the Station Commander, and Colonel Anderson met Mrs. Eleanor Roosevelt, wife of the U.S. President. Mrs. Roosevelt inspected the guard of honor provided by the WAAF. She then spoke to all United States Pilots who were lined up near the watch office.

Mrs. Roosevelt next spoke to members of the British ground forces and witnessed a fly past of 12 Spitfires of 336 Squadron. After the fly past, she was a guest at tea in the Officers' Mess.

6 Nov - W/C Woolley led a mission to Caen A/D. No e/a were seen, and the Group returned in poor weather.

Mrs. Eleanor Roosevelt, wife of President F.D. Roosevelt, speaks to the 4th Group Pilots. Col. Edward Wharton Anderson - First Commanding Officer of the newly constituted 4th Fighter Group - is in the center. Bruce Zigler collection.

7 Nov - The Group by now had 100 Officers and 24 Enlisted Men.

8 Nov - W/C Woolley led a Circus to Lille/Fives locomotive works. E/a were encountered, but they broke away and the Group continued to escort.

9 Nov - W/C Woolley again led the group on a mission to LeHavre where 10/10 cloud cover limited action. No e/a were seen.

10 Nov - Again the mission was Le Havre with no e/a seen and no action.

11 Nov - Lt. Anderson led a Shipping Reconnaissance from Ostend to Knocke with no vessels sighted.

The Color hoisting was combined with an Armistice parade. Last post and reveille were sounded and special prayers were said by the Padre.

16 Nov - Lts. Anderson and Potter led an attack on an encampment, which was followed by a second attack led by Lts. Clark and Boock over St. Valery. Lt. Clark, attempting to avoid enemy flak, struck a tree top. He managed to maintain control and returned safely.

Lt. Jerik, a recent OCS (Officer Candidate School) graduate, was assigned to 335 Squadron as an Administrative Officer.

18 Nov - Lts. Anderson and McMinn attacked and blew up a railway engine.

19 Nov - While returning from a Rhubarb to France, Lt. Smolinsky, 335, with Lt. Willis, shot down a FW 190 over the English Channel. This was Lt. Smolinsky's first victory.

20 Nov - While on a Rhubarb (low level strafing sweep) into France, Lt. Evans, who was flying with Lt. Smolinsky, got a FS 156. The Jerry, on his way down after being hit, tried to ram Lt. Evans. Evans ducked out of that one, but he was hit by flak while coming out over the coast of France. Evans bailed out over the Channel just a few miles off the English coast and was picked up by rescue ships. Lt. Smolinsky covered Lt. Evans until Evans was picked up by the rescue vessel.

22 Nov - Captain Blakeslee from 336 Squadron was named Commanding Officer of 335 Squadron. He replaced Major Daley who had completed his tour and was returning to the States

26 Nov - A Shipping Recco was undertaken by Lts. Hopson and Boehle, but no enemy vessels were seen.

Captain Sprague crashed on a non-operational flight and was killed.

4 Dec 1942 - Group was airborne on a Rodeo (bomber escort with bombers as bait to draw up e/a), sweeping the enemy coast. E/a were sighted about 5,000 feet above the Group, but no contact was made.

Lt. Frank J. Smolinsky, 335 Squadron - Later KIA when his P-47 crashed in flames while taking off. Charles Konsler collection.

6 Dec - Group supported Forts on a raid to Lille/Fives loco works. Lt. Fetrow, 335, attacked and damaged one locomotive. He then shot down a Jerry while on his return from France.

8 Dec - Officers and Enlisted Men from Atcham were transferred to Debden.

11 Dec - Lts. Anderson and Beeson took off for a Rhubarb to Ghent/Bruges area. They attacked troop concentrations and targets of opportunity.

12 Dec - The first contingent of Enlisted Men arrived from the States, via Atcham. Until now, the Group, still flying Spitfires, was provided mechanical service by British personnel. These were mostly women of the British WAAFs. As American Enlisted Men arrived from the States, they had little or no training, and began to learn their technical specialties under the tutelage of the British WAAFs.

One of the exceptions to this program was Ervin Brill. He had been with the Group from the spring of 1942 as a part of the Eagle Squadron. "The American Pilots were still wearing RAF uniforms and flying Spitfires. I lived and worked with the RAF armament crew. They were teaching us how to take care of the armament on Spitfires. When the 4th Group was formed, I was there. I was there when the first mission was flown, and I was there when the last mission was flown."

As the American numbers grew and their expertise developed, they gradually assumed the maintenance duties. By 31 December, the maintenance staff took on a totally different aspect. These newly trained men were destined to become as fine a group of maintenance men as had ever been assembled. They were to be challenged by the quirks of the Spitfires, the P-47s, and the P-51s, and they were to master them all with competence and distinction.

The Group, led by Major Daymond, escorted Liberators to Romilly with no action.

14 Dec - Little flying - First snowfall. Pilots are restless. More EM arrived.

15 Dec - Lts. Anderson and Boock, on a Rhubarb to the Bruges/Ghent canal area, intercepted a JU 52 that was flying at a low level. They attacked the JU 52. As they closed, heavy flak was encountered, and the port wing of the JU 52 fell off. The plane went into a flat spin and crashed into the water.

20 Dec - A Diversion was flown to east of Dunkirk where many e/a were encountered well up-sun. No engagement took place.

21 Dec - Lts. Anderson and Boock carried out a Rhubarb to a camp under construction. They blew up a locomotive and damaged construction equipment.

Another group of Enlisted Men arrived from Atcham.

Among them was Pinckney Lackey from Lenoir, North Carolina. A typical recruit,"Pink" had walked resolutely into the recruiting office in Charlotte, where he was immediately enlisted and sent to Camp Croft for two days. He was pleased to be issued a set of wool uniforms, knowing this meant he would most likely be sent to the European Theatre.

On 21 September, "Pink" was sent to Miami Beach for Basic Training, which he completed in less than five weeks. He then was sent to another "resort," Atlantic City. There he fired rifles on a golf course and trained in Convention Hall, where normally Miss America was crowned. He pulled night guard duty. Where? The Boardwalk!

Next, he went to Hoboken to embark, with 950 other men, on the Queen Mary. There he spent Thanksgiving Day before disembarking in Scotland, only 67 days after entering the recruiting station in Charlotte, North Carolina.

After a short stay in Atchem, "Pink" ended up in Debden in time to celebrate Christmas, the first of three Christmases that he would spend in England. Here, he received his "on the job training" from the British technicians who were providing the ground support to the Group.

The Debden base was, to say the least, unusual. It contained both American and British service people. The planes were British Spitfires bearing American colors. The British Union Jack flew over the Base, which was still British. The not-too-pleasant daily diet included brussel sprouts and afternoon tea. "Pink" was, however, housed in comfortable brick living quarters and worked in substantial maintenance buildings.

The Pilots wore British gear and had Bitish ways. They enjoyed the nickname of the "Debden Eagles." Pinkney remarked,"Here I was, a 'Buck Private' in the USAAC, serving under the Union Jack, in essence an American in the RAF. Boy was I happy on 3 May when the Union Jack was lowered for the last time and the Stars and Stripes was raised for the first time. I was an American on an American Base with the American flag proudly flying over us!"

The 335 Squadron Intelligence Section soon assigned "Pink" as a clerk typist to keep squadron records and to provide Pilots with escape photos, maps, and escape kits. Pilots were not allowed to carry anything of a personal nature on their missions. "Pink," therefore, was responsible for gathering all the Pilots' personal belongings, such as pictures, wallets, and letters, before each mission. He provided them with escape articles and checked to see that they had their "dogtags," compasses, and a waterproof packet of 500 French franks. The money was to help with bribes, clothing, and/or transportation to Spain if shot down over France. Once in Spain, a Pilot could return to Debden in a very short time.

He also typed up the Pilots' Combat Reports (seven copies) and kept the Squadron Diary, which, incidently, included the results of the softball teams' efforts.

Pinkney obviously served well, since he rose from the rank of Private to that of Staff Sergeant by the time he was discharged from the service.

During this same period, Ed Nelson, who had been studying in an aircraft engine school, received his "Presidential Greetings." After the usual "bend over and spread your cheeks routine," he boarded a train to Camp Grant, at Rockford, Illinois. He there endured the usual testing, introduction to military life, shots, and training which was fondly referred to as "Basic Training."

Ed soon was assigned to an Aeronautics School and eventually wound up in Atlantic City. There he married his hometown girl friend on Labor Day weekend. He embarked shortly on the Queen Mary and arrived in Scotland on 30 November. A train ride delivered him to Atchem, where he was reassigned to Bovingham to learn about the new fighter, the P-47. Since the P-47s had not arrived, Ed busied himself with overhauling all the inoperative little one cylinder engines which powered the battery carts.

His next stop was Debden. He arrived with the rest of the group who had accompanied him on the Queen Mary. He was first assigned as Assistant Crew Chief to George Fite's Spitfire. When George returned to the U.S. for Pilot's training, Ed became Crew Chief on the P-47 flown by Gerald Montgomery, a position he was to hold until the end of the war.

Meanwhile, the 334th received a very talented man, who "Uncle Sam" had greeted and sent to Fort Hayes in Columbus, Ohio. Although he had completed a four-year major in art, the Army, in its infinite wisdom, determined that Don Allen was to become an Aviation Mechanic. Like others who arrived with him via the "Queen," he arrived in December and trained under British tutelage until the P-47s arrived. His first assignment, while still a Private, was to be Crew Chief on the P-47 shared by Lts. Steve Pisanos and Aubrey Stanhope.

At this time his talent took over, and he painted his first "nose art," a black panther, superimposed on a fleur-de-lis, on "his plane." The response was immediate and orders poured in. Don's extra job kept him busy in his spare time and also helped his finances at the rate of approximately $35 per illustration. His artwork eventually appeared on over thirty planes.

At the time, Don had no idea that his nose art would become widely recognized in aviation circles; be featured in many books and magazines; and would fifty years later be a featured display in the Air Force Museum in Dayton, Ohio.

25 Dec - Christmas Day. The Officers served in the Airmens' Mess. All approved. Later, after a sumptuous turkey dinner, the Officers all got drunk.

27 Dec - Sgt. Robinson became the first AWOL of 335. This was his first military offense.

LT. AUBREY STANHOPE
WD-O P-47 41-6233
335th Fighter Squadron
4th Fighter Group

Pvt Don Allen's first "nose art" on the P-47 he crewed for Lts. Steve Pissanos and Aubrey Stanhope. He eventually produced "nose art" for over 30 planes. Don Allen collection.

30 Dec - Anderson and Boock damaged a locomotive and box cars, one of which blew up, and debris from it damaged Lt. Anderson's plane. Both Pilots returned safely.

31 Dec - Monthly Personnel Report:

334 Squadron	34 Officer	258 Enlisted Men
335 Squadron	35 Officers	195 Enlisted Men

"Tomorrow is another year, we hope it bodes Hell for Hitler!"

1 Jan 1943 - No flying - snow. This was good, since everyone complained of severe headaches, the aftermath of too much celebrating. We had a good dinner with turkey and Christmas Pudding.

2 Jan - Convoy Patrol, no contact with "Hitlerats." Our 1st Sgt. has been accepted for OCS. "May God help him if he ever becomes an Adjutant."

4 Jan - Uneventful shipping patrol was flown. Lt. Ellington "Pranged one."

6 Jan - Bad weather, no flying. Sixty-five new men rolled in— Air Mechanics and Armorers.

7 Jan - Bad weather. One new "Corporal became a Private"; another Private was placed under arrest for insubordination. "There's hope for a better day tomorrow."

10 Jan - The hangar was filled as the personnel of the three Squadrons lined up in formation to view the presentation of the Air Medal to Lt. Anderson. It was for meritorious achievement in the destruction of a FW 190 over occupied Continental Europe on 2 October 1942.

12 Jan - Captain Blakeslee was appointed Major, which makes us mighty happy.

13 Jan - Two large scale actions, escorting bombers, were undertaken. No e/a were engaged. Papers state that 400 fighters took part in raids on this day, and it is the first big raid of 1943.

14 Jan - Lts. Anderson and Boock, while flying below 400 foot clouds in driving rain, crossed out to sea near Ostend. Two FW 190s attacked Lt. Anderson, who skidded violently with reduced throttle, causing the Huns to overshoot. Anderson then followed the e/a in a right turn, firing at 200 yards astern. The e/a skidded and crashed into the sea. The #2 evaded into the cloud.

Lt. Boock saw two more FW 190s approaching Lt. Anderson from astern. Boock turned into them firing a three-second burst, at which time the leading FW 190 climbed 150 feet and dived into the sea. Lt. Boock climbed rapidly into the cloud to avoid colliding with the #2. Emerging alone, Boock found himself over land and fired his remaining ammunition at a truck and a lorry full of enemy soldiers. He then returned to base and found his plane had two bullet holes in his port wingtip.

Lt. Carpenter nosed over while taxiing to 335 dispersal. The cause was laid to heavy morning rain, which softened the ground where the accident occurred. There was only minor damage to the prop.

15 Jan - Returning from a local flight, Lt. Harrington crash-landed at Watton because his motor cut out. He was uninjured. This was his first flight with 335. He had just been assigned from 334.

17 Jan - Several of the Pilots left for Atcham for training in the P-47s that were soon to replace the Spits which the Group had been flying.

20 Jan - The 335 Squadron was scrambled, but they missed the Jerries, 90 of which were reported up the Estuary. The 334 Squadron, with 24 Pilots on the roster, is now commanded by Major Gregory Daymond.

Lt. Boock, now flying with 335 Squadron, with a #2, led a Rhubarb to Le Pogue where the Squadron shot up several locomotives and enemy troops. He returned to base completely out of ammo.

Lt. Pisanos crashed on take-off. He wrecked the plane and was hospitalized for minor injuries. Probable cause—engine failure. Pilots and Mechanics now call him "Crash Pisanos."

21 Jan - The 335 and 336 Squadrons had Escort missions, but encountered no combat.

22 Jan - The 335th flew an Escort mission to St. Omer. Over the French coast, they were intercepted by FW 190s. A violent dog fight ensued. Lt. Boock destroyed a FW 190, which crashed into the sea. Boock's canopy and goggles were shot off in the fray. Lt. Anderson shot the belly out of a FW 190, and it went down in flames.

Lt. Grimm of 335 was last seen going down about five miles this side of Dunkirk. Operations claimed that he had bailed out and was seen in his dinghy just before dusk. His aircraft was knocked down by flak. (He was KIA).

Lt. Ross landed at Manston to refuel. He stated that he was jumped by at least eight to ten Jerries at different times and was lucky to get back. He said that, "the sky just seemed to be full of Jerries."

Lt. Fetrow's guns jammed just when he had a Jerry in his sights.

Maj. Oscar Coen and Lt. Joseph Matthews of 335 Squadron each downed one e/a.

26 Jan - The 336 flew a Ramrod to Bruges. Lt. Boock's plane, hit by flak over the coast of France, caught fire and fell into the Channel six miles from the coast. He was soon picked up by a naval vessel.

Because of the presence of FW 190s, Lts. Fetrow, Fink, Kelly, and France covered Lt. Boock until he was picked up. All the Pilots, of necessity, had to stop at Channel airdromes to refuel.

Lt. Boock's boots were all burned on the toes from the flames in the plane, and he reported that he had trouble with his dinghy. He also reported,"the water was very cold."

27 Jan - Lt. Boock returned today. He related that his controls went, and he bailed out when his boots started to melt from the fire. Boock asked Col. Anderson to write a letter of thanks to the crew of the vessel and to the others who extended aid. While in the water, he was worried because the vessel did not move for about ten minutes. Boock did not realize the reason for the delay was that they had to lift the anchor. He did try the R/T before he bailed, but it was out of commission. Lt. Kelly, flying over-head, called for other vessels when he saw that the one there was not moving. Lt. Boock got brandy after he was picked up. (Lucky Dog!)

29 Jan - Lt. Foster crash-landed a P-47 near Chipping Warden. He was not hurt, and the plane could be salvaged. Lt. Gover, attempting to take off, nosed over due to faulty brakes. He was uninjured, and the plane could be salvaged.

Lt. Ellington, on a test flight, made a forced landing at Castle Camp. A rag was found in the oil line. He returned by motor car and left the ship at Castle Camp, where a new motor was installed in the aircraft.

30 Jan - All ships grounded due to high winds. A B-17 landed at this field due to adverse weather conditions. The plane attracted a large crowd. It had more guns than a battleship. Major Blakeslee was asleep at the time, but he insisted that he see it before it took off.

Lt. Fetrow returned from Kings Cliffe, where the boys think the Eagle Squadron "is hot stuff." He states that the Pilots there, who have over 200 hours on P-47s, say that the P-47s are better than the Spits. Most Pilots, not in this Group, would give their eye teeth to be assigned here at Debden.

31 Jan - General Hunter presented ten of our Pilots with Air Medals:

Five were from 334, and the other five were from 335 and 336.

In early January, Jim Goodson, 336 Squadron, "Hoppy" Hopson, 334, and "Snuffy" Smith, 335, went on TDY to 8th Fighter Command Headquarters by orders of Col. Anderson. Their mission was to check out the P-47, the P-38, and a P-51 equipped with a Merlin engine. The P-51 had been modified by the RAF. They had removed the Allison engine and had replaced it with a Merlin. After subsequent tests, the P-51 was put into production.

After testing the planes, the three Pilots returned to Debden flying the first P-47s to be assigned to the Group.

During January, 24 Pilots of 334 completed Transition and Formation training on P-47s. The Squadron received 25 P-47s during this period.

"Every night, our mechanics talk 'barracks talk,' usually beginning with women and ending with heated discussions on how I keep my ship better than anyone else's."

To date, 334 Squadron has credits for 8 1/2 FW 190s Destroyed: Anderson, three; Coen, two; Clark, one-half; and Boock, three.

Squadron strength at the end of January was:

334 Squadron	39 Officers	248 Enlisted Men
335 Squadron	39 Officers	250 Enlisted Men

2

We Go American

1 Feb 1943 - The Officers' Mess changed from British to American rations. Farewell to sprouts, cabbage, kipper, and imitation sausage. The Officers went on American rations with a sigh of relief, but with a dubious look in their eyes over the increased cost. After the change, only Pilots could go to tea at 1630 hours.

2nd Lt. Mitchellweis, 336 Squadron, was killed flying a P-47. The plane caught fire at an altitude of about 5,000 feet. He bailed out, but his chute was not strapped on tight enough. He was jerked out of it by the force of the opening. The accident occurred near Duxford, and the plane was a total wreck.

The 335 Squadron diary says, "Lt. Mitchellweis of 336, flying with 334 in a P-47, crashed today and was killed. Didn't have oxygen with him and went up too high. Passed out, recovered in dive, but couldn't pull ship out. Tried to bail out, but wind pressure pulled chute off his back."

*****

Capt. Andrews and Lt. Powell of 336 were on Convoy Patrol when they sighted two FW 190s, but they were too distant to be engaged.

2 Feb - The 335th was on a Ramrod to St. Omer, but returned due to bad cloud conditions. No e/a sighted.

3 Feb - Cameras arrived for our P-47s. Each carries 50 feet of film with an exposure rate of one foot per second.

4 Feb - Major Blakeslee congratulated Lts. Halsey, Fetrow, Evans, and Kelly on having been promoted to Captain as of 28 Jan. Two Privates from 335 Sq.- AWOL today.

5 Feb - While returning from Flak Island, Capt. Kelly, who was leading a Roadstead (attack on enemy shipping or ports), spotted a large convoy. He climbed and immediately called for a hom-ing. Reporting to Ops, he dove on the convoy and received a direct hit by flak from a destroyer. Although the other Pilots urged him to bail out, he tried to make the Dutch coast. He couldn't make the coast, so he turned to fall near the convoy.

Kelly tried to roll his ship on its back, but only made it half way. He plunged into the drink half-way out of the cockpit, apparently unable to get clear. The plane sank immediately and nothing came up. The plane was in flames when it hit the water. The Jerries kept firing at him the entire time until he went in, even though it was clear that he was out of the scrap and fighting for his life.

Kelly probably could have saved his life if he had bailed out immediately when hit. "Old Kelly wasn't in the groove for the last couple of weeks. Didn't seem to be in the mood for this trip."

The Group raked the convoy with machine gun and cannon fire. The 11th Group was immediately sent out to get the convoy.

Tonight, the Squadron mourns for one of its best Pilots. Kelly went down fighting to the very end.

Capt. William "Wild Bill" Kelley. A former Eagle, he was KIA attacking a convoy. Zigler collection.

7 Feb - Weather very bad—snowing. Squadron 335 was supposed to get Spit 9's until the Squadron could convert to P-47s. Flyers were definitely against the P-47. Pilots already on them called themselves the "Suicide Squadron."

8 Feb - No flying—terrible weather. Our Intelligence Office was moved from Major Daymond's office to the B Dispersal on the line.

The order of "Confused Kati-pillers" was founded on this date. The members were Peterson, Fetrow, Evans, Boock, and Anderson.

9 Feb - 2nd Lt. Conklin started Rifle School to train about 25 men each week until all members of 334 Squadron have taken the course. The course included: cleaning the rifle, lectures on the use of the sling, firing positions, trigger squeeze, and firing from each position. A prize of ten shillings was offered for the highest score in each group.

11 Feb - Lt. Ross did local flying in the Tiger Moth. The kite got away from him in a wind gust and smashed into a garage.

12 Feb - Captain Evans and Lt. Willis stood night readiness.

Girls from MOR (Main Operations Room) were here on a visit to see what makes us tick. "Likkee!"

Consensus of opinion seems to be that a P-51 is better than a P-47.

"Peace reigns over the Administrative front."

13 Feb - All Pilots were given an Aircraft Recognition Test in the projection room.

2nd Lt. Jap Powell of 336 was KIA when his engine quit while he was on convoy patrol. He bailed out, but he was dead when picked up.

The 335 Squadron rumor is that we will not do any more shows. We will just do convoys. We haven't done a show since 5 February.

Girls from MOR were here again today. They are being shown around by Lt. Gowan, Intelligence Officer. Major Blakeslee was also present on this visit.

Information Board quotes our 335 Squadron as "Best One in England."

The 335 Squadron has lost 15 Pilots since it was formed.

14 Feb - Main Operations Room girls were up again to look at our dispersal. Sgt Hubbard explained the Spitfire's controls to them.

It was rumored that this base was to become a bomber base, and we were to leave.

15 Feb - Gales expected tonight. Snow in the next 24 hours.

The Enlisted Mens' Mess changed from British to American rations. They were as glad as the Officers to say farewell to "hot" milk, imitation sausages, mushy sprouts, mutton, and tea. The boys had their first breakfast, which consisted of: a dipper of tomato juice (this was the first taste of fruit or vegetable juice for many of the boys in over two months), powdered eggs, oatmeal with cold milk, plenty of sugar, and coffee.

Regarding mutton: the *Stars and Stripes* had this to say in the February 23 issue,

"I find that if lamb is cut and soaked in salt water overnight, the water makes an excellent cleanser for garbage cans. The lamb is then placed on a board, seasoned with salt and well heated in a warm oven. Then take the lamb, toss it in the nearest can, garbage GI 32 gallon, and serve the board."

Gerald Hunter, 336 Squadron Armament, found the switch to American Mess a welcome change. Gerald had grown up on a farm in central Illinois, and he knew the delights of good food. After several months of eating British rations, he was disenchanted to say the least. One side of the Debden Base, near the Mess, happened to be adjacent to a farm. The Base was separated from the farm by a barbed wire fence. On the other side of the fence was a herd of beautiful Holstein cows.

The Mess Sergeant, named Gilbreath, constantly griped about the inadequacies of trying to cook with powdered milk. He bragged about the possibilities of cooking if he only had fresh milk with which to cook. Hunter conceived of an idea. Hunter approached Gilbreath with the idea that if the Sgt would give up some of his supply of British origin, barely edible rolled oats, he possibly could solve the Sergeant's problem.

The oats were poorly milled and the sharp hulls that remained on them made them uncomfortable to eat. Gerald knew, however, that this would not be objectionable to a cow. He suggested that Gilbreath take some of the oats in a bucket and hold the bucket over the fence for one of the cows to eat. Meanwhile, Gerald would climb through the fence and milk the cow while she was eating.

The cow was extremely cooperative, and on the first try yielded about three gallons of milk. The Sgt was delighted, and in celebration even baked a cake to show off his culinary talent.

Every day at 1530 hrs, they repeated the process. Hunter began to be concerned that if this were to continue, the farmer might sell the cow, since it would appear that she was no longer producing to her capability. The two conspirators then decided to start using a second cow, but unfortunately their secret had become so public and had attracted such a group of spectators that the base health authorities put out a "cease and desist" order on the basis of "an unsanitary milk collection process." This order was reinforced with the threat of removal of stripes and/or the preferring of charges. Reluctantly, they gave up the project and went back to the drudgery of the powdered milk route.

*****

S/Sgt John Beyrooty, 336 Admin. Specialist Eng., also had his problems with the British Mess. He had always been a lover of olives. Since none were included in the menu, he sent an appeal to his home for a "Care Package" containing olives. In due course, a package arrived. It contained a large jar of olives. John, by now completely starved for olives, proceeded to down the whole jar in one sitting.

John became so sick that he went on sick call, and they immediately hospitalized him. While there, he speedily recovered, but the doctor insisted that he must have his tonsils removed before discharge from the hospital. He was incarcerated for ten days for this operation. During that time, he developed a need for ice cream. The Mess Sgt miraculously provided a daily portion of ice cream for John for the remainder of his stay in the hospital. Conjecture had it that the cooperative cow, with the help of Hunter and the Mess Sgt, had a bit to do with this largesse.

*****

M.O.R. girls visited again today. They were shown around by Lt. Cowan. Lts. Merritt and Pisanos explained the controls of the Spits to the visitors.

16 Feb - Ops. scrambled two Sections. It turned out that they were friendly kites over Cromar.

Lts. France, Boehle, and Beeson walked across the field and the runways to the Dispersal. Duty Pilot called Major Blakeslee about it, and Blakeslee gave them hell.

MOR girls were down to look things over again.

18 Feb - A British Mosquito bomber crashed as it was landing on the N/S runway. Trouble with the right engine caused the plane to veer to the right off the runway. The bomber flew over one P-47, causing slight damage. It struck the next plane with its landing gear, tearing a hole over two feet wide in the tail and damaging the canopy. It then crashed into the gun turret and caught its tail on the south end of our A Dispersal building. The tail was pulled off, and the plane stopped on the east side of the building. Both wings were off, as well as both props and one motor. The wreckage was strewn all over the place.

The dispersal wall was badly damaged, but no U.S. personnel were injured. The British crew of two escaped miraculously with only slight injuries. Because the bomber carried four 500-lb fused bombs, the area was cleared until the fuses were removed.

"The code-word 'Woodcock' was introduced. It was an exercise between land based aircraft which are to protect the ships and a land based aircraft which is to attack the ships."

Warning came through from Ops to expect long range bomber activity from Jerry today.

New Insignia Markings

19 Feb - About noon, a fourth bomb was located under the wreckage of the Mosquito. All personnel in the area were removed for two hours until the fuse was removed.

Major Blakeslee led a Ramrod to St. Omer. No e/a were sighted, and no action was reported.

The 335 Squadron was the first off with Lt. Willis and Capt. Fetrow making grand stand takeoffs. The Squadron circled the field and was formed before it was half way around. The Squadron came right over the field in a beautiful formation and headed straight for France. "They sure looked swell and a great group of well trained Pilots. The 335 stood out over 336 head and shoulders."

20 Feb - "Weather very bad, soup very thick. Now we know why Chamberlain always carries an umbrella."

Since the P-47s sometimes have been mistaken for FW 190s, effective this date, the following markings will be painted on them:

1. leading edge of engine cowl with white band 24" wide
2. regulation star insignia on upper surface of left wing
3. star insignia on lower side of each wing 59" in diameter; center line of star 6' 10" from wing tip
4. regulation star insignia on each side of fuselage 36" diameter; center line of star 20" to rear of intercooler door; 2" yellow band around star
5. white stripe 12 inches wide parallel with longitudinal axis on each side of fin and rudder from leading edge of fin to trailing edge of rudder; center line of stripe 26" from top of fin
6. white stripe 18 inches wide parallel with longitudinal axis on upper and lower surfaces of both stabilizers; elevators from leading edge of stabilizer to trailing edge of rudder; center line of stripes 33" from stabilizer tip

"The Pilots are getting uneasy over the several accidents that have occurred. Quite a few glycol leaks, a rag in the oil pan, and claims of iron filings in the oil have been reported."

22 Feb - "Weather stinks. Impossible to fly. A lovely day—in Chicago."

Some of our "boys" were issued Thompson submachine guns. Lt. Conklin started a course of instruction on these guns. About 25 men took the first course, consisting of field stripping, use of sling, firing positions, and firing on the range.

"Even the ducks are squawking about the weather now."

Lts. Pierce McKennon, Ward Wortman, and James Dye were assigned to 335 Squadron; all 2nd Lts., none of them have seen combat.

1st Sgt. McIntyre and Lt. Beeson started feuding. Lt. Beeson started thus: *"There was a 1st Sgt. named Mac, with a mind as sharp as a tack. He'd send them to school, and then as a rule, give them guard before they got back."* To which the Top Kick replied: *"Lts. Beeson, Lanning, and Gale, do nothing but moan, gripe, and wail; They sweat out promotions, raise a hell of a commotion, if I put one of their men on detail."*

23 Feb - The feud continued—Ye Historian wrote one as follows: *"A Top Kick named McIntyre, arouses everyones' ire. If his smile we won't mar, we must give a cigar, if we don't our predicament's dire."*

Another from an unknown source: *"There once was a Top Kick named Mac, whose heart, like his stogie, was black. Every guy that he'd detail, his soul he'd retail. Yes men—he should be shot in the back."*

24 Feb - Two German aircraft, a HE 111 and a ME 110, not to be shot down, arrived at this station for a two day inspection. These were part of the RAFs "Flying Circus" of captured Nazi planes and equipment. All personnel, combat crews in particular, were urged to look the craft over.

The Me 110 still bore its German tires carrying the name "Continental" and marked in English, "Made in Germany." The Heinkel was all patched up where it had been hit. It was riddled with bullet holes. Both ships seemed well built and very formidable in the air. "Jerry has good kites, that's something no one can deny."

Fourth Group personnel inspecting a captured German HE-111. Zigler collection.

In the afternoon, both aircraft went up to practice combat exercises with the P-47s.

25 Feb - More of our Pilots were honored with decorations. Assembled on the parade ground, many of us saw for the first time "Old Glory" carried as colors. Added to the occasion was a U.S. military band.

The Feb 26 *Stars and Stripes* commented:

"Sixty American Pilots, ex-members of the Eagle Squadron, today received from Air Marshal Sir Trafford Leigh-Mallory, Commander-in-Chief of the RAF Fighter Command, Medallions in appreciation of their service to the RAF. Eight Air Medals and four Oak Leaf Clusters also were awarded to Fighter Pilots."

The Pilots were addressed by their Commanding General Frank O.D. Hunter, who told them what the ceremony meant to him. He praised them for having become a fully trained nucleus of operational Pilots around which he had built "our fighting machine." "You have given the USAAC everything the RAF has learned in 3 years of fighting the Huns in preparation to finally annihilating them."

During the proceedings, General Hunter presented the **American DFC** to RAF Wing Commander Raymond Myles B. Duke-Wooley, who for two months had led an American Fighter Group.

The sky was full of big bombers on their way to enemy territory. They had been droning over for two hours. "Old Jerry is going to get a good headache tonight."

26 Feb - Starting today about 50 men, in two groups per day, were required to go through the gas chamber. The course was conducted by Sgt. Haray. Before entering the chamber, all masks were carefully tested.

Morning and afternoon were taken up with three missions escorting bombers, which were attacking the docks and an armed raider in the harbor of Dunkirk. Thousands of pounds of bombs were dropped, and the intense flak damaged many bombers, but all returned safely.

27 Feb - Lt. Gover, flying a P-47 above 20,000 feet, reported that his engine started throwing oil and caught on fire. He dove the plane, which put out the fire, cut his engine, and came in on a dead stick. Although he attempted to bail out, he landed hard with little damage to the undercarriage. "More power to a swell pilot for proving that a P-47 can be safely landed on a dead stick."

Another Roadstead against Dunkirk found the raider gone, but the bombs were dropped. All planes returned intact.

Due to continuing problems in landing after shows, Major Blakeslee threatened to have 335 Squadron practice takeoffs and landings.

28 Feb - The 334 Squadron finished its 45th day of non-operational flying since 14 January 1943. Although they were sorry to

Captain Leroy Gover 336 Sq. proved a P-47 could be landed dead-stick. Much decorated, he flew 257 Combat Sorties in Fighters. Konsler collection.

say farewell to the Spitfires which had carried them over enemy territory so often, and although they naturally disliked changing from known to new aircraft, our Pilots were hopeful that the new Thunderbolts would give them an even better weapon. This date marked the approximate completion of their 30 hours of training. We were all on our toes, anxiously awaiting the first day our boys could go operational. Many besides our Group will be watching them that day.

Squadron strength report:

| 334 Squadron | Officers 40 | Enlisted Men 246 |
| 335 Squadron | Officers 41 | Enlisted Men 250 |

Major Blakeslee had completed 119 sorties to date.

"The air offensive, which many considered the second front, has really driven a few shots home the latter part of February. Germany, Italy, and occupied Europe were bombed continually for 72 hours the last few days of February."

Rumors of P-47s for 335 Squadron filled the air.

A Squadron party was planned for 17 March, St. Patrick's Day, and many of the boys were already staggering around in anticipation.

1 Mar 1943 - "The weather is definitely better, and the field is now dry enough to taxi across it safely."

Lt. Pisanos, 50 feet in the air with wheels up on takeoff, lost power, crashed, and nosed over when his wheels buckled. While being towed to the hangar, the cart on which it was being towed broke down, and the plane again crashed to the ground.

The 336 Squadron spent most of the day on Convoy patrol. They were rapidly moving to Martlesham. Operations, Ground Crews, and Pilots had moved.

2 Mar - A formation of our P-47s took off for a tour of surrounding dromes in order to better acquaint their personnel in recognition of our new planes.

The 334 Commanding Officer, Major Daymond, left for the States. He was replaced by Major Oscar Coen.

Capt. Evans, 335 C.O., also left for three months' duty in Washington. We have lost one of our steadiest men.

"We had a gang of promotions: it may be said with satisfaction that Pfc (should be Staff) Schubert made Corporal. We made one M/Sgt, four T/Sgts, two S/Sgts, and 52 Cpls. Many GIs were a lot happier."

3 Mar - We had a complete black-out, and flak and bombing were clearly heard. It was a raid on London and Cambridge by an estimated 60 e/a.

Many of the boys were proudly sporting their new stripes.

4 Mar - Lt. Stanhope undershot while landing his P-47, and it was badly damaged when muddy ground caused his wheels to collapse. He was unhurt.

More Convoy Patrol—No incidents.

8 Mar - Twenty-five Spitfires of 335 and 336 Squadrons were airborne on a Ramrod to Rouen. Col. Peterson developed engine trouble and had to return. This left Major Blakeslee in command. The Group warded off an attack on the bombers by seven FW 190s, but they did not engage. Many planes had to land at forward bases to refuel. "With all our sweeps, France should be a tidy place soon."

9 Mar - An uneventful Rodeo was flown by 335 and 336 Squadrons. For the past couple of months, nothing much has happened, but work has continued with Flights in readiness. There have been Convoy Patrols and uneventful Sweeps; however, things are picking up. "That's what the street cleaner answered when asked how business was."

10 Mar - Major Blakeslee led 12 Spitfires of 335 on an uneventful Rodeo to St. Omer. Meanwhile, Lt. Col. Peterson led 334 on the first operational flight in P-47s to Ostend. All returned from an uneventful mission, but it was an important day because our Thunderbolts attacked Flak Island.

Although 334 Squadron was operational with P-47s, 335 still received Spits for replacements.

12 Mar - There was an uneventful morning mission, after which 335 and 336 Squadrons, in Spits led by Col. Peterson, engaged two FW 190s. They damaged one.

Lt. H.S. Anderson bailed out near St. Omer. "He was flying 'tail-end Charlie' and lagged too far behind." (He became a POW).

13 Mar - The 334 Squadron had not been flying missions in March due to so many Pilots temporarily being assigned to 335 and 336 Squadrons. The 334 was not to fly missions until their Pilots returned. Throughout the month, 335 and 336 had been flying Convoy Patrol, Standing Patrol, and Readiness almost daily.

The 335 took off for a Sweep and Escort mission. The bombers missed the rendezvous point by about 50 miles; "a pretty poor show for the Forts."

15 Mar - Two Sections returned from Readiness after dark. They ran into trouble since they had no knowledge that the runway had been changed, and the flare path had not been lighted. "The Duty Pilot and Ops both were definitely off the beam tonight."

Major Blakeslee reported that,"tomorrow was to be the last day for 335 to be operational in Spitfires." All 334 Pilots were to return to their own Squadron. The 335 Pilots, flying with 334, would return to their own Squadron with their own new P-47s. Each Pilot would then have assigned to him two Pilots as students. The 335 Pilots would have the responsibility for training the student Pilots in flying the P-47s.

17 March - One of the Red Cross's 48 Clubmobiles arrived today. Free coffee, doughnuts, and a piece of chocolate were served to all comers.

Nine of 334's Pilots were returned to their Squadron.

The 50 calibre machine gun, installed outside of Dispersal on 10 March, became operational and had a gun crew standing by.

The Squadron party was a huge success. All the men got just a little tight, and there were a few funny moments. For example, S/Sgt Quinn tried to get one of his two London "Beauties" to sing a song and failed in the attempt. Lt. Jensen grabbed the best looker at the dance, and our Adjutant didn't do badly either. The high spot of the evening was the scuffle which ensued between two Officers from another Squadron. One kept stepping on the other's blouse and the other parried by giving him dirty looks. It seems that one

was hesitant, and the other was damn glad of it. The next day, we all had big heads and very few reported to work on time. The boys were eagerly looking forward to another such affair.

18 Mar - Lt. Rafalovich, 334 Squadron, returned from his seven-day leave during which he was married. Lt. Bunte had also asked for a seven-day leave in which to get married.

"Looks like the Spits are about done here—off operations."

19 and 20 Mar - "Weather stinks, which is a break for the Thunderbolts. They'll need the rest before the boys get at them and start tearing them apart."

The men were utilizing their time out at Dispersal by making odds and ends, such as rings, cigarette lighters, wrist watch bands, etc. They turned out some fine work. The Pilots jealously observed and were trying to get their Crew Chiefs to make them souvenirs such as these.

21 Mar - Seven P-47s were flown to Burtonwood near Liverpool for crankshaft repairs. We had experienced problems due to insufficient lubrication on the crankshafts.

"Someone ought to invent a fog disperser of some kind. Looks as thick as the soup one gets at 'Sloppy Joes.' This weather may be comparable to New England weather, but I'll still take New England."

The 335 got its first P-47, and Lt. Boyles flew it. He was really tickled at its performance.

22 Mar - The 335 received word today that of the five men who had applied for Flying Cadet, four passed the preliminaries. This was the best Squadron record in the ETO. Cpl Buie received the highest grade on the written exam (highest in the ETO)—115 out 150. "Golly, we're proud!"

23 Mar - Today was the transition from Spits to P-47s for 334 Squadron. We hated to see them go, but we felt that these new kites would be better fighters.

The 335 received six new P-47s from Burtonwood.

A list was posted of all Enlisted Men qualified to start, warm up, and operate aircraft engines. Also posted was a list of all Sgts qualified to taxi aircraft.

Pfc Richard A. Claspell was designated Squadron Mail Clerk.

At the height of a drinking party in the Officers' Mess, Lt. Kalberg, Squadron Supply Officer, demonstrated his ability to execute backflips from a table top. Not up to par, he broke his knee-cap. We were now missing a Supply Officer.

Something must have gone wrong with the food. At three o'clock AM, there was a queue extending outside the latrine in C block.

Lt. Alexander Rafalovich 334 Sq. upon return from his leave to get married. Konsler collection.

24 Mar - Each day 335 had completed about twice as much transition training time as 334. The "335 Squadron was, unofficially, understood to be the best Squadron on the field."

Thought for the day—"Think not, for it will be thy undoing." Psalm 6, Chap. 5, "Book of McIntyre." And for this bit of wit, this writer nearly had to scrub the floors. "Comes the revolution, there'll be no 1st Sgts."

27 Mar - Twelve P-47s and a B-17 landed today, flown by ferry Pilots. Shortly thereafter, the B-17 took off with the ferry Pilots. The mechanics were all hopped up about these new "American machines."

The 335 Squadron was released until 29 March so all kites could have modifications installed.

All Pilots were issued side arms and knives.

28 Mar - Lt. Goodson returned to 334 Squadron.

A Chemical Warfare Class for all personnel of 334 was started. It covered chemical agents and the proper use of the gas mask.

The Enlisted personnel, assigned to the married quarters, were required to plant some kind of garden and to be responsible for it. "It looked like we were going to eat a lot of brussels sprouts."

Out on the line, a soft ball game had been cooked up between the Pilots and the Mechanics. It was to be played sometime the following week.

29 Mar - "Weather pretty bad. Bad weather and England; Potatoes and the Army; are the same, inseparable."

31 Mar - "Weather bad, kites bad, but it was payday so everything was fine." Boys hung around all day, as the English would say, "shooting a line." With the new armament issues, they now had "knives, knuckles, and 45s."

All Pilots of 334 had now started or finished their training course on the P-47.

Two of the Pilots went up in the Thunderbolts with newly modified radios. They reported good reception as far away as 60 miles from base.

Squadron Strength Summary:

334 Squadron	Officers 39	Enlisted Men 246
335 Squadron	Officers 41	Enlisted Men 248

"March is over, wish the war was. Slow, very slow. Hitler may be catching hell, but it certainly isn't our fault. But then, we may get there some day, at least so the brass hats tell us. We are now in possession of the 'master of the Luftwaffe' and will chase Jerry from the skies. Or so we have been reading. (Our country publishes no propaganda)."

1 April 43 - The RAF celebrated its quarter-century birthday. Against odds of seven to one they won the Battle of Britain. In honor of the occasion, a party was held in the Officers' Mess, and the RAF contributed five barrels of beer for the Airmens' Mess.

On our February payday, all Enlisted Men contributed to a fund to adopt a British war orphan. The fund reached 72 Pounds, 12 Shillings, and 10 Pence. Donations had to be in units of 100 Pounds or more, which would care for an orphan for three years.

The boys were up to the usual April Fools' tricks. The most imaginative one, promoted by Lt. Fink, had everyone searching for a crashed Spitfire.

3 April - Major Coen, on an aircraft recognition flight with B-17s, had his supercharger catch on fire at about 25,000 feet, and he was forced to bail out. His arm caught in the shroud lines, and he fractured his shoulder. His P-47 exploded on impact.

The 335 Squadron letters were changed to WD.

"Still having an awful lot of trouble with these Thunderbolts. God only knows when they'll become operational."

Major Coen 334 Sq., seated on stove discusses the mission with Col. Pete. Zigler collection.

Lt. Frank Smolinsky was killed while trying to land his Thunderbolt at Sawbridgeworth. His kite had engine trouble and was smoking. As he was making an emergency landing, his engine suddenly cut at about 150 feet, and the kite fell straight down like a rock. It immediately burst into flames. Lt. Smolinsky was killed instantly. The impact of the crash broke both his legs and arms, and he was badly burned. "His loss is really felt for 'Old Smo' was liked by everyone. Yes, Sherman must have had days like this in mind when he said "War is Hell!""

4 April - The 334 Squadron changed its numbering system to the letters QP followed by a separate given letter.

All clocks were set ahead one hour at 0200 hours, 4 April, making them two hours ahead of the sun.

5 April - 200-gallon belly tanks were to have been installed on the Thunderbolts, but since they only had 3" ground clearance, they were changed to 100-gallon tanks.

New regulations required Pilots to fly 100 sorties instead of 50 for the DFC. The boys were plenty hot about this. "Seems all the Generals and Colonels have their medals and are now trying to make it as hard as possible for the boys that are doing the fighting." The boys here at the Eagle Squadrons have been very conservative about their claims, unlike some other Squadrons.

It was decided that, until further notice, no passes would be issued to anyone on the field. To further expedite operational flying, clerks, wherever possible, were to take over KP and Guard Duty to relieve mechanics and line men.

The 334 Squadron presented a show at the station cinema. The proceeds went to the Squadron Orphan Adoption Fund. Receipts amounted to about 40 Pounds. This added to the amounts collected from the Officers since 1 April, made the total about 132 Pounds.

The cast of "Commandos" was assisted by Cherry Lind, a talented young English singer; Lyle Evans, a tall Canadian comedian; and Forsythe, Seaman, and Farrel from the U.S.A. The show was produced by S/Sgt Arthur G. Brest, and Pvt Spencer C. Smith was musical director.

8 April - Col. Peterson led the 2nd operational Sweep in Thunderbolts to Abbeville, leading P-47s from 334, 335, and 336 Squadrons. The Mission was uneventful due to 10/10ths cloud cover over the Continent. Many Majors and Colonels from here and Kings Cliffe were on this show. Lack of formation practice certainly showed up. After going through a few clouds, there just wasn't any formation, and no one knew "which was following what." They cruised back at 400 mph. What ships!

Col. Peterson kept the usual flow of his characteristic letters coming in the last few days. We wondered if the boys read them because of the issuing authority or because of the choice phrases the author used in them.

A dawn to dusk Airdrome Defense schedule was posted for Spitfires.

All Officers and Enlisted Men were required to carry their fire arms to and from work until further notice.

10 April - The Distinguished Flying Cross was awarded to Lt. Boock

Two 335 Pilots flew the last Spitfire mission—it was a Convoy Patrol.

11 April - The restriction of no passes until further notice was lifted.

Major Blakeslee led six a/c from this base on a Sweep over France. The idea was to draw the Jerries up prior to the bombers' arrival. This was the first P-47 Sweep the Major flew, and he liked the kite very much.

The much desired Distinguished Flying Cross. Prerequisites for this award kept increasing. Speer photo.

13 April - Lt. Col. Peterson led a Ramrod to Bruges and later a Rodeo to Berck. Both were uneventful. Half of the kites had to abort because of problems.

A Thunderbolt went in over Dover at 300 feet and was hit by British A/A (antiaircraft fire.) The Pilot was too low to bail, and he crash landed on a farm. Everything was wrecked. The Pilot was lucky that he wasn't killed. Regulation was that no aircraft was allowed to come over the coast under 1,000 feet. A/A opened fire without warning on any aircraft that did.

14 April - The Intelligence room had a blessed event today. "Poppa" Cowan was delightfully happy. It was a radio loudspeaker. Now he could keep in touch with Pilots while they were on Ops.

There was a big air raid during the night. Night fighters and A/A claimed a few kites.

15 April - Capt. Anderson, while on a test flight, had his plane catch fire. He was able to put it out, and he belly landed at Langham. (335 Sq. reported that he had bailed out.)

Lt. Col. Peterson led a Rodeo to Cassel. They encountered five FW 190s near Ostend. Three were destroyed by Col. Peterson, Major Blakeslee, and Lt. Boock, and another was damaged. Capt. Anderson and Capt. McMinn were reported missing. (Both were KIA).

Flying at 27,000 feet, the Squadron sighted five FW 190s at about 24,000 feet. Peterson led the attack. He shot down one FW 190 in flames. A cylinder head blew out, and he headed for home. He had to bail out 30 miles off the English coast. Just before he bailed out, he heard a "May Day" from Capt. Anderson. Lt. Col. Peterson's kite caught fire, and he bailed out over the Channel with his chute opening just as he hit the water. He was pretty shaken when picked up by a Walrus. (Col. Pete's two wingmen reported that his chute never opened. The hospital discovered he had suffered only two black eyes and a cut lip.)

Lt. Boock saw a P-47 under attack by a FW 190 and turned to attack. The FW did a split-S after the P-47 was struck. Boock followed and gave a four-ring deflection shot, which caused the e/a to burst into flames. It then crashed into the sea.

Lt. Clark, with Lt. Mills, met two FWs beneath the clouds and turned to give chase. Closing to about 400 yards, Lt. Clark gave short bursts at the e/a on the right. Lt. Mills gave a short burst to the one on the left. At that time his gunsight went out and his guns jammed. Clark followed his e/a through a half roll to the deck. He then observed strikes as he fired the last of his ammo at about 300 yards. His gunsight had gone out on the first burst.

Major Blakeslee dove on three Jerries who tried to dive away from him. He easily followed them down and cut through one of them twice. The e/a caught fire and crashed. This gave him four destroyed.

Capt. McMinn was reported to have shot down a FW 190 during the combat. Capt. Lee Gover 336 also destroyed one FW 190.

It was rumored that General Hunter was taking Thunderbolts off Ops because too many of them were catching fire.

16 April - General Hunter and staff members visited Debden for a conference on strategy. Col. Pete atttended sporting two very black eyes. "Long underwear is now out of season—weather is fine and boys have spring fever."

17 April - General Hunter presented several awards to Pilots for meritorius service, including the **Distinguished Flying Cross** to Capt. Anderson.

Major Blakeslee led two uneventful Sweeps over Europe.

The Major put his gun switch on firing position and his guns unloaded. That "shook him" for if he had been behind someone he would have shot the hell out of him. Also, it came to light that Blakeslee got his last Jerry with practice ammunition on the fifteenth.

"Jerry got it last night. Bombers were droning overhead for about an hour and a half."

The 334 Squadron received two new a/c today. One was a P-47-D, which was supposed to be 1,000 pounds lighter. It was to be the Major's kite.

18 April - A three-hour course in Chemical warfare was held for all Officers and EM.

The guns on WD-T accidently went off while the plane was parked in front of Dispersal. There was no damage because of the angle, but the burst barely missed a passing gasoline truck. It seemed an electrical engineer was working in the cockpit and got a couple of wires crossed.

The report that Blakeslee shot down a Hun with practice ammo was wrong; the guns were loaded with combat ammo.

On a Rodeo this morning, Lt. Gover of 336 fired on Lt. Hopson of 334 at 150 yards. He mistook the Thunderbolt for an FW 190. Lucky for Gover that he missed Hopson, for if he hadn't, Gover might as well have stayed in France.

20 April - "A" Dispersal was renamed "Times Square."

21 - 30 April - Bad weather held the Group to training missions, miscellaneous Hq duties, and one boring Sweep.

Several awards were handed out.

The P-47s' armor plate behind the Pilot was removed because it restricted visibility.

One noteworthy event occurred on 25 April when Lt. Terry, Armament, found a nest of colored, wooden eggs on his desk. The eggs bore the greeting, "To one good egg from five bad eggs— Happy Easter."

"We wondered what the Old Easter Parade down Fifth Avenue looked like this morning."

Armorer Leroy "Ol Nick" Nitschke, a former Navy man, prepares to put the "Sting" in a P-47. Weckbacher collection.

26 April - A rumor started that 60 colored WAACs were moving into this Station after the first of the month. The boys really thrashed this one out. "Snuffy resolved that he'd sleep here in Dispersal when that happened."

27 April - Lt. Chatterly attacked Red Section in a mock combat. He misjudged and crashed into the tail of Lt. Wilkinson. Wilkinson then bailed out, and he wrenched his back when his chute was torn in descent. He was unconcious when he hit the ground. He was darn lucky to be alive. Chatterly made a dead-stick landing.

It was now official that Wing Headquarters would move here on the third of May. We would then have a General on the field at all times as Wing Commander.

28 April - The Pilots spent the PM playing "Sieg Heil," an a/c identification game.

"Bright news for the 30th is pay day. There'll be plenty of drunks around tonight with pay day and release coming at the same time."

Squadron Strength Report 30 April:

334 Squadron	37 Officers	245 Enlisted Men
335 Squadron	38 Officers	242 Enlisted Men

3

The Thunderbolts Prove Their Worth

1 & 2 May 1943 - No operational flying due to unfavorable weather.

Seven 335 Pilots were promoted from 2nd Lt. to 1st Lt.

The Squadron now has 1 Major, 3 Captains, 17 1st Lts., and 6 2nd Lts.

3 May - Air Medals and/or clusters were awarded to several of the Pilots.

The pet cat "QP" gave birth to four kittens in a lowly coal bin. Simultaneously at 1200 hours, the American flag was hoisted on the parade ground. Major Osborne, Medical Officer, was in attendance at the birth. Sgt. Hedrick, of Operations, won a four-shilling wager for guessing the exact number of kittens to be born.

The Stars and Stripes was raised, incidentally, as Group Capt. Nixon officialy handed over the Station to Col. Anderson. It will now be under U.S. Control.

The transfer was celebrated in the Officers' Club with a dance and a buffet supper at which RAF officers were guests of the USAAF Group.

The *Stars and Stripes* carried a front page picture of 1st Lt. Spiros Pisanos taking the oath of allegiance to the United States before U.S. Commissioner Dr. Henry Hazard in London.

"Yesterday, 1st Lt. Spiros "Steve" Pisanos, of Athens, Greece, and Plainfield, N.J., became the first American soldier in the British Isles to become a U.S. citizen under the provisions of the modified overseas naturalization law. He was sworn in by Dr. Henry Hazard. In 1938, Steve Pisanos landed in New York with $8 and no knowledge of English. Among other things, he was determined to fly. He got a job for $13 a week. He spent $12 of it for every hour of flying instruction he received at a flying school.

In 1941, with a private pilot's license, he joined the RAF. He has been in 19 operations with the RAF and the U.S. Fighter Squadron to which he was transferred in October."

Said Steve at the close—"This is the most happiest day of my life." The night of the 4th, the following sign was displayed at the bar in the Officers' Club:

"FREE BEER ON STEVE PISANOS - AMERICAN"

The PX is now run by Americans with a large batch of American supplies.

Lt. Spiros "Steve" Pisanos 334 Sq. stands next to his plane Miss Plainfield. Steve was the first American soldier in the British Isles to become a U.S. citizen. He also was an evader for several months. Zigler Collection.

4 May - Major Blakeslee led a Ramrod to Antwerp. Upon return, the Pilots of 334 Squadron were assigned new call signs of "Scandal" plus a two-digit number.

A misguided Jerry flew through the Squadron and Major Blakeslee dove on him, overshooting. Lt. Carpenter of 335 Squadron followed and polished him off. He claimed a FW 190 destroyed.

On the same show, Lt. Lutz' plane (334) started smoking and losing speed. At 2500 feet, his a/c went over on its back and dove straight into the Channel. He bailed out, but he was seen to be unconcious as he lay in the water. Later search was unable to find any trace of the Lt. (He was KIA)

Word arrived that a Thunderbolt from Horsham shot down a Spit IX over France.

Also heard was that Clark Gable, accompanied by two Generals, acted as Bombardier in one of the Forts on this show.

Lt. Anderson, previously reported shot down, is now reported as being a POW in Germany.

8 May - At 0730 hours it was announced that e/a were approaching the field. Three JU 88s flew over at about 3,000 feet. They were later attacked by Spitfires who shot down two of the 88s over England and one over the Channel.

Sixteen of 335 Squadron's airplanes will have their motors replaced due to new modifications.

9 May - Gales - no flying.

One hundred plus of our men paraded in Safron Walden with RAF regiments, WAAFs, ATS, and Red Cross Workers in conjunction with the city's "Wings for Victory" Campaign. This was followed by church services for U.S. and British forces.

13 May - Col. Peterson led a Ramrod to Le Touquet, no action. Pilots commented that this was the most devastating bombing mission they had seen. Eighty Forts "Blew Hell" out of St. Omer.

Major Blakeslee today qualified for the American DFC to add to his British DFC.

About 160 men of a Fighter Control Squadron arrived today, straight from the States. "As 'Rookies,' these guys take the cake; God help us now!"

News claims that the "Boys from the Eagle Squadrons" are the only ones to have shot down Jerries with the P-47.

14 May - Col. Peterson led the group on a Ramrod to Antwerp. The 334 Squadron, flying high cover, had to restrain desires to mix it up when e/a came in at 20,000 feet. However, 335 Squadron bounced Jerries with Blakeslee getting one Destroyed and Lt. Stanhope a Probable. Lt. "Zoot Suit" Carlow chased a Jerry off the tail of a P-47, but then he blacked out in pulling out of his dive and apparently missed. Col. Peterson also got one, but he suffered supercharger damage in the scrap. Lt. Gover added one to give the Group 3 Destroyed with no losses for the day.

About 0300 hours, Chelmsford, 15 miles from Debden, was raided by enemy bombers. About 250 newly arrived EM (enlisted men) witnessed the raid with mixed feelings.

15 May - The Group, again led by Col. Peterson, conducted a Rodeo to Amsterdam. It was the longest over-water trip yet undertaken by the Group. (Over 200 miles)

Today's show made the 40th for Capt. Fetrow, and with his one destroyed, he is eligible for the DFC.

16 May - Major Blakeslee led the Group on two uninspired missions; Rodeos to Walcheren Island and to Abbeyville.

Lt. Beatie attacked two FWs. Seeing the canopy and pieces fly off but not seeing the Jerry go in, he claimed a probable. Lt. Stanhope also attacked two Huns and gave them deflection shots. He saw hits on the tail and fuselage of one, which then went into a spin. He claimed a Damaged. Capt. Halsey and Lt. Patterson damaged one of a flight of four. Ross and McKennon both returned with bullet holes in their kites.

Col. Donald Blakeslee, the much decorated 4th Fighter Group C.O., was a no-nonsense Pilot whose innovative tactics and stern discipline created the top-scoring Allied Fighter Group in WWII. He transferred from the RCAF to the USAAC flying Spitfires, P-47s, and P-51s for a total of over 500 combat missions. USAF collection.

17 May - 2nd Lt. Alfred Markel, F/O Clyde Smith, and F/O Gerald Montgomery were assigned to the Group.

The Wing was led by Major Blakeslee on a Rodeo to Brest. He landed enroute to refuel both on the way out and on the return. He flew over 900 miles on the mission.

18 May - Major Blakeslee led the Wing on a Rodeo to Bruges, with many aborts for mechanical problems. Capt. Andrews intercepted several Me 109s which had attacked a P-47. It was thought to be Lt. Boock, whose plane crashed into the sea. (It was Lt. Boock, and he was KIA). Andrews fired and then went into a spin from which he recovered, but he could find neither the P-47 nor the Me 109. In the meantime, Lts. Clark and Beeson dove on three e/a and were followed by two 109s. The duo in turn attacked the e/a with Lt. Beeson scoring one 109 Destroyed.

19 May - Major Blakeslee replaced Lt. Col. Peterson as Group Executive Operations Officer; Col. Peterson was relieved of Flying duties with nearly 200 Operational sorties to his credit.

A Ramrod to Holland saw no flak and no e/a.

A FW 190 landed at Manston tonight and was captured. Some of the boys went to see it. It seems the FW was allowed to fly over England without any flak and then permitted to fly back towards France. While still over English territory, the RAF cluttered his R/T, getting the Pilot confused, at which time they gave him a homing to Manston. At the proper moment, they turned on the runway lights at Manston; whereupon he came in for a landing. Result: one FW 190 and a very bitter Nazi Pilot.

21 May - Major Blakeslee led the Wing on a Rodeo to Ostend.

E/a were sighted, and Lts. Care and Morgan broke off to attack. Care fired on one of them, and Morgan destroyed one. Capt. Andrews then broke off to attack the other e/a followed by Lts. Pisanos, Whitlow, and MacFarlane. Andrews went into a tight turn and fell off into a spin. Pisanos was able to get off a short burst and observed white smoke from the e/a.

Morgan, Whitlow, and MacFarlane, all of 334 Squadron, have not returned. (MacFarlane and Whitlow were KIA, and Morgan became a POW).

25 and 26 May - Two uneventful missions were flown.

27 May - Eleven Pilots from 334 and 6 from 336 were awarded 12 Air Medals or Oak Leaf Clusters. This is the first such occasion with "Old Glory" fluttering over the parade ground.

Major Blakeslee led a no contact Rodeo to Knocke.

29 May - On a show to the coast near Brest, six FWs were engaged by Evans, Padgett, and Fink. Although hits were seen, no claims were made pending film assessment. Being low on fuel, they returned immediately.

Lt. Carlow flying WD-Q, "a jinx kite," had a Hun on his tail; his kite suffered considerable damage from a 20mm HE and an AP shell. The only thing that saved Carlow was the armor plate behind the cockpit.

All planes stopped at Predannack to refuel.

30 May - Today there was rain, thunder, and lightning to enliven Memorial Day.

There was an informal service at the flagpole on the parade ground. Old Glory went back to full mast.

31 May - "Finally got off to a 'Ropey Do.' With aborts and ending up in the wrong place, 335 had only four men on the show."

"Our strength here keeps increasing with all kinds of Control Squadrons and Service Squadrons moving in. This place is packed worse than Times Square on New Year's Eve. If nothing else, we can certainly subdue Jerry by weight of numbers."

"Forts, Stirlings, Lancasters, Halifaxes, Spitfires, and several other types land here almost daily. It has been noticed that the English kites get here just before chow time."

Squadron strength:

334 Officers 41		Enlisted Men 243
335 Officers 41		Enlisted Men 245

June 1-6 1943 - The 334 flew no Missions, preferring to make reassignments and to engage in various administrative duties.

The one notable accomplishment was the first Squadron party which was held at the old "Sgts' Mess." All crowded around the free beer until the refreshments were offered. These consisted of cakes, doughnuts, and sandwiches. (Nobody would have guessed that the deviled ham was our old friend Spam in disguise or that the cake contained powdered eggs.) The goodness of the doughnuts will remain a military secret, known only to the bakers.

A good time was had by all. A vote of thanks was extended to the cooks, the RAF Station Band, and the committee.

During this period, Sgt. "Grease Ball" Bonitati left on a pass to London; the cinema showed "Stage Door Canteen"; a couple of Balboas were flown; more rookies arrived from the States; and Major Blakeslee made Lt. Colonel. The boys were beginning to agitate for HE (high explosive) ammo.

7 June - Col. Blakeslee led a Rodeo to Blankenberghe which was recalled due to unfavorable weather.

Lt. Ross made the doghouse again. He was Rhubarbing over Cambridge and beat up a Tiger Moth. He was so close the Moth's Pilot got Ross' serial number and complained to Ops. Notice was posted that there were to be no more flights below 10,000 feet within ten miles of Cambridge.

8 June - Returning from a Squadron Balboa, Lt. Clark pulled off the runway, striking a parked jeep and injuring Corp. Ballinger in the head. Dr. Blackburn patched Ballinger up and placed him under observation.

Orders were issued that, "Every Pilot will take 45 minutes of exercise daily." Capt. Halsey had all Pilots out running this morning. "There are a lot of lame Pilots around tonight."

11 June - Col. Blakeslee led a Ramrod to Thielt. The Group set a record by taking off and up in five minutes. The 334 Squadron made a record 16 plane landing in four minutes.

An afternoon Rodeo to Hazebrouck and Courtrai was also uneventful as far as e/a were concerned.

The Pilots have been playing volleyball every day in preference to running for exercise.

12 June - A radio message was received stating that Lt. Morgan, MIA 21 May, was a POW, wounded but otherwise well.

On a PM Rodeo to Roulers and Ypres, 1st Lt. E.D. Beatie, 335, developed engine trouble and bailed out; he was rescued from the Channel by a Walrus from Martlesham ASR (air sea rescue.)

Group was currently putting up 48 a/c on each show.

14 June - Lt. Garrett King was practicing a homing with MOR when he suddenly failed to answer. Efforts to contact him proved futile. His plane crashed in flames near Swaffham. It is believed that he flew into a Thunderhead and was struck by lightning. An English soldier witnessed the accident. The soldier claimed that he saw the kite go into a cloud, a loud clap of thunder followed; after which, the plane came out of the cloud and crashed straight into the ground.

15 June - On an aborted Ramrod, Lt. Hively turned back and bailed out into the Channel due to engine trouble. He was later picked up by a launch from Portsmouth. The launch was directed by "Eagle Eye" Padgett, who kept circling the area.

16 June - Five Generals, U.S. Ambassador Winant, and Aides inspected 334 Dispersal, which General Hunter described as "the best G—D— Dispersal in England."

Later, with appropriate ceremony, General Hunter awarded 16 Air Medals and Oak Leaf Clusters to Pilots of 334.

The Distinguished Flying Cross was awarded to Capt. Fetrow

Flash recognition training classes were held in Group Intelligence. Images of aircraft were projected for from 1/5 to 1/50th of a second to improve the Pilots' power of observation.

The Confirmed Enemy Casualty Reports for the period of 2 Oct 1942 to 21 May 1943 were released showing 334 Squadron credits of eight 1/2 FW 190s and two Me 109s Destroyed.

19 June - Lt. Mills bellied in while attempting a landing. His gear did not extend properly, although his dash lights showed everything was in order. Shortly thereafter, Lt. Castle flew past A flight.

As he climbed in a turn for landing, his plane dove straight for the ground and went up in flames. He was killed instantly.

"The boys are still playing volleyball; it's more fun than running."

All Pilots were required to be sent home immediately upon completing 200 hours of operational time. They were to leave within 48 hours.

Lt. Beatie produced a masterpiece—a mounted gunsight that worked on a joy stick and rudders. It worked the same as if one were sitting in the cockpit. He was to be awarded the "Brussel Sprout Cluster" at the earliest convenience.

22 June - Col. Blakeslee led the Group on a Ramrod to Antwerp. R/V was not made due to an unannounced change in timing, but Group made contact with bombers on their way out from target and under attack by about 20 Fw 190s and Me 109s. The 334th flew top cover while 335 and 336 attacked. The 336th Destroyed one FW 190, and 335 Destroyed two FW 190s and one Me 109. Lt. Beatie got one FW 190 and one Me 109, but was hit in the left wing by a 30 caliber which cut the hydraulic line to his brake. This caused him to run off the end of the runway upon landing, but there was no damage.

Lt. Ernest D. Beatie transferred from the 121st E.S. to 335 Sq., 4th Fighter Group. Konsler collection.

This is the first time that one Pilot has downed two e/a on a single mission since 335 Squadron was organized. (About 16 months)

Lt. "Snuffy" Smith got the other Hun and nearly bought it himself when he found two Huns on his tail. He outran them on the way home, pushing 70" of Mercury. Lt. James Goodson, 336, destroyed a FW 190 near Hulst, Netherlands.

Capt. "Chief Longhair" Fetrow, a really great guy, left for the States, having completed his tour.

24 June - The Duchess of Kent, with appropriate ceremony, presented plaques to the three Squadrons for their part in the Eagle Squadrons under RAF command.

The Duchess said;

"To commemorate forever the part the Eagle Squadrons played in those critical days (of the war), the King has gladly given permission for the RAF crest to be designed for those Squadrons and has approved and signed them."

The Officers and Enlisted Men marched in review, and this was followed by Thunderbolts passing over in formation.

At 1615 hours, a briefing was held, and a Rodeo was flown to Doullens with no contact made with e/a.

26 June - Col. Blakeslee led a Ramrod to Gisors to provide withdrawal support for Forts with R/V at Gisors. They proceeded after landing at Thorney Island to refuel. Group made R/V with bombers near Dieppe, at which time e/a were encountered and attacked. Lt. Care claimed one Me 109 Destroyed; Lt. Beeson, one Me 109 Probably Destroyed; and Lt. Leaf, one Me 109 Damaged.

28 June - A practice invasion of the drome was held, after which an uneventful Ramrod to St. Nazaire was flown.

Upon returning from the Do, Lt. Smith landed at Lee on Solent to refuel and met his Waterloo. He came in high and attempted to go around, but his engine failed to respond. With wheels up, he made a belly landing in a potato patch. "Mashed potatoes!" Luckily "Snuffy" was not injured. He returned to Debden the next day by train.

30 June - Still lots of volleyball by the Officers.

Around the latter part of next month, Uncle Sam has promised Jerry a 45 percent increase in bombs. "Let's get into the month of July and help deliver that order!"

1 July 1943 - Major Blakeslee led the group on a Rodeo to Abbeyville. Individual sections broke up a couple of attacks on bombers, but no claims were recorded.

After returning from the Rodeo, four sections went on a search mission for ASR, but they were unable to find the downed Pilot.

3 July - All aircraft grounded for radio frequency changes.

Bob Hope and his party arrived at the base. He cracked jokes, sang, and danced on an improvised platform on the parade ground. He was assisted by Frances Langford, Jack Pepper, and Tony Romano. The Group turned out "en masse" to see them.

4 July - The following call signs were instituted:

Saffron Walden (MOR)	"MORELIGHT"
Debden Homer*	"CARMAN"
Group**	"UPPER"
334 Squadron	"PECTIN"
335 Squadron	"GREEENBELT"

*Airdrome Control Tower will use this call sign followed by the word Control.

**For use of Leader of formation (Group) in R/T contacts with ground station (Saffron Walden).

Bob Hope meets a Squadron mascot prior to entertaining the base personnel. Zigler collection.

Each of the Pilots was assigned a call number - "A" Flight numbers were 30 through 49 and "B" Flight numbers were 50 through 69.

An Independence Day Parade was held. Following the parade, Colonel Anderson and Corporal Blair (of Group Intelligence) addressed the troups. The troops then passed in review.

Major Dufour led a Ramrod to Le Mons which, due to cloud cover, was unproductive.

6 July - All enlisted men were treated to a lecture on the Articles Of War followed by a lecture on veneral diseases.

An uneventful mission was flown to Ghent.

Most Pilots played volleyball, checkers, and bridge; no poker today.

9 July - F/O Nicholas Megura made his first operational flight with the Group on a Rodeo to Ghent, with no action.

Lt. Hively and Sgt. Don Allen of 334 Squadron received credit for the finest party yet. It was held at the Officers' Lounge; it featured a buffet dinner and a dance with music by Geraldo's orchestra (the best in England) and the Cuban band of Edmundo Ros. Flowers were everywhere. The Air Corps wings in white with gold carnations adorned the stage above the musicians. There were Station paintings by English artist Frank Beresford. Over the fireplace was a huge American flag made of roses. At the other end of the lounge, there was a draped silk flag illuminated by flood lights.

The game room was transformed into a "Trading Post." It simulated a log cabin with Indian cartoons of Post Officers on the walls with model planes, German relics, and cartoons as decorations.

The buffet was served in the "Snooker" room. A very popular attraction was the huge tent which was erected in the triangle in front of the lounge. Drinks and sandwiches were served there until blackout time. In the choice of "les Femmes," the Officers showed unusual discretion. All in all the party was "tops."

12 July - The first class in first aid for chemical warfare casualties was held in the Decontamination Center. All personnel were required to attend these classes.

"Hedy Lamar, the old 'birthday suit kid,' showed here in a couple of flicks lately. She is sure 'some piece of meat' and what the boys would like to find under the tree on Christmas morning."

A committee was appointed to make the necessary arrangements for a 335 Squadron party. It is to be a stag party and will be financed by the Officers.

13 to 17 July - Several uneventful missions were flown.

Unofficial information indicates that on a "Do" to France a Me 109 got on the tail of a Thunderbolt and shot hell out of the supercharger. The kite was only able to pull 25" of Mercury at about 10,000 feet. The Hun, surprised that the kite did not go down, pulled alongside to see what was keeping him up. He waved, dropped

Frank Beresford, a famous British artist, painting one of his many depictions of the 4th Fighter Group. Zigler collection.

back, and continued to shoot until he ran out of ammo. The Yank landed at an advanced base. "I'm from Missouri. He'll have to show me. All these stories have to be taken with a grain of salt. Americans, by their nature, are likely to brag and exaggerate a little."

"This seems to apply to that story about the Fort boys cleaning their guns the minute they spotted their fighter escort while still over France. A few Huns jumped them, and they were in a hell'va fix."

Lt. Wortman is missing from the show 14 July. He was last seen chasing some Hun off to the right. (He was KIA).

18 July - The 334 Squadron has raised 200 Pounds for the British War Orphan Fund, which will finance the education and clothing of two children for five years. Capt. Heene decided on case No. 603-Dorothy H., born 2 April 36, and case No. 604-William H., born 16 September 33.

Their father was a gunner in the Royal Artillery from December 1939 until his death in action February 1942. Prior to service, he had been a house painter, earning about 4 Pounds per week. Mrs. H's pension for herself and four children is 2 Pounds, 18 Shillings; plus, she receives 15 Shillings per week as a domestic. Her rent is 16 Shillings Sixpence, with other costs of 6 Shillings Twelve Pence.

The mother is needed at home at this time in the children's lives, and this grant will enable her to be with them.

The ARC accompanied the children to the Station where they had lunch in the EM mess. Each child received a chocolate cake with his or her name on it. After lunch, they toured the Airdrome by Jeep, had an archery exhibition, and went to the Squadron offices where they received many gifts—candy, gum, dolls, drawing sets, picture books, and model airplanes. Dorothy received a dress and accessories to match. They returned home after about 3 hours.

S/Sgt Marsh and Cpl Schneider left for the States today for Aviation Cadet Training.

On the 18th, Lt. Beatie broke his ankle playing volleyball. He has the toughest luck of any Pilot in 335.

19 July - New insignia for easier recognition will be placed on all a/c.

(a) The straight line formed by the top edge of the two star points will be parallel with the leading edge of the wing or top of the fuselage.

(b) Two white rectangles, each one radius long and one half radius wide, will be blocked on each side of the circle. The inner ends of the rectangles will be concave to conform to the Blue Circle. The top edge of the rectangle is to form a straight line with the top or side of the white star. The star is parallel with the top of the fuselage or leading edge of the wing. The entire design will be outlined with a red border one-eighth radius wide.

20 July - Twenty-one Pilots were released individually from closed vans on a six-mile radius from the base to simulate bail outs and to practice evasion tactics. They carried chits indicating when and where they were apprehended if captured. Entrance to the airdrome undetected constituted a successful evasion. Three of the seven who were successful were from 334 Squadron: Lts. Sobanski and Markel, and F/O Montgomery.

The 335 and the 336 each had 2 evasions.

Lt. Ross managed to find a scarecrow in a field from which he used the clothes for a disguise. He sneaked back into camp without being detected.

Lt. Fink reversed his leather jacket, rolled up his pant legs, and was able to move about. However, not knowing where he was, he went to the public library to ascertain his location. It turned out to be a jam-making center, and the wife of the commander of the 11th Home Guard Battalion recognized him; he was apprehended.

Lt. Smith, using fence rows and wooded areas, returned safely.

25 July - Due to unfavorable weather, there has been no operational flying since 17 July.

Major Halsey led a Rodeo to Ghent with no action.

The 335 Squadron was chosen to be the guinea pig for the experiment with the new belly tanks. The boys worked like hell to get 16 of them on in time. Half of the tanks are to be flown until empty and dropped into the Wash. The other half are to go to 30,000 feet. One tank wouldn't draw, and one, when dropped, dented the underside of the plane. Well, that makes 16 gone and only 1,129 to go. We'll be glad when the last one is gone.

26 July - Major Halsey led a Rodeo to Numansdorp. NW of Rotterdam, four FW 190s were bounced with Lt. Mills, claiming one FW 190 probably destroyed. Later, several other e/a were bounced with no definitive results.

On a second Rodeo, e/a were again encountered, but they all managed to evade into clouds without contact.

Benito Mussolini threw in the "Sponge" today and resigned. The king has accepted. At the rate it is going, the war in Italy should not continue too long. We Hope!

27 July - On a Rodeo to support B-26s, the Group was forced to leave prematurely due to low gas supplies. No e/a were seen. After this mission, 200-gallon external tanks were installed on all serviceable a/c.

In a volleyball game today, the ground Officers were trounced by the Pilots. "Literally, our 'Eaglets' were—on the ball!"

28 July - Major Halsey led a Ramrod to Westhoofd-Emmerich during which three new records were made for an operational flight in this theatre of operations.

1. It was the first on which the new belly tanks were used.
2. It was the first fighter mission into Germany.
3. It was the longest non-stop fighter flight. The round-trip was over 575 miles.

(335 Sq. took off first, making them the first to start off on an operation over Germany with belly tanks).

On the way to R/V, the Group encountered a Wing of Forts being attacked by upwards of 30 FW 190s and Me 109s.

The Group attacked and destroyed nine e/a in a running battle over German and Dutch soil. The 336 Squadron lost one—Lt. Ayres. (Ayres became a POW).

"What a surprise this must have been for Jerry, having us get into his back yard."

The B-17s attacked various a/c factories, destroying 66 e/a, and meanwhile losing 23 Fortresses. E/a were bounced as they were attacking the forts. Forty-five FW 190s and Me 109s were encountered during the course of action.

Results were:

334 - Lt. Beeson claimed one Me 109 Destroyed; 1st Lt. Care one FW 190 Destroyed.

335 - Capt. Evans one FW 190 Destroyed; Lt. Boyles one FW 190 Destroyed; Lt. Blanding one FW 190 Destroyed.

Lt. Leon Blanding 335 Sq., transferred from 121 E S and became C.O. of 335 Sq., leading the Sq. on the Russia Shuttle mission. Konsler collection.

336 - Capt. Miley one Me 109 Destroyed; Capt. Gover one Me 109 Destroyed; Col. Anderson two Me 109s Destroyed.

Combat Reports: "I was flying Red 3 with no wingman and saw two FW 190s attacking a straggling B-17. I opened fire on the rear 190 at about 700 to 1,000 yards to keep him from shooting at the B-17. I saw strikes on the front part of the fuselage and port wing root. The e/a practically stopped. I closed fast to 100 yards, seeing strikes and parts flying off all the time and the a/c breaking up. Both his wheels came down, and his canopy flew off. It was all busted up, and there wasn't anything left but the frame.

I had to pull away because the other a/c had swung out to the left and then came back at me. I broke hard left and hit him with a couple m/g bullets. Red 1, who had covered me, could have taken him, but he was out of ammo, having just shot down a FW 190 himself. I carried on and fired at four other 190s, all with deflection shots, but I observed no results. We gave the Forts all the help we could, but apparently were too late. I saw four chutes open right beneath me and behind the crippled fort. I then dove for home alone. I claim one FW 190 Destroyed."

Leon Blanding 1st Lt., Air Corps.

*****

"I was flying Red 1 when I saw two FW 190s about 2,000 feet below preparing to attack the bombers. I dove behind them and opened fire on one from about 400 yards dead astern. I closed to about 50 yards, seeing strikes all over his wings and fuselage. After about a nine-second burst, my tracers started to go into him. There was a brilliant flash and a puff of smoke. As I pulled away, his engine was smoking badly. My number two man, Lt. Hupe, saw flashes and strikes all over the a/c, a very bright explosion, and flames inside the cockpit.

Lt. Frank Boyles 335 Squadron, formerly 121 ES, was subsequently KIA October 1943. Konsler collection.

A moment later, I covered Red 3, who was firing at a pair of FW 190s. As he fired, the wheels of one of the a/c came down. I tried to fire, but was out of ammo. I claim one FW 190 Destroyed."

Frank Boyles 1st Lt., Air Corps.

*****

"I was flying 335 Sq. Blue Leader, West of Arnheim, when I saw two FW 190s about to attack the bombers from the rear. I dove on them, and one turned into my attack. I got about a one-second burst into each one without result. I pulled up towards the bombers when two Me 109s came in to attack them. I got behind them, and the #2 e/a pulled away and ran. I got into line astern to #1 and gave him a short burst with no result. I closed to within 100 yards and gave him a second burst, and I saw glycol start to spurt and a lot of pieces fly off the wing and right radiator. I gave a little left rudder and eased back on the stick. I saw more parts fly off, and the plane seemed to blow up in a cloud of smoke. I pulled away to keep from ramming him and blacked out. When I came to, two FW 190s flew across in front of me. I gave the last one a full deflection shot with about a half-second burst, and I saw a piece fly off from the vicinity of the cockpit. I claim one Me 109 Destroyed and one FW 190 Damaged."

Roy Evans Captain, Air Corps.

Capt. Roy W. Evans 335 Sq., a former Eagle, became 335 Sq. C.O. and later became C.O. of the 359th Fighter Group prior to becoming a POW. Konsler collection.

*****

After returning from the mission, Col. Anderson presented 25 Air Medals and/or Oak Leaf Clusters to the Pilots.

A Circus to St. Omer was then flown with no action.

"So ends the best day we have had yet: may we have many more of them! Amen!"

29 July - Major Halsey led an uneventful Rodeo to Ghent area.

After lunch, all available personnel were assembled on the parade ground where General Hunter introduced Captain Eddie Rickenbacker who spoke for 40 minutes. He predicted that Italy would be out of the war in 30 days, but it would take until the fall of 1944 to whip the Hun.

Another uneventful Circus was then flown.

"In the past 72 hours the Allies have dropped over 5,000 tons of bombs on Hamburg, which is Germany's second largest city.

During the blitz of London, which took 11 months, Germany only dropped 7,500 tons. Hamburg must be hamburger by now!"

30 July - Captain Thomas J. Andrews was awarded the **Distinguished Flying Cross** for extraordinary achievement

He has accomplished 40 fighter combat missions and Destroyed one e/a in combat.

The Group, led by Major Halsey on a Circus to Westerhoofd-Emmerick, encountered upwards of 150 e/a. Although heavily outnumbered, 335 Squadron destroyed five FW 190s and damaged two more. One of their planes, with Lt. Merritt, is missing. Four Pilots aborted due to faulty belly tank problems. (Lt. Merritt was KIA).

The scorers today were: Capt. Young, Lt. Stanhope, Lt. Boyles, Lt. K.G.Smith, and Lt. Mc Kennon. Each claimed one FW 190 Destroyed. "We are rapidly becoming a 'Crack Outfit,' aren't we?"

Combat Reports: "I was flying Green 3 and dove to attack a FW 190. I gave him a short burst as he dove away. I started to climb and saw three FW 190s in vick formation. I attacked the one on the right, getting hits on his tail and left wing. He side slipped and went down. I then turned to the one on the left, closing from 250 yards to within 100 yards, firing a long burst from 15 degrees deflection to dead astern. I saw strikes on his tail and left wing. Then there was a violent explosion in his left wing where his gun was. There was a huge flash, pieces flew off, and all his wing outboard of his gun came off clean. The plane then tumbled tail over nose and spun down, smoking badly. I broke away; the third plane did a half roll downward.

I was then attacked by two Me 109s coming from the right. I turned into their attack and fired a burst at both of them. They half rolled and dove away. I then came home. I claim one FW 190 Destroyed and one FW 190 Damaged."

Aubrey Stanhope 1st Lt., Air Corps.

*****

"I saw a bomber being clobbered by two FW 190s. I cut my throttle and dove on one as he broke away and went into a diving turn. I went after him, closing rapidly as he turned into a sharp climbing turn to port. I firewalled everything and closed to within about 150 feet and got in a three or four second burst with 15 degrees deflection. Something flew off his port side and large quantities of white smoke came pouring out. He flicked violently to starboard, and I almost hit him. Passing within just a few feet of him, I saw his engine on fire with long streamers of flame and smoke. He went into a straight dive. I watched him till he went out of sight. He was still trailing smoke. He never recovered.

This plane was painted a dull sooty black with no camouflage, and it had a yellow nose. I claim one FW 190 Destroyed."

Pierce McKennon 2nd Lt., Air Corps.

Lt. Pierce "Mac" McKennon 335 Sq. Much decorated, he flew 560 combat hours and was credited with 21 plus e/a. He became Squadron C.O., was shot down and evaded back to England. Shot down the second time, he was picked up by G. Green and flown back to England in Green's P-51 with Green sitting on his lap. He was killed in a flying accident in 1947. Konsler collection.

*****

"I saw an aircraft ahead and below me about 4,000 feet. I was not sure it was a Jerry, so I throttled back. I maneuvered back and forth to stay behind him as I closed directly behind him. When I determined it was an FW 190, I opened fire at about 75 yards. I immediately saw flashes at the wing root and cockpit area. I broke off at about 50 yards as he rolled and went into a spin. I was directly opposite him and saw the yellow nose and even the exhaust slits. A chute came out but tangled in the tail plane. The Pilot came out and fell free without the chute. The plane kept spinning straight down, and I saw it crash into the deck. I claim one FW 190 Destroyed."

Kenneth Smith 1st Lt., Air Corps.

*****

"I was flying Red 1 in 335 Sq. when a FW 190 crossed in front and 500 feet below me. I closed and opened fire from dead astern at about 300 yards, closing to about 100 yards, and firing about an eight-second burst. I saw strikes on the fuselage and an explosion in the cockpit. The FW 190 went slowly into a vertical dive and crashed into the Rhine near Zaltboomel. I claim one FW 190 Destroyed."

Frank Boyles 1st Lt., Air Corps.

*****

Major Eugene Roberts made 8th AF history by shooting down three e/a in one operation. Capt. London shot down two e/a, (the second time he has done this), making him the first 8th AF Ace.

Two Pilots from 336 were flying around the field together when one of them accidently shot off his guns. He hit the wing of the other plane and damaged it considerably; however, no one was hurt.

At 1845 hours, 111 Officers and Enlisted men marched around the perimeter. Officers carried side arms and Enlisted Men carried rifles. It was announced that such hikes would be continued as part of the P.T. program.

31 July - Col. Blakeslee led a Circus to Doullens with no action.

The Aero Club of the American Red Cross held an open house which was attended by most of the Base personnel. The Red Cross quarters were newly decorated and were enjoyed by all.

1 Aug 1943 - The 335 Squadron has been notified that they will receive two gliders and six C-47s to move the air echelon in a hurry if necessary.

Lts. Patterson and Fink got into a little argument with a crew on a visit to a bomber station. One of the bomber boys asked them, "What the hell are you guys doing up there at 70,000 feet? Why don't you come down and get into the fight?" Pat immediately answered with, "We will when you guys take a little more aircraft recognition."

2 Aug 43 - Five U.S. Senators arrived on station today with visiting Generals. They arrived at 1610 hours, and they left at 1710 hours after stating that they intended to "see and talk with as many American troops as possible."

4 Aug. - All Officers and Enlisted Men attended a showing of training films.

7 Aug - **The Distinguished Flying Cross** was awarded to: 1st. Lt. Duane W. Beeson

Seven new kites arrived this morning and were air, gun, and radio tested by our pilots.

Lt. McKennon, slow timing a plane, crash landed in a potato patch at Chesterford when his plane caught fire at low altitude.

12 Aug - After days of inactivity due to poor weather, Col. Blakeslee led the group on a Ramrod to Sittard. They attacked and broke up small formations of e/a attacking the bombers. As a result, Capt. O'Regan claimed one Me 109 Destroyed, and Capt. Clark claimed one FW 190 Destroyed. Lt. Pisanos dispatched one Me 109.

Lt. Padgett got credit for one Me 109 Destroyed. "Ole Padgett went right up on him and got him with one quick burst. The Horrible Hun kept flying straight and level, and he took no evasive action. Only 280 rounds did the trick, confirmed by Lt. Ellington."

13 Aug - The Distinguished Flying Cross was awarded to
Captain James A. Clark - 50 Combat Missions
1st Lt. Raymond C. Care - 40 Combat Missions- 1 e/a

15 Aug - Double summertime ended today, we will now be only one hour ahead of Greenwich mean time.

A Rodeo to St. Inglehette and Knocke was eventful. It was the first time that all Pilots were issued a bar of chocolate and a pack of gum before taking off. This will be a standard practice on all future missions. It's much appreciated.

A second mission, a Rodeo to Brussels, was uneventful.

"The weather was excellent today so we splurged and put on two shows; yes, peoples, two whole double features for the price of one. Both turned out to be the usual bus run or milk run. Belly tanks were again dropped outside of Antwerp and the following words were painted on them: 'Schickelgruber is a bastard'."

16 Aug - The Group, equipped with belly tanks, was led on a Ramrod to Paris by Col. Blakeslee. E/a were engaged on the way in and out, attacking in flights of six and eight with no regular pattern. Most of our planes stopped at advanced bases to refuel because of damage.

Battle Damage: Lt. Rafalovich crash landed safely near Newromey. His plane was hit by 20 mm cannon in the starboard ammunition box, causing the box to explode and damaging the wing and tail plane. In spite of the danger, the Pilot chose not to bail out.

Capt. Clark's plane was hit by 20 mm cannon, tearing a three-foot hole in the port wing.

F/O W.B. Smith's plane was hit in the tail by MG bullets.

F/O Markel's plane was hit by flak in the engine cowling. His was the first plane of our Group to be hit by flak.

Lt. Matthews of 336 failed to return. (He evaded capture and subsequently returned to England).

Results of Engagement:
Following are claims of e/a Destroyed:

Capt. Clark	two FW 190s
F/O. Smith	two FW 190s
Lt. Mills	two FW 190s
Lt. Hively	one FW 190
Lt. Care	one FW 190
Lt. Happel	one FW 190
Capt. Evans	one Me 109
Lt. Stanhope	one Me 109
F.D. Smith	one FW 190
Capt. Young	one FW 190
Capt. Young and Lt. Fink shared	one FW 190
Lt. Matthews	one FW 190
Lt. Goodson	two FW 190
Maj. DuFour	one Me 109

Combat Reports: "My #2 and I were up-sun from bombers being attacked by FW 190s. I saw a FW, painted black, pull up under me to the right. I looked around and told my #2 to cover me while I slid in dead astern of the FW 190. I fired about a three and one half-second burst at 150 yards. The e/a had explosions all along the fuselage and cockpit. Flames and heavy black smoke trailed back from around the engine. I don't think the Pilot got out. My #2 kept a Hun off me, but he was hit himself, sustaining minor damage. My Wingman saw me shoot the FW 190, causing it to start a slow spiral, go onto its back, and into a spin. I claim one FW 190 Destroyed. (Night Fighter)."

Fonzo Smith Captain, Air Corps.

*****

"I was leading 335 Squadron White section covering the front box of bombers near Paris. Three Me 109s, coming out of the sun, started attacking a straggler. I went down to attack these e/a, picking out one. My #2, Lt. Stanhope, took another. I started to fire at 350 yards at about 15 degrees deflection astern. The first burst hit the e/a in the tail, so I moved my bead up and gave him a two or three-second burst, ceasing fire at about 250 yards. I observed strikes around the cockpit, on the engine, and at the left wing root. As I closed fast, I flew past very close to the e/a, less than 20 yards away. I saw the Pilot slumped over in the cockpit with smoke and flame coming from the left side of the engine cowling. He started a diving turn to starboard when I lost sight of him. I was using tracer one to ten in alternate guns. I claim one Me 109 Destroyed."

Roy Evans Captain, Air Corps.

Captain Fonzo "Snuffy" Smith with Pistol Packin Mamma. A colorful Pilot from the 121st E S, transferred into 335 Sq. His tour ended when he became a POW. Zigler collection.

*****

"I was flying #2 to Blue Leader who dove to attack several FW 190s positioning themselves for attack on the Forts. I followed Blue Leader at about 125 yards and witnessed him firing at a FW, which he apparently damaged. I then pushed the attack, firing a full eight-second burst. I closed in from a banking 15 degree turn astern at 250 yards to a full diving line astern at about 100 yards. I saw strikes on wing roots and cockpit and intermittent streams of black smoke. The cockpit hood flew off, and the e/a broke up in the air. It whipped into a violent inverted spin, streaming smoke as it disappeared from my view at about 5,000 feet. I claim one FW 190 Destroyed."

Frank Fink 1st Lt. Air Corps.

*****

17 Aug - On a Ramrod near Antwerp, the Group broke up several attempts by e/a to attack bombers, but the Group did not close on any of them since the e/a did not stay around to fight.

A memorandum was received from Col. Edward Anderson, addressed to the ground crews, this Station, dated 16 Aug 43.

1. This morning the Pilots of the 4th Fighter Group destroyed 17 enemy aircraft, probably destroyed 2 more, and damaged 4.

2. Much of the credit for this impressive score belongs to the ground crews of this Station, and this is as it should be. Too often the efforts of the men who put the planes in the air are overlooked; but the Pilots know, and I know the value of their work. To accomplish the results we achieved today means that ground crews were right in there pitching.

3. It is my desire to thank all ground personnel for today's success and to express my sincere appreciation for a job well done.

Col. Peterson is to replace Col. Anderson as Group Commander, with Col. Anderson becoming Brigadier General as Wing Commander.

20 Aug - Lt. Conklin returned from hunting in Scotland. He furnished the venison for a dinner for Squadron Officers. Fresh corn on the cob and salad completed the meal.

24 Aug - Seven of the new escape kits were received from Group Intelligence. These were given to Pilots flying with the U.S. Mae Wests.

25 Aug - The 334 Squadron was the only operational Squadron. They completed the installation of racks to handle the new 75-gallon metal belly tanks or bombs.

The Distinguished Flying Cross was awarded to:
Capt. Alfred H. Hopson
Capt. William O'Regan
1st. Lt. Henry L. Mills
1st. Lt. Robert L. Priser
Each for completion of 50 Combat Missions

Lt. Col. Peterson, formerly Commanding Officer 71st Eagle Squadron, is now Commanding Officer of the 4th Fighter Group. He succeeds Col. Edward Anderson effective 20 Aug 43.

In a tail chase exercise, Lt. Fraser, a new recruit, experienced difficulties in a high speed dive from 30,000 feet with the IAS showing more than 400 mph. He regained control at 1,500 feet. Wing seams were torn open and rivets forced out by the speed of the dive.

28 Aug - General Hoyt presented Air Medals and/or Oak Leaf Clusters to 15 Pilots of the 334 Squadron. In addition, 34 Medals or Clusters were presented to Pilots of 335 Squadron.

The Distinguished Flying Cross was awarded to:
Capts. Evans, Young, and F.D. Smith
Lts. Padgett and Stanhope

31 Aug - Major Dufour led the Group on a Ramrod to Support bombers near Dieppe. In the vicinity of Beauvais, eight to ten e/a dove towards 336 Squadron head on from 27,000 feet. Apparently surprised, the e/a broke in all directions. In the ensuing combat, Capt. Miley and Lt. Stanhope each claimed one FW 190 Probably Destroyed. As the Group headed for base, they encountered another group of about 40 Forts with 12 to 15 e/a lining up for a head-on attack on them. Capt. Evans, 336 Squadron leader, led his Squadron in front of the e/a, breaking up the attack, with Goodson claiming one.

The enemy casualty report confirmed 15 e/a destroyed from 26 June through 16 Aug by eight Pilots of 334 Squadron.

Another notable event took place this month. It all started shortly after a group of enlisted men arrived in Debden in December. A short bicycle ride from Debden, there was a little town named Thaxted. The town had an annual celebration, the highlight of which was a drawing of a lucky number and the award of a prize to the lucky winner. S/Sgt Gerald Hunter, of previous cow milking fame, had decided to leave the Armament Shop, nicknamed "Slaves in the Woods," and together with a Texan, Supply Sgt Bill Pearson, he decided to attend the celebration. Since they had both become well acclimated to the language and ways of the locals, they felt comfortable in attending this affair. They knew all the unique words of the RAF such as; kites, gen, pukka gen, gremlins, and mild and bitters. They knew that it was taboo to discuss the value of having a King and Queen, and that the cost of the Royal Family was not a subject for discussion. The two, however, were totally unprepared for what happened next. Quite by surprise, Bill won the grand prize—a thirty pound live pig, which had been donated by a local farmer.

Gerald tried to convince Bill that he should give up the pig and let some British family have an opportunity to enjoy it. Bill insisted on keeping the pig, which he dutifully carried back to the Base. They then built a pen behind the Mess Hall and daily fed the pig the scraps from the Mess.

The pig prospered and gained weight rapidly: 30-40-50 pounds came quickly, and continued until eventually the pig weighed over two hundred pounds. Unfortunately, during the process a setback occurred when the Base Health Officer discovered the pen behind the Mess Hall. He demanded that it be immediately removed from the vicinity. Bill conceived of an idea to build another pen at a little auxilliary field nearby. This was accomplished. He daily carried the swill to the pig, and the pig continued to thrive.

It soon became time to bring the original program to fruition. Bill sent out invitations to all the men, in the Base Squadrons, to come and bring their girl friends to a big Pig Bar-B-Que. Pfc Burly Grimes, an Alabaman from 336 Ordinance, was assigned to build a magnificent spit on which the whole pig could be roasted. Volunteers were then requested to shoot, bleed, scrape, and gut the pig in preparation for the roasting.

No one volunteered or had any knowledge of the process, so the duty fell to Gerald, the "Good old farm boy." He enlisted the aid of a nearby farmer to provide the hot water and a flat bed hay wagon on which to scrape the hair off the pig. Gerald took a carbine and several large butcher knives, from the Mess, to the scene. He then outlined the procedure to his helpers. Gerald shot the pig in the head, cut its jugular, and had it lifted onto the wagon where the pig was scalded, scraped, and gutted.

The pig was then installed on the spit, back at the BBQ site, and roasted all day and all night in preparation for the following day's festivities. The picnic was held in a nearby pasture, and the celebration continued throughout the entire afternoon and evening. The Mess Sergeants provided all sorts of appropriate accompaniments and topped the meal off with cake with fruit frosting. The icing was made by draining the juice from canned fruit cocktail, which was then mashed and thickened with sugar.

All participants agreed that the Bar-B-Que was the high point of the month.

Squadron strength 31 Aug:

334 Squadron	40 Officers	244 Enlisted Men
335 Squadron	40 Officers	241 Enlisted Men

1 Sept 1943 - Saffron Walden homing changed from MORELIGHT to JACKNIFE.

All Officers were required to attend a mobile exhibit of German Aircraft Equipment. The Enlisted Men also attended.

2 Sept - *Life Magazine* photographed the dispersal and the Pilots who scored on the raid to Paris. *Gaumont British News* took motion pictures for release to movie houses all over the world.

On a Group Sweep, near Formerie, e/a attacked 334 Squadron, which then evaded but was unable to score any kills. During this engagement, one P-47 was seen to dive straight down followed by four FW 190s. 1st Lt. Dale B. Leaf was reported NYR. (He was later reported as KIA).

Returning early due to engine trouble, Lt. Fiedler, attempting to land, pulled up to avoid hitting another plane. In so doing, he pranged his ship at the end of the runway. He was not injured.

Lt. Boyles was promoted to Captain as of 1 September.

This was Lt. Fraser's first operational flight.

3 Sept - By request of His Majesty the King, a National Day of Prayer was observed to commemorate the Fourth Anniversary of Britain's entry into the war. A service was broadcast over the Tannoy.

A Ramrod to support 1st Task Force, encountered e/a near Abbeyville. The 336 Squadron broke up the attack on the bombers. Later, another attack was intercepted by 336 Squadron with Lt. Goodson claiming one FW 190 Probably Destroyed.

It appears that the Huns have a new tactic. They send in a small number of planes to attack the bombers and draw off the escort, while a large number awaits up-sun in position to bounce the bombers.

The 335 Squadron did not have enough serviceable kites to send a full Squadron.

This was F/O Blanchfield's first operational flight.

6 Sept - On a Withdrawal Support mission, the Group arrived at the bomber location to find them under attack by 15 yellow nosed FW 190s. The 190s dove away as the Group approached. Later, a FW 190 attacking a B-17 was destroyed by Capt. Evans of 335 Squadron (As of yesterday, Evans is now a Major.)

Thirty-four Forts were lost on this show. Twenty-four of them were in the Channel out of gas.

Pvt Edward Rupnick was transferred to await transport to the States for Aviation Cadet Training.

Col. Edward Anderson was presented with the Silver Star by BG O.D. Hunter.

In a farewell party following the ceremonies, the "Flying Eagles," with Lt. Ben Ezzell at the piano, entertained and introduced the new song—"*Lilly from Piccadilly*," by Cpl Mickey Balsam. It was received with gusto.

Mickey had composed the musical score and written eight verses of the song, extolling the merits of a "Piccadilly Commando." Mickey sang the song at this party and was quickly invited to perform in the Debden Cinema. He also joined the "Flying Eagles Band" and appeared in the show "*Glad to See Ya*."

7 Sept - Escorting bombers near Deynze, 335 Squadron chased e/a about to attack bombers. Later, near Hulst, 334 Squadron drove off another attack. Heavy flak was encountered, and 1st Lt. Aubrey Stanhope was knocked down. He dove on a Hun and was heard to yell either "Hit" or "Help." He was not seen again. (Stanhope became a POW). Capt. Smith sighted two kites on the deck. It looked like a P-47 and a FW 190. Both of them blew up. Tonight the Squadron, with Mrs. Stanhope, mourns the passing of old Stan.

Lt. Stephenson of 336 claimed three e/a Damaged. One FW 190 was Destroyed by German flak.

8 Sept - Cecil Blackburn was promoted from 1st Lt. to Capt.

Hostilities between Italy and the Allied Forces ended when General Eisenhower, Supreme Allied Commander-in-Chief, announced the "Unconditional" surrender of the Italian forces by Marshall Badoglio.

9 Sept - On a morning Ramrod, near Elbeu, upwards of 30 e/a attacked the Forts head-on from up-sun. The 334 and 336 Squadrons broke up these attacks, reformed, and continued escort towards Paris. The 334 again climbed and headed off an attack by about 16 e/a, again head-on. Long range deflection shots were made, but there were no claims of damage.

Lt. Boehle peeled off and was not seen again. He was reported as NYR. Lt. Fink bailed out over Paris due to engine failure. He told the boys he was going out, and he bid them farewell. He seemed calm and under control. (Fink became a POW). At least three Forts were seen to peel away from the formation, and several chutes were seen.

11 Sept - After spending two nights and a day in a dinghy, Lt. Boehle was picked up by a Torpedo Boat this morning.

Sgts Tabb, Threet, Simmons, and Penn, and Cpls Bartel, Natheny, and Ward are transferred to U.S. for Aviation Cadet Training. "Lucky Boys!"

2nd Lt. Gangemi, 1st Lt. Moon, and F/O Biel are assigned to 334 Squadron.

The Group celebrated its first anniversary as an "All American" Group with a Field Day featuring everything from football to a pie eating contest. There was a Cabaret and a Stage show, plus free beer and a banquet in the Base mess hall.

These events were followed by a Ball at the Red Cross Aeroclub with music by the "Flying Eagles." Col. Peterson awarded prizes.

14 Sept - A few minutes prior to "press time," for an uneventful Escort to Roulers, Lt. Boehle appeared dressed in "civies." He was welcomed by all and turned himself over to the I.O. (Intelligence Officer)

Lt. Boehle recalled: "On our escort to Paris, we turned into several FW 190s attacking head-on. I pulled up to avoid a collision with another P-47. Shortly thereafter, I dove after a FW 190 that was attacking a Fort. I followed to 15,000 feet, but pulled up unable to get in firing range. Climbing back up, another FW 190 dove to attack me. I took evasive action, ending up in a spin and dive,

The Flying Eagles Band was manned by 4th Group personnel. The band was very popular and played at many Station functions. They frequently had engagements at other Stations, and they went on a one month tour near the end of the war. Ray Pool collection.

coming out at 10,000 feet. The FW followed, firing at every opportunity as I maneuvered. I was able to get in a short burst at him, but saw no strikes. I then dove for the deck. He followed, still firing, until apparently, out of ammo, he broke off and climbed.

During the fight, I felt no hits, but noticed a hole in my port wing. I headed for home. In a gentle dive, at 19,000 feet, there was a terrific vibration; the engine broke loose and plunged down. The plane, out of control, went into a flat spin. I tried a "May Day," but I found the R/T was u/s. With some difficulty, I then bailed out at about 15,000 feet. I landed in the water about 30 miles off Dieppe.

I released the Dinghy, inflated it, and climbed into it. I pulled the cover over me and got as comfortable as possible. At dusk, I fired one of my flares. I rationed my food to one bit of chocolate, two malted milk tablets, and a stick of gum per meal. The rain each night provided enough water to drink, but I could not sleep either night. I saw two Spits and fired a flare, which was not seen. After midnight, I heard MTB boats and flashed the torch on my British Mae West at intervals. They finally saw me and picked me up at 0450 hours after 43 hours in the water."

15 Sept - Col. Blakeslee led a Ramrod to Paris. Just West of Paris, Lt. Sobanski led his Section in an attack on several FW 190s attacking the bombers. Although hindered by fire from the bombers, the Section fended off the attack and rejoined the Squadron. No claims were made.

18 Sept -

An **Oak Leaf Cluster to the Distinguished Flying Cross** was awarded to Captain James Clark for completion of 70 fighter combat missions and the destruction of three enemy aircraft.

Lt. Vernon Boehle 334 Sq. transferred from 71st E S. While returning to Debden from a fight, his engine fell out of his plane forcing him to parachute into the Channel. He spent 43 hours in the water before he was rescued. Konsler collection.

The **Distinguished Flying Cross** was awarded to the following Officers

1st Lt. Douglas Booth	Lt. Robert Messinger
1st Lt. Winslow Sobanski	Lt. George Mirsch
	Lt. Don Gentile
F/O Clyde Smith	Lt. Donald Nee

F/O McGrattan was assigned to 335 Squadron.

22 Sept - A Rodeo to Lille was uneventful with no e/a seen.

A British Sterling blew up 1 1/2 miles north of base. No one got out.

Ingold of 336 crash landed.

24 Sept - Thirty-six Sgts and Cpls from 334 Squadron were awarded the Good Conduct Medal.

F/O Riley and F/O Waterman were assigned to 335 Squadron.

A Group Balboa (practice mission) was flown for the benefit of visiting dignitaries.

27 Sept - A Ramrod was flown in support of Forts over Rottumeroog Island. On the way out, two FW 190s were seen positioning to attack. Lt. Millikan destroyed one, but the other one evaded.

In the afternoon, Lt. Douglas, while attempting to take off, pranged (crashed or damaged a plane) on the runway. He damaged his prop and undercarriage.

F/O Ralph K. Hofer and F/O David W. Howe were assigned to 334 Squadron.

29 Sept - The Chemical Warfare lecture series continued, as required, for all personnel.

A Mustang (P-51) was assigned to 334. Major Coen and Captain Clark immediately made experimental flights in it. Captain F.D. Smith followed for 335.

F/O Brandenburg and F/O Church were assigned to 335 Squadron as replacements.

30 Sept - Today is pay day, which is the only thing good about today. It continues to be a long spell of cloudy weather with intermittant rains.

Captain David Van Epps and F/O John McNabb were assigned to 334 Squadron, and Don Gentile made Captain.

2 Oct 1943 - **The Distinguished Flying Cross** was awarded to Major Oscar H. Coen for 30 Combat missions and the destruction of two enemy aircraft.

A Ramrod was flown to Emden to support 180 Forts. At the target area, six Me 109s attempted to attack the bombers. The 336 Squadron diverted the attack. Near Aurich ten FW 190s prepared to attack, but were chased off by 334 Squadron. Lt. Beeson claimed one FW 190 Destroyed. Three other Pilots fired but made no claims.

Lt. Schlegel, 335 Squadron, claimed a Probable. Peterson, of 336 Squadron, also claimed one Destroyed.

Two Pilots reported they had been fired on by two P-47s with UN letters.

4 Oct - Lt. Col. Peterson presented "**Oak Leaf Clusters to the Air Medal**" awards to 14 Pilots on the parade ground.

The ceremony was followed by an uneventful mission to Eupen.

6 Oct - The Group held Open House for 75 distinguished civilian and military Officials from various countries. Eleven of the Pilots, who hold the DFC, were seated with the visitors. Later there was an inspection of the planes on the flight line by the visitors.

7 Oct - Oscar H. Coen was promoted from Major to Lt. Colonel; Robert L. Priser from 1st Lt. to Captain.

Cpl. Eugene Heath was transferred to U.S. for Aviation Cadet Training.

8 Oct - After refueling at an advanced base, the Group led by Col. Blakeslee flew a Ramrod to Bremen.

The 334 Squadron attempted to climb to attack 30 plus e/a up-sun of the rear boxes of bombers. As they attempted to climb, they were continually bounced by sections of four to eight Huns, who were apparently trying to break up the Squadron and draw them away from the bombers. A P-47 was seen to go straight down from 24,000 feet, and two chutes were seen to open. It is believed one was F/O Clyde D. Smith and the other an enemy pilot. Lt. Patterson, of 335, is also MIA. He has not been heard from or seen. (Both Smith and Patterson became POWs).

Near Amsterdam, F/O Hofer destroyed a Me 109 that was shooting up a P-47, both of which went into the Zuider Zee. Capt. Clark claims one Me 109 Destroyed; Lt. Beeson claims two Me 109s Destroyed; and Lt. Mills one Me 109 Probably Destroyed.

On a second mission, again e/a attempted to intercept, but they were driven off. Lt. Ross saw a Me 210 below the bombers. He attacked and Destroyed it. Major Evans Destroyed a FW 190, thereby becoming the first Ace in 335 Squadron.

Lt. Blanding was attacked and evaded with damage to his kite, but he made it back to base. "Talk about coming in on a wing and a prayer." Blanding's engine, cockpit, and tail were damaged. He had thrown away his helmet and was ready to bail when he noticed Jerry had left.

10 Oct - Ten EM, graduates of the A/A School, were ordered to the British East Coast Gunnery Range for further training.

2nd Lt. Willard R. Terry was assigned to 334 Squadron.

F/Os Ward, Barnes, and Clotfelter and 2nd Lt. Reed were assigned to 335 Squadron.

A Ramrod was flown to Munster to escort 180 B-17s.

Bombers were under attack by 30 plus e/a attacking in pairs. The 336 Squadron went to their aid while 334 and 336 Squadrons fended off another attack. No e/a were destroyed.

The following Officers were assigned to 334 Squadron: 2nd Lt. Charles Carr, F/O Robert Hills, and F/O Frank Gallion.

15 Oct - "Kingo" exercises were held by the Pilot Officers. Thirty-seven Pilots were released about six miles from base. They were told to return and to evade police and guards. F/O Howe was the only one from 334 Squadron to make it.

Sgt Halpin was transferred out to return to the U.S. for Aviation Cadet Training.

20 Oct - A practice "Commando" raid caught two Polish soldiers in civies preparing to light a "bomb" in the blister hangar. The saboteurs promptly "surrendered."

All personnel were scheduled to have chest x-rays.

A Ramrod to Duren was uneventful except for F/O Megura's plane. It sustained battle damage from two unidentified planes while he and his wingman were escorting a straggler across the Channel. The a/c continued on toward England.

Lt. Carr and F/O Hills made this their first operational mission.

23 Oct - **Oak Leaf Clusters to the Air Medal** were awarded to 1st Lts. Hively, Robert Williams, Allen Bunte, Alexander Rafalovich and F/O William Smith. An Air Medal was awarded to 2nd Lt. Robert B. Fraser.

Lt. Duane "Bee" Beeson became the first Ace of 334 Sq. He was credited with 24 plus e/a Destroyed prior to his becoming a POW in April 1944. He is pictured with Don Gentile (in Cockpit) another top scoring Ace with 27 plus e/a Destroyed to his credit. Zigler collection.

27 Oct - Lt. Beeson's claim of two Me 109s Destroyed and one Damaged, 8 Oct 43, near Mepple-Zwolle was confirmed. Also confirmed was his claim of one FW 190 Damaged, 10 Oct, Annhem area.

These confirmations give Lt. Beeson the honor of being the first Ace of 334 Squadron with six e/a Destroyed and three Damaged.

29 Oct - James A. Clark was promoted from Captain to Major.

With appropriate ceremony, with all Pilots and Enlisted Men on base in attendance on the Parade Ground, Col. Auton, 65 Fighter Wing, presented the following awards:

The Silver Star
Major Roy Evans
Major Carl Miley
1st Lt. Duane Beeson
The Distinguished Flying Cross and/or Oak Leaf Cluster
Major James Clark
1st Lt. Duane Beeson
1st Lt. Raymond Care
1st Lt Victor France
1st Lt. Winslow Sobanski
1st Lt. Vernon Boehle
1st Lt. Archie Chatterley
1st Lt. Alexander Rafalovich
F/O William Smith

30 Oct - A Halloween Party was held at the American Red Cross "Aeroclub" with bundles of hay, pumpkins, masks, fortune tellers, apple bobbing, a horror house, and games. The "Flying Eagles" band helped make this a typically American party.

31 Oct - For more than a week there has been nothing but fog and bad weather with no operations possible. There has been some slow-timing, local flying, and lots of cards.

The **Air Medal or Oak Leaf Cluster to the Air Medal** was awarded to the following Officers:

1st Lts. Ivan Moon, Vasseure Wynn, Alfred Markel, and Spiros Pisanos, and F/O Herbert Blanchfield

2 Nov 1943 - "A new month, and we hope better weather is in store. This morning doesn't bring much hope."

"An 8-pound boy was born to Lt. and Mrs. A.H. Markel. Lt. Markel's claim of being the first father in 334 Squadron is hereby confirmed by the Squadron Medical and Intelligence Officers acting as the Credit Board. The new mascot was named Robin-Adair."

All available Pilots attended an Aircraft Recognition Test followed by a Dinghy drill at Saffron Walden Baths.

The 335 football team came through in great style as they tramped over the 45th Service Squadron team to the tune of 20-0. This victory made the 335th the Station Champion.

3 Nov - 2nd Lt. Robert A. Breaux and 1st Lt. George W. Adams were assigned to 334 Squadron.

At Halesworth, where the Group refueled, Lt. Waterman took off; he immediately spun back to terra firma with his plane in flames. He was rescued by the crash crew with only slight injuries, but considerable blood loss.

On a Ramrod to Wilhelmshaven, 334 and 335 Squadrons were engaged in combat with e/a while 336 flew cover. The e/a, Me 109s, attacked from 3,000 to 4,000 feet above from out of the sun. The 109s attacked by zooming down, firing, and climbing back up. The 109s dive speed enabled them to out climb our a/c and get into position to zoom down to attack again. The enemy tactics appeared to be designed to cause our a/c to drop their external gas tanks. With the loss of this gas, our planes would be unable to continue to escort the bombers.

Lt. Moon and F/O Gallion were lost as their planes were shot down. Captain Julius Toy, (Assistant Intelligence Officer) reported in the Mission Summary Report, "A P-47 was seen going down in flames, vicinity of Opmeer, after attack by a Me 109. Another aircraft, believed to be a P-47, went into the Zuider Zee just off Hypolitushoef. No chutes were seen in either case."

These planes were believed to be piloted by Lt. Moon and F/O Frank Gallion respectively. (On 10 Feb 1995, Frank Gallion's plane, with his body still in it, was recovered from the shallow water in this vicinity. The whereabouts of Lt. Moon remain a mystery. (Moon was KIA).

Lt. Rafalovich claimed one Me 109 Destroyed, and Lt. Fraser claimed a Probably Destroyed.

5 Nov - The red trim bordering the plane insignia was ordered removed and replaced by blue on all a/c.

The Group, led by Major Evans, flew a Ramrod to Dortmund. As the bombers turned onto the target run, 12 FW 190s, flying four line-abreast, attacked the lead box. Major Evans, leading 335 Squadron, diverted them. He fired, sending one e/a into a spin. The remaining e/a reformed for another attack. As 335 Squadron turned to engage them, another force of eight FW 190s attacked from the rear. During this engagement, Captain Smith destroyed one FW 190 by firing from 300 yards down to 200 yards. He got many strikes, and a large section of empennage flew off the e/a. He had to break off the engagement to avoid fire from the Forts. The e/a were aggressive and persistant.

Miscellaneous notes: Lt. Waterman may lose his left eye as a result of his 3 Nov accident at Halesworth.

11 Nov - There were several days of bad weather, during which only flight testing and local flying was accomplished. Combat films and training films were shown each morning.

The Distinguished Flying Cross was awarded to 1st Lt. Robert G. Williams

Lt. Ivan Moon 334 Sq. was shot down on 3 Nov 1943, on the same mission as Frank Gallion. His body was never recovered. Frank Gallion collection.

F/O Gallion 334 Sq. with RCAF trainer, was shot down on 3 Nov 1943. His body and plane were recovered from the Zuider Zee in 1995 during dredging operations. Frank Gallion collection.

An Oak Leaf Cluster to the DFC was awarded to 1st Lt. Henry L. Mills

The Group flew an uneventful Ramrod to Wesel.

The 8 Oct claims were confirmed for Lt. Mills, one 109 Probably Destroyed; Lt. Fraser, one 109 Damaged; and F/O Hofer, one 109 Destroyed.

14 Nov - A **2nd Oak Leaf Cluster to the DFC** was awarded to Major Roy A. Evans

16 Nov - The November Overseas Edition of *Life Magazine* featured our 334 Squadron Commanding Officer, James A. Clark, on the cover in front of a Thunderbolt. Inside, three of our Pilots, Lt. Howard Hively, Captain Henry Mills, and Lt. Raymond Care were shown with pictures of e/a they had destroyed.

20 Nov - **The Distinguished Flying Cross** was awarded to 1st Lt. Earle W. Carlow

21 Nov - **The Distinguished Flying Cross** was awarded to 1st Lt. Spiros N. Pisanos

All available Pilots viewed films of:

Forts attack on Norway

Shuttle raid on Regensburg—England to Africa

23 Nov - An article appeared in *Stars and Stripes* 22 Nov 43 relating how F/O Hofer, 22, scored a kill on his first mission into enemy territory.

25 Nov - A letter was received from Major General W.E. Kepner, commending the 4th Fighter Group for completing operations in the month of October—1507 hours of flight without a single accident.

26 Nov - After refueling at Hardwick, the Group, led by Col. Blakeslee, flew a Ramrod to Bremen. The R/V encountered B-24s strung out with as much as one mile between individual a/c, making cover very difficult. Near Hude, Lt. Padgett Destroyed a Me 109 attacking a lone Lib. The e/a, equipped with a large belly tank, blew up in mid-air. Several subsequent attacks by e/a were diverted without incident.

The Distinguished Flying Cross was awarded to 1st Lt. Howard D. Hively

1st Lt. Edmund Whalen and 2nd Lt. Herbert Kneeland were assigned to 334 Squadron.

29 Nov - Major Edner led the Group on a Ramrod to Bremen.

Eighteen 334 Squadron planes left for refueling at Bungay. Ten aborted the mission for various mechanical problems. Six aborted from 335 Squadron. The remaining members encountered various hit and run e/a, attacking and diving into the clouds before interception could be accomplished. Lt. Beeson was able to close on one Me 109. He probably destroyed it. Capt. F. D. Smith jumped a Me 109, firing and knocking off several pieces as the e/a went into the clouds. He claimed one Destroyed.

Miscellaneous Notes: Stanhope, Merritt, Fink, and Wortman were all unofficially reported as POWs. Mrs. Stanhope has received a letter from Lt. Stanhope from a POW camp.

30 Nov - An uneventful Rodeo was flown to the Dutch Islands.

The Assessed Enemy Casualty Report Confirmed six e/a Destroyed from 12 Aug 43 through 3 Nov 43 by Lts. Beeson and Rafalovich, Capt. Clark, and F/O Hofer. Lt. Beeson led with three Destroyed.

Captain F.D. Smith was promoted to Major and has completed his tour. Blanding and Padgett were both promoted to Captain.

The Monthly Squadron Strength Report:

334 Sq.   Officers 41   Enlisted Men 240

336 Sq.   Officers 43   Enlisted Men 236

1 Dec 1943 - December started with a Ramrod to Solingen led by Major Edner. One e/a was seen but evaded into clouds. Two of our planes suffered minor damage. Lt. John Godfrey got his first e/a, a 109.

2 Dec - Airborne on a test flight, F/O John McNabb was killed when his plane crashed near Kenton. It was reported that his plane burst into flames and hit the earth at a low angle, spreading debris over three or four acres.

3 Dec - The 334 Dispersal Flag was flown at half-mast in memory of F/O McNabb.

2nd Lts. Lawrence Grey and Nicholas Megura were assigned to 334 Squadron.

The 334 Squadron celebrated the first anniversary of its arrival in England with a party given by the Officers. It was chaired by "Deacon" Hively. Music was provided by the "Flying Eagles," and there were many attractive girls present from Saffron Walden and the WAAF and ATS organizations.

There was chocolate cake, chocolate ice cream, doughnuts, sandwiches, and coffee. There was a continous supply of beer throughout the evening with no casualties. Don Allen supplied cartoons on the walls showing GIs and their girls.

7 Dec - The Distinguished Flying Cross was awarded to 1st Lt. Alfred H. Markel

A letter was received from Capt. Heene. He commended and thanked all those who helped make the recent anniversary party a success. Named specifically were: 1st Sgt Morris and T/Sgt Nickerson for their efforts; S/Sgt Mastos and Sgt Golden for preparation of the supper; Sgts Wehrle and Lewis for the liquid refreshment service; the band for its fine entertainment; and S/Sgt Don Allen for the excellent decorations.

10 Dec - An order was received promoting Lawrence Orin Grey and Nicholas Megura to 2nd Lts. and assigning them to EAD as of 27 November.

Raymond C. Care and Henry L. Mills were promoted from 1st Lt. to Captain.

11 Dec - Major Evans led a Rodeo to Emden. On the way to R/V, four Me 109s attacked the lead Squadron, 335. Eight other Me 109s attacked 334 and 335 Squadrons. Lt. France destroyed one during an engagement that lasted to the limit of endurance of the Group. The Group then returned to base not having reached the R/V.

After the big Hun raid on the 9th, hitting Andrews Field, the Station was placed on a semi-alert basis. All personnel are to carry helmet and gas mask. All kites and vehicles are to be fully dispersed.

13 Dec - A report was received concerning the status of the following Pilots:

2nd Lt. Hazen S. Anderson - 12 Mar 43 - POW

1st Lt. Gordon H. Whitlow - 21 May 43 - Buried in France

1st Lt. William B. Morgan - 21 May 43 - POW

Col. Edner led an uneventful Ramrod to Bremen.

Many Pilots practiced dive-bombing in preparation for future missions.

Miscellaneous Notes: Of the P-51s on yesterday's sweep, one stayed up for over four hours.

15 Dec - Lt. Hofer was picked up by MPs in London for failure to wear bars on his trench coat and for not carrying his AGO card. It took several hours to prove his identity to the authorities.

16 Dec - Orders were received of the appointment of the following as 2nd Lts. and placing them on EAD (extended active duty): Hipolitus Thomas Biel, Herbert Jude Blanchfield, and Gerald E. Montgomery.

Col. Edner led the Group on a Ramrod to Bremen during which new tactics were introduced. Each Squadron was to be 2,000 feet from the next Squadron and to add a fifth section (purple). The Purple Section was to fly 500 feet above the Squadron, act as Scout, report, and attack any approaching e/a.

E/a were encountered by 336 Squadron, and Gentile, Norley, and Garrison each destroyed a Ju 88.

Lt. Ballew crash landed at Horham, damaging his prop and one wing.

18 Dec - Robert Fraser was promoted from 2nd Lt. to 1st Lt.

With appropriate ceremony, Col. Chesley G. Peterson presented awards to Pilots in the briefing room.

20 Dec - Major Evans again led the Group on a Ramrod to Bremen. On the way in, F/O Hofer turned back due to engine trouble. He was bounced by three Me 109s and chased to mid-channel where he evaded into the haze.

Lt. William W. Millikan of 336 claimed one Me 109 Destroyed.

22 Dec - Capt. Heene wrote a memorandum to detail that on 19 Dec the two children sponsored by 334 Squadron, Dorothy and William H., were entertained in London by Sgt Morris, Sgt Nickerson, Cpl Ettner, and himself. They were given many gifts from the Squadron and five Pounds each. On their ride through London, they were fortunate enough to see the King leaving Buckingham Palace. Later they were taken to lunch and a show. The Squadron has seen to it that at least two children had a "Merry Christmas."

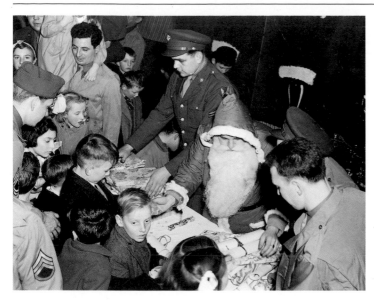

Santa Claus, believed to be John Cross 335 Sq. entertaining English children 25 Dec. 1943. Pool collection.

Col. Blakeslee led a Ramrod to Munster. Near Enschede, Lts. Bunte, Wynn, and Godfrey made a diving attack on four Me 109s. Wynn and Godfrey each destroyed one, and shared a third.

Miscellaneous Notes: Col. Blakeslee has returned after doing six shows in P-51s.

24 Dec - Major Clark led a Ramrod to Calais where the bombers were trying to take out Hun rocket guns. It was a record raid with over 1,300 American kites and over 2,000 Allied Kites. Not one a/c was lost.

Miscellaneous Notes: President Roosevelt in his Christmas Eve "Fireside Talk," named Ike Eisenhower "Second Front" C in C. The Second front was to start in 90 days.

25 Dec - The first three-graders were guests at the Officers' Mess for punch and lager, which was served from 1030 to 1200 hours.

At 1200 hours, over fifty Officers, with Lt. Col. Malone acting as "Head Waiter," served a sumptuous dinner to the Enlisted Men in the Airmens' Mess.

At 1430 hours, 60 Enlisted Men entertained seven large truck loads of English children. They were treated to cartoons in the Cinema, then ice cream, candy, and cake. They next visited with Santa Claus, (Sgt John Cross, 335), who presented a gift to each child. The children, to their delight, were then allowed to crawl all over a Thunderbolt.

At 1600 hours, the Officers were treated to a heavily laden Christmas dinner table in two separate sittings.

This was the second Christmas away from home for many of them, and everyone hoped this would be their last Christmas spent away from their loved ones.

27 Dec - **The Distinguished Flying Cross** was awarded to 1st Lt. James D. Dye

The **Purple Heart** was awarded to Lt. Lloyd W. Waterman

30 Dec - An Enemy Casualty Report was received, confirming the claims of e/a Destroyed or Probably Destroyed for Capt. Henry Mills, Lt. Robert Fraser, and Lt. Rafalovich, on 8 Oct and 3 Nov 1943.

Col. Edner led an uneventful Free Lance and Withdrawal Support to Mannheim.

31 Dec 1943 - Col. Blakeslee led a Ramrod to Paris.

The USAAF put up 1,700 planes today, which was a record. They have dropped over 11,000 tons of bombs this month in spite of the bad weather. This was almost double the tonnage of any previous month.

Col. Pete was assigned to the 9th AF. Col. Blakeslee took over as Group Commander, with Col. Edner as his Group Operations Officer.

Winslow M. Sobanski was promoted from 1st Lt. to Captain.

4

Another New Kite

1 Jan 1944 - An announcement was posted on the 334 Squadron bulletin board headed:

"COMMUNICATIONS RENEWED WITH SCOTLAND AFTER THREE GENERATIONS - DOUR DESCENDANT OF ANCIENT CLAN MARRIES BEAUTIFUL EDINBURGH LASSIE"

The announcement explained that the great grandfather of Lt. Walter P. Young left Scotland for a life in the U.S. He never dreamed that his grandson, scores of years later, would marry the former Janet Dorothy McDonald Tomes, of Edinburgh, thus uniting these two Scottish Clans. Janet is a WAAF, and after their honeymoon in Aberdeen, they will be spending their leaves together at a nearby WAAF Station.

Our "Condogratulations" to them!

4 Jan - Target Munster - 335 Squadron, "This was the third Sweep running with no aborts; no spares; short on Birdmen."

5 Jan - On an ATF Support to Tours, four FW 190s were encountered. The 336 Squadron bounced them and destroyed two and damaged one. Capt. Gentile and Lt. Messenger each claimed one Destroyed.

Lt. Raphel of 336, crashed on takeoff. His rudder stuck, and he headed toward 335 dispersal. He hit a kite and ended up in the bomb dump. Both kites were badly damaged, but Raphel was unhurt.

7 Jan - Col. Blakeslee led a Withdrawal Support to Ludwigshafen. Near Hesdin, 12 FW 190s dove out of the sun and attacked straggling bombers. Col. Blakeslee bounced them. In the ensuing combat, Blakeslee destroyed one, as three others attacked him from the rear. His a/c was seriously damaged before Capt. Goodson shot down two of the e/a on his tail. Lt. Garrison damaged the other e/a. Blakeslee's kite was badly shot up, and he barely

made it back to Manston. He was escorted home to protect him from the Me 109s that kept jumping him. This was his seventh kill.

9 Jan - **The Distinguished Flying Cross** was awarded to: 1st Lt. Allen F. Bunte

13 Jan - A Ground Defense Platoon was established with 28 Enlisted Men under the command of Major Booth.

S/Sgt George M. Fite was transferred to the U.S. for Aviation Cadet training.

One of the 335 Squadron Enlisted Men received a Montgomery Ward catalog through the mail. It created quite a stir. The most popular section was the women's section.

14 Jan - On a Free Lance to Northern France, led by Col. Edner, the Group bounced 15 FW 190s. The 336 Squadron claimed four Destroyed in the ensuing combat. Near Soissons, 12 FW 190s were

1st Lt. Duane W. "Bee" Beeson, formerly of 71 ES, became 334 Squadron CO in March 44 with a rank of Major. "Bee" was an Ace with over 24 e/a to his credit. On 5 April 44, while strafing a German A/D, his P-51 was hit by flak and he had to bail out becoming a POW. Zigler collection.

engaged in combat. Later, Lt. Richards of 336 claimed one FW 190 Destroyed. Gentile claimed two FW 190s Destroyed; Garrison and Norley claimed one FW 190 shared; and Garrison, one FW 190 Destroyed.

The 334 Squadron claims were: Lt. Whalen one FW 190 Destroyed and one-half FW 190 Destroyed, shared with Lt. Rafalovich. Lts. Beeson, Biel, and Montgomery each claimed one FW 190 Destroyed.

R/T interference, the worst it has been, made messages from "Ginfizz" unreadable.

Combat reports submitted:

1st Lt. Beeson - "Flying Green 1, We dove on 10 or 12 FW 190s and closed at about 6,000 feet. I picked one of the last four and opened fire at about 250 yards down to 50 yards, when I broke over him. I saw severe strikes and large flashes in the wing roots and observed a large hole in his cockpit hood. The a/c fell into a dive and exploded when it hit the ground."

*****

2nd Lt. Biel - "Flying Green 4, I and Green 3 each singled out one FW 190 as we dove. Mine pulled off in a steep climb as I gave him a three-second deflection burst. He immediately exploded and burst into flames. The Pilot bailed out while the plane was on its back."

*****

2nd Lt. Montgomery - "I was flying White 3 when Pectin Sq. bounced 12 FW 190s. I closed and fired on one FW that broke formation. I saw only one strike. I continued firing as the e/a dove steeply. I pulled out with IAS 500-550 mph. The FW crashed, leaving a high column of smoke."

*****

1st Lt. Rafalovich - "Flying Green 3, I attacked an FW 190 at the rear of the formation. I observed severe strikes on both wings as I closed to 100 yards. Seeing fire coming from his engine, I pulled away to avoid explosion."

*****

1st Lt. Whalen - "I was flying Pectin Red 3 with Lt. Blanchfield as my #2. We turned into the group of Huns and I followed one who had turned out of the formation. I fired short bursts, as he took violent evasive action. I saw no strikes. He rolled onto his back and dove vertically, and I followed. #2 and I reached compressibility and could not pull out until we reached about 5,000 feet. The Hun just continued his dive and went straight into a field."

Major George Carpenter of Oil City, Pa. transferred from 121 ES and became 335 Squadron CO in Feb 44. He had Destroyed over 17 e/a, two of which he shot down on his last flight 18 April 44, prior to going down himself and becoming a POW. Zigler collection.

W. B. Smith and Charles Carr were promoted from 2nd Lt. to 1st Lt.

The Huns have put into use a dangling bomb or mine which they drop over our bomber formations to break them up so their fighters can get at them.

Three new Mustangs arrived, and each of the Squadrons was assigned one. Major Carpenter of 335 was the first to fly one.

15 -20 Jan - Fog closed all aerial operations, but routine a/c recognition tests and the study of operational bulletins kept all hands busy. Viewing combat films was a more pleasant duty.

On the 17th, Captain Don Gentile and 1st Lt. Willard Millikan were awarded an **Oak Leaf Cluster to the Distinguished Flying Cross**

Nine Pilots of 336 Squadron were awarded an **Oak Leaf Cluster to the Air Medals** previously awarded.

The 336 Squadron held a party for the enlisted men and S/Sgt Beyrooty retained his title of "Squadron Jitterbug."

21 Jan - Blakeslee led a Free Lance to Pas De Calais. In the Arras area, 12 e/a were sighted. In the ensuing combat, F/O Richards claimed one FW 190 Destroyed and Lt. Peterson one Damaged.

"Lt. Brandenburg will soon be awarded the 'Air Mud Plowing Medal' due to his heroic efforts in aiding a Land Army girl to plow a field. His gallant action was above and beyond the call of duty and was accomplished with the lower six inches of his prop blades while in aerial flight. In addition, he was awarded the unenvied distinction of flag waving for one week; being grounded for one week; and being restricted to the post for one month."

"Oh, what a wonderful morning it is??? Ho! Hum!"

23 Jan - **The Distinguished Flying Cross** was awarded to 2nd Lt. Nicholas Megura

29 Jan - On a Penetration Support to Frankfurt, the Group encountered 16 plus Me 109s and bounced them. Later they engaged four FW 190s. Some of the e/a were equipped with rocket guns and belly tanks.

Results: Capt. Mills claimed two Me 109s Destroyed;

Lt. Beeson claimed one Me 109 and one FW 190 Destroyed;

Lt. Chatterley and Lt. Whalen each claimed one Me 109 Destroyed; Lt. France claimed one FW 190 Destroyed and Lt. Pisanos claimed two Me 109s Destroyed.

Lt. Wyman is MIA; nobody knows what happened to him. The unofficial version is that he chased a Hun down through the clouds but that another Hun got on his tail. (He was KIA).

30 Jan - On a Penetration Support mission to Brunswick, 335 Squadron bounced 15 e/a and in turn were bounced by eight new type FW 190s. Lt. Anderson got one Me 109 Destroyed and one Damaged.

Lt. Mead was involved in the dogfights and he is MIA.

(He became a POW).

Combat Report:2nd Lt. Charles Anderson - "Flying Blue 4, near Lingen, we encountered 12 Me 109s and FW 190s at 26,000 feet and about 15 more at 12,000 feet. As we climbed in a circle towards the upper group, two 109s dove down between my #3 and me. Upon seeing us, they immediately started to climb away. I followed and fired at the one on the left from about 350 yards. I saw hits, and he started smoking badly as he turned off to the left. Since the e/a were flying line abreast, I could not follow the smoking Hun for fear the others would then be on my tail.

I then attacked the other e/a, but my guns on the starboard side jammed, making my fire very ineffective. I saw strikes on the fuselage and tail as the a/c went over on its side and then continued straight. I saw a 109 above me, so I broke off to rejoin my Section. I saw the first e/a spinning and burning as he went into a cloud. I joined up with Red 4 who had just seen an e/a falling out of control. He thought possibly it was the second a/c I had engaged. I claim one Me 109 Destroyed and one Damaged."

Captain Raymond C. "Bud" Care a former member of 71 ES was assigned to 334 Squadron where he became CO 6 April 44. On 15 April he had to bail out near Celle, Germany and he became a POW. Konsler Collection.

1st Lt. Paul M. Ellington of Tulsa, Oklahoma, formerly of 121 ES, was assigned to 335 Squadron. On 4 March 44, his P-51 developed engine trouble while returning from a mission to Berlin, and he had to bail out. He spent the rest of the war as a POW. He seldom shaved before a mission to avoid the irritation caused by several hours of wearing an oxygen mask. Konsler collection.

*****

31 Jan - Capt. Care led the Group on a Dive Bombing mission to Gilze Rijen A/D with 500 pound bombs. Two Sections were armed with bombs and two Sections flew as fighter cover. The Group dropped 17 bombs, hitting a fuel dump and the E/W runway.

The fighter cover was engaged by 15 to 20 Me 109s, then eight Me 109s, and still later six Me 109s. Capt. Sobanski and Lt. Beeson each claimed one Me 109 Destroyed. Lts. Carlson and Garrison each claimed one.

Lt. Clotfelter Destroyed a 109, and Lt. Ellington also Destroyed one. Both of these Pilots scored their first victory, and they were so excited they could hardly make sense when they gave their report.

Combat reports: Lt. Clotfelter - "Seeing a Group of Me 109s, we went into a Luftberry as three of the e/a dove through us, one staying above to cover them. I told Green #1 to follow them and I would watch the one above. Green #1 was unable to close. I saw a Me 109 coming at us from 9 o'clock. As he started to pull deflection on me, I called break and flicked into a tight turn. At that time, I saw three other e/a off to my right approximately 1,500 yards away. I pushed everything to the firewall and closed quickly.

One of the e/a started to pull to the left. I pulled deflection and fired a short burst with no effect. A second burst straightened him out, and I closed to 100 yards. I saw strikes all over the cockpit, causing pieces to fall off and a fire to start. I passed within a wing span as the e/a went into a dive and continued into the ground where it exploded on contact. I watched closely, but I saw no parachute. Apparently the Pilot was killed."

*****

1st Lt. Paul Ellington - "We engaged six to eight Me 109s and three of them dove for the deck. I attacked one of them and made several head-on passes, but I could not get a shot. I saw a Me 109 attack a P-47 and then dive for the deck. I followed and attacked this e/a and closed to about 500 yards. I gave him a two-second burst with insufficient deflection. I indicated 500 mph as I closed rapidly. I gave him another burst and saw strikes along the wing, engine, and cockpit. The e/a started to burn, and a lot of stuff blew off from the engine area. He half-rolled at about 800 feet and crashed in flames."

*****

2nd Lts. Howard Moulton and Shelton Monroe were assigned to 334 Squadron.

1 Feb 1944 - With appropriate ceremony, on the parade grounds Col. Auton made the following presentations: The **Distinguished Flying Cross and/or Oak Leaf Cluster to the DFC** to Capt. Mills,

1st Lts. Pisanos, Hively, Markel, Williams, Rafalovich, and Bunte, and 2nd Lt. Megura

Captain Heene then presented the Good Conduct Medal to thirty-seven Enlisted Men in the hangar.

The January issue of *Air Force Magazine* gave a graphic account of Capt. Winslow M. Sobanski's experiences prior to and after joining 334 Squadron.

3 Feb - Col. Edner led a Bomber Support to Emden with no action. However, F/O Cox became separated from Capt. Sobanski due to clouds and icing conditions, and F/O Cox was NYR. (He was KIA).

2nd Lts. Robert Hills and David Howell were assigned to 334 Squadron.

4 Feb - Hipolitus Biel and Herbert Blanchfield were promoted from 2nd Lt. to 1st Lt.

An **Oak Leaf Cluster to the Distinguished Flying Cross** was awarded to: Major James A. Clark

5 Feb - The 335 Squadron had a party at the Red Cross honoring their victorious football team. The Flying Eagles supplied music for dancing. Girls were transported from neighboring RAF Stations. A sumptuous table was set, and Lager was supplied in ample amounts. The team received a medal for winning not only the Field Championship but the Wing Title as well.

6 Feb - On a Bomber Support to Romilly, 15 to 20 Me 109s and FW 190s were engaged in a running battle for about 40 miles. Lt. Hofer claimed one Me 109 Destroyed near Paris. Garrison and Hobert each claimed a FW 190 for 336 Squadron.

Combat Report: Lt. V.J. France: -"Pectin Red Section bounced five FW 190s diving head-on through the lead box of fortresses. Red Leader took the first two. I, flying Red 3, started chasing one of the others. Throughout the encounter, which lasted from 20,000 to 12,000 feet, I was never able to close on the FW 190, although I had the engine wide open. Only once did I observe strikes on the fuselage between his cockpit and tail. I expended my ammunition as the e/a dove through the clouds, and I returned to base."

*****

Lt. Ballew was attacked. He had to bail out near Paris. "Happy landings to the 'Frost, Texas Flash,' and heaven help the French damsels in Gay Parrie!" (He became a POW).

10 Feb - Col. Edner led a Bomber Support mission to Brunswick. The Group engaged 25 to 30 FW 190s and Me 109s from Lingen to Nienburg, from 28,000 feet to the deck. E/a attacks against the bombers were head-on and aggressive. They dove to attack, and then climbed up to reform.

Results of the engagements: Lt. France claimed one FW 190 Destroyed; Lt. Montgomery and Lt. Biel each claimed one Me 109 Destroyed; Lt. Anderson and Lt. Schlegel claimed a shared Destroyed; and Lts. Manning, Millikan, Garrison, and Norley each claimed a Destroyed.

Lt. Brandenburg had his plane shot up badly and was lucky to get back to an advanced base.

Combat Report: 1st Lt. Gerald Montgomery - "I was flying Pectin Red 3 as we approached the rear box of bombers east of Zwolle. Pectin Red Leader sighted five Me 109s at two o'clock and went down on a bounce. The 109s pulled into a tight starboard turn. After about two turns, the e/a worked around onto the tails of me and my wingman. As we continued turning hard starboard, I flicked and spun about five times. I had the opportunity of getting in one head-on shot, but I observed no hits. Pectin Blue Section came down to our aid, and the e/a broke off the engagement and started down. I again fired a long shot at a Me 109 but observed no hits.

Off to my starboard, four P-47s were chasing two Me 109s, so I tacked on. At about 10,000 feet the e/a split up, going in different directions. I caught one of the e/a at about 3,000 feet. I fired several short bursts and observed one large flash. The motor on the e/a quit and I overshot. On the second attack, the Jerry was in a glide and skidding back and forth violently. I got only one short burst at close range, but evidently shot under him. I overshot again. I made a third attack, firing at very short range (about 25 to 50 yards), but the 109 went into a tight turn. Again I overshot. As I passed him, about 20 feet away, he jettisoned the canopy and went over the side. A small flame was coming from the engine. At this point, I was jumped by a Me 109, but I climbed up and joined four P-47s; my Wingman and three others, which were marked 'MX'. The 109 turned away, and we crossed out at 16,000 feet, north of the Hague."

*****

When our Pilots returned after the mission on 31 January 1944, the number of planes destroyed by 334 Squadron had reached 48. Lt. Ezzell asked each Pilot for a contribution of one Pound. This 30-Pound pool was to be paid to the Pilot that claimed the 50th plane Destroyed. F/O Hofer came close to winning this pool when he Destroyed a Me 109 on the Romilly mission 6 Feb. There were three claiments today when the boys came back from the Brunswick mission—France, Montgomery, and Biel.

At 1600 hours Lt. Ezzel presented ten Pounds to each of these Pilots. The Base Photographer took a picture of the three winners who split the pot.

From 29 Nov 44 to date, our 334 Pilots have made the following claims: 22-1/2 Destroyed, one Probable, and two Damaged. During this period, we have lost only one Pilot - F/O William Cox, who was reported NYR from the Emden mission on 3 February.

We have had two Officers who married in the ETO prior to joining our 334 Squadron. 1st Lt. Allen Bunte was married to Grace

On 10 Feb. 44, three Aces (l-r) 1st Lt.Thomas Biel, Major Gerald "Monty" Montgomery, and Captain Victor France, Split the 30 Pound "pot" for destroying the 50 e/a claimed by 334 Squadron. Two months later, Lt. Biel was shot down and KIA. In March, Captain France was KIA when he hit the ground and his plane exploded while chasing an Me 109. Major Montgomery was the only one of the three to survive the war. Zigler collection.

Miller in Slamannan, Scotland, and 1st Lt. Alfred Markel to Anne Murray Adair, in Shropshire, England, prior to joining us. Two have married since they joined us. 1st Lt. Alexander Rafalovich married Margaret Hewett, Surrey, England, and 1st Lt. Walter Young married Janet McDonald Tomes, Edinburgh, Scotland, after joining our Squadron.

Since joining our Squadron, the following Enlisted Men have married in the ETO: T/Sgt Joe A. Bridges, T/Sgt Leroy P. Hadden,

1st Lt. Allan F. Bunte was one of the few Pilots who had been married prior to assignment to 334 Squadron. He became a POW when he crashed into a lake near Pottsdam after hitting a high tension wire 5 April 44. A F Museum collection.

T/Sgt Jack H. Howerton, S/Sgt Joe Ciciulla, S/Sgt Wolford Katz, Sgt Walter Gukeisen, Sgt Kuykendall, Sgt Richard S. Rowe, Cpl John R. Lakin, Cpl Robert H. Riggle, Cpl Anthony Sprague, and Pvt Stanley Widdows.

13 Feb - The first of our looked-for Mustangs arrived and was assigned to 334 Squadron.

Tech Orders for the P-51s have been received. This usually precedes the delivery of the kites. (We hope!)

Patterson's name and serial number were given over the Hun R/T as being a POW. "Good Show—! Ballew also was said to be a POW, unofficial."

The following article appeared in the *London Evening News*, 14 Feb.1944:

"EARL'S DAUGHTER TO MARRY U.S. AIRMAN"

"Lady Bridget Elliot, 22 year old daughter of the Earl and Countess of Minto, is to marry Major James Averill Clark, DFC, an American airman. For some time Lady Bridget worked at an aircraft factory near London."

17 Feb - Duane W. Beeson was promoted to the rank of Captain effective 15 February 44.

Groups of 30 Enlisted Men reported to the firing range with their new Carbines. Each man shot 20 rounds for familiarization.

19 Feb - The Victory Credits Board Report credited claims of 29 Jan of seven Me 109s Destroyed; Mills and Pisanos - each two; Whalen, Beeson and Chatterley - each one; and two FW 190s by Beeson and France.

Further claims were confirmed for the month of January for: Wynn, one and one-half Me 109s; and four FW 190s (one each) by Montgomery, Beeson, Biel, and Whalen.

All available Pilots attended an Air-Sea Rescue lecture, and later a lecture on procedures followed by WOR, while they are out on missions.

All available Enlisted Men attended a meeting to hear Commendations from General Doolittle and General Spaatz. They were read by 1/Sgt Morris to all personnel who participated directly or indirectly in the 10 Feb mission.

Station Defense warnings were sounded for full alert at 0120 hours as approximately 90 e/a operated over England. Incendiaries and HE bombs were dropped in the woods about one mile south of the base. They started fires, but there were no casualties. A large number of the incendiaries and bombs dropped did not explode. Metallic Leaf was dropped by Jerry, borrowing this device from us. This interferes with our radio location of planes for defense.

20 Feb - On a Withdrawal Support to bombers from a raid on Leipzig, the Group led by Capt. Goodson, encountered five Me 109s and Me 110s attacking with rockets. The 335 Squadron engaged. Lt. McKennon claimed one FW 190 Destroyed; Lt. Ellington

one Me 110 Probably Destroyed; Lt. Fiedler one 110 Probable; and Lt. Riley one 110 Destroyed, shared with Lt. Reed.

Later, 334 attacked eight FW 190s. Capt. Mills and Capt. Beeson each claimed one FW 190 Destroyed. This brings Beeson's score up to 11 Huns.

Lt. Reed is missing. He was seen shot down in the vicinity of Aachen with two FW 190s on his tail. (He was KIA).

Lt. Rowles crash-landed at Eastchurch due to severe combat damage.

The Distinguished Flying Cross was awarded to: 1st Lt. Vasseure H. Wynn

An **Oak Leaf Cluster to the Distinguished Flying Cross** was awarded to:

    1st Lt. Duane Beeson

    Capt. Raymond Care

    1st Lt. Archie Chatterley

    1st Lt. Alexander Rafalovich

21 Feb - Col. Blakeslee led a Bomber Support mission to the Dummer Lake area. They encountered 15 FW 190s and attacked. Lt. Howe and Capt. Care each claimed one FW 190 Destroyed. Lt. Clotfelter claimed one Me 210 Probable.

"The guys are working the new Mustangs to death. Everyone wants a ride."

22 Feb - Col. Blakeslee led a Withdrawal Support to bombers returning from Schweinfurt. Eight FW 190s were seen circling a disabled bomber near Aachen and were attacked by 335 Squadron. Major Carpenter and Lts. McGrattan, McKennen, and Schlegel each claimed one Destroyed.

Major Beckham, the leading ETO ace with 18 Huns to his credit, was shot down by flak while beating up an enemy A/D.

24 Feb - Col. Edner led a Withdrawal Support mission for bombers returning from Schweinfurt. They encountered four FW 190s making head-on attacks against the B-24s. Upper Squadron engaged, chasing them off. Four FW 190s and six Me 109s were engaged near Koblenz. Lt. Schlegel claimed one FW 190 Destroyed. Gentile of 336 also claimed one Destroyed.

Lt. Sullivan, on his second show, is NYR. (He was KIA).

Lt. Read returned with a small wound from a 20 mm.

Reed, Steele, and Rowles had their kites badly shot up and landed at advanced bases.

Ten Mustangs were assigned to 334 Squadron; eleven Mustangs were assigned to 335 Squadron.

25 Feb - Col. Edner led a Penetration Support mission for bombers to Regensburg, Nurnburg, Stuttgart, and Augsburg. Five FW 190s made a frontal attack on a B-17, shooting out one engine. It dropped out of formation and seven chutes were seen. The e/a were attacked and three were destroyed. Later, four FW 190s were engaged at the same level. Two more were bounced 6,000 feet below; two were destroyed.

Capt. Beeson and Lt. McKennon each claimed one FW 190 Destroyed.

Garrison, Herter, and Gentile, of 336, each claimed one Destroyed.

Five more Mustangs were assigned to 334 Squadron. By morning, our Squadron lettering was painted on all Mustangs.

Fifteen more Mustangs were assigned to 335 Squadron. The crews were called out and worked until three or four in the morning to get them operational.

27 Feb - An **Oak Leaf Cluster to the DFC** was awarded to Capt. Winslow M. Sobanski.

All available Pilots attended a lecture on "Escape," followed by a session with a representative of the Rolls Royce-Merlin people, who answered technical questions for Pilots.

28 Feb - Fourteen more Mustangs were assigned to 334 Squadron.

Major Clark led our first sortie with Mustangs, using 75-gallon wing tanks. They supported bombers to Noball. Near Paris one

Major James Clark Jr. transferred from 71 ES and was assigned to 334 Squadron where he became CO 1 March 44. An Ace with 16 kills, he made headlines in the London Evening News when he married Lady Bridget Elliot. He was later transferred to Headquarters Squadron. A F Museum collection.

Colonel Don Blakeslee arrives piloting the first Mustang assigned to the Group. It was turned over to 334 Squadron.

section went down on an A/D and destroyed a Ju 88 about to take off. The kill was shared by Beeson, Smith, Megura, and Garrison from 336 Squadron.

The 4th went into combat with P-51s with an average of 40-minutes flying time in these new planes.

The 335 Squadron could only put up 11 planes. Seven of them aborted, leaving only four to complete the show.

· Lt. Fraser, on a local flight, was making a turning approach into the field when his plane stalled, flicked over on its back, and nosed straight in. The plane was enveloped in flames. He was killed instantly.

Capt. Sobanski of 334 belly-landed on the runway yesterday. He had his wheels down on approach; overshot; went around; pulled his wheels up; and landed. *Then Col. Blakeslee landed on him.*

29 Feb - Thirty Officers and thirty Enlisted Men stood at attention at the Main Gate and saluted as the remains of Lt. Fraser passed slowly through the formation on its way to Cambridge Cemetery.

Our 334 Squadron now has 29 Mustangs on hand and five Thunderbolts.

Capt. Goodson led a Bomber Support to Brunswick. Thirteen planes from 334 Squadron took off and eight aborted due to mechanical problems.

The 335 Squadron was able to put up only seven kites.

The **Distinguished Flying Cross** was awarded to:

Lt. Robert B. Fraser

Lt. Gerald E. Montgomery

P-51 Mustangs of the Fourth Fighter Group in flight.

5

The Struggle Broadens

1 March 1944 - The 334 Squadron had a roster of 28 Pilots:

14 Enlisted in RCAF

1 Enlisted in RNAS

4 Enlisted in USAAF

9 Enlisted in RAF

These Pilots consisted of one Major, James A Clark, Jr. CO; four Captains; sixteen 1st Lts.; six 2nd Lts.; and one F.O. In addition to the Pilots, there were 12 Administrative Officers and 232 Enlisted Personnel.

The Victory Credits Board listed confirmed credits for the Squadron for 3 Nov 43 through 6 Feb 44 as follows:

12-1/2 Me 109s Destroyed

7 FW 190s Destroyed

2 Me 109s Probably Destroyed

1 FW 190 Damaged

Lt. Beeson led with four Destroyed. Whalen had 2-1/2. France, Mills, and Pisanos each had two; Wynn 1-1/2; Montgomery, Biel, Chatterley, Sobanski, and Hofer one each; and Rafalovich had 1/2 Destroyed.

The **Distinguished Flying Cross** was awarded to: 1st Lt. Herbert J. Blanchfield

An **Oak Leaf Cluster to the Distinguished Flying Cross** was awarded to:

1st Lt. Victor J. France

1st Lt. Spiros N. Pisanos

2 March - Col. Edner led the Group on a Target Support Mission to Frankfurt. There were several early returns due to leaking belly tanks and rough engines. Near St. Goar, six e/a, several miles ahead of the bombers, turned and made a head-on attack. Three were engaged and one was destroyed. Shortly after this encounter, ten FW 190s came in head-on from above, and one of these was destroyed and one was damaged. After escort was broken off, a P-47 fired at Lt. Megura's plane; fortunately, Megura was not hit. Lt.

Lt. Col. Seldon R. Edner 121 ES transferee to 336 Squadron, became 334 Squadron CO in Nov. 43. In Jan. 44, he was transferred to 4th Group Headquarters to become Group Executive Officer. On 8 March 44, while leading the Group on a mission over Berlin, he went down and became a POW. Konsler collection.

George Villinger of 336 was missing and subsequently listed as KIA.

Anderson and Freeburger of 335 shot up an airdrome.

Col. Blakeslee issued an order that any crew chief who has a belly tank fall off will be placed under arrest. This order really "shook" the boys, but it was completely superfluous. The boys were already doing their best.

Any pilot pranging a kite, and found personally at fault, would be considered for transfer.

Combat Reports:

F/O Ralph K. Hofer - "I was flying Pectin Purple #1 when we R/V'd with bombers at 1150 hours, south of Koblenz. We intercepted and chased 15 plus e/a that attacked bombers from 1 o'clock. I saw Lt. Wynn fire on a Me 109; the Pilot bailed out. In positioning myself on four FW 190s, I was bounced by four e/a from above. I dropped wing tanks, broke sharply port and evaded. I positioned for a bounce on one e/a, and I was in turn bounced by two e/a. I evaded sharply down into a cloud and continued to chase the first e/a. I climbed back on top, hoping to find him there. I again broke down through cloud, where I observed two Me 109s to my port. I dodged up for a while and then went to the deck. I fired on a locomotive and observed many strikes. I tested my guns on a power pylon and a control tower near Koblenz."

*****

1st Lt. Vasseure H. Wynn - "I was flying Pectin Red #3. Five minutes after R/V with the lead box of B-17s, 15 miles south of Koblenz, we attempted to intercept 15 plus e/a attacking from 1 o'clock. We were unable to engage. I climbed back to rejoin, and I saw five Me 109s positioning at 11 o'clock to bombers at 15,000 feet. "Upper" instructed us to attack. I positioned astern the last e/a. I started firing at 250 yards and closed to 50 yards. I chopped the throttle to keep from overshooting. The e/a took slight evasive action and dived for a cloud as I observed strikes. I fired very long bursts and kicked rudder. Strikes from my unharmonized guns caused glycol to start streaming from the e/a. I followed thru, and I saw the e/a pull back up. I gave him another long burst and observed strikes on the fusilage. I circled under the cloud base (9,000 ft.) and soon the e/a came down, followed by the Pilot and chute. I joined Capt. Petersen and Lt. Garrison at 14,000 ft. We escorted a straggling B-17 for 15 minutes until we were bounced by P-47s. We came home, but Capt. Petersen landed at a forward base. This claim was confirmed in writing by F/O Ralph K. Hofer."

*****

There was a military funeral at 1100 hours for First Lieutenant Robert B. Fraser at the Cambridge American Cemetery. Chaplain Brohm and Captain Blackburn attended. A Color Guard was present, and the firing squad paid a final tribute to Lieutenant Fraser.

All officers and EM reported to the Station Sick Quarters for immunization shots.

All available Pilots attended a showing of combat films in the projection room at 1615 hours.

3 March - 2nd Lt. Herbert D. Kneeland was assigned effective 29 Feb 44.

The following Sergeants were promoted to the rank of Staff Sergeant:

Robert J. Bowen
Wallace C. Carrier
Grant O. Brown
Dale L. Hall
Ernest J. Pfankuche

Corporal William L. Rickerson was promoted to Sergeant.

Colonel Blakeslee led the Group on a Target Support mission to Berlin. No e/a were seen by the main force, but units from 335 and 336 Squadrons broke off. They, subsequently, encountered Huns. Squadron 335 lost Lt. Barnes; 336 lost Garrison, Herter, and Dunn. Squadron 336 claimed eight e/a Destroyed. (Barnes and Herter were KIA, and Garrison and Dunn became POWs).

On his way back, Lt. Hively was vectored by "Tackline" to ASR search. He sighted a Pilot and dinghy 15 miles off Deal and directed a Walrus and a launch to the location.

4 March - Col. Blakeslee led a Target Support mission to Berlin. Due to engine problems, half of the group aborted on the way in. Prior to I.P. (Bomber's Initial Point), about 20 Me 109s and FW 190s were encountered. Eight attacked in fours head-on and were dispersed, while the rest remained up as cover. The cover then bounced our Group. E/a attacks were half-hearted, and the Me 109s were easily outclimbed. Some Pilots were hampered by windscreen frost and jammed guns.

At 1330 hours, Lt. Ward, 335, was seen chasing a Me 109. He and the e/a dove from 31,000 feet. Lt. Megura followed Lt. Ward to 18,000 feet where the wing, tail, and canopy of Ward's P-51 came off. The debris hit Lt. Megura's a/c. Ward was not seen to bail out. Immediately, Lt. Riley chased the same Me 109 and probably destroyed it.

Megura chased a Me 109 to 3,000 feet above an A/D where its Pilot bailed out. A Ju 52 on an A/D, believed to be Meresburg or Bernburg, was destroyed on the ground by Lt. Megura. Lt. Megura attacked and damaged a locomotive in the same area.

Casualties: Ellington and Ward were both missing. Ellington was last heard over the R/T by Major Clark. He was heard to say that his engine was cutting and that he was undecided about bailing out. (Both became POWs).

Richards of 336 was killed as he crash-landed at an advanced base.

Squadron 335 has lost eight men in the last five days.

"One P-51 Group lost 11 men, most due to weather. The Hun will send 11-51s against us one of these days. We made the 8th column in fine print, in one of the daily papers—quote, 'The former Eagle Squadrons now flying the famed Mustang, gave cover to the bombers over Berlin.'"

Results of engagement:

Megura, 334, claimed one Me 109 Destroyed, one Ju 52 Destroyed, and one locomotive Damaged.

Lt. Ward, 335, claimed one U/I S/E e/a destroyed.

Sooman, 336, claimed a Ju 52 Destroyed.

Battle Damage: Pieces of Lt. Ward's P-51 damaged Lt. Megura's plane. The pieces dented Megura's stabilizer and tore off his antenna.

Combat Reports:

1st Lt. Nicholas Megura: "I was flying Pectin Blue #1 when we R/V'd with the Combat Wing of B-17s west of Berlin. As we positioned ourselves ahead of the Bombers, we saw many single and double smoke trails coming from all directions—at our level and above. Fifteen plus Me 109s and FW 190s made a frontal attack on the bombers and were driven down. We gave chase from 27,000 to 22,000 feet and up again along-side the bombers. I investigated eight plus a/c, which I identified as FW 190s. They were going away from the bombers. I was unable to close after chasing from 27,000 feet to 5,000 feet. I found myself alone, and I took a good look around. At 12,000 feet, I noticed three Me 109s very close at 8 o'clock. I easily outclimbed them and reached 31,000 feet about 25 miles behind the bombers. Seeing two smoke trails at 9 o'clock, I bounced the nearest. It turned out to be a P-51 ("WD"-335 Squadron). The other a/c was a white-nosed Me 109. I joined the P-51, and I gave chase to the e/a as it half rolled into a vertical

dive. I followed the P-51, "WD" Squadron, clocking 550 IAS. At 18,000 feet the P-51's port wing came off at the root and disintegrated. The canopy and tail came off as I dodged past. Pieces carried away my antennae and hit my stabilizer.

My controls were frozen, and I had to use trim to pick up the nose. This brought me behind the e/a, but I was overshooting. The canopy frosted on the inside, but disappeared when I opened the window. The only evasive action taken by the e/a was a weave to right or left. I barrel-rolled and positioned myself 1,000 feet above and to the side of him. I dropped flaps and dove astern. This engagement brought us down to 2,000 feet. Just as I was about to fire, the e/a pulled up sharply to 3,000 feet, and jettisoned its canopy. The pilot bailed out. The e/a crashed and burned. The pilot landed 50 feet from the wreckage. I cleared my tail and saw that I was right over a grass A/D. Directly ahead of me was a large hangar with a Ju 52 parked alongside. I pushed everything to the firewall and hit the deck. I opened on the Ju 52, observing only one gun fire. Shooting low, I brought my fire into the e/a itself and noticed flames leaping out as I hopped over the hangar and hit the deck weaving. A few miles away, I saw a locomotive pulling 10 or 12 cars. I pulled up to 50 feet, looked back at the A/D, and saw black smoke rising behind the hangar. I opened fire on the engine and noticed strikes. The train came to a halt. Seeing that it was time to "leave out," I set course for home."

*****

Lt. Hugh Ward filed this report, June 45, upon return from POW Camp: - "I started to return to base because my oxygen light was on, indicating only about five more minutes supply. I saw another P-51 going west and joined him. It turned out to be Lt. Megura. As we were flying along, we were suddenly attacked by a lone Me 109 firing steadily. We both broke into the 109. Because of the 109's excessive speed from his dive, he could not turn tight enough to pull deflection on either of us. He then climbed steeply, and I put everything to the wall and followed him. At about 30,000 feet, I had closed to about 400 yards. I opened fire as he started a slow turn to the left. I observed strikes on his wing root. He realized the situation and flicked over, and he dove straight down with me on his tail. I gave him a three-second burst with good strikes. He continued straight down, heading for heavy clouds, as I began to overrun him. I pulled back on the throttle and gave him another blast. I got a heavy concentration of strikes all over his engine and cockpit, tearing off his canopy and engine covering. I kept firing as the 109 started to come apart. I attempted to back off but was too late.

A large section of the e/a smashed my canopy and windscreen, and it must have sheared off most of my tail section. My plane began to snap viciously, end-over-end, and my right wing snapped off. I was stunned momentarily, but I managed to jettison my canopy. I pulled my harness release, which threw me out of the cockpit. I delayed opening my chute because of the speed, and I fell through

1st Lt. Nicholas "Cowboy" Megura, an ex RCAF Pilot, was assigned to 334 Squadron. On 22 May 44, as a Captain, "Cowboy" was attacking 3 Me 109s near Kiel when a P-38 badly damaged his P-51 with gunfire and he was forced to head for Sweden where he was interred. An Ace, he had 15 e/a to his credit. Pool collection.

the cloud layer. I opened my chute just in time. I landed in the suburbs of Berlin, and I was captured by civilians."

Hugh Ward 1st Lt. Air Corps.

*****

5 March - Major Carpenter led a Bomber Escort mission to Bordeaux. Because of 10/10ths cloud cover over the target, the bombers diverted and bombed a grass A/D near Limoges. South of Bordeaux two long-nosed FW 190s and four Me 109s came in head-on to the bombers. They were engaged with one destroyed and two damaged. Later, climbing for an underneath attack on the bombers, two Me 109s were destroyed. A FW 190 and a Ju 88 on Fontenay Le Comte A/D were strafed and damaged.

Lt. Pisanos bailed out 10 miles south of Le Havre. His claim, of one Me 109 Destroyed, was confirmed by Captain Beeson. True to his Eagle Squadron training, "Steve" was wearing a British chute and a British Mae West. He was reported NYR. (Pisanos evaded and eventually returned to Debden).

Several planes either aborted or returned to forward bases because of problems. Lt. Lange landed at Matching because of an unservicable wing tank. Following a patrol car leading him to the watch tower, he did not see the 2-1/2 ton truck parked on the perimeter. Lt. Lang ran into this truck, damaging his starboard wing and prop. Lang left his plane at Matching and was flown back to Debden.

In addition to the claim of Lt. Pisanos, Lt. Hively claimed two Me 109s Destroyed; Lt. Carr claimed one Ju 88 Damaged; and Capt. Beeson claimed one Me 109 Destroyed and one FW 200 Damaged. Blakeslee Destroyed one Me 210.

Steele of 335 Squadron claimed one FW 200 Destroyed; Smith and Freeburger shared a FW 200; and Freeburger Damaged two FW 200s on the ground. Dye claimed one FW 190 Destroyed.

Peterson, 336, claimed a FW 200 Destroyed.

"These FW 200s are used for long range convoy work: they are huge four motor a/c. Unconfirmed reports state that the RAF would give their Pilots the DFC and six months off Ops whenever they destroyed one of these aircraft."

Battle Damage - Capt. Beeson's plane was hit by flak, which tore a large hole in the vertical stabilizer and damaged the rudder.

Combat Reports -

Capt. D.W.Beeson - "I was flying as Pectin Green leader. Col. Blakeslee was forced to abort due to engine trouble. This left me leading the Squadron. The bombers turned back about 60 miles south of Bordeaux. Just after they had completed their turn, they were attacked by about six Me 109s. I sighted two e/a who had just gone through one box of bombers and were turning to go through another. Our Section immediately dove toward them. They saw us coming and whipped into a tight turn. I took a head-on shot at them, then pulled up above for another pass. They again turned into us, and I took another head-on shot and pulled up again. There were now several other Mustangs around who were trying to get these Me 109s. As the e/a went over into a dive, the Mustangs went after them. I had managed to keep my speed pretty high and was able to get on the tail of one. Lt. Pisanos also got on the tail of one. We broke up their line astern formation. Before I opened fire, I saw Lt. Pisanos getting very good strikes on his e/a. I had evidently struck my 109 in one of the head-on attacks, for he was already smoking slightly. After opening fire at about 150 yards and getting more strikes, he began to smoke quite badly. As I overshot the e/a, the pilot bailed out. I began an orbit and called for the other Mustangs to rejoin.

We were now at about 7,000 feet, so we climbed to 12,000 feet. We flew near Bordeaux and saw FW 200s, a He 111, and other a/c sitting on an aerodrome. As we had already awakened the flak gunners, it would have been foolish to attack after flying over. So, we flew on. Shortly afterwards, we sighted an aerodrome about 60 miles north of Bordeaux. We dove to the deck and approached at about 400 mph. I opened fire on a FW 200 and saw strikes around the engines. We headed across the aerodrome with a little flak bursting around us. As I reached the other side, I felt a heavy blow on the a/c and was thrown over on my side. I had great difficulty regaining control. I checked my engine instruments, which were OK, and I reduced speed for better control. The rudders were very stiff, and I was forced to hold hard left rudder all the way back to base. I had been hit by flak, which left a large hole in my rudder.

About five minutes after our attack, Capt. Peterson shot down a FW 200, which I confirmed. He and Lt. Carr joined me as we came out. Three hours later, we landed at our base. I also confirmed one Me 109 shot down by Lt. Pisanos. I claimed one Me 109 Destroyed and one FW 200 Damaged. This claim was confirmed in writing by Capt. Kenneth D. Peterson of 336 Squadron."

*****

1st Lt. Charles D. Carr - "I was flying Green #2 to Capt. Beeson. Capt. Peterson of 336 was also flying in the Section. We were flying at 8,000 feet, North of Bordeaux. Capt. Beeson called over the R/T that we were going down to strafe an aerodrome. We dove down to the deck about a mile from the A/D. We approached it at about 400 mph IAS. Capt. Beeson and Capt. Peterson turned to port to attack a FW 200 on the ground. I was on the inside, and I could not turn with them, so I continued to fly straight. I pulled up over a hill and saw what I thought was a Ju 88 in front of a hangar. I fired and saw strikes in front of the e/a. I raised the nose and kept on shooting. Three of my guns stopped at about this time. I did not see any more strikes. I had no reflector sight and was using the mechanical sight. I pulled up over a hangar and continued on for a few hundred yards before pulling up. I saw Capt. Peterson on my starboard. Capt. Beeson called over the R/T saying he had been hit by flak. I looked back, and I saw him behind and to the port."

*****

1st Lt. Howard D. "Deacon" Hively from 71 ES was attached to 334 Squadron and became CO in June 44. He was wounded on the return trip of the Russian shuttle. As a Major, he was appointed Acting Deputy Group CO in Aug 44. Pool collection.

1st Lt. H.D. Hively - "I was leading Pectin Red Section south of Bordeaux, near the rear of the bombers at 15,000 feet. When e/a were reported coming through the formation, I turned port and followed Pectin leader in an attack on two Me 109s. I could not break into the queue because there were about six P-51s after these two. I was circling above the fight, and I was waiting for a chance to break in when I noticed four a/c approaching from the South at about 8,000 feet.

I turned toward them and identified them as Me 109s. I attacked from their 9 o'clock. They broke into me, and we went around and around in a port-climbing orbit. At about 13,000 feet, I started getting deflection. Two of the e/a broke starboard out of the turn and started for the deck. I picked up my flaps, turned, and chased. For a second it looked as if I wasn't closing, so I took two short bursts at about 800 yards just for meanness. I noticed I was closing rapidly. I chopped everything, let down my flaps (20 degrees), and closed to about 50 yards on the #2 e/a. He turned starboard as I fired, and I observed many strikes on the bottom and the top-side of the fuselage and the wing root. When I closed my throttle, I screwed my trim so that I started sliding out to the left. As I slid by, I saw his starboard wing crumple about two feet from the wing-root. I then

slid right into the #1 e/a and fired. I observed five or six good hits on his fuselage, underside, and just back of the cockpit. I slid on past to his port, picked up my flaps, and followed him down in a gentle diving turn from 3,000 feet. He never pulled out. The e/a went in with a large column of dust and black smoke. Neither pilot bailed out.

The Me 109s were a dirty-green color with bright orange spinners. It was also my observation that a P-51 can out turn, out climb, out dive, and out run Me 109s at those altitudes, especially above 12,000 feet. Also, I would like to caution those concerned to go easy on the trim in these airplanes, because it really takes hold at high speeds."

*****

1st Lt. Pisanos - This claim is submitted by Lt. Benjamin Q. Ezzell, 334 Squadron Intelligence Officer, on behalf of Lt. Pisanos, who was NYR after combat in the area south of Bordeaux,

"Lt. Pisanos was flying Pectin White #3, escorting B-17s just after the bombers completed their turn 60 miles south of Bordeaux. Me 109s attacked, and he and Capt. Beeson each closed in on an e/a. Lt. Pisanos Destroyed one." This claim was confirmed in writing by Captain D.W.Beeson and Captain Kenneth D. Peterson of 336 Fighter Squadron.

*****

"Old Jim Steele raised merry hell with the Huns. His kite went U/S while deep in enemy territory, so he dove to the deck and started back on his own. He saw tracers coming over his wings. Looking back, he saw four 51s, the leader firing at him. He broke off. The 51s, seeing he was friendly, pulled away. He then came upon eight FW 200s in a circuit and shot down one before a S/E e/a took off to challenge him. Steele then took off. Soon two FW 190s jumped him, but he went flat out and left them without them firing a shot."

"Smith and Freeburger caught their FW 200 in the same circuit and forced it to crash-land in flames. As the crew piled out, they came around and mowed them down. They continued to shoot-up some FW 200s on the ground. Good show for Smith and Freeburger."

Wehrman of 336 was injured when he crash-landed his a/c.

All Officers and Enlisted Men turned in their gas masks, both Service and Diaphragm, to Squadron Supply in exchange for the new type masks.

6 March - Col. Blakeslee led the Group on a Target Support mission to Berlin.

Thirty S/E e/a made head-on attacks on the bombers from 27,000 feet while 40-50 T/E e/a attacked from beam and astern at about 1240 hours. The Group engaged these a/c. In the process, the Group became separated. They returned by Flights and Sections.

While returning to base, 334 Squadron attacked two A/Ds and three locomotives in Germany.

Major Mills reported on R/T that he was having engine trouble and was going to bail out, but no chute was seen.

Lt. Whalen's a/c was struck by debris from an exploding Me 110, and a back-type chute was seen to open in the immediate vicinity.

One B-17 blew up after a rocket attack southwest of Berlin - no chutes were seen. One B-17 exploded after a cannon attack by FW 190s northeast of Brunswick - six chutes were seen. One B-17 attacked by Me 109s, went down south of Genthin - four chutes were seen. One B-17 went down, north of Dummer Lake - five chutes were seen.

Battle Damage - The elevator and stabilizer on Capt. Van Epp's plane was hit by MG bullets. The fuselage was peppered with flak holes.

Exhaust valves on Lt. Rafalovich's plane were damaged by flak.

Lt. Chatterley's plane was damaged by four MG bullet holes in the stabilizer; two MG bullet holes in the prop; a cannon hole in the port aileron. MG bullets also ripped the underside of the starboard wing.

Missing in Action:

Major Henry I. Mills, reported NYR.

"Old Hank told Jim Clark to write and tell his wife that he is OK." (He became a POW)

1st Lt. Edmund D. Whalen, reported NYR.

(Subsequently reported KIA)

Cecil Manning, said over R/T that his engine was cutting and that he was bailing out over Holland.

(He became a POW)

Robert Messinger reported missing.

(He became a POW)

Manning stands by a P-47. Captain Cecil Manning of 335 Squadron bailed out of his burning P-51 6 March 44 after a Do 217 slug hit his engine. He became a POW. Konsler collection.

Results of Engagement: The following Pilots claimed e/a Destroyed:

Capt. Van Epps / shared with Lt. Moulton	1 Me 110
Lt. Whalen	1 Me 110
Major Mills	1 Fw 109
Lt. Chatterley	1 Me 110
Lt. Rafalovich	1 Me 109
Lt. Megura	2 Me 110s
Lt. McKennon	1 Me 109
Lt. Anderson	1 Do 217
Lt. Waterman	1 Me 110
Lt. McGrattan	1 Ju 88
Lt. Dye	1 Do 217
Lt. Godfrey	1 Me 109

Combat Reports -

1st Lt. Chatterley: "I was flying Pectin Blue #3 behind Maj. Mills. On approaching the IP, south of Berlin, we saw many vapor trails collecting at 12 o'clock to us. They were swinging towards the bombers. Six Me 109s passed underneath, going 180 degrees to us. Our Section dropped our auxiliary tanks. Immediately afterwards I saw a Me 110 attacking a Fort that had pulled out of formation. I attacked and saw strikes with my deflection shots. When I closed to line astern, I saw many strikes, and pieces were flying off as much smoke came back over my wind screen.

A Mustang called and said that a Ju 88 was on his tail. I was then at 12,000 feet; the Ju 88 at 28,000. As I climbed up, I began to pull deflection. He broke away from the Mustang and began to pull very tight, diving turns. The Ju 88 turned out to be a Me 210. The 210 dove from 28,000 feet to 2,000 feet doing tight turns. He never straightened out of his turn until the very last. I was on the red line of my air speed following him when someone said the 210 was shedding pieces. It seemed he pulled out, made a zoom, dove, and crashed.

I formed up with three other Mustangs, and we were setting course for home when a FW 190 met us head-on. All four of us turned and started wide-open racing for him. The 190 started a shallow climb, and we gained on him quickly. I asked Major Mills if we were going to queue up. 'Hell no, first one there gets him,' he answered.

Major Mills edged the rest of us out and I confirmed his claim, after seeing many strikes all over the e/a as it dove straight in. Major Mills called on R/T - 'I got the pilot, I got the pilot.' (Lt. K.G. Smith and I heard this).

Lt. Godfrey of 336 and I then went down on a train. We pulled up and attacked an airdrome. We saw strikes on a Ju 88 parked behind the Watch Tower. Lt. Godfrey states that he saw strikes on two other unidentified e/a. Due mainly to excessive speed, I only saw the one.

We stayed low over the drome and crossed a field. We met a train head-on. My shots were low, but as I went up the tracks I saw strikes on the engine. After this, we settled down to the trip home,

1st Lt Archie W. Chatterly, 334 Squadron, was hit by flak near Tours, France and bailed out. Prior to becoming a POW, he was an Ace with 5 1/2 e/a destroyed. A F Museum collection.

flying line abreast. About ten minutes out from the target, I had to urinate badly and was just beginning to relieve myself when tracers passed on each side of me, converging in front. Lt. Godfrey called to break, which I did without putting any of the relief equipment back in place. Strikes hit me just as I broke. Lt. Godfrey then shot the e/a down."

*****

1st Lt Megura - "As a spare, I saw no vacancy in Pectin Squadron, so I filled in with 335 Squadron as White #2. We R/V'd south of Berlin and positioned ourselves on the lead box. We saw twelve plus smoke trails coming from 12 o'clock and high, 30 miles ahead. 'Upper' positioned the Group up-sun, below condensation height, and waited. The trails finally converged at 9 o'clock to the bombers and started to close on them. Six thousand feet below the trails were 20 plus S/E e/a, line abreast, sweeping the area for 20 plus T/E rocket-carrying a/c. 'Upper' led the Group head-on into the front wave of e/a. I passed over on top and started after three Me 110s. They split and headed for the deck without firing their rockets. I started to follow, but I took a good look around and noticed some Me 110s of the cover coming down.

I broke into an a/c closing from 8 o'clock, but I identified it as a P-51. I jumped three others, which were Me 110s, just as they let go their rockets, which burst behind the last bombers. I raked the three Me 110s which were flying wing-tip to wing-tip. As the #1 e/a broke into me, I saw strikes all over his cockpit and both engines as he disappeared under me. I cleared my tail and saw a P-51 covering me 500 yards behind and to the side. I closed on the Me 110 and fired. I saw strikes with pieces falling off, and I saw an explosion in the cockpit. I pulled up over him and saw him go into a vertical dive, pouring out black smoke. I climbed starboard toward a Me 110 who was climbing up behind the bombers. The e/a started

violent evasive action toward the deck. There I closed on him with one working gun. He led me over an A/D. I saw strikes on his port engine and cockpit. I pulled aside, overshot, and closed firing. The e/a was hugging the deck as I got hits on his wing and cockpit. His port wing tore off as the e/a hit the ground and nosed over. I got away fast and pulled up behind a FW 190 carrying a belly tank. I pressed the teat and nothing happened. I closed fast and pulled up to keep from ramming him. I hit the deck; tried my guns on a train, again with no results; and came home."

*****

Major Mills - Lt. Benjamin Q. Ezzell, Intelligence Officer, submitted the claim of one FW 190 Destroyed, in behalf of Major Mills who was NYR after leading Pectin Blue section in an attack, in the Brandenburg area. This claim was confirmed in writing by Lt. A.W. Chatterley and Lt. K.G. Smith of 335 Fighter Squadron.

*****

1st Lt. Howard N. Moulton, Jr. - "I was flying Pectin Red #2 to Lt. Whalen at 25,000 feet, SW of Berlin. White #3 went down because he was out of oxygen. Lt. Whalen and I went down with him. The three of us circled at 15,000 feet, below and to the front of the lead box. A Me 110 came diving down at 2 o'clock to us. As we went after him, I followed about 500 yards behind Lt. Whalen. I saw Lt. Whalen get very close, line astern to the e/a. He gave a short burst which was very accurate. The e/a blew up and many pieces flew back. This was the last time I saw Lt. Whalen. At this time, 'A' Channel on my radio went out. The e/a did a three-quarter spin and crashed.

Major H. L. "Hank" Mills of 334 Squadron had transferred from 71 ES. He bailed out near Berlin with engine trouble 6 Mar 44. Hank was 334's second Ace with 6 destroyed, prior to becoming a POW. Konsler collection.

I pulled up to about 6,000 feet. After a turn, I saw another Me 110 diving down. I did a turn to cut him off and fell in astern. I fired a long burst but saw no strikes until I was directly line astern. I overshot and looked down. His left engine was smoking badly. A short time later, Capt. Van Epps (White #4) came in and fired a good burst, getting strikes, after which both engines were smoking. We pulled off the e/a and attacked a nearby locomotive. I did not see any strikes.

We came back at minimum altitude. At one time, we came over an airfield. There were FW 190s and Me 110s in the air and a lot of Me 110s on the ground. I pulled up and fired at a FW 190, but scored no hits. I saw one or two strikes as Capt. Van Epps fired. We again dove to the deck. The cloud layer became solid so we climbed above it line abreast. I was flying about 1,500 feet above the cloud layer, and Capt. Van Epps about five hundred feet. I looked back. I saw a FW 190 come out of the cloud directly in back of Van Epps, but some distance behind, closing rapidly. I did a turn left then right, and pulled out in back of the Hun.

The e/a started firing a second before I did, and I saw strikes on Capt. Van Epp's left wing. I fired as soon as possible and saw strikes on both wing roots. The e/a broke into the clouds. I ran out of ammo after a burst of about ten rounds. My radio was out, so I stayed above the cloud and came home."

*****

1st. Lt. Rafalovich - "I was flying Pectin Blue #4, as we R/V'd with the front box of bombers southwest of Berlin. We were weaving in front at 23,000 feet when 20 plus Me 109s and FW 190s attempted to come in from the left and above. I flicked as I positioned myself. I recovered and climbed toward smoke trails. I flicked again, (caused by too much gas in fuselage tanks), recovered, and climbed. I closed in on the last of three Me 109s.

I held my fire until I was sure it was not a P-51. I opened fire at 250 yards and blew his belly tank off. My gun sight burned out. I pulled up and saw smoke coming from his engine. I then gave him another short burst and saw strikes again on his wing roots. He went into a slow sliding turn. I gave him another burst and saw strikes. He split-S'd and crash-landed in the woods. Range - 250 yards to 100 yards. The pilot was very cool and had a lot of experience.

I attacked a locomotive but made no claim. This locomotive was armed with machine guns. One of them hit me in my port wingtip."

*****

Capt. David Van Epps - "I was flying Pectin White #4. Over the Zuider Zee. White #3 turned back, and I filled his position. Soon Red #1 and #2 joined us - making five in white Section. Fifteen minutes after R/V with the lead box of B-17s, west of I.P., I ran out of oxygen. White leader instructed Red #1 and #2 to follow me down. At 12,000 feet, Red #2 and I formed on Red #1 line abreast, sweeping out in front of the lead box of bombers.

A Me 110 dove in front of us, and we gave chase. As I pulled up, I saw it hit the deck and burn, apparently from Red #1's fire (Lt. Whalen). I noticed a pilot swinging violently in a back-type chute at 1,000 feet. About that time an explosion occurred about 2 o'clock to me as if an a/c blew up in the air. I presume that Lt. Whalen had bailed after his encounter with the e/a. His P-51 exploded.

Another Me 110 dove past us. Red #2 and I gave chase. I saw strikes from Red #2's fire (Lt. Moulton). After he fired and pulled up, I saw strikes from my fire. The canopy and odd pieces flew off the e/a, and both engines were streaming white glycol. I had to pull up to avoid ramming into the e/a and the ground. I received no answer from Red #1 as Red #2 joined me. We started home at 6,000 feet. We saw a train. We attacked and saw strikes but no steam. We stayed on the deck from then on and attacked another locomotive. I observed strikes on the cab and telegraph poles in front of it. We saw e/a circling to land nearby. We pulled up and dove on the A/D. I fired on a FW 190, scattering mechanics who were working on it. The circling FW 190 turned into me as I took a short ahead-of-beam deflection shot at him. I observed one flash on his cockpit. I pulled starboard and saw a Me 110 turning into me. I took a shot at him and observed strikes. After I stopped firing, I observed more strikes and concluded Lt. Moulton was firing also.

We hit the deck and crossed a lake where three flak posts of a nearby factory opened on us. We jinked, flew roof-top height across a large town, and pulled up into clouds at 4,000 feet. We saw three FW 190s turning toward us. We broke through the clouds and leveled off on top at 5,000 feet. I noticed an e/a on my tail. I broke down, felt strikes, and saw that my left aileron was half shot off. I blacked out as I pulled up from a vertical dive. The e/a was 1,000 yards to port. I, again, evaded into clouds. I changed course, and I emerged later because of icing. I came home without further incident."

*****

1st Lt. E.D. Whalen - A claim of one Me 110 Destroyed was submitted in behalf of Lt. Whalen who was NYR after combat in the Nienburg area. It was submitted by Lt. Benjamin Q. Ezzell, Squadron Intelligence Officer, and it was confirmed in writing by Capt. David Van Epps.

*****

1st Lt. Cecil Manning - (Upon return from POW Camp, 5 June 1945) "Flying Blue #3 in Greenbelt Section, we attacked an e/a which had been firing rockets at the bombers. I followed a section of three Do 217s as they broke downward. I opened fire on the starboard e/a at approximately 300 yards and closed to the point I had to break away to keep from colliding with him. I observed lots of strikes on the cockpit and out to the port engine, which immediately burst into flame. He flicked into a spin, and I saw two chutes come out.

I turned into the other two e/a and fired at one with 20 degrees deflection. I observed strikes from the rear gun to the cockpit and wing roots. The rear gunner had been firing up to the point where I observed strikes which must have killed him. The Pilot must also have been killed because the e/a mushed and fell into a fast spin. One chute came out before the e/a crashed and burned. I climbed up to attack the remaining Do and fired, but I ran out of ammo as another Mustang closed on him getting strikes. On the way home, my oil pressure dropped; the engine overheated; and the glycol caught fire. I must have caught a slug from the Do 217 which caused me to lose my oil. I bailed at 3,000 feet at Sogel, 16 miles inside Germany."

*****

Misc. Notes: Our Group's outstanding achievements:

1. The first Group in the ETO to go on Ops after the African invasion

2. The first Group to fly P-47s on operations anywhere

3. The first Group to lead the bombers over Berlin

4. The first Group to transfer from P-47s to P-51s without losing one day of operations

"Now we are going for the lead of the ETO, and the boys will do their best to get it."

7 March - A new type spark plug was received in the hangar at 0200 hours. It was expected to improve engine operation. All crew chiefs who had operational planes were awakened, and they installed these new plugs before morning.

The new type plugs were an attempt to overcome some of the problems associated with the high octane gas needed for the operation of the Merlin engines.

Edward Richie, an unusual man, had jumped in rank from Pfc. to WO, JG. in just over a year after enlistment. He was an octane tester, and he explained the problem. "The fuel we needed for the Rolls Merlin Engine, in order to resist detonation, had as much as six cc's of Tetra Ethyl Lead to the gallon. This raised the equivalent octane value to 130 performance number. Unfortunately, this amount of lead oxide would foul the plugs so that after every long mission the plugs had to be changed. Since there were not enough plugs to have two sets for every plane, after each long mission the plugs had to be pulled, cleaned, and regapped. Sand blasting was no problem, but regapping 24 plugs for each plane took a great deal of time and became a real bottle neck." W/O Richie went to work on this problem and soon designed a regapping tool which speeded up the process and eliminated the bottleneck. (After several months of use

and hundreds of crew hours saved, the Engineering Department said there was no need for this regapping tool and consequently would not have them manufactured.)

Richie's tool was just one of the many inovations which the crews of the 4th devised to save time and to help keep the planes flying. Many of these shortcuts would not pass inspection but were really helpful when needed.

An example of this ingenuity was shown when Al Landon was presented with a prop which had a large nick in the end of one of the blades. He needed the plane to be ready but there was no replacement prop available. He carefully filed the notch out of the damaged blade. This left that blade somewhat shorter than the other three. He found a stick and marked the length of the blade on the stick. He then used the stick to measure the other three prop blades so he could file them to the same length.

A preliminary run-up of the engine indicated that the prop was OK. The Captain in charge of maintenance, however, called for an air check to be sure that the engine would not run rough. A Pilot volunteered to fly the plane on a test hop. He returned and reported that the engine was too rough. A second Pilot took it up for a flight. When he returned, he said that he would take this plane in trade for his since it ran so much smoother than his. "So much for differences of opinion."

Under a new Table of Organization for the Squadron, the number of Enlisted Personnel was changed from 252 to 245.

An extract was received announcing that the 4th Fighter Group was entitled to battle credits for participation in the Air Offensive of Europe.

The following letter was received from Major Clark, addressed to all ground personnel, it stated:

"The Pilots and myself wish to express our thanks to you for the extra work you have been put to these last few weeks. The only way we feel that we can show our appreciation properly is by destroying more Huns. We will do it."

8 March - Col. Edner led the Group on a Target Support mission to Berlin. "This was another record 2,000 plane raid. Looks like Toohy Spaatz and Jim Doolittle want to chase the Luftwaffe to Russia."

Southwest of Brandenburg, the lead Combat Wing of bombers was attacked by five or six Me 109s; three were destroyed. Shortly thereafter, 60 plus e/a approached and attacked in pairs and fours. Combats ensued and claims were made as listed below. Southwest of Berlin, Col. Edner and his Wingman were bounced by four Me 109s. Col. Edner was not seen again. Eight B-17s were seen to go down with sightings of 57 chutes. (Edner became a POW).

There were more S/E e/a than usual, with a few twins down low. East of Berlin, many Ju 88s were seen parked on an unidentified A/D.

There was very little battle damage.

Results of Engagements:

334 Squadron claims:

Major Clark	1 Me 109 Destroyed
Lt. Bunte	1 FS 156 Destroyed
Lt France	1 Me 109 Destroyed
Lt. Howe	1 Me 109 Destroyed
Lt. Megura	1 Me 109 Destroyed
	1 FW 190 Destroyed

335 Squadron claims:

Lt. Clotfelter	1 FW 190 Destroyed
Lt. Smith	1 Me 110 Destroyed
Lt. Dye	1 Me 109 Destroyed

336 Squadron claims:

Lt. Tussie	1 Ju 88 Destroyed
Capt. Gentile	3 1/2 Me 109s Destroyed
Lt. Godfrey	2 1/2 Me 109s Destroyed

In addition, many additional e/a were Damaged.

"Fiedler's score: Several broken windows in Berlin."

Excerpts From Combat Reports -

1st Lt. Bunte - "Our Squadron approached five Me 109s from seven o'clock low. As the e/a broke for the deck, in my excitement, I opened fire at about 1,000 yards but observed no strikes. I fired another short burst at 500-600 yards, observing a few strikes. I fired again at 200-300 yards and observed several strikes as the e/a spun and jettisoned his hood. I spun and lost the e/a, the Squadron, and the bombers. I dove to the deck and started home. I saw a small a/c just above the tree-tops and gave a short 90-degree deflection burst and hopped over it to avoid ramming it. Looking back I saw him in a tree. I claim one Me 109 Probably Destroyed, and one FS 156 Destroyed."

*****

Major James Clark - "We attacked five 109s from below. I followed one down to 8,000 feet where I fired three short bursts. I observed a few strikes in the cockpit area. The e/a flicked and dove straight into the ground. I claim one 109 Destroyed."

*****

1st Lt. Victor France - "We saw five 109s above us turning to bounce us. We climbed to attack them, and I discovered my oxygen was completely gone. I had to go down, and I hoped I might find an e/a diving down. One did dive, but I lost him, so I continued to orbit below the bombers at 15,000. I saw two 109s spinning down, one burning, after attack by two Mustangs: Capt. Gentile and Lt. Godfrey, of Shirtblue Squadron. I also saw the tail section of a Mustang floating down. Two e/a soon came down out of the fight, and I closed rapidly on one to about 100 yards. I opened fire dead

astern. After many strikes, I hit his belly tank which exploded in a mass of flame and debris. He crashed in a forest as I overshot him. He had been carrying rocket guns. On the way out, I damaged a large electric locomotive."

*****

2nd Lt. David Howe - "Two 109s crossed at right angles to us, and I picked the second one. He started to dive at about 60 degrees. As I closed, I got strikes. The e/a either jettisoned the belly tank or had it shot free. It exploded close to me. I continued to fire until his engine was smoking so badly I could no longer see the target. He went into a dive past the vertical and crashed near a small stream."

*****

1st Lt. Nicholas Megura - "The first box of bombers asked for help so Major Clark led us up to 33,000 feet where five plus e/a passed through us. I gave chase to a Me 109. I closed at 8,000 feet and started to fire. At about 25 yards range, I got strikes on his wing and engine, which exploded. Heavy black smoke poured out.

Skidding in a turn, I found a 109 on my tail, but I lost him in a couple of turns. I went to help a Fort and closed on a FW 190. I got strikes on his starboard wing and engine. He bailed out, and the a/c crashed in smoke and flame. I closed on another Me 109, which led me in a circuit. He kept breaking gently into others that were around us. As long as I behaved like one of them, they did not attempt to engage, and they ignored me. A FW 190 was landing with flaps and gear down. As I was just about to fire, two 109s came at me from 3 o'clock, very business like. I broke hard into them, came back, and shot at the first FW 190 just as he was touching down. I broke into three others; balls out; hit the deck; and headed east with the e/a still chasing me. Later, I fired on a train, leaving it in a cloud of steam. Still on the deck, I was chased again by six U/I a/c, which I finally lost.

Over the Ruhr at 14,000 feet, I saw a Ju 88 and gave chase. Flying at house level, flak was intense, but I kept firing with only one gun operating. I got strikes all over the e/a, with no return fire, until I was out of ammo. I pulled alongside to find him flying only on his port engine. Out of ammo and oxygen, I returned home."

*****

1st Lt. W.B. Smith - "We attacked two Me 109s, and I became separated from the Group. I joined up with Lt. Howe and attacked a train west of Berlin. Pulling up, we saw and attacked another train after which we spotted an A/D with quite a few planes. We dove in from the sun, going so fast I managed only a few strikes on a Ju 52."

Captain W.B. Smith, 334 Squadron, was KIA 9 Sept 44 when his flak riddled plane hit the ground and exploded on an airdrome strafing run near Ulm, Germany. He was an Ace and he was on his second tour. Konsler collection.

*****

"Fiedler chased two FW 190s, a Me 109, and a Me 110 all over Berlin, squirting at them as he went. The people on the street would stop running and stare at him as he whizzed by. Clem was pulling tight turns around Berlin's best buildings and having one hell'va time for himself.

Old Don Blakeslee got a write up in today's S&S for being the first Pilot to lead the bombers over Berlin. Major Halsey, also, was mentioned for tackling 60 Huns with eight of his boys from 336.

Old Don said that as long as we can get one kite over Berlin, we'll stay on Ops. You can bet your last hay penny that we will.

"A penny for Old Adolph's thoughts at the moment."

9 March - Col. Blakeslee led the Group on a Target Support Mission to Berlin. The mission was uneventful and no e/a were seen.

"There was a solid overcast to 20,000 feet, so Goering grounded all his boys. It would be absurd to think that he grounded them because of the beating they took the two days previous.'

Four new boys in 335 Squadron today. The old boys heave a sigh of relief."

All enlisted personnel reported to the Station Gas Chamber to test the newly issued gas masks.

10 March - The Victory Credits Report Board confirmed the following e/a Destroyed between 31 Jan and 21 Feb 1944:

One Me 109 each Lt. Moulton, shared with Capt. Sobanski; Lt.Biel, and Lt.Montgomery

One FW 190 each Lt. France, Lt.Howe, Capt. Mills, Capt. Beeson, and Capt. Care.

12 March - Capt. Mills was promoted to Major; 2nd Lt. Breaux and 2nd Lt. Terry were promoted to 1st Lt.

A General Order was received authorizing all personnel assigned to this Group, from 4 July 1942 forward to a future date to be announced, to wear the "**Bronze Star**" on the ETO ribbon.

1st Lt. Dale B. Leaf was officially listed as killed in action on 2 Sept 1943.

15 March - The following Officers were assigned to 334 Sq.:

2nd Lt. Robert P. Kenyon

2nd Lt. Leonard R. Pierce

Complying with a verbal order from Group Material, the noses of all our Mustangs were painted bright red.

16 March - Col. Blakeslee led the Group on a mission to Munich. There were a major number of abortions and early returns. "Still quite a few bugs in the aircraft." Upon return, two ounces of medicinal whiskey were issued to each of the Pilots.

After R/V, seven Me 110s were engaged as they attempted a rear-on attack on the bombers. Five were destroyed, and below the clouds, five more were encountered and two more were destroyed. A mixed Group of 12 to 20 Me 109s and Me 110s were subsequently engaged, and six Me 110s were destroyed. Two B-17s were seen heading for Switzerland.

Results of Engagements:

334 Squadron	
Hofer	1 Me 110 Destroyed
Chatterley	1 Me 110 Destroyed
335 Squadron	
Carpenter	2 Me 110s Destroyed
Smith	1 Me 110 Destroyed
Riley	1 Me 110 Destroyed
336 Squadron	
Goodson	2 Destroyed ME 110s
Glover	2 Destroyed ME 110s
Carlson	2 Destroyed ME 110s
Godfrey	1 Destroyed ME 110s

Combat Reports:

1st Lt. Chatterley - "While firing on a Me 110, which was attacking a bomber, I was bounced by a Me 109F. This caused me to break off. Later I engaged a Me 110 and saw strikes around the cockpit cover and fuselage. It tumbled straight down as if the pilot had been hit. Cloud cover obscured the e/a as it descended, but F/O Fred Glover of 336 confirmed my claim."

*****

F/O Ralph K. Hofer - "I was flying #2 to Major Clark when we bounced a Me 110. As Major Clark closed, he discovered his guns would not fire and told me to take over. I attacked two Me 110s that jettisoned their rockets and dove for the clouds. I followed one and noticed that my gunsight was out. The rear gunner of the e/a was firing all the time and hit my prop. I fired and saw strikes followed by explosions as the Me 110 nosed down from 300 feet and crashed."

*****

Battle Damage: "Major Carpenter was shot up by the rear gunner on the second Me 110 he destroyed. The Hun really drew a bead on Carp and peppered hell out of him. One .303 struck on the brace between the first and second panel on the canopy. An inch either way and it would have been fatal to Carpenter."

Lt. Skilton of 336 was lost today. (He was KIA).

"We now have passed the 200 mark in Destroyed for the Group: Hq. has five; 334 has 79; 335 has 58; and 336 has 60—making a total of 202.

"This was the first time the boys were over Adolph's Beer Hall, but it certainly won't be the last. The bombers didn't get the primary target, which usually means a second trip. This was the longest trip in the 51s so far. Munich is just slightly farther than Berlin from this base. Jerry doesn't bother much about coming up unless it is a deep penetration of his fatherland. He tries to catch the bombers when they have insufficient or no fighter escort. However, the quality, courage, and desperation of the Hun pilots hasn't shown any slacking. The Hun is still a smart, wily pilot."

18 March - Major James Clark was appointed Group Operations Officer, and he was assigned to Headquarters, 4th Fighter Group.

Capt. Duane W. Beeson was appointed Commander of 334 Squadron.

The Victory credits Board Confirmed the following for 25 Feb to 4 Mar:

Capt. Beeson	1 FW 190 Destroyed
Capt. Beeson, Lt Megura, and Lt Smith,	
	shared 1 Ju 88 Destroyed
1st Lt. Wynn	1 Me 109 Destroyed
1st Lt. Megura	1 Me 109 Destroyed
1st Lt. Chatterly	1 Me 110 Destroyed

Col. Blakeslee led the group on a mission to Munich. This was Lt. Pierce's first operational sortie. Two hours into the mission, four

Sections dropped tanks and bounced eight to ten Me 109s, 5,000 feet below them. Afterwards, the same Sections went down and strafed an A/D. This upset the Col. since he said a few men, not a whole squadron, should attack. This reduced our maximum strength over the target since those who dropped tanks had to go home early due to low gas reserves.

Subsequent skirmishes left only six aircraft over the target. They were engaged by 60 plus SE e/a who were attacking the bombers head-on. These e/a were aggressive in attacking both the bombers and the fighters. The Huns appeared to have used time-fused explosive 20 mm canon fire. "Our boys made a stab at breaking up the attack, but were completely overwhelmed."

Capt. Beeson's plane had its elevator and rudder damaged by flames from the Me 109 he Destroyed.

"Bomber targets included Oberphoffenhoffen and Lansberg, where, incidently, Herr Adolph was interned and wrote Mein Kampf."

Results of Engagements:

Claims of e/a Destroyed were made as follows:

Capt. Beeson	1 Me 109
Lt. Chatterley	1 Me 109
Lt. Megura	1 Me 109
Maj. Carpenter	1 Me 109
F/O Hofer	2 Me 109s
Lt. McGrattan	1 He 111
Lt. Smith	1 FW 190
Capt. Gentile	1 FW 190
Col. Blakeslee	1 FW 190
Maj. Goodson	2 He 111s

Combat Reports:

Capt. Beeson - "Leading Pectin Sq. just under the second layer of clouds at 17,000 feet, we spotted nine Me 109s directly below. As we started down on them, they were darting in and out of the clouds. I closed on one, and my second burst must have hit his belly tank, because the whole aircraft immediately blew up in my face. A large sheet of flame suddenly appeared in front of my a/c, and I was unable to avoid it. I had to fly through it, and I felt pieces of the Me 109 strike my a/c before I could break clear. I could feel the heat in my cockpit, and I immediately checked my instruments. I looked down and saw what was left of the 109 going down, covered in flame.

Later I made two passes at Me 109s, which evaded into the clouds. When I came out of the clouds, I saw one of them appeared to have been hit by a nearby burst of flak.

I claim one Me 109, which is confirmed by Lt. Chatterley, in writing."

*****

1st Lt. Biel - "We sighted nine to ten Me 109s, and we broke down at them. I picked one and attacked. I gave him three bursts with no success. I then closed to 300 yards and used 35 degrees of deflection to fire on him. I saw strikes around his right wing root as his belly tank dropped off, and he headed into the overcast. I then saw Lt. Megura clobbering a 109, which broke into a mass of flames."

*****

1st Lt. Chatterley - "As we dove on nine 109s that just popped out of the clouds below us, I met one head-on. I stall-turned onto him and opened fire at 400 yards. I saw strikes on the fuselage and wing roots as I closed to 300 yards. A burst of flame appeared, presumably from his belly tank. It died down a little, then became continuous as he went into the clouds where we could still see the glow as he disappeared. This claim is confirmed by Lt. Montgomery."

*****

F/O Ralph Hofer - "As we dove, I saw a good bounce on a Me 109 and dropped W/T and went after him. I saw strikes and an explosion as pieces flew off and black smoke poured out of the falling e/a. I saw an A/D with a four engine a/c that looked like a Liberator. I fired on a Me 109 which went into the clouds but popped out again as the canopy came off. The pilot bailed out. Major Goodson confirmed this a/c.

I bounced another 109 but lost him in the clouds. I set course for the target, and I saw two 109s in front and above me. I climbed to attack them. At about 600 yards, my prop ran away, and I lost flying speed. I was recording a terrific amount of boost and rpms, so I set course for Switzerland. As I passed into Switzerland, I started to climb to bail out, and my prop came back to normal. I decided that with a little luck I could make it back home. On the way, I saw three 109s shoot down a Mustang before I could help. I landed at Manston with six gallons of gas."

*****

1st Lt. Megura - "As we dove on nine e/a below us, I closed on one on the port side of their formation and gave him a squirt. I skidded over to one on the right, an intrepid type who was working his way behind us. Firing, I closed fast and saw strikes on his port wing with pieces falling off. I then saw strikes all over the fuselage, engine, etc. I slid aside to avoid a collision, as flames appeared below the engine. The plane staggered, flipped over on its back, and started down gushing flame and black smoke. Just before he hit the clouds, his belly tank exploded.

I pushed everything to the firewall and climbed up with my wing tanks still intact. I saw two Me 109s attacking a P-51; broke down; and opened fire on one of them. Because of the wing tanks I could not turn tight enough, so I dropped them. I started to fire as he went under my nose and did a skidding roll off to the side, but the Huns disappeared in the clouds. With my tanks gone I could not continue on the show, so I headed home with several others in the same predicament."

*****

Lt. K. G. Smith reported on Freeburger as follows: "We spotted a bunch of Huns. I told Freeburger that I'd take the one on the right, and he should take the one on the left. He answered 'OK Ken.' Just as I opened fire, he yelled, 'Ken there's four on our tails, break!' I broke right and presumed that he broke, also."

*****

Major Henry Mills was reported NYR on 6 March. He became 334's second "Ace" with confirmation of his 20 Feb destruction of one FW 190.

"We lost Lt. Edward Freeburger who was last seen by Capt. Smith, 20 miles SSW of Ulm. He was being chased by four Huns." (Freeburger was later confirmed as KIA).

Lt. Sooman of 336 was also lost today. (Sooman became a POW)

"Show really shook the boys today. They really needed that double shot they're getting after every mission. Col. Don called a meeting of all pilots immediately after landing."

"The Red Nose Command nightly resume" of the day's activities is now given each night over the Tannoy. "Makes the GIs feel better and is going over big. Many thanks to Col. Don."

19 March - 334 Squadron led by Capt. Sobanski, supported Thunderbombers (which never showed) on an uneventful mission to Brussels. This was the much talked of "Milk Run."

This was Lt. Don Patchen's first combat mission. Don was a member of the class of 43-I. He had gone through the usual flight training, but in addition to learning to fly, he had picked up a few other bits of knowledge during his Cadet training.

His first bit was, "*Play cards with strangers, not friends.*"

Next, "*Don't play cards with anyone if you aren't a card player.*"

The last was that, "*Cheating was not to be tolerated.*"

Don did not cheat, but experienced the never to be forgotten degradation of one who had cheated. At 0200, the Cadets were assembled in full uniform on the parade ground. They then stood at attention for a prolonged period of time. The errant Cadet was brought before the assembled group. His insignia was unceremoniously removed, and the group was advised that the Cadet's name was never again to be spoken.

20 March - Major Carpenter led the group on a Target and Withdrawal Support mission to Frankfurt. Lt. Kenyon made his first Ops on this mission. No e/a seen. "These bus rides are really getting awfully boring. Tally Ho!"

21 March - Authorization was received to increase 334 Squadron strength by 12 flying Officers.

Major Clark led the Group on a Fighter Sweep to the Bordeaux area, a mass "Rhubarb." This was a show the boys wanted and got permission from Fighter Command to do. The idea was to penetrate France at about 28,000 feet and then come back on the deck shooting up whatever they came across.

The 334 and 335 Squadrons attacked a grass field (A/D), destroying three e/a. During the attack, five FW 190s came down on 334 Squadron, which then destroyed three of them. Later a Ju 88 was destroyed near Langon.

Casualties: 1st Lt. Alex Rafalovich bailed out north of Bordeaux. (He became a POW).

The 335 lost Smith, Carlow, Brandenburg, Goetz, and Hawkins. (Smith and Carlow became POWs, Brandenburg and Goetz were KIA, and Hawkins evaded and returned to the Group)

1st Lt. Robert Williams bailed out north of Angers.

Lt. Williams was interviewed by CWO Edward Richie in Aug 45 upon his return from POW Camp. Lt. Williams recalled: "I came to England in November 41, and I was in the 611 Eagle Squadron. I was one of those unlucky blokes who never was in the right place at the right time. I got mine on 21 Mar 44, on that special show Col. Jim Clark dreamed up after we spotted all those damn FW 200s on that A/D on our mission to Bordeaux.

I was leading Green Section, and Shell Monroe and Anderson went down with me. I picked up a load of ground flak. After about a minute and a half, my engine packed up, and I hit the silk. I was knocked out cold when I hit the stabilizer as I bailed out. When I came to, my chute was open, and I was in a cloud. I landed in a plowed field, and when I tried to get up, I found that I couldn't. Some kids helped me into a nearby peasant's home, which soon became full of their relatives.

I had the darndest time trying to get a glass of water.

They tried to give me wine, which I turned down. Then they gave me a glass full of clear stuff, which I guess was turpentine or some very strong liquor, which I spit out. I had a bad gash on my leg, and my ribs were bruised. They wanted me to get medical attention. They sent for the Gendarmes, but the Gestapo arrived instead.

After some interrogation and a few threats, they put me in a French hospital where I received good care. I got more verbal abuse and threats from the Gestapo, including the threat of a firing squad. However, after I was able to walk, about a week later they put me on a train for Paris. From there we went to Frankfurt, where bombing had just killed about 40,000 people. My guards had to raise their guns to keep the civilians away from me.

We arrived at a new interrogation center where they took my watch and gave me a receipt for it; they always give you a receipt, but you never see the watch again. Supper arrived; two pieces of bread with such a thin coating of jam that it must have been sprayed on the bread.

At an interrogation by a man named Scharf, I met Peterson and Clotfelter—some reunion! We got the usual rundown, which brought us up to date on the news from the 4th. The Germans knew more about the 4th than we did. We were then shipped to a POW Camp where we stayed until the Russians arrived. When they showed up, they looked like a bunch of gypsies. By golly, they were riding bicycles, horses and wagons, carriages, walking, and shooting off their Tommy Guns in the air. They brought their women right with them, and they were a motley looking crowd.

When they became more or less organized, they took us on a visit to the concentration camps. I'll never forget it. It's hard to reconcile such brutality and outright cruelty with modern civilization. Meanwhile, they had a detail of German civilians clearing the booby traps and mines from the nearby airfield so Forts could come in and pick us up. When it was cleared, the Forts arrived, and in two days they evacuated all nine thousand of us by air."

*****

Lt. Dye was hit pretty badly while being attacked by eight Huns. Hawkins was with him when they were jumped and Dye told him to get out of the scrap and beat it home if he could. This is the last that was heard of Hawkins. Dye will be out for five or six weeks with his wound. He climbed out of the scrap and started for home. "The bleeding was so bad, old Jim tied his belt around his leg to stop the bleeding. This probably saved his life. This show was only the second for Hawkins."

F/O Goetz was hit at zero feet while shooting up an airdrome. McKennon saw him crash; the kite did not catch on fire, but both wings were off, the engine was out, and the fuselage was on its

1st Lt. Robert G. "Digger" Williams of 334 Squadron, became a POW when he bailed out near Angers, France 21 Mar 44. Konsler collection.

Captain Earle W. Carlow of 335 Squadron became a POW when his plane was hit by flak near Bordeaux, France, 21 Mar 44. He subsequently escaped and made it to Spain, returning to England 10 June 44. Konsler collection.

back. McKennon does not believe Goetz could have survived. He turned back and took a picture of the crash.

Capt. Carlow was hit while shooting up the second airdrome. This was seen by Church. He was hit either by Bofors or MG. His kite was streaming glycol about 15 minutes after being hit. He bailed out; his chute opened alright; and he was last seen gathering his chute on the ground. His aircraft crashed about one mile north of him.

Lt. Brandenburg was hit while attacking an A/D thought to be Caen. His engine was on fire and sweeping around the cockpit, so Waterman told him to get out. Brandenburg then climbed to 1,000 feet and bailed. His chute opened at about tree top level, but he floated the last few feet.

Lt. K.G. Smith was last seen leading Brandenburg and Waterman over the Caen A/D. "Don't know if he was hit or not."

"Sure a rough day for 335, but our victories kind of offset the losses. Sure hope the boys made it OK."

Battle Damage: Near Langon, Lt. Wynn hit an antennae, damaging both wings.

Lt. Godfrey was hit by 20 mm just back of the cockpit, and Major Goodson picked up a flak hole in the oil cooler.

Results of Engagements: Claims of e/a Destroyed:

Major Clark	2 FW 190s
Lts. Chatterley and Megura	shared 1 FW 190
Lt. Megura	1 He 177
Lts. Hively and Goodwin	1 Ju 88
F/O Hofer	1 He 177
Lt. France	2 FW 190s
Lts. Rafalovich and Capt. Van Epps	1 Do 217
Lt. Fiedler	1 FW 190
Lt. Hawkins	1 Me 110
Lt. McKennon	1 FW 190
Lt. Schlegel	1 He 111
Major Carpenter	1 FW 190
Lt. Anderson	1 FW 190
Anderson and Carpenter shared	2 Fw 190s
Anderson, Carpenter and Church	1 Ju 52
Smith and Brandenburg shared	1 Fisler Storch
Major Goodson	1 Me 410
Capt. Hobert	1 FW 190

Combat Reports:

1st Lt. Chatterley - "We pulled up after strafing and were attacked by four FW 190s. As I was pulling inside of one of them, they all broke off and started to run off on the tree tops. I was pulling strikes on #4 man when Lt. Megura went past me and also got strikes. The Hun's wheels started to come down, he hit some tree tops and spread the plane over a field where it burst into flames. Regaining height, we saw five FW 190s below us. I attacked the last one. He dove and I closed very fast. I fired short bursts and saw strikes. I was still firing as he pulled up, jettisoned the hood, and bailed out."

*****

1st Lt. Victor France - "I saw about five aircraft on an A/D and picked a Me 109 near the Control Tower. I fired at point blank range, setting it on fire. We broke port and saw two FW 190s. A Mustang was chasing one of them, and there were two Mustangs chasing the other. I saw a 190 firing at a Mustang at close range and called for him to break. Smoke started to come from the Mustang. I fired a burst at the 190, but it was out of range. I saw an A/D ahead and attacked a FW190 taxiing. I made two runs and left him burning fiercely."

*****

Capt. Howard Hively - "I attacked a Ju 88 that was taxiing out on a runway. I got strikes and observed a fire start under his starboard engine, which soon engulfed the whole plane."

*****

F/O Ralph Hofer - "I came in very low over an A/D near Bordeaux, flying line abreast with Lt. Wynn. I fired at an e/a which I believe was a He 177. It was smoking very badly, and I saw many strikes as it burst into flames. The a/c was destroyed. I claim one e/a shared with a person unknown."

*****

1st Lt. Nicholas Megura - "As we strafed a few buildings on an A/D, Pectin White 3 and I were jumped by four FW 190s. We broke into them and chased them to the deck. We closed on one, both firing at intervals with pieces flying off the e/a. His undercarriage came down, and he crashed in a field and blew up. I came across another airfield and fired a long burst into a He 177 which started to burn."

*****

2nd Lt. S. W. Monroe -"I was flying Pectin Blue 2 to Lt. Williams. We dove on an A/D at St. Jean d'Angely, and we fired on a FW 200. As I pulled away from the field, a number of tracers passed over my port wing. I dropped to the deck wide open for a couple of minutes and then zoomed up into cloud cover. Later Lt. Williams had to leave his kite because of a glycol leak. Lt. Carr and I were with him when he bailed out safely near Angers, France."

*****

2nd Lt. Pierce - "I was flying on Lt. Hively's wing as we attacked an A/D South of Bordeaux. He fired on a Ju 88, and I observed hits on the e/a. I took a short burst at another Ju 88 but saw no strikes. I then attacked a Me 110 near a hangar and observed hits and also saw the hangar catch on fire."

*****

1st Lt. Alex Rafalovich - A claim of one Do 217 Destroyed, shared with Capt. Van Epps, was submitted in behalf of Lt. Rafalovich, who is NYR from Ops in the Bordeaux area. The claim was submitted by Lt. Benjamin Q. Ezzell and was confirmed by Capt. Van Epps.

*****

Capt. David Van Epps - "I followed Lt. Rafalovich down on an A/D east of Bordeaux, and we both shot at a Do 217 that was landing. I observed strikes all over it from both of us. Lt. Blanchfield reports that the a/c was burning badly when he came across the drome behind us."

*****

Lt. Braley, 336, "I fired at a hangar and managed to scare a horse and wagon out of it." (Lt. Emerson flew with Lt. Braley and confirmed his actions on the horse and wagon, and the personnel strafing.)

*****

2nd Lt. William C. Hawkins - (Filed in July after he returned to the U.K. from enemy territory.) "I was flying Greenbelt 2. My element leader and I bounced four FW 190s near Bordeaux. Later four other FW 190s came in, and I lost my element leader as I was trying to shake two of the FW 190s from my tail by tight maneuvers below the tree tops. When I finally lost them, I ran into a Me 110 taking off from a grass-covered field. This e/a was flying at about 50 feet. I made one pass and gave him a short burst at 45 degrees deflection. I got strikes on the wingroot and canopy. The e/a then crashed and burned at the end of the runway. I came back to take a picture of the wreckage before continuing on my trip home. I ran out of gas before I reached home base, and I had to parachute to safety at 1630 hours."

*****

22 March - Col. Blakeslee led the Group on an easy Penetration and Target Support to Berlin. No e/a were seen. "Now even Berlin seems to have become a Bus Ride except for sweating out the engines and the flak. About 600 Bombers and 1,000 Fighters went on this raid. The boys said that it was the most accurate and the heaviest flak they had encountered. It harassed them all the way in and out. There was a huge black cloud over Berlin caused by flak bursts. Over Berlin someone was heard to comment on the excitement of the mission, "Ho, Hum.""

23 March - Col. Blakeslee led a Target Support mission to Brunswick. When the Group R/Vd near Steinhuder Lake, the bombers were under heavy attack by 25 plus Me 109s and FW 190s. In the following combats which took place down to 3,000 feet, the Group destroyed eleven and damaged three. Two more e/a were destroyed near Brunswick. Three B-17s were seen going down, and one was seen with only one engine operating. The 336 lost one P-51.

Results of Engagement: Claims of e/a Destroyed:

Major Clark	1 Fw 190
	1 Me 109
Capt. Beeson	2 Me 109s
Lt. Pierce	1 Me 109
Lt. Bunte	1 Me 109
Lt. Godfrey	1 Me 109
F/O Hofer	1 FW 190
Lt. Megura	1 Me 109
Capt. Gentile	2 Me 109s
Major Goodson	2 Me 109s

Hofer is the only FO in the ETO that is an ace!

Beeson and Gentile are tied for top honors in the Group, each having 17 Destroyed. This puts them exactly five behind the leading ETO ace, Johnson of Zemke's Group. He has 22 destroyed. The ETO record is held by Capt. Eddie Rickenbacker with 26.

Combat Reports:

Capt. Beeson - "As we approached the bombers, there were many e/a around. One Me 109 made a head-on pass through our Squadron. He then circled to come at us again, so I turned after him. He dove, and as I closed he pulled up into a steep climb. I followed; closed; and got good strikes on him. He began to smoke and headed for the clouds. I followed and clobbered him again as he came out of the clouds. He stuck with his plane and crash-landed in a field where I strafed him. His engine began to flame as the pilot got out of the cockpit and ran across the field. He fell behind a fence post as I made another pass.

I made a pass at a freight train and got good strikes on the engine. I then climbed after a Me 109 with its wheels down, but he went into a cloud just as I saw tracers going past my port wing. I quickly broke to starboard and saw a Me 109 behind me. He pulled into a cloud from where he again dove, but I was able to get on his tail and saw many flashes as I fired.

He jettisoned his hood, but I kept firing. Oil from the e/a covered my windscreen. He bailed out, but his chute did not open. His plane crashed nearby and burst into flames."

*****

1st Lt. Allen Bunte - "I bounced three 109s in a dive, and just as they entered a cloud I saw strikes on one. I saw another 109, and we fought for three or four minutes. I got quite a few strikes, and he started smoking and headed for the deck where he made a wheels-up crash landing."

*****

Capt. Howard Hively - "Three e/a were attacking a B-17 straggler, and I managed to get on the tail of the last one. As I closed rapidly, I observed strikes on the fuselage and starboard wing. He flicked over on his back at 3,000 feet, so I figured he was destroyed. I climbed back up to look for the other two e/a. My #2 said the e/a had pulled out and that it had been carrying some sort of wing racks."

*****

F/O Hofer - "I picked out one of the e/a attacking the bombers and followed him through the clouds getting strikes. A dog fight followed and ended when the FW 190 flicked into the deck."

*****

1st Lt. Megura - "At the R/V, I picked a FW 190 and gave chase. As I overtook him in a tight turn at tree-top level, a Me 109 joined the scrap. He couldn't get deflection on me, so I climbed as I fired at the FW 190. I observed large pieces coming off him as the e/a plunged into the ground and exploded. The Me 109 attacked, and I worked around in back of him. I was closing as he entered the clouds. Two FW 190s joined the fight, so I entered the clouds and flew on instruments for 10 minutes. I then set course for home."

*****

2nd Lt. Leonard Pierce - "I was flying Capt. Beeson's wing, but in a fight I became confused as to which one was Beeson. I started to join an a/c, but recognized it as a Me 109. I turned inside him and took a short burst as he turned to the right. I was directly line astern. I continued to fire until I saw him catch fire and spiral down as the pilot bailed out."

*****

24 March - Major Clark led the Group on a Penetration, Target, and Withdrawal Support mission to Schweinfurt. A lone Ju 52 was engaged, but escaped in 10/10 cloud cover.

Two Forts were seen to collide over Germany, and two P-38s collided over France.

Capt. Blackburn gave a sex morality lecture to the first three grades of EM, and then introduced and issued the new "PROPAK" prophylactic kit made by Lilly and Co, Ltd.

25 March - All available EM reported to the hangar, and Capt. Heene commended the Squadron for the exceptional job done in getting the Mustangs operational. He also stressed the need for thought in writing letters so as not to give any military information or to make any derogatory remarks about the British. He then announced that the 3rd Squadron party would be held 5 April.

General Auton awarded the following decorations to the Pilots on the parade ground:

2nd and 3rd
Oak Leaf Cluster to the Distinguished Flying Cross
Capt. Beeson
Oak Leaf Cluster to the Distinguished Flying Cross
1st Lt. France
1st Lt. Chatterley
Distinguished Flying Cross
1st Lt. Montgomery
1st Lt. Blanchfield
1st Lt. Bunte
1st Lt. Wynn
F/O Hofer

General Auton then read the following Commendation:

1. I desire to commend the 4th Fighter Group for its outstanding victory against the German Luftwaffe during an aggressive attack in the area of Bordeaux, France, during which there were claimed 21 e/a Destroyed and 4 Damaged for the loss of 7 pilots and 7 P-51s.

2. A Special Commendation is hereby given to Major James A. Clark, Jr., who first thought up this mission, planned it in detail, led the attack in a thoroughly aggressive manner, and claimed two FW 190s Destroyed.

3. The great distance of this smashing attack took the enemy completely by surprise. It took savage destruction into his training base area, brought damage to blister hangars, airdrome buildings, wagons, soldier personnel, and power lines, and convinced the enemy that no part of his territory will henceforth be safe from attack; thereby bringing great fear to the enemy and lowering his will to continue the war.

The following order was received:

The Distinguished Flying Cross was awarded to 1st Lt. Charles Carr

The Victory Credits Board confirmed the following for 5 Mar and 8 Mar 1944:

Capt. Beeson	Me 109 Destroyed
1st Lt. W.B. Smith	Ju 52 Damaged
2nd Lt. Howe	Me 109 Destroyed
1st Lt. Bunte	FS 15 Destroyed
1st Lt. Megura	FW 190 Destroyed

26 March - No operations.

27 March - Major Clark led the group on a Target Support and Free Lance to Pau.

The 334 and 336 Squadrons escorted three CWs of bombers at Cazaux A/D. They saw 75 or more parked e/a undamaged by the bombing, and strafed the A/D, destroying 21. Later, near Angers, a lone S/E e/a dove through the bomber formation. Lt. Megura chased it, but broke off after being attacked by four long-nosed FW 190s and three Me 109s. They were unable to close on him as he dove to the deck.

Brigadier General Jesse Auton was 65th Fighter Wing CO. Although he never personally flew with the 4th, he was a frequent visitor and presented many awards to members of the Group. Zigler collection.

Capt. Chatterley was hit by flak and bailed out ten miles south of Tours. (He became a POW).

Results of Engagements: Claims of e/a Destroyed:

Capt. Beeson	one Ju 88
	one He 126
	one Ju 88 shared Lt. Biel
Lt Biel	one Me 410
	one Ju 88
Lt. Monroe	one Me 410
Capt. Chatterley	one Me 109
Lt. Smith	two Me 109s
Capt. Hively	one Ju 88
Lt. Markel	one Ju 88 shared Lt. Megura
Lt. France	one Ju 52
	one Ju 88
Lt. Montgomery	one Ju 88
	one Ju 52
	one FW 190
Lt. Wynn	one Do 217
	one Ju 88

Major Carpenter	one FW 190
Lt. Anderson	one FW 190
Capt. Gentile	two Me 110s
Lt. Millikan	one He 177
Lt. Norley	one Ju 88
Major Clark	one Ju 88
Major Clark	one Ju 88 shared with Lt. Emerson

"Col. Blakeslee wasn't here for this show, but he'll sure be tickled when he hears of it. The boys really went flat out. The boys now have to get at least 15 on a show to get free beer. Previously it had been 10, but like all good businessmen Col. Don raised the quota."

Major Blanding has now officially left for Atcham to instruct the boys in the fine art of how to duck Hun lead. God help those poor rookies!

28 March - Major Clark led the Group on a Target and Withdrawal Support mission to Chateaudun. One Squadron attacked an A/D with Lt. Markel claiming a Me 109 Destroyed. Anderson got one U/I a/c destroyed.

Lt. Raymond Clotfelter was lost during this action. He leaves a wife in the States. War is sure getting rough on the married men. (He became a POW).

One pilot from 357 Group shot down a mosquito over France.

"Our Group score now stands at 283 to Halesworth's 372. The boys at Halesworth must be tearing their hair out for we're closing fast. They seem to be making a suicidal attempt to stay ahead of us by shooting up airdromes, but they are paying for it and not making any headway.

Our boys are doing their share to destroy the Luftwaffe before the Invasion begins. In one month of operations in P-51s, our Group score is well over 100 Destroyed."

29 March - Lt. Col. Clark led the Group on a Target and Withdrawal Support mission to Brunswick. Near Grifhorn, 30 plus e/a approached the bombers from the Northeast at the same time as 15 plus S/E e/a were making a rear attack from the South. Our Group bounced and combat ensued from 24,000 feet to the deck. Later near Celle, four S/E e/a attacked and were engaged. Twelve silver Me 109s with red noses were seen in the target area.

Lt. Smart had to bail out about eight miles off the English coast. He went into a cloud, and his instruments went out at 2,000 feet. Luckily, a Spit and a Walrus were in the vicinity and saw a Mustang come out of the cloud and into the water. They waited around until they saw Smart come out of the cloud in his parachute. He was in the water about ten minutes all tangled up in his chute. He was nearly frozen to death. If the Walrus had not been so close, he might easily have drowned.

Lt. Newall is missing on this show. Godfrey saw him bail out, NW of Dummer Lake. He left a wife back home and had the dis-

tinction of being our youngest pilot, only 19. (Newall became a POW)

Capt. Peterson of 336 was also lost today. (He became a POW).

Combat Report: (The following information was taken from a report submitted on 29 June 1945 by 2nd Lt. William Newell while stationed at "Lucky Strike," Le Havre, France.)

Lt. Newell was flying Greenbelt White, #4, near Brunswick, when he engaged a FW 190 at 5,000 feet. He closed on the e/a, fired, and observed strikes along the left side of the fuselage and left wing root, which caused the e/a to explode. After he destroyed the e/a, Lt. Newell was hit as a 20 mm exploded beside the canopy. The explosion blew the plexiglass out of the left side of his canopy; cut him; and caused a coolant leak in his A/C. After about 15 minutes, his engine quit and caught fire. He bailed out and was taken prisoner.

*****

Results of Engagements:	Claims of e/a Destroyed:
Lt. Col. Clark	one FW 190 Destroyed
Lts. Bunte, Howe, and Biel @	One FW 190
Capt. Sobanski	One Ju 52
Major Carpenter, Lt. Godfrey, and F/O Glover	shared one He 111
Lt. McKennon	one FW 190
Lts. Fiedler, Saunders, Church, and Riley @ one Me 109	
Lts. Anderson, Godfrey, and Capt. Peterson @ two FW 190s	
Capt. Gentile went to town;	three destroyed!
F/O Glover	one FW 190
LeJennessee	one Ju 88

A Lib crashed at Halesworth today, and shortly after caught fire and exploded, killing several people who had run to watch it. It also killed a pilot who had completed his tour and was waiting around to go home.

A commendation was received from 65th Fighter Wing as follows:

"Special commendation is given to the 334th Fighter Squadron and to Capt. Duane Beeson, who led on this mission, for the highest claim of any Fighter Squadron in this theatre of operations to date, on which there are claimed 18 enemy aircraft destroyed and 6 damaged. This record establishes a standard for other Squadrons to emulate and strive to attain.'

30 March - There were no operations.

An order was received awarding the **Distinguished Flying Cross** to 1st Lt. Hipolitus T. Biel

31 March - No operations.

All available pilots attended an aircraft recognition test, after which there was a showing of combat films.

6

The Offense Begins

1 April 1944 - Early today we had snow.

The Victory Credits Board confirmed the following March claims:

Victor France	1 Me 109Destroyed
Nicholas Megura	1 Me 110Destroyed
Spiros Pisanos	1 Me 109 Destroyed
James A. Clark	1 Me 109 Destroyed

The Group conducted a Fighter Sweep to the Ludwigshafen area, led by Col. Blakeslee. E/a were engaged near Lake Constance as they were attacking two boxes of Liberators. Capt. Beeson destroyed his 21st Hun. Lt. Megura and F/O Hofer each claimed a Me 109 destroyed. Gentile of 336 got his 22nd Hun, which tied him with Johnson, who was the leading ETO ace. Major Carpenter damaged a Me 109.

Today the boys saw the snow covered Alps. This was the first day that we were able to put a full Group in the air since we went operational in Mustangs.

One Wing of Libs got off course today and bombed some Swiss city. "Someone is sure going to catch hell." One hundred-ninety-five Libs made today's show with a loss of twelve.

Claims on the ground are to be discouraged as much as possible from now on.

Lt. Lehman, son of New York's governor Lehman, was killed yesterday on a local flight. He was dog fighting with some P-47s. He rolled twice and then flicked into the deck.

Lt. Hupe has been taken off flying status.

The Group set a new record with 155 e/a destroyed last month. This tops all Groups in the ETO. Wing also credits us with the record of 26 e/a destroyed on one show. Our official Group score now stands at 300 1/2.

We are really rolling now and should catch Halesworth by the end of the month. As Col. Don would say, "They're a good bunch, but just the second best in the ETO."

2 April - The following EM were promoted to Master Sergeant:
Joseph D. Coady
Herman J. Hager
Paul F. Riddle
The Victory Credits Board confirmed the following March claims:

Major Mills (MIA)	1 FW 190 Destroyed
1st Lt. Whalen (MIA)	1 Me 110 Destroyed
Capt. Van Epps	1 Me 110 Damaged
	2 FW 190s Damaged
1st Lt. Rafalovich	1 Me 109 Destroyed
2nd Lt. Moulton	1 FW 190 Damaged
Capt. Hively	2 Me 109s Destroyed

All Pilots attended a lecture on the geography and history of various parts of France. This information might be helpful in attempts to escape if shot down.

3 April - All available Pilots were assembled for the British press to have a picture taking session.

4 April - Col. Clark led a discussion on ground strafing and airdrome attack for all available Pilots. Combat films were shown.

Twenty-one new Pilots arrived today. Nine were assigned to 335 Squadron: 2nd Lts. Hunt, O.R. Jones, Lines, Perkins, Ross, Russel, Scarbrough, Sensibaugh, and Shapleigh.

5 April - The **Distinguished Flying Cross** was awarded to: Capt. David A. Van Epps

An **Oak Leaf Cluster to the Distinguished Flying Cross** was awarded to: 1st Lt. Gerald E. Montgomery

Col. Blakeslee led a Jackpot Operation to Juterbog A/D, Friedersdorf A/D, a large A/D near Potsdam, Stendal A/D, Plau A/D, and an A/D near Brandenburg. During the attack, Capt. Beeson, 1st Lt. Charles D. Carr, and Lt. Allen F. Bunte were hit by flak and forced down.

Casualties: MIA

Capt. Duane W. Beeson, QP-E near Drummer Lake

1st Lt. Charles D. Carr, QP-I near Drummer Lake

1st Lt. Allen F. Bunte, QP-L south of Berlin

Capt. Robert Hobart of 336 was lost in the Channel. He was picked up by ASR, but died in the hospital of exposure.

(Carr, Bunte, and Beeson became POWs).

Results of Engagements:

Capt. Beeson, and Lts. Biel, Carr, Wynn, Monroe, Megura, France, Pierce, Blanchfield, Montgomery, and Markel, all of 334 Squadron, combined to destroy nine e/a and damage thirteen. They also destroyed or damaged various A/D installations and shipping.

The 335 Squadron claimed ten Destroyed, through the efforts of Goodwyn, Riley, Saunders, Carpenter, Anderson, Fiedler, F.C. Jones, and Schlegel. They also claimed one Probable and 14 Damaged.

The 336 Squadron claimed 26 e/a of various types destroyed. Major Goodson led with four, and two shared with others of the Squadron. Capt. Gentile had three, and one shared. Lt. Simon had two, and Lts. Carlson and Nelson each had one. Lts. Gover, and Johnson each got one and also shared one. Lt. Godfrey got four. Captain Hobart, Lts. Patchen, Emerson, and Tussey had two apiece and damaged six. In addition to the destroyeds, 336 damaged 16 of various types, with most of the Squadron participating.

Combat Reports: "I was flying Greenbelt White 3 when we came across a small grass A/D about 20 miles SW of Berlin. There were seven T/E planes on it. We circled on the deck and came in low, strafing, and receiving very light fire from the ground, from what appeared to be one gun post. I fired at two a/c which caught fire and began to burn. We made six or seven passes but received no ground fire after the first pass.

When we left, all seven planes were burning furiously, leaving absolutely no question as to whether or not they were destroyed. I claim two U/I Training Planes Destroyed."

Charles Anderson 1st Lt., Air Corps.

*****

Col. Clark led a flight of six Pilots on an air-sea rescue mission to look for Capt. Robert D. Hobert of 336th Squadron. They found that he had already been picked up by a Walrus when they arrived on the scene.

Lt. Schlegel was hit by a 40 mm shell which tore "one beautiful hole in his wing."

"Today's score puts us within a very few of the 'Zemke' outfit, and they'll have more than a fit when they see it. One more good show and 56th was the leading outfit in the ETO."

Gentile claimed three Destroyed and two shared to raise his total to 27 e/a Destroyed. This makes Gentile the ETO leading ace.

A commendation was received from Brigadier General Jesse Auton concerning the 4th Fighter Group's achievements on this day:

1. For the highest single day score of enemy planes destroyed by any Group, (45) plus (3) probably destroyed, and (39) damaged, along with various locomotives, barges, and miscellaneous equipment.

2. The 336 Squadron for the highest score of any Squadron for a single mission, (26) e/a destroyed, (2) probably destroyed, and (16) damaged.

3. Particular commendation to Major Goodson for (6) e/a destroyed, the greatest achievement of any Pilot in the Theatre.

4. Special commendation to 1st Lt. John Godfrey for (4) e/a destroyed and (5) damaged.

5. Particular attention to 1st Lt. Thomas Biel, who claimed (3) destroyed and (4) damaged, and to Captain Don S. Gentile for (3) destroyed and (2) probably destroyed.

6. Special notice is taken of Captain Robert Hobart, 1st Lt. Donald Patchen, Lt. Robert Tussey, and Lt. Donald Emerson, each of whom claim (2) e/a destroyed and (6) damaged; F/O Fred Glover and Lt. Robert Nelson, each claiming (2) destroyed and (2) damaged, Lt. Albert Schlegel, with (2) destroyed and (1) damaged, Lt. Paul Riley, with (2) destroyed and (1) probably destroyed, Captain Duane Beeson, Lts. Frank Jones, Charles Anderson, Reuben Simon, and Warren Johnson, each claiming (2) e/a destroyed.

All passes and furloughs were canceled and a station defense dry-run was held.

Photos of the new "G" suit were shown to all available pilots, and combat films were shown.

The Officers held a party for the entire Squadron with the "Flying Eagles" dance band furnishing the music and a group of attractive girls from surrounding villages as guests. S/Sgt. Allen decorated the walls with cartoons. The amenities included a buffet sup-

Captain Don S. Gentile prior to completion of his tour. With 350 combat hours, Don was top scoring U.S. Ace with over 27 confirmed e/a Destroyed when he returned to the States. Weckbacher collection.

per featuring sandwiches, coffee, a delightful three-decker chocolate cake, chocolate ice cream, and cookies. Cold lager beer was served throughout the evening with no reported casualties.

6 and 7 April - Various defense dry-runs were held each day.

8 April - Major Carpenter led a mission to support Bombers over Brunswick. The Group attacked three separate gaggles of e/a consisting of 75 to 100 FW 190s and Me 109s. The Group battled the Huns over a 30 mile area, from 23,000 feet to the deck. The Group destroyed 33 and damaged 9.

Four to six B-24s were seen going down in flames with 15 to 20 chutes seen in the air at one time. Two P-51s collided in the air west of Wittengen, and one chute was seen to open. One red-nosed P-51, believed to have been piloted by Lt. Moulton, was shot down west of Wittengen. The pilot was seen in his chute.

A Ju 52 was destroyed on an A/D SW of Celle.

This was Lt. Kolter's first operational sortie.

Casualties: 2nd Lt. Howard N. Moulton, Jr. 2nd Lt. Robert P. Claus, Capt. Frank Boyles, and 1st Lt. Robert Hughes

(Claus and Boyles were KIA, and Moulton and Hughes became POWs).

Battle Damage: Lt. Kolter landed at Becles with damaged instruments and bullet holes in the fuselage. A silver P-51 was seen to crash head-on with a Me 109 in the target area. No one knows who the pilot was in the P-51. McGrattan received slight battle damage, and Rawles nearly ground looped when landing. Rawles brushed his wing tip on the ground.

Results of Engagements: Captain Care and Lts. Markel, Moulton, Smith, Biel, and Monroe, and F/O Hofer of 334 Squadron, combined to destroy seven Me 109s and FW 190s, and a Ju 52. They also damaged seven Me 109s and FW 190s, and one Ju 52.

The 336 Squadron destroyed 13, and the 335 Squadron destroyed 12.

The 335 victories were claimed by: Carpenter and Fiedler, two each; Riley, McKennon, Anderson, Stanford, McGrattan, and Happel, one each; and Schlegel, three (2 Shared with Monroe).

The 336 victories were claimed by: Gentile, Norley, and Millikan, three each; and Simon, Bennett, Glover, and Hughes, one each.

Combat Reports: "I was leading the Group near Celle, Germany, when Lt. Fiedler reported many a/c at 10 o'clock. They were flying close formation and looked like a box of bombers. We turned toward them, meeting them more or less head-on. They were 75 to 100 FW 190s and Me 109s. We attacked at once with all Squadrons, but were unable to prevent some of the e/a from attacking the bombers and knocking down four or five of them.

I picked out a FW 190 and followed him down to about 6,000 feet where I got in a couple of good bursts with good results. The e/a went into a spin, and I kept stalking him, thinking it was an eva-sive maneuver. However, the FW 190 did not recover, and I saw it crash in a field with a great orange ball of flame. I then pulled up, saw another FW 190 and got behind him. I followed him through some rather violent actions down to the deck. I got a couple of good bursts into him, with several strikes in the cockpit area. He jettisoned his hood, but I did not see him bail out. I saw him crash three or four seconds later.

I claim two FW 190s Destroyed."

George Carpenter Major, Air Corps.

*****

"I was flying Greenbelt White 3 when we tangled with 85 plus e/a heading towards the bombers. I cannot give a very coherent description because it's the first fight like it I have ever been in. FW 190s were all over the place, and every time I turned around I started shooting. I made attacks on about five different FW 190s; one of these I got strikes on. Looking over at one side of the fight there was a FW 190 and a P-51 going round and round, neither getting deflection on the other. I dove towards the FW 190 and clobbered him pretty good. (about a 40 degree shot). He straightened out, and I got in some more strikes on wing root and fuselage around the cockpit. He went into a sharp dive, and then I overshot him. I turned sharply. Looking down, I saw him hit and litter a field with pieces. The fight started about 23,000 feet and finally ended up on the deck. Boy! It sure was a honey. I claim one FW 190 Destroyed and one Damaged."

Pierce McKennon 1st Lt., Air Corps.

*****

"I was flying Greenbelt Red 3. As we were approaching the target area, I reported a 'Gaggle' at 10 o'clock. We turned toward them and found about 100 Huns flying in close vic formation. As we bounced these e/a, I took on a Me 109 that started diving and closed slowly at first, firing short, long range bursts. I closed till I was dead astern, and fired again observing strikes on the tail and fuselage. After that the e/a emitted an enormous cloud of glycol that covered my entire plane. We were at 13,000 feet when I broke off his tail as he spiraled straight down, trailing smoke, and crashed. The plane exploded and burned in a wooded area N of Celle. I did not see the Pilot bail out. I claim this Me 109 destroyed.

I climbed back up to bomber level and found another Me 109 attacking a small box of B-24s. I closed behind this e/a in a port turn. When I opened fire on this Me 109, I observed immediate strikes around the cockpit, and after a very short burst, the Pilot bailed out. I claim this Me-109 Destroyed."

Clemens Fiedler 1st Lt., Air Corps.

*****

Today Fighters claimed 92 e/a Destroyed for a loss of 25 Fighters and 34 Bombers in the Brunswick area.

Our boys saw a formation of about 30 Huns, in close formation, go right through our bomber formation with all their guns blazing. They took out five Libs, after which our Group really tore them apart.

Colonels Blakeslee and Clark were down here when the boys landed and they sure were happy; they extended their congrats on a very fine job. "The beer will flow tonight. It really should be Scotch!"

Narrative: "Frankie Boyles of Hq. was flying today, having asked to be put back on flying status. Boyles was last seen in the battle near Celle. He is NYR. Frank has had a lot of bad luck lately, and this was his first show since being put back on flying status. He leaves a lovely wife behind. (Boyles was KIA)

Mead is now officially reported as a prisoner of war, and Merritt is listed as killed in action. Too bad about old Freddie, and sure surprising about old Mead who everyone thought had bought it.

The boys are really pouring the coal to it, and there's no stopping them now. Don Blakeslee sure has something to back him up when he says this is the best group in the ETO. It looks like Hubert's (Zemke) last quarter pep talk will be to no avail. Cheers, me lads."

9 April - Col. Blakeslee led a Bomber Withdrawal Support Mission to Tutrow Airdrome. The Group got off once in a hell'va fog and was recalled. It was a real sweat job landing. They were finally airborne at 1050. After leaving the bombers, the Group strafed two unidentified grass A/Ds. There were no claims for 334 Squadron, pending film assessment. The reason was that there were dummy a/c on the fields. The 335 Squadron claims were: Godfrey, one, with Blakeslee, Glover, Godfrey, McKennon, and Happel sharing two Ju 88s. The 336 Squadron only had two kites on this show.

Captain Van Epps was seen to pull up to 1000 feet after the last attack. He was not seen again. (He became a POW).

10 April - Lt. Col. Clark led a Type 16 Control mission and Rodeo. The Group wound up strafing Romorantin A/D, which had a large number of trainer type aircraft dispersed about the field and in the woods. Light flak was encountered as the group attacked in several passes.

Results of Engagements: Lts. Montgomery, Siems, Blanchfield, Hills, Biel, and Howe, of 334 Squadron, combined to destroy six e/a and various field installations.

The 335 Squadron Pilots destroyed a total of 9 e/a. Happel destroyed two, Stanford one, Riley two, Anderson one, Schlegel, two, and Russel, one. In addition, four were damaged.

The 336 Squadron destroyed nine, with Goodson claiming 5 1/2, Shilke, 1 1/2, and Nelson, two.

Battle Damage: Clem Fiedler was hit as he was shooting up an A/D near Vendome A/D in France. He was streaming black oil and said he was bailing out. Waterman watched him, but did not see him get out. Clem climbed and put the kite on its back, and went

Three heavy hitters discuss the day's mission. (l- r) Major James A. "Goody" Goodson 336 Squadron CO with 30 e/a Destroyed prior to becoming a POW, 20 June 44; Captain Don Gentile 336 Squadron with 27.8 e/a Destroyed prior to completion of his tour, 13 April 44; Major John Trevor Godfrey 336 Squadron with 30.6 e/a Destroyed prior to becoming a POW, 24 Aug 44, when he was hit by his Wingman's fire and bellied in near Nordhausen, Germany. Pool collection.

into a dive. He then leveled off for a few seconds and went into another dive, after which many objects were seen to come out of the cockpit. Fiedler was seen hanging half way out of the cockpit. Waterman circled until the plane crashed, but saw no parachute. Fiedler has had 50 missions. (It was later determined that he was KIA).

McKennon was hit by ground fire.

Goodson now has 26 e/a, Gentile 30, and Godfrey 19.

This was Lts. Malmsten and Siems' first operational sortie.

Narrative: "This show really puts us out in front. Old Zemke will have to get crackin' if he even wants to stay with us. His boys are now carrying 400 gallons of gas externally so they should be able to go nearly as far as we do. On this beat up stuff they may even have an edge for they have paddle props, water injection, six guns, and all this added fuel. Their a/c, being more durable, will sustain much more damage before going down. However, we'll stay out in front, for as Don said, 'This is only the beginning.' Cheerio!"

The **Silver Star** was awarded to Major John T. Godfrey

"For the support of bombers over Germany, 8 March 1944, during which he and his section leader attacked e/a, destroying two. Upon climbing back, he destroyed another, and with his section leader, they then attacked and destroyed a third."

11 April - Capt. Raymond C. Care was appointed 334 Fighter Squadron C.O.

The following Officers were assigned to AAF Sta. F-356 effective 4 Apr 44:

2nd Lt. Mark Kolter
2nd Lt. Donald M Malmsten
2nd Lt. James F. Scott
2nd Lt. Robert C. Sherman
2nd Lt. Grover C. Siems, Jr.

Generals Eisenhower, Spaatz, Doolittle, Kepner, and Auton, and Commander Butcher arrived at the post and attended a mock briefing conducted by Col. Blakeslee, Capt. Conrad, and Lt. Swope. This was followed by a showing of combat films.

Generals Kepner and Eisenhower praised the Group and their accomplishments. Eisenhower personally decorated Col. Blakeslee and Capt. Gentile with the **Distinguished Service Cross**.

Following a press photo opportunity, they had lunch at the Officers' Mess and then a tour of various installations of the A/D. General Eisenhower had a short ride in a P-38, after which the party left the post.

Major Carpenter led the Group on Withdrawal Support for Bombers over Cottbus and Sagan. Several small engagements were fought, and an A/D south of Stargard was strafed. Capt Care, F.O. Hofer, and Lts. Smith, Biel, and Hills, claimed nine e/a Destroyed and five Damaged.

Narrative: "There were 64 bombers lost today with the Huns coming up before the Bombers hit Berlin. We, unfortunately, were scheduled for Withdrawal Support. This was the longest escort job of the war to date, going approximately 60 miles past Berlin, and then north almost to Sweden. After seven hours, we really were sweating out the gas."

The 357 certainly got on the gravy train today, getting 23 e/a.

"McKennon and Goodwyn threw a scare into the Fort boys. Up over the Baltic, they went right into the Bomber formation and the gunners let go. Old Mac and Goodwyn did some mighty fast wagging to identify themselves as friends. Schlegel reported Mac and Goodwyn as two Huns attacking the Forts. Evidently the Fort boys do not realize how Mac adores them and wants to get as close as possible to them."

"It sure looked like a Hollywood first showing around here. Ike told the boys, 'Shortly, I will demand everything that you've got; you'll have to forego eating and sleeping for weeks.' This statement made the headlines in all the morning papers."

"Carroll McColpin and Michael McPharlin, two of the original Eagle boys, were here today. Wee Michael is real wee."

The ground crew boys were really sweating out today's mission, but the boys all made it.

The Victory Credits Board Report confirmed the following claims for February and March 44 for 334 Squadron:

Lt. Col. Clark	2 FW 190 Destroyed
Capt. Sobanski	1 JU 52 Destroyed
	1 FW 190 Probably Destroyed
Capt. Beeson	3 Me 109s Destroyed
	1 JU 88 Destroyed
	1 He 126 Destroyed

Capt. Hively	1 1/2 JU 88 Destroyed
1st Lt. Chatterley	2 Me 110 Destroyed
	1 Me 109 Destroyed
	1/2 FW 190 Destroyed
	1 Me 210 Probably Destroyed
1st Lt. Megura	1 Me 109 Destroyed
	1 1/2 FW 190 Destroyed
1st Lt. Bunte	1 Me 109 Destroyed
	1 FW 190 Destroyed
1st Lt. France	1 Ju 52 Destroyed
1st Lt. W.B. Smith	1 Me 109 Destroyed
2nd Lt. Pierce	1 Me 109 Destroyed
F/O Hofer	1 Me 110 Destroyed
	2 Me 109s Destroyed
	1 FW 190 Destroyed

12 April - Col. Blakeslee led the Group on a Target Support Mission to Castricum. Near Celle, four Me 109s were encountered and destroyed by 335 Squadron. The 335 Squadron only had enough planes to put up three Sections. Sharing in the victories were Carpenter, Jones, and Anderson.

"The Huns keep getting clobbered 'as time goes by'."

Combat Reports: "I was leading Greenbelt Squadron, and I took White Section down to attack four Huns. I fired at the tail end Hun and overshot. Lt. Jones destroyed it. I attacked a Hun trying to get Lt. Anderson, who was firing at another e/a. I hit the e/a well in the left wing and cockpit and again overshot. I watched him go down toward the ground, well under control but with no power. Then another Mustang, Lt. McKennon, came in and hit him a few times. The e/a had his wheels down and was trying to force land on an A/D just beneath us. He was unable to make it. He went into a very small field, and his airplane broke up into many pieces. The plane spread itself over a considerable area. Lt. McKennon makes no claim on this A/C because he feels that I destroyed it.

A half hour later, I attacked an A/D in the same area and damaged a JU-88. In this attack I sustained a 20 mm hole in my right wing."

George Carpenter Major, Air Corps.

*****

"I was flying Greenbelt White 3 when we bounced four Me 109s flying line astern. White Leader took #4, and I took #3. He started to turn left and I fired, seeing one strike right in the cockpit. He fell off on his left wing and did a spiral dive into the deck. The plane did not explode, but the a/c broke up into small pieces. A large cloud of black smoke rose to three or four hundred feet into the air. I then went after #2. While firing at him, I saw #1 coming at me from nine o'clock. I could see he was not getting any deflection, so I kept after #2. I believe #1 was trying to ram me, but he passed about five feet behind my tail. I saw many strikes on #2, and he started streaming glycol from his starboard radiator. Number 1 came in behind me and started firing, but he was still pulling no deflection. As he began closing in, I tightened my turn for a few seconds until Major Carpenter attacked him and made him break off. I then returned to my attack on #2 and fired once more as he pulled up to about 5,000 feet and bailed out. His a/c crashed and exploded."

Charles Anderson 1st Lt., Air Corps.

*****

13 April - Col. Blakeslee led a Target and Withdrawal Support mission to Schweinfurt. South of Aschaffenburg, 20 plus FW 190s were engaged and vigorous combats took place from 24,000 feet down to 10,000 feet. One red-nosed P-51 was seen shot down by a FW 190, which in turn was destroyed by Lt. Megura. The P-51 Pilot was seen in his chute.

Casualties: Capt. Vasseure H. Wynn NYR. Saunders of 335 was last seen by F.C. Jones at 1400 hours about 20 or 30 miles NW of Schweinfurt. Nothing was heard over the R/T, and he seemed to be O.K. (Saunders was KIA and Wynn became a POW).

Results: Capt. Sobanski and Lt. Megura each claimed one FW 190 destroyed for 334 Squadron, while Carpenter and McKennon each got one for 335 Squadron. Norley from 336 destroyed one.

About 750 Bombers and 1,000 fighters went out from England, and 1,250 a/c took off from Italy to targets in Germany and occupied territory, a total of 3,000 on the raid. The Germans countered with fighters with approximately 200 a/c over Schweinfurt alone.

Scores of the leading aces now stand at: Gentile 30, Johnson 25, and "Bing" Bong 27.

This was Gentile's last show. Many correspondents were here waiting for him to land, and he did beat up for them with a real buzz job. He came in so low that he chewed up about 50 yards of dirt in

The remains of Captain Gentile's P-51 "Shangri-La" after "buzzing" too low for the newsmen who had gathered to cover his final mission before returning to the States for a bond drive. Weckbacher collection.

front of the dispersal, pulled out of this and crashed out in a field. The kite was a total washout, and he was darn lucky to be able to walk away from it. "Old St. Pete was watching over Donnie Boy that time." Pictures of the accident were in the following days' papers. "Turned out to be an inglorious and almost disastrous finish for the Publicity Kid."

14 April - Orders were received, effective 1 April, promoting - 1st Lt. to Captain - William B. Gabrilson.

Combat films were shown to all available pilots, followed by an Air-Sea rescue drill in the Saffon-Walden Public Baths.

15 April - Captain Care led a Jackpot Operation to Juterbog A/D. Due to bad weather, the Group became split up into small sections, and three different A/Ds were attacked by small groups of our a/c. Capt. Care and Lt. Biel attacked an unidentified A/D northeast of Celle and destroyed a yellow nosed Ju 52. Capt. Care was heard to say he was bailing out.

Results of Engagements: Capt. Care and Lts. Biel, Montgomery, and Blanchfield, of 334 Squadron, claimed four e/a Destroyed, plus three locomotives, assorted flak posts, water, and transmission towers Damaged.

1st Lts. Anderson, Jones, and Schlegel of 335 Squadron upped the score by three.

Lt. Milliken, 336 Squadron, led nine a/c against an A/D that might have been Hagenow, destroying four He 177s, one FS 156 and one Me 110. They also damaged three He 177s. Lts. Millikan, Nelson, and Tussey, and F/O Glover shared in these kills.

Seifert, 336 Squadron, is MIA. He was yelling for a Mayday, but the Group could not find him. He apparently spun out in the clouds over the Channel. Capt. Care bailed out near Celle. (Seifert was KIA and Care became a POW)

Bennet, 336, ditched and was picked up by an A/S/R boat.

Battle Damage:

Lt. Montgomery's plane was hit by flak, damaging the prop, aileron, and port wing.

Lt. Biel hit a tree in Germany. He damaged his port wing, which required a wing change.

Church, 335, was hit on the wingtip by enemy ground fire.

Narrative: Capt. Care, 27 years old, from Angora, Indiana, has been in England since March of 1942. He transferred from the 71st Eagle Squadron, of the RAF, and was in the 334 Squadron. He had seven confirmed and one probable e/a to his credit prior to being shot down. He was the 3rd 334 CO lost in a month. He was picked up by German civilians immediately upon landing. They even helped him out of his chute. He was put in solitary confinement in an interrogation center for seven days, on bread and water, without cigarettes, or any luxuries such as a bath. He then transferred to a permanent camp near the Polish border.

*****

About 750 Fighters were out today and met no opposition in the air, but 30 are missing, most due to collisions in the clouds and spinning out. There were more Maydays on "B" than there have been in months.

Halesworth got 17 today to raise their score to 406. Our score went to 433 1/2 today, and so we remain the leading Group in the ETO.

The **Distinguished Service Cross** was awarded to Captain Don S. Gentile

"For extraordinary heroism in action 8 April 1944, while leading a Squadron of P-51s supporting bombers near Ruhrburg, Germany. Displaying great courage, Capt. Gentile led his Squadron in an attack against 50 to 60 German aircraft attacking a box of Liberator bombers, dispersing the enemy that outnumbered him by more than three to one. He became separated and was attacked by three enemy aircraft, which he skilfully evaded and maneuvered into position on one of the FW 190s, following it to 8,000 feet where he destroyed it. Climbing, he encountered another e/a which he destroyed in vigorous combat. Again he encountered a third e/a and, although he had expended excessive amounts of gasoline and ammunition and his supply of both was critical, he engaged the e/a in combat which lasted for fully 10 minutes, finally destroying the e/a at zero altitude."

E.P. Curtis Brigadier General, U.S.A., Chief of Staff

16 April - Orders were received promoting Fred L. Heene from Captain to Major.

The following Officers were awarded **Oak Leaf Clusters to the Distinguished Flying Cross**:

1st Lt. Nicholas Megura
1st Lt. William B. Smith
1st Lt. Robert Wehrman
1st Lt. Willard Millikan
Capt. Donald Gentile
Maj. James Goodson

The 334 Squadron call-sign was changed from PECTIN to COBWEB.

17 April - Orders were received promoting the following Officers from 1st. Lt. to Captain:

Victor J. France
Vasseure H. Wynn

"Six bright-eyed and bushy-tailed new officers arrived from Goxhill. They carried their ever present gas masks and new mussette bags with their names neatly stenciled on each, like children off to their first day of school. They arrived lugging their bulging B-4 bags. They were full of eagerness and apprehension at having been chosen to be a part of such a famous and daring Group. The day

was filled with the usual hum-drum—checking into the various operational entities, getting room assignments, etc."

Narrative: Frank Speer - "The culmination of the routine was the welcome by our new (to us), awe-inspiring Group Commander, Col. Blakeslee. He made an imposing entrance in his leather flight jacket and forty mission crush hat. He looked like he had just come back from a mission. He bruskly stated the general routines we were to follow and gave us a brief rundown of how we were to fit into the Group. It was all quite routine until he arrived at the summation. Warming to his subject, he said, 'You have just transferred from the States to the Eighth Air Force. While in the States, you had a myriad of rules and regulations governing your conduct while flying. Here in the 4th Group, we have additional S.O.P.s (Standard Operating Procedures). Don't get caught breaking any of them or you'll never fly with us again. The same is true if you prang an aircraft because of Pilot Error. We want aggressive Pilots, but we will have discipline.' He saluted and left, but, needless to say, his talk made a lasting impression on each of us."

18 April - The Victory Credits Board Report confirmed the following claims for March 1944:

1st Lt. Howe	FW 190 Destroyed
1st Lt. Biel	Ju 88 Destroyed
	Me 410 Destroyed
1st Lt. Montgomery	Ju 52 Destroyed
	FW 190 Destroyed
1st Lt. Markel	Me 109 Damaged

Col. Blakeslee led a Penetration, Target, and Withdrawal Support mission to Berlin. Twenty-five plus Me 109s and FW 190s were engaged as they attempted to attack the bombers. They were chased into the clouds, and one was destroyed by 334 Squadron. Two B-17s were seen going down on fire north of Berlin, and two more exploded. Two others were observed smoking and spinning in the same area.

The Group then strafed Juterborg A/D, destroying eight and damaging six Ju 52s. Fassberg A/D was then strafed and three He 177s were destroyed. Three twin engined a/c were damaged. North of Genthin, four Me 109s were caught landing; one was destroyed, and two others were damaged. Capt. France struck the ground while chasing a Me 109, and his plane burst into flames. The e/a was, in turn, destroyed by Lt. Megura.

Casualties: Capt. Victor J. France KIA.
Major Carpenter, NYR
Lt. Henry, NYR
(Henry was KIA and Carpenter became a POW).
Battle damage:
Lt. Siems- Oxygen system shot out by flak.
Lt. Blanchfield- Oil tank and intake damaged by 303.
Lt. Scott- Fuselage, wing, and canopy damaged by flak.
F/O Hofer- Firewall, gear, and wing damaged by 303s.

Lt. Kolter- Supercharger damaged by 303s.

Lt. Monroe- Oil radiator damaged by 303s.

Lt. Biel- Aileron, wing, gun bay, and crank case damaged by 303s.

Results of Engagements:

F/O Hofer	2 He 177s Destroyed
Lt. Malmsten	1 Ju 52 Destroyed
Lt. Howe	2 Ju 52s Destroyed
Lt. Monroe	2 Ju 52s Destroyed
Lt. Kenyon	1 He 111 Destroyed
Lt. Lang	3 Ju 52s Destroyed
Col. Blakeslee	1 He 177 Destroyed
Lt. McKennon	1 FW 190 Destroyed
Major Carpenter	1 Me 109 Destroyed
	1 FW 190

Lts. Meguira, Siems, and France

shared 1 Me 109 Destroyed

Lt. Emerson	1 Me 109 Destroyed
Lt. Nelson	1 Me 109 Destroyed

Lts. Van Wyk and Logan shared 1 FW 190 Destoryed

Combat Reports: "I was Caboose Blue 1, and we lost the Squadron in the clouds. Fifty to seventy-five FW 190s attacked the bombers and came in under us. Several Huns stayed to attack the bombers. We went in, and I latched on to one that was beginning an attack. It was different from any I had seen before. The fuselage seemed longer and smaller from the cockpit forward. After several bursts, I finally hit him, knocking off a few pieces. He flicked and went into a dive with me following. He hit the deck at about a 45 degree angle and burned. Three FW 190s then jumped me on the deck, but I outran them, climbed up, and came home."

Pierce McKennon 1st Lt., Air Corps.

*****

These two reports were given to Maj. Jenks, Assistant S-2, on behalf of Major Carpenter, who is NYR.

"I was flying Caboose Blue 2 and lost my Section Leader, so I pulled up among a Group of Red-Nosed P-51s, one of which was attacking two Me 109s. This P-51 (which must have been Major Carpenter), broke away after both e/a were smoking and in a diving turn. I fired at the rear Me 109, which half rolled and split S'd. I followed it down, thinking it was not damaged badly, but it never pulled out. It hit the ground and exploded a few miles NW of Nauen.

I confirm this Me-109 destroyed for the Major, as at no time did I get any strikes on it. Both 109s were in line at the time, and I assume Major Carpenter also damaged the other."

William Hunt 2nd Lt., Air Corps.

*****

"I was No. 3 in Caboose White section led by Major Carpenter. We jumped seven or eight FW 190s, and I saw Major Carpenter fire at one of them. There was an explosion on it, and I saw it spin down. As the e/a was going down, the complete elevator and stabilizer on the port side fell away from it. There was also much smoke coming from the e/a. I confirm this e/a destroyed on behalf of Major Carpenter."

Unsigned.

*****

19 April - Capt. Sobanski led a Target and Withdrawal Support mission to Eschwege. Fifty plus single-engined e/a attacked the bombers. They were being covered by ten other e/a. As our Group attempted to head off the attack, they were fired upon by the bombers. The ensuing battle ranged from 25,000 feet to the deck. Capt. Sobanski, and Lts. Kenyon and Megura accounted for three e/a destroyed. McKennon and McGrattan of 335 each accounted for one. Lt. Millkan added one for 336.

Lt. Anderson, highest scoring ace of 335 Squadron, is NYR. (Anderson was subsequently reported as KIA)

Combat Reports: "I was flying Caboose Blue 1 as we came over a box of bombers. We spotted smoke trails at 6 o'clock. We turned and started climbing, and at 30,000 feet these 25 plus e/a were still three or four thousand feet above us. We sighted 15 plus e/a coming in from 10 o'clock below us. We went after these, but we saw four Me 109s much closer and went after them instead. I looked back to clear my tail and to see what the bunch at smoke trail height were doing, and I saw them dive towards the bombers.

I started diving and got behind two silver colored Me 109s. I was very low before I closed to good shooting range. I shot two bursts and missed, but at 75 yards I got strikes all around the cockpit and wing roots. Parts went flying in every direction, and at 4,000 feet the e/a half-rolled and went into a cloud almost straight down. We were clocking 475 IAS. I didn't see him crash, but I'm quite sure he never pulled out.

I started to climb after the #1 who was ahead and to one side. I chased the son of a b—— all over the place, but I couldn't hit him. He finally shook me by going into a cloud at about 3,000 feet. I claim one Me 109 Destroyed."

Pierce Mc Kennon 1st Lt., Air Corps.

*****

"We were climbing to intercept 12 e/a approaching the bombers. They started to dive, but were intercepted and their formation was broken up by some other P-51s. I turned and dove on three Me 109s flying line abreast. Two of them broke right and one broke left. I went after him. He tried to evade by a steep turn to the left, but after two complete turns, I was able to draw deflection. I fired a burst. I saw hits on his port wing and fired again. I saw many hits around the cockpit, and the a/c fell earthward from the turn. We were at 3,000 feet when he went straight down, apparently out of control, gaining more and more speed. He crashed almost straight down from where he was hit.

I went down to the deck and was joined by Lt. Megura as we flew line abreast looking for another Jerry. I sighted a FW 190 at 7 o'clock to Megura, and I broke in that direction. Because of my speed, I couldn't get onto his tail immediately, and he went past me and head-on toward Megura. He straightened out and went into a port turn as my speed slowed down, and I was able to get behind him. After turning through 180 degrees, I was about to fire when pieces flew off from behind his cockpit. I thought Megura had gotten him with a beautiful deflection shot, but Megura had not fired his guns. The pieces were, evidently, from his fuselage and had been knocked off by the jettisoned canopy. The Pilot came out; his chute opened; and Megura shot pictures of his a/c crashing. It was probably the presence of both of us that made him panic and bail out, neither of us having fired at him. I claim one Me 109 Destroyed and one FW 190 Destroyed, (Shared with Lt. Megura, 334 Squadron)."

Bernard McGratten Lt., Air Corps

*****

Word was received that 1st Lt. Ivan R. Moon, reported MIA on 3 Nov 43, was killed in action on that date.

Narrative: Crew Chief "Sy" Koenig had come to the 4th in Dec 42. He was to stay until Sept 45. He commented, "Our primary mission was to keep that kite in top condition and 'mission ready' at all times. My normal time on the flight line was from 0800, or two hours prior to an early flight, until well after the last mission returned, seven days per week. While the aircraft was on a mission, we would prepare for the next mission. We would assemble a new set of drop tanks, prepare a new set of spark plugs, plus many other details.

In addition, we had our normal Squadron detail duties, such as K.P., C.Q., Guard Duty, and Black-out check. I had a unique experience on the last of these. I missed doing the Black-out check while working on my plane until midnight. I was promptly charged, and was 'invited' to sign an Article 15 Courts Martial. No excuses, no warnings!"

*****

20 April - Capt. Sobanski led the Group on a Type 16 Control mission to Noball. No e/a were seen.

The Tower (T-0000 hours) diary begins. Lts. Simpson, Newman, Shoemaker, and Overstreet rotated shifts as Tower Con-

trol Officer. The diary was previously coded "Secret." (This diary is available through the foresight of Pinkney Lackey. At the end of the war as Pink was burning extraneous records, according to orders, he happened to notice this Tower Diary and thought what a shame it would be to destroy such an interesting piece of history. Accordingly, he approached the CO for permission to save this book. Written permission was granted, and Pink smuggled the Diary into the States upon his return from England.)

T-1810 Caboose 67 (Lt. Homuth) crash landed on South Coast 5 miles east of Eastbourne. Pilot seemed OK. Fricton nearest A/D taking necessary action. Intelligence informed.

T-1915 Becky 31 having trouble. Landed OK.

T-2035 All Group landed, except Caboose 67 that crashed and Caboose 56. Caboose 56 called for homing, but could not receive us.

T-2055 Flying Control at Newmarket called and said Lt. Hunt, Caboose 56, landed there and will come here as soon as he refuels.

T-2200 Saffron Walden, operator, called and said someone gave him a message to pass to Wing. He couldn't get Wing, so he called us. Information was that 2nd Lt. James N. Allen, in P-47, crashed at 1915 at Park Farm, Selsey. Plane burned and Pilot was killed. They told him plane was in 355 group. Said plane was supposed to belong to "Little Middle Wallop." Pilot belonged to Bealieu and had crashed on takeoff.

Pilots are now flying their extra time in the new "G" suits to become acquainted with them. It will be required that they have five hours of non-operational time in them before they can be worn on Ops. They are form fitted silk-lined rubber suits worn next to the skin. They have a water reservoir in the chest area that flows to bladders in the lower extremities and abdomen during violent maneuvers, and in effect, keeps the blood from rushing there, which deprives the brain. The suit thus helps prevent blackout.

This was Joe Higgin's first mission. He was introduced to flak on a fighter sweep. It was somewhat different from training in the States. He had gone through the usual Pilot training program and had graduated as a 2nd Lt. He eventually found himself in Fort Hamilton, New York, along with hundreds of others awaiting shipment overseas. One cold morning in February, he and the others were loaded into Army trucks; crossed Manhattan; and soon found themselves at the Cunard Line Piers at 56th Street. They were awed by the sight of the majestic Queen Mary towering over them. So awed were they that they barely noticed the unassuming little British fruit boat moored on the opposite side of the pier.

They soon discovered that this "fruit boat" was the *HMS Arawa*, and that it was to become their home for 12 long days and nights,

1st Lt. Joseph W. Higgins 336 Squadron finished his tour with 63 missions and 270 combat hours 30 Sept 44. He survived the rigors of the invasion and the Russian shuttle mission in his P-51 Meiner Kleiner. Weckbacher collection.

while they painfully struggled across the dismal, cold, North Atlantic. Joe and hundreds of others were crowded onto this ship and vied for places in the dining area, the toilets, the showers, and the sleeping areas.

After several days at sea, Joe had an assigned shower time shortly after midnight. In the middle of his shower, he heard the loud clanging of the bell, which meant, "We're under attack, everyone on deck immediately." "Since I did not want to be on deck in my birthday suit in February, I turned off the water; dried myself; put on my clothes and shoes, my overcoat, and hat, and was on deck, all in 12 seconds. It's amazing what adrenalin can do for your performance.

After 13 days at sea we landed in Bristol, England. Thirty-four of us Pilots from 43-I, who were destined to be assigned to the 4th Fighter Group. We were shipped off to places like Stoke-on-Trent to continue our Combat education. Little did we know what destiny

had in store for us. Of the 34 Pilots in our program, 11 were KIA, 11 were to become POWs, 3 were disabled, and only 9 were to complete a tour of operations and return to the States intact.

Three of these 34 Pilots became Aces; Donald Malmsten, Grover Siems, and Frank Speer, with a combined score of 24 e/a Destroyed. The Group of 34 Destroyed 42 e/a in addition to innumerable locomotives, trains, trucks, and miscellaneous equipment by strafing and bombing."

Joe had the good fortune to team up with a very capable crew chief in the person of Glesner Weckbacher. This was a fine relationship that lasted throughout Joe's 63 missions. Glesner kept Joe's plane, Meiner Kleiner, in tip-top shape throughout Joe's tour.

21 April - Mission aborted due to weather.

T-0553 Darkey called from—D-Dog. Was answered "This is Debden." Replied "Roger, Thank you, off."

T-1530 Group recalled, 13 a/c landed, the remainder are to stay airborne and do practice section flying until they have used up gas in their wing tanks.

22 April - Col. Blakeslee led a Sweep to Kassel - Hamm. The Group bounced 20 plus Me 109s with Capt. Sobanski damaging one and Lt. Smith destroying one (shared with Lt. Paul Riley of 335 Squadron). Lt. Schlegel got two Me 109s, and Lt. Jones got one Me 109 for 335 Squadron.

The 336 came through with flying colors with a total of 14 Destroyed for the day, all Me 109s. Lt. Millikan led with four, Lt. Godfrey three, Lt. Norley and Col. Blakeslee, two each. Lts. Carlson, Simon, and Emerson each Destroyed one.

Lt. Nelson was lost near Kassel. He is believed to have bailed out. (He became a POW).

Combat Report: "I was flying White 4 of Caboose Squadron when we turned into two e/a above us. They broke upwards, with my leader taking one and I the other. I followed the e/a to the deck where he joined another e/a. They went into a Luftberry, and I put down flaps and circled slightly above them. Being alone, I could not get in, but was soon joined by another Mustang who forced one of them into a position where I could get in and get a shot at the other e/a. I fired a couple of high deflection bursts and saw strikes from the nose to the cockpit. The Pilot must have been badly wounded because he broke from the Luftberry and looked like he was going to make a forced landing. Three times he came so close to the ground that dust flew up, and I thought he was going in. Finally, he dipped a wing which caught the ground, and he cartwheeled and spread pieces of his a/c for several hundred yards.

Caboose Red 2 was having trouble with his e/a so I joined up with him. They were in a tight circle, and I fired at the e/a but could not hit him. Some other Mustangs came in, and I saw strikes on his fuselage as he leveled out and crashed on a nearby hill.

We formed up and saw another Me 109 and went after him. I was the fourth man in the Section. The first man got some strikes, and the e/a rolled over on his back as if to crash. However, he pulled out right on the deck and kept going. One and two fired until they were out of ammunition, and number three then lost him. The e/a was flying in a deep valley, and it was almost impossible to get a shot. I kept closing till I was about 300 yards away when the men behind me warned of possible flak traps. I fired until I saw tracers, but got no strikes, so I broke off."

F. Jones Lt., Air Corps.

*****

"I attacked a Me 109 from about 80 degrees, allowing a little over 2 rings (100 MPH sight). I opened fire under 200 yards and saw strikes in the area just above the wing root. The 109 started smoking immediately. Someone called 'Damn good shooting' over the R/T. I climbed and returned to the fight. Just about then, I saw a Me 109 that looked like he was about to crash-land. The P-51 that was chasing him overshot, and the e/a pulled up behind him and attacked. I started after him, firing at deflection of 30 to 40 degrees at long range, but observed no strikes. The e/a broke and turned into me. I opened fire at about 150 yards at about 70 to 80 degrees, allowing about 2 rings. I could only see the spinner of the e/a, but the rest was hidden under my wing. I couldn't see, but it is very possible that I was hitting him. He slid under me. When I did a tight turn back onto him, I found that he had straightened out and was heading for the ground. I remembered his former tactics, so I slowed up and followed him down, getting strikes. When he was just a few feet off the ground, I clobbered him. His right wing hit and tore off, and the rest of him I lost in the dust and smoke."

Albert Schlegel Capt., Air Corps.

*****

T-2040 All down except Becky 54—334 Squadron will do night flying.

T-2100 Night-flying briefing—four pilots reported that one red-nosed Mustang was seen to go into deck—Thought to be Becky 54 (Nelson).

This morning the Group practiced with the "G" Suits and soon they will probably be operational with them.

On today's show, six Pilots came back early due to u/s external wing tanks. The Group was testing a new fabric tank, and it is not certain whether or not the problems were from inexperience with the tank or mechanical difficulties.

23 April - Pfc. Crossett had his right foot run over by the oxygen truck.

Pilots were given a lecture on the proper R/T procedure and on how fixes are obtained. It was also explained how air-sea rescue operates and the proper use of the "pip-squeak."

T-0807 Called duty electrician about half of outer circle being out. He says they must have shot the wire down yesterday. They will start work immediately.

T-1000 Rocket firing, unseen fire, up to 20,000 feet in R-4849 till 1130.

T-2058 Night flying starts—12 pilots taking part.

T-2348 Night flying ends without incident.

24 April - The following Officers were assigned: (as of 17 April)

2nd Lt. Eacott G. Allen
2nd Lt. John L. Barden
2nd Lt. Preston B. Hardy
2nd Lt. Aubrey E. Hewatt
2nd Lt. Pete R. Kennedy
2nd Lt. Frank E. Speer
Col. Blakeslee led a Free-Lance Support to Munich.
The Group engaged 34 FW 190s and Me 109s north of Worms.
Casualties : 1st Lt. H. Thomas Biel reported as MIA. His plane was shot down in combat, south of Dormstadt.
One red-nosed Mustang was seen going down in smoke.
Lts. Riley and Scarbrough were lost, and they are NYR.
(Biel was KIA and Scarbrough and Riley became POWs).
Results of Engagements: Lts. Lang, Megura, and Howe claimed four Destroyed and one Probable. The 335 Squadron claimed ten Destroyed and one Damaged. Lts. Riley and Schlegel each got two 190s, Col. Blakeslee one, and they shared another. Capt. Happel, Lts. McGrattan, Read, and Stanford each Destroyed an FW 190.
Lt. Godfrey, of 336 Squadron, Destroyed one Fw 190. Major Goodson destroyed two 109s while flying with 31 FG.
Combat Reports: "After I fired at two different e/a and missed them, I encountered a single FW 190 in a gradual port turn. I came in line astern, and as I started to fire, he straightened out, pulling his nose up. At the instant I fired, he jettisoned his canopy and bailed out. I fired only a short burst from about 200 yards. I continued the burst for about a second after the Pilot had bailed out. I did not observe any hits on the e/a. There were three other P-51s to my starboard at the time. I claim one FW 190 Destroyed."

Leighton Read 1st Lt., Air Corps.

*****

"As we dove to attack several e/a, my leader picked one and went after him. Another e/a came up behind him, and I opened fire on it at about 300 yards from dead astern. I closed to 75 yards, getting many hits throughout the attack. The FW 190 exploded in front of me, throwing oil and debris all over my windscreen. What was left of it fell towards the ground in flames. I claimed this FW 190 Destroyed.

I tried to position myself on several other e/a, but each time lost them as I could not see through my windscreen. I climbed to 34,000 feet and headed home."

George Stanford, Jr., 1st Lt., Air Corps.

*****

"Waiting outside the big Luftberry circle for a stray, I latched on to a FW 190. I fired at him, but had to break off when an e/a came to his rescue. I picked up another 190, and the same thing happened again. I attacked the third FW 190 and fired several bursts in a medium to fairly steep turn. I was giving him deflection that put him almost entirely under my wing. He lessened his bank, and at that point another e/a came at me from 8 o'clock. I turned into him, and he immediately turned away. I turned back to the a/c I had been firing at, and he went into a split-S from about 1,500 feet. He did not pull out, but crashed with an explosion of flames."

Captain Bernard J. McGrattan 335 Squadron Ace, prior to being shot down as he was leading Blue Section when all were shot down by enemy aircraft who bounced them out of low clouds, 6 June 44. Konsler collection.

Bernard McGrattan 1st Lt., Air Corps.

*****

One thing noted in particular was that the e/a that were shot down fired their cannon into the ground before crashing.

T-0750 Lt. Overstreet and Newman on duty; Lt. Shoemaker off. Some a/c over field, but could not land as vis and cloud base too bad. Aerodromes to the east are open. Told all a/c to fly east and land at first suitable airfield.

T-0830 All planes landed elsewhere OK. Becky Red section (4) landed at Ruienhall, Cobweb Red section (4) landed at Warminford, Becky 31 and Caboose 52 at Wethersfield. All a/c told to remain there until we notify them.

T-0930 Called all the above Aerodromes and told pilots to return.

T-1030 Caboose 52 lands from Wethersfield, which makes all planes down here at base.

T-1517 Group landed. Everyone accounted for except Caboose 49, Caboose 59, Cobweb 55. Caboose 46 landed at Lymphe, R/T trouble.

T-1600 Caboose 46 returned to base, still no news of the other three.

T-2050 First ship airborne for night flying with seven pilots taking part.

T-2300 All a/c down—lights turned off and all crews released. Q site off.

Combat Report: (Submitted by 1st Lt. Paul Riley upon his return from POW Camp, 31 May 1945) "I was flying Green #3 in Caboose (335) Squadron when we bounced 20 plus FW 190s flying a perfect V formation. I immediately got onto one who started to dive and then pulled up again. I caught him in the cockpit and engine with a two-second burst, and he went into a slow left spiral straight into the deck. At that point, another FW 190 made a head-on pass at me without firing and then broke to my left.

Another FW 190 came in on my tail, and I broke down hard left just as another one came directly into my flight path. I was boomeranged through the air by a collision with this a/c. The stick was wrenched from my hand, knocking my leg against the side of the cockpit and injuring the leg. I recovered control and found that 1/4 of my left wing had been sheared off. Below me, I could see the Pilot of the e/a with red parachute silk streaming after him, but the chute did not open. He went straight into the deck.

I set course for home, and while climbing from 10,000 feet I had my left wing tank blown off by A/A. I immediately bailed out and landed about 600 yards from the A/A battery. My a/c crashed and burned about 1,000 yards away. I claim two FW 190s Destroyed."

Paul Riley 1st Lt. Air Corps.

*****

2nd Lt. Milton Scarbrough, (Upon return from POW Camp to Camp Lucky Strike, France): "I was flying Green #2, 335 Squadron, south of Manheim when we bounced a formation of 50 plus FW 190s. They broke formation, two coming up astern of Green Section. We broke and I blacked out temporarily. Coming to, I discovered the only planes in sight were FW 190s. One was climbing into my flight path and I fired, observing strikes in the left wing root, cockpit, and engine. The e/a immediately went into a lazy spin and crashed.

Shortly thereafter, an e/a made a stern attack on my plane, hitting the engine and setting it on fire. Before I was able to jettison my canopy and bail out, my right arm was burned by fire from the fusilage tank, and my face was burned from hot coolant. I claim one FW 190 Destroyed."

Milton Scarbrough 2nd Lt. Air Corps.

*****

25 April - The Confirmation of Victory Credits Board Report confirmed the following claims for March 1944:

1st Lt. Carr	1 Ju 88 Damaged
1st Lt. Megura	1 Me 110 Destroyed
	1 Me 110 Damaged
	1 FW 190 Damaged
	1 Me 109 Damaged
1st Lt. Biel	1 FW 190 Destroyed
Capt. Van Epps	1 FW 190 Damaged
Capt. Chatterley	1 Me 109 Destroyed

Col. Blakeslee led a Penetration, Target, and Withdrawal Support mission to Mannheim. No e/a seen.

T-1245- All Group back but Caboose 40.

T-1256- Homing Caboose 40.

T-1302- Caboose 40 landed.

T-2130- All planes down. Crews released or stood down. Flarepath laid W to E and S to N.

T-2400- Enemy action seen in the south. No Alert.

26 April - Lt. Millikan led a Fighter Sweep to the vicinity of Trier. It was uneventful and no e/a were seen. Lt. Pierce's plane was damaged by accurate flak from Ostend. The Group participated in practice bombing flights off Bradwell Bay.

T-0830- Lt. Lang (Cobweb 63) landed at Raydon with his glycol gone. He wants someone to bring his crew chief down. Have called Capt. Toy's office, and he is taking care of it.

T-1145- Group all returned with exception of Lt. Lang at Raydon—Oxford has gone down to pick him up.

T-1415- Group on dive bombing show, (practice), until 1630.

T-1700- Raydon called that 10 Becky planes had landed there without clearance. Said they had gone to Martlesham chasing Flying Circus, (FW 190, Me 110, etc)

T-1756- Becky 44 (VFA) landed awfully hot, runs off runway. Plane OK, Pilot OK. All informed.

T-1800- Martlesham called that Lt. Tussey in a/c VFP had a crash on landing there. His left wheel collapsed and plane went down on a wing. Pilot OK. Plane pretty badly damaged. All informed.

T-2111- Night flying begins—called Bovindon and Lt. Braley (Becky 33) will remain there for 2 or 3 days.

T-2130- Someone has an open transmitter on Channel "A." All transmission from here and other a/c are hard to understand.

T-2142- An A-20 lands from operations, belongs to Little Walden. He was short of fuel. He is refueling and returning to his home base. Little Walden notified.

T-2200- Caboose 53 lands without permission. Found out later he was the one with the open transmitter—Channel "A" is OK again.

T-2213- Nightgale 11 (General Auton) lands from Gosfield.

T-2215- Nightgale 17 (Capt. Gebhard) in Cessna is also doing night flying.

27 April - A gas casualty film was shown to all available personnel.

Capt. Duane W. Beeson (MIA) was awarded the **Distinguished Service Cross**.

Capt. Howard D. Hively was awarded an **Oak Leaf Cluster to the Distinguished Flying Cross**.

Col. Blakeslee led the Group on a Support, 1st ATF mission to Nieuport. Col. Blakeslee led 335 Squadron on an attack of Toul A/D, while 334 and 336 escorted the bombers out at Dunkirque.

Results of Engagement: Lt. Read Destroyed an U/I, S/E, a/c. Captain Happel Damaged a JU-87 as did Lt. O. Jones. Lts. O. Jones and F. Jones each Damaged a FW 190.

T-0006- The last a/c lands from night flying. All lights doused; all crews released.

T-1112- 335 Squadron told us to recall their a/c which were taking off. Complied.

T-2130- Took it upon the Tower to call off night flying as wind is cross and haze coming in.

28 April - The full station alert was sounded at 0310 hours; the all clear at 0440 hours.

Orders dated 15 April awarded the **Distinguished Flying Cross** to: 2nd Lt. Robert L. Hills

2nd Lt. (now 1st Lt.) David W. Howe

An **Oak Leaf Cluster to the Distinguished Flying Cross** was awarded to Capt. Victor J. France

29 April - Capt. Sobanski led a Penetration, Target, and Withdrawal Support mission to Berlin. No e/a were seen in the air, but Blue Section of 334 and Red Section of 336 strafed an unidentified A/D west of Berlin. They left five a/c burning. Lts. Godfrey, Patteuw, and Grounds claimed three Destroyed and four Damaged. Megura, Barden, and Monroe destroyed four Ju 52s. Trains at a nearby M/Y were strafed and buildings were shot up. One of our a/c was hit by flak from the A/D, and the pilot bailed out.

Casualties: 2nd Lt. John Leighton Barden reported as MIA.

2nd Lt. Pete Ralph Kennedy reported as MIA due to engine failure. Pilot had to bail out.

1st Lt. Nicholas Megura was treated upon landing for a bullet wound in the left arm.

(Barden and Kennedy both became POWs)

Battle Damage:

Lt. Scott - Flak hole under engine

Lt. Megura - Bullet hole in canopy, right wing, and elevator

While taxiing off the runway, Lt. Monroe collided with another plane.

T-1330- Group returning — many homings.

T-1407- Cobweb 67 called in for permission to land immediately as he didn't have enough fuel to go around. Gave him permis-

sion and told all other a/c to let him land. He made a good landing, but when he turned off R/W he collided with Becky 64, who was waiting to cross runway. Crash crew and ambulance responded immediately. Both pilots OK. All concerned notified.

T-1500- All down or accounted for except Becky 59 at Castle Camps, Becky 40 at Martlesham, and Caboose 61 at Marston. Cobweb 50 and Cobweb 34 reported to bail out.

T-1645- Lt. Millikan called requesting that all 336 a/c be instructed to taxi to the end of the R/W when landing. This is to be done in the future for all 336 a/c. per Lt. Col. Clark, it's the impression of the Duty FCO that all a/c will be requested to do likewise in the future.

T-2155- F.C. Martlesham Heath called. They have three or four planes airborne that they may not be able to land when they return in a couple of hours. Want to get an idea if we might be able to take them if they do send them here. They will give us at least half an hour notice. They will check with their Meteorologist and don't want an official forecast from here now.

T-2300- Called Martelsham regarding their diversion. Their planes all just landed.

30 April - Col. Blakeslee led the Group on a Free-Lance General Support mission to Lyon. A Me 109 was bounced by three P-51s and destroyed. A section of 334 Squadron strafed Lyon/Bron A/D destroying several e/a.

Results of Engagements:

Capt. Sobanski	1/3 Me 110 Destroyed-Shared
Lt. Monroe	1/3 Me 110 Destroyed-Shared
Lt. Lang	1/3 Me 110 Destroyed-Shared
	1 Me 110 Destroyed

Lt. Glover and Lt. Frederick   shared one U/I T/E a/c

Col. Blakeslee, Capt. Godfrey, Lt. Harris, Lt.Patteeuw, and Lt. McDill 3 Seaplanes Destroyed-Shared

This put the Group score over 500 Destroyed; over 200 in April alone.

Lt. Glover was last seen N of Lyon, streaming glycol. He later bailed out. (Glover evaded capture and returned to England).

The Pilots returned to find the a/c grounded and the Pilots restricted to the base. "Maybe the Col. wants to make certain the Pilots will attend the party at the Officers' Mess tonight in honor of their achievements."

Battle Damage: Capt. Sobanski—Hole in fuselage.

Lt. Johnson—flak hole in gas tank.

T-1200- Group returning. Several homings. Apparently many are short of fuel and are landing at advanced bases.

T-1300- Marsten called that Lt. Frederick in VF-H had made a belly landing there. Pilot is reported OK. Oxford will go to Marston to see about him.

T-1400- All a/c accounted for except Becky 34. Lt. Glover is reported to have a glycol leak and to have headed for Switzerland.

T-1534- Becky 342 landed from Deanland where he had stopped for gas returning from operations. All operations a/c now here except Becky 34 and Becky 36 (Malmsten).

1 May 1944 - Effective 0200 hrs, pilots will no longer receive double sortie credit for one mission completed. Each mission will be one sortie only. Where formerly 10 sorties were required for an Air Medal, the pilot must now complete 40 operational hours for the Air Medal and 200 operational hours for the DFC.

Col. Blakeslee led the Group on a Bomber Withdrawal Support to Saarbrucken. After leaving the target area, east of Luxembourg, the Group sighted twelve Me 109s. Lt. Godfrey chased one of them down to the deck where the Jerry bailed out. Lts. Hofer, Jones, and McGrattan each scored one Me 109 destroyed.

Combat Reports: "I followed a Me 109 into a cloud, firing but not getting any hits. When I pulled out, I saw three e/a with a Mustang in front of the one farthest to my right. I turned on this one and fired a good deflection shot as he turned into me. I saw only one strike in the cockpit just above the wing root. He rolled over on his back and went straight down. His canopy came off, but I did not see him bail out or a chute open. I followed him straight down and saw him hit and blow up in a great ball of flames. He crashed in a large town behind some houses. When I returned to base, I found that only two of my guns had been firing."

Frank Jones 1st Lt., Air Corps.

*****

Lt. Hofer, with Lt. Speer as Wingman, claimed one Me 109 Destroyed. Lt. Speer reported,"The pilot bailed out in front of me so close that I could see his dress uniform and his black shiny boots glistening in the sun. He waved as I flew by within 50 feet of him."

T-1655- Lt. Col. Clatinoff called and asked how many unauthorized personnel were in the tower today when the Group took off. I told him "None," as the only one in the Control Room besides FC personnel was the Duty MO, Capt Blackburn. All others were on the balcony. He said to advise him if we were bothered in the future—that no one was to be here except authorized personnel.

T-1711- Caboose Green 4, Lt. Waterman, called Green 3 to take over because he had been hit by flak and was coming back. Called Duty MO to be on hand in case pilot was injured.

Lt. Willard G. "GI" Gillette 334 Squadron, was a colorful Pilot who survived a mid-air collision, taxi accidents, and the loss of his P-51's tail section in a dive. He also lost a Wingman to enemy action, prior to completing his tour 25 Oct 44. Konsler collection.

T-1745- Caboose Green 1 landed OK. Had flak holes in wings but pilot was not injured.

Narrative: Today seven new Pilots were assigned to the Group and one of them, Lt. "G.I." Gillette, gave his impression: "I came into the unit and was assigned to 334 Squadron. Capt. Sobanski was the Squadron CO, and Capt. Hively was the Ops. Officer. The first day we did our paperwork, toured the base, and were assigned to the Squadron. We were told Col. Blakeslee wanted to speak to us personally, but he was on a mission and would return soon.

When he arrived, we waited for him as he taxied up, climbed out of the cockpit, and got out of his chute and dinghy. As he approached us, I noted his nurtured fighter Pilot image: the swagger, the leather jacket with the inevitable white scarf, and the fighter Pilot attitude. I was impressed by his operational tan; dark around the eyes and white on his nose and lower face, which was normally covered by the oxygen mask; a definite helmet line on his forehead. He reminded me of a raccoon as he began to speak. He talked to us for about five minutes. I don't remember much about his talk, except the last thing he said, "I'll see you guys at the bar tonight. I don't want anybody in my outfit that won't drink, because a man who won't drink won't won't fight, and I don't want any son-of-a-bitch in my outfit who won't fight!" He waved his hand and walked out. That made an impression on me. I resolved to go out and do the things he said we should do."

2 May - The Red Cross Aero Club was jammed to capacity as over 500 G.I.'s gathered to hear our Group Comander, Col. Blakeslee, announce that the 4th had confirmed more than 500 enemy aircraft Destroyed, 207 during April alone. This was an all time high for any U.S. Group in one month.

In an exciting program Sgt. R.A. Meyer, acting as Master of Ceremonies, introduced Major Trippet of the 65th Fighter Wing, Lt. Col. Clark, Capts. Conrad, Gabrilson, and Mead, and Lts. Swope and Ingold. They, in turn, described the various facets of the operations of the Group and how they all fit together to form an efficient and successful unit.

Col. Clatanoff finished the program by stressing the importance of having a well administered station, after which Combat films were shown to the delight of the audience.

T-1102- Thunderbolt, UN-L, from Boxted landed. Tire blew. A/C taxied off R/W to right and stopped about 40 yards off the R/W. Called Base Flight. They will fix it as soon as possible.

T-1122- VF-U, Lt. Tussey, came in for a landing. Made a good landing, rolled approximately 1,000 yards on R/W when his undercarriage apparently collapsed. Crash crew and ambulance on way to crash. All concerned notified.

T-1530- Watten called about Lt. Foster in Master 672, who landed there without a clearance, and left without getting a clearance, taking off against a red light. He then cleared here for a local flight. It was reported to Wing, and he was assigned to Maj. Trippett for disciplinary action.

3 May - No Group activity. Dawn and local flying only.

T-1549 Becky 34, Lt. Lynch, came in for a landing. Just before reaching the intersection, he bounced the a/c, and it went up into the air about 10 feet. It looked as if he might have partially stalled out. He came down on his left wing tip and made a wonderful recovery. He then proceeded towards 335 dispersal still rolling quite fast. He cut in between two planes parked there and came to a stop just in front of 335 dispersal. Ambulance and crash crew were there, and all concerned were notified.

4 May - Seven new pilots were assigned:
Capt. Thomas Joyce
2nd Lts. James Callahan
Thomas Fraser
Willard Gillette
Thomas Sharp
Jack Simon
Edward Steppe
S/Sgt Cleo E. Phillips was promoted to Tech Sgt.
Sergeants Raymond Mayorga, Max Mintz, and Fred Taylor were promoted to Staff Sergeant.
Corporal Joseph P. Langlois was promoted to Sergeant.
After an aborted mission, the Group returned and landed.

All available pilots were given a talk by a POW interrogator explaining how Dulag Luft interrogators attempt to trick captives into devulging information.

All available personnel attended a "500" Victory party with free beer and hot dogs. After the party there was a good USO show in the cinema.

T-1135 As Lt. Allen, in QP-K, was landing, apparently both brakes locked as they were smoking badly. The pilot kept the ship well in control and turned off the R/W to the left just beyond the intersection. The right brake seemed to release, and the ship stopped just north of 335 dispersal. Lt. Allen did a swell job in not cracking up.

5 May - Movies of ground strafing were shown to all available Pilots.

6 May - The following commendation, dated 1 May 1944, was received from Brigadier General Jesse Auton.

"I desire to commend you for your loyalty, diligence, and attention to duty during the months of March and April 1944. There are many duties required by the Army for the successful prosecution of the war against the enemy that seem small, such as: guard, K.P., clerk, and orderly. However, each of these duties were well performed and thus were important in the destruction of the enemy by the units of AAF Station F-356."

Col. Donald Blakeslee endorsed this commendation as follows:

"It is a pleasure for me to forward to all members of my command this commendation in which I heartily concur. During the month of March, the 4th Fighter Group established a new tactical record by claiming 155 Destroyed enemy aircraft, 13 probably Destroyed, and 51 Damaged. During April, this Group claimed 207 Destroyed, 4 probably Destroyed, and 111 Damaged. This is the largest number of enemy aircraft Destroyed by one Fighter Group in one month in the history of aerial warfare. In the words of Major General Kepner, it is an "Outstanding contribution to our Allied objective of winning the war.""

Since the activation of the 4th Fighter Group in September 1942, our total claims to 30 April 1944, are as follows: Destroyed - 505 1/ 2 - Probables - 39 - Damaged - 232.

"This makes us 'top' Group of the war by a comfortable margin, and the same is far from over."

An **Oak Leaf Cluster to the Distinguished Flying Cross** was awarded to:

1st Lt. Alfred H. Markel

2nd Lt. Ralph K. Hofer

Captain Hively returned from Southend where he tested the new secret gyroscopic sight.

7 May - Capt. Millikan led a Target and Withdrawal Support mission to Berlin. No e/a were seen. The mission was fouled up by late arrival of orders and inadequate briefing. Practice glide and dive bombing missions were flown.

8 May - Orders were received promoting Ralph Kidd Hofer to 2nd Lt. and assigning him to the 4th Fighter Group, as of 22 April 44.

Sergeants Vincent Baietti and Murphy Gower were ordered to RAF Station Fainborough, Hants, for a course in K-14 Gun Sight Maintenance.

1st Lt. Vernon A. Burroughs was assigned to 334 Squadron.

Col. Blakeslee led a Target and Withdrawal Support mission and Bomber Escort to Berlin.

North of Ruhr, one straggling B-17 at 10,000 feet was seen being attacked by three Me 109s and one FW 190. Our Red section attacked. Hardy, Speer, and Howe engaged the e/a, damaging two before they evaded into clouds and were not sighted again. They made no claims pending assessment of the film. Prior to R/V, two B-17s were hit by flak and exploded. Near Wittenberge, three B-17s collided, and only three chutes were seen.

Flak at Berlin was intense and accurate as to altitude only; heavy type, heavier than usual.

There was a wet dinghy drill at 1600 hours for all Pilots who had not previously attended.

T-2148 Night flying begins.

T-2245 Becky 44 called that brakes are locked at west end on Perimeter Track.

9 May - Mission: Sweep and A/D Strafing to St. Dizier, led by Capt. Millikan. The Group beat up the Airdrome and inflicted much damage, but only one plane was claimed Destroyed, that by Lt. Grover Seims.

Lts. Simon and Patchen teamed up to damage a Me 410.

Lt. Allen sustained slight battle damage. As he came in for a landing, his starboard tire blew.

Lt. Robert S. Sherman 334 Squadron belly landed his A/C after his prop hit the ground while strafing St. Dizier A/D, 9 May 44. He is pictured with his crew chief S/Sgt E. G. Haning. Sherman Photo.

T-1143 Lt. Allen came in for a landing. As he touched down, his right wheel buckled under him. He held the plane up on one wheel until he passed intersection, then it sagged down onto right wing and swung to right. He came to a stop about 50 yards off runway. The Pilot was not hurt.

T-1200 All Group landed except 4 planes: Cobweb 53 in QP-N, Lt. Burroughs, and Cobweb 44 in QP-E, Lt. Blanchfield, bailed out. Cobweb 31 in QP-D, Lt. Sherman, crashed in Germany. Caboose 40, Lt. Waterman in WD-A, is unaccounted for. (All four became POWs).

Combat Report: Filed 11 May by Lt. Frank Speer:

"Flying line abreast in #3 position to Lt. Blanchfield, we dove at 1000 hours onto the airfield. We came over the field in a dive from 200 feet down. I believe Lt. Blanchfield was shooting at a Flak Tower, as was his #2. I was shooting at hangars and buildings, and I didn't see Lt. Blanchfield get hit. As we passed the field, I saw his plane streaming white smoke as he pulled up to about 3,000 feet, very slowly, on a course of 240 degrees from the field. His jacket was covered with oil, which also covered the side of the plane. He seemed to have lost both his oil and glycol, and the engine was detonating violently.

Blanchfield climbed out of the cockpit as the plane rolled in a half roll to the left. His radio seemed to have been shot out, also, but he was using both hands and making signs. He seemed to be unhurt. When he left the plane, it was going about 150 mph, and his chute opened almost immediately. He landed in a small woods. We didn't stay around to see him get out because he was near a small town, and we didn't want to attract attention to him.

His plane immediately burst into flames and burned furiously about a half mile from where he landed."

Frank E. Speer, 2nd Lt. AC

*****

Lt. Blanchfield recalls: "Two small missions were scheduled for the morning of 9 May 1944. This was unusual, as our group always made the long escorted penetration raids. I planned the morning trip in order to visit a friend who was in a nearby hospital after crashing a Mustang on a ferry trip. The mission was Bomber Escort and Strafing to St. Dizier Aerodrome south and east of Paris. Our Squadron was designated to be the first to go in after the bombing. I found myself flying down the enemy runway 50 feet off the ground. The coolant system was hit immediately, and the cockpit started to fill up with an amber vapor. It was only a matter of time before the engine would freeze up or catch on fire. I pulled the plane up to about fifteen hundred or two thousand feet, put it in a slight turn, and jumped out. My parachute was barely opened when I hit the ground. It was fortunate that I had a backpack and not a seatpack, as the backpack opens a fraction of a second quicker.

I hid my chute and started to run toward the nearest cluster of woods. I heard many dogs barking and imagined they were after me. After running about another half mile, I came to a small stream in a lightly wooded area. I ran down one side as far as the woods would hide me. I then crossed over and ran up the other side so I would have ample warning if the dogs followed my trail. Since there was no action, I knew I was not being followed. I then laid down to have a rest. After a couple of hours, I decided to look for some help."

Herb soon made contact with a Frenchman who hid him in a haystack until he could return. The Frenchman returned and gave him some cider, brown bread, and some fried rabbit. He then guided Herb to a village where he waited in a cemetery until daylight. Previous information indicated to Herb that the safest way to contact the Underground was through a priest or a prostitute. At daybreak it was a little early for the latter. In the church cemetery, he was close to the former, so Herb waited for the Priest to come to say Mass. The Priest never arrived, and so Herb made further contact with a French farmer. He eventually ended up with a Frenchman who subsisted by making soap for German Officers out of dead horses and making black market runs to Paris. He also hid downed American Airmen.

Unfortunately, a Gestapo informer discovered the operation and Herb found himself in the hands of the Gestapo. It was rather frightening to be in the control of drunken German officers whose constant companions were bleached blonde French prostitutes. It was like a scene from a sleazy class "B" movie. There was an atmosphere of complete depravity. Screams were heard from time to time, but fortunately downed Airmen were low on the list for involved interrogation. After five months in the hands of the Gestapo, during which Herb managed prodigious mental arithmetical feats to pass the time, Herb was shipped out to a POW camp, Stalag Luft #1.

There the food was meager, with small fractions of Red Cross parcels to supplement the sawdust laden bread and thin soup. One special day a good soup was made from the head of a horse that was boiled in water.

In due course, the Russians liberated the camp. Herb, along with the other POWs, arrived at Camp Lucky Strike, where all returnees were processed and shipped out for the U.S.

10 May - Mission aborted due to bad weather conditions.

The members of the post dance band,"The Flying Eagles," which included Sgts. Brong, Kirkpatrick, and Schroeder, from 334 Squadron, were put on orders for London to play an engagement.

11 May - Weather recco to Strasbourg—Uneventful.

Orders were received of the promotion of the following Officers from 1st Lt. to Capt:

Alfred H. Markel

William B. Smith

Nicholas Megura

Gerald Montgomery

A **Silver Oak Leaf Cluster to the Distinguished Flying Cross** was awarded to:

Major Duane W. Beeson

An **Oak Leaf Cluster to the Distinguished Flying Cross** was awarded to:

Capt. Archie W. Chatterley

1st Lt. Vasseure H. Wynn

Major Goodson led a Sweep to Saarbrucken with no e/a seen.

1st Lt. Tussey bailed out in the Channel and was picked up by ASR, but he died shortly thereafter.

T-1000 Major Cadill called about VIPs coming, also 3 Aircraft for display—2 P-38s, (One droop snoot), and a P-47.

T-2010 Ops "B" called that Becky 56 (Lt. Tussey) bailed out at N-2108. Picked up by Dover boat, seriously injured, he was being taken to Ramsgate Hospital south of Manston. Intelligence and Hospital notified.

T-2100 Stansteel called that a red-nose Mustang flew low over their field and as he pulled up, it seemed that his motor started spitting. He was seen to disappear behind some trees north of their field, about 5 miles from us.

T-2110 Ambulance and Crash truck dispatched in search of the Aircraft.

T-2120 Capt. Megura was up at the time. I contacted him. He said he did fly over Stanstead, and he saw a B-26 flying low. He cut his motor and dropped down to fly formation with it. It seems that this was the Aircraft.

12 May - 2nd Lt. Leonard R. Pierce was promoted to 1st Lt.

Mission: Penetration, Target and Withdrawal Support: 1st ATF, Brux.

Lts. Hofer, Pierce, and Siems, along with Capt. Hively, claimed three Me 109s Destroyed in an attack on eight Me 109s maneuvering to attack the bombers. Lt. McDill and Major Goodson each Destroyed a Me 109. Capt. Happel, and Lts. Homuth, Lines, Shapleigh, and Stanford combined to knock down six 109s.

Narrative: Lt. Gillette recounts: "This was my third mission; I was flying on Deacon Hively's wing. We sighted four Me 109s out there and Deacon said, 'Let's go get 'em.' Man! We went charging out there right at them, two of us and four of them—good odds? I found out later that these were very good odds for the 4th. I dropped my tanks and the Huns started to turn. They were just as scared as I. I knew my job, just stay back there and watch Deacon's tail. Deacon gets on one, and there's fire all over the plane before he stops shooting at him, and he pulls up and says, "Why the hell don't you go shoot one?" Now here I am, this is all new to me, and by the time I got my thing together, they were too far away. If only I hadn't broken off and pulled up with Deacon. No, I didn't get one, but it really helped me to find I no longer had the fear and apprehension that I had on the first two missions."

Combat Reports: "I was flying Caboose Blue 3. At 10,000 feet, we spotted three Me 109s below us and went down to attack them from the rear. I picked the one in the middle, and he broke right and down onto the deck. I fired at him continually, starting at about 350 yards. I observed only one group of hits on his starboard wing. For some reason, however, he seemed to think his jig was up, for he pulled up in a steep climb, started to roll over, and as he was rolling, he jettisoned his canopy.

Half-way through his roll, as his canopy came off, Lt. Shapleigh, who was flying Caboose Red 2, came up and fired at the e/a, hitting it in the mid-section. The Me 109 completed his roll and went into the ground on its back. I saw the Pilot's chute come out of the cockpit before the plane hit, but I did not see the Pilot come out. We then set course for home. I claim one Me 109 Destroyed, shared with Lt. Shapleigh."

George Stanford 1st Lt., Air Corps.

*****

"I was leading Caboose Green Section when we heard the bombers were under attack. We headed in to intercept the e/a, and bounced three Me 109s. We chased them to the deck, and I took the one on the port. My wingman, Lt. Homuth, took the one in the middle. I fired about a three-second burst at approximately 400 yards and had a good strike in his wing root. He turned to the starboard, and I closed more, getting a few more good strikes on his wing root and engine. I closed to about 250 yards. I saw fire coming from his engine. The Pilot jettisoned his canopy and bailed out. His chute just opened as he hit the ground. His a/c crashed a few hundred yards away from him. I took a picture of what was left of the burning a/c and the chute on the ground. Lt. James Russel, my #4 man, saw the Pilot bail and the a/c crash."

James R. Happel Captain, Air Corps

*****

"I was flying Caboose White 2 on Horseback's wing. Horseback sighted two Me 109s, and we dropped tanks and went after them. When we jumped the 109s, they split up and headed for the deck. I saw Horseback get his 109, and just then, the other 109 cut right in front of me. I got on his tail and started firing just as my gun-sight bulb burned out. Since we were on the deck, I didn't have time to change it. I followed the e/a for about 20 miles, and he led me into a flak area. By that time, I was out to get him. I cleared my tail and just as I faced forward, I saw this Me 109 hit the ground and blow up. I claim one Me 109 Destroyed."

Ted Lines 2nd Lt., Air Corps.

*****

"I was flying Caboose Green 2 when we sighted three Me 109s heading for the deck. Capt. Happel, Green 1, took the one to port, and I went after the middle one. I fired out of range and missed. The e/a made a tight turn to port on the deck, and I got a four-second deflection shot at him as he leveled out with his engine smoking. He went over a grove of trees and down into a field. Evidently he was trying to mush me into the ground. I stayed behind him firing one-second bursts and getting strikes at the wing root. His engine stopped, and he tried to crash-land; his speed falling rapidly. I closed too fast and had to pull off to port, but I kicked back down and fired again, observing strikes in the cockpit. His canopy came off, and he tumbled out at ten feet. I observed no chute. The e/a began to burn and went in on the starboard wing. It exploded when it hit. I claim one Me 109 and Pilot Destroyed. Lts. Russel and Jones, Caboose Green 3 and 4, witnessed this attack and saw the e/a crash and the Pilot come out."

Robert H. Homuth 2nd Lt., Air Corps

*****

"I was Caboose Blue 2 when we saw three Me 109s on the deck. We started down after them, "S"ing back and forth to lose some speed. Blue 1 was to take the one on the left; Blue 3 the one in the middle; and I was to take the one on the right. I opened fire getting strikes on the wings and fuselage. I pulled up as the e/a went into the deck and exploded. I made a starboard turn and found a Hun right in front of me. I opened fire, getting strikes on his fuselage and wings. He half rolled and tried to get out. The chute opened partially, but he wasn't able to free himself from the cockpit. The plane hit the deck and exploded, but he didn't get free. I found out later that Lt. Stanford, Blue 3, had also been shooting at this e/a and had gotten strikes on it. I claim one Me 109 Destroyed and one Me 109 Destroyed (Shared with Lt. George Stanford)"

Eliot Shapleigh 2nd Lt., Air Corps

*****

13 May - Lts. Pierce and Simon were airborne at 0645 hours for a local flight and landed at 0740 hours. Lt. Simon submitted the following report:

"Lt. Pierce and I went up on a local flight this morning. I was flying on his left wing, and we went down for a little low flying. I moved out a little, and as I took a look at his ship to check his position, I hit a tree. We were about ten to fifteen miles south of the field at the time. After checking the instruments, it looked like I could make it back to the field, so we came in and landed. The throttle wouldn't retard to less than 40 inches of mercury at the time. After working it a little, I got it down to 25 inches of mercury. I made 2 passes at the field, and on the third try, I cut back the idle cut-off and landed." Lt. Simon was flying QP-O, plane Cat "AC."

*****

T-0740 Cobweb 33 (Lt. Simon) lands after several attempts. His throttle was stuck.

T-0800 One of crash crews' men reports that Lt. Simon's aircraft (QP-O) is damaged pretty bad, prop, air scoop, and wings. He did not do it landing. The pilot says he hit a tree while doing local flying this morning. No one notified as yet—too early.

Mission: Withdrawal Support, Target: Posen. One FW 190 was seen. He disappeared in haze, and the Group returned to base.

Casualties: 1st Lt. Leonard R. Pierce, O-813221, MIA. Lt. Pierce bailed out 30 miles east of Southwold at about 1335 hours, reason unknown. Leonard was reported to have been last seen by a spotter, as Leonard was struggling with his chute 150 yards from his inflated dinghy. The chute pulled him in before rescue could be effected. (He was KIA).

All available EM attended a meeting in the hangar at 1430 hours. Major Heene announced that, effective 2400 hours, 14 May 1944, all passes will again be canceled until further notice. He then read extracts from secret communications stressing security and handling of crashed enemy aircraft. He also read a report from Lt. General Carl Spaatz. He concluded the meeting by announcing that we all may be called upon to re-double our efforts as some of us may be sent to other outfits on detached service, and there would be no replacements.

T-1345 Ops Controller advises they have a "May Day" on Cobweb 33, Lt. Pierce in QP-G. They have a good fix and there is a launch near. Notified those concerned.

T-1350 Ops called that Lt. Pierce has been sighted—He's in his dinghy and should be OK. They will let us know.

T-1445 Called Ops Controller about Lt. Pierce. His dinghy with his name on it was picked up in the Channel inflated, but he wasn't in it. They are still looking. ASR launch was only five miles away when Pierce went in.

T-1843 All group back but Lt. Pierce. Last report from ASR is that he couldn't get into his dinghy and went down.

14 May - The report was received from the Confirmation of Victory Credits Board confirming the following claims for the period 6 Mar thru 18 April:

334 Squadron - 26 e/a Destroyed of various types; Me 110s, Ju 88s, Ju 52s, Me 109s, and FW 190s.

The pilots registering kills were: Capts. Van Epps, Care, and Beeson; Lts. Megura, Montgomery, Smith, Markel, Moulton, Biel, France, Pierce, Monroe, Care, Lang, Blanchfield, Malmsten, and Howe; and F/O Hofer.

In addition to these kills, many claims of damage to both e/a and other military equipment were confirmed.

The crews were occupied making the changeover from 75 gallon to the new 108-gallon wing tanks, which will greatly extend our range.

15 May - The following Station Defense plan went into effect 15 minutes before dawn. "Until further notice, four pilots of the group are to be on continuous readiness, at their Dispersals, from 15 minutes before dawn until 15 minutes after black-out time, alternating among the three Squadrons."

All available pilots reported to the briefing room at 1500 hours. Col. Blakeslee reported that: "Effective 2400 hours, 15 May, the new operational tour for fighter pilots will be 300 hours and soon may become unlimited. Anyone having 180 hours or more, as of 2400 hours today, will complete their tour on the 200-hour basis."

The Colonel also called to the pilots' attention the fact that there have been too many avoidable flying and taxiing accidents recently, and that if they continue, those responsible may expect to be fined and/or possibly grounded.

The matter of military courtesy and proper uniform was discussed by Blakeslee. He cited specific violations which were to cease immediately. All were reminded that information given out in the briefing room is secret and will be communicated to no one prior to completion of the mission. The unauthorized dissemination of such information has resulted in some members of air crews, from other stations, being tried by courts-martial.

The Articles of War were read, and a sex morality lecture was given to all available EM in the Station Cinema at 1700 hours. All EM of the Squadron, who were not present because of other duties, were to attend a second meeting at 1700 hours, 16 May 1944.

T-1425 Major Booth called in regard to men on the gun sites. From now on, here is what we are supposed to do.

On every sweep or show, we are to call the Intelligence switch board operator four times.

1) At least 15 minutes before sweep takes off.

2) After sweep is off.

3) At least 15 minutes before Group returns.

4) After the main Group has landed, we notify the main switch board operator, and he will notify the men on the gun sites. The guns will be manned 15 minutes before takeoff until Group takes off and 15 minutes before Group returns until the main force has landed.

T-1727 Cobweb 30, QP-Z, Lt. Scott, had his right brake lock in landing. He pulled off the R/W to the left and came to a stop 20 yards off the R/W. Squadron informed.

T-1815 Captain Toy called about a teletype regarding four A\C to stand readiness. Every day one of the Squadrons will be responsible for the above A\C and Pilots. Today 334, tomorrow 335, etc. The Pilots and A/C will be standing by 1/2 hour before dawn until 1/2 hour after dark. The order to scramble A/C will come from the Controller at Ops B. All A/C in air (if in the daytime) will be told to stay off "H" Channel as Ops B will be controlling the 44 A/C on A. If at night, all A/C will be told to land. Capt. Toy suggests that the duty FCO will be on call from 1/2 hour before dawn until 1/2 hour after dark, as the readiness A/C may take off any of the above times. The A/C will not use a specific R/W, but will take off from their dispersals. Capt. Toy is sending the teletype and a schedule over tomorrow.

16 May - An **Oak Leaf Cluster to the Distinguished Flying Cross** was awarded to Capt. Nicholas Megura and to Lt. David Howe

T-0716 Dawn flying begins.

17 May - The pass restriction effective 2400 hours, 14 May 44 was rescinded, effective 0600 hours today.

18 May - All available personnel attended a meeting in the hangar at 1600 hours. 1st/Sgt Morris announced that our Squadron was to furnish 12 enlisted men every night, effective this date, for the "Readiness Platoons." Hours of duty are to be from 2030 hours to 0600 hours the following morning. Members of the Platoon are to be ready for their station defense duties 30 seconds after an alert is announced. All Enlisted Men from Private to 1st/Sgt. are to take a turn on this detail, as well as all Administrative Officers in the Squadron. These Platoons are being used to combat any reprisal measures that may be taken by the enemy. Major Heene pointed out that this new Station Defense plan was the first detail to affect all enlisted grades and Administrative Officers of the Squadron.

19 May - 1st Lt. Benjamin Q. Ezzell was ordered to London to attend the Monthly Escape Meeting.

1st Lt. Orrin C. Snell was assigned to 334, effective 13 May.

Mission: Target and Withdrawal Support: Berlin.

Bombers were escorted over target and to the Baltic coast. West of Wismar 334 Squadron bounced three Me 109s and destroyed one. West of Lubeck at 1530 hours, they sighted six Me 109s flying north in two vics. The Squadron attacked and destroyed five of them. One unidentified single engine a/c was destroyed at 700 feet by Lt. Lang. Two of the e/a destroyed collided when a #2 made a violent port turn, cutting the tail off his #3.

Results: Seven e/a Destroyed and two Damaged by Capt. Hively, Major McPharlin, and Lts. Scott, Howe, and Lang. (Hively destroyed three)

Lt. Don Patchen was hit by flak over Berlin and bailed out near Hanover. He was seen to hit the ground OK. Later, when Don was liberated from a POW Camp, he told of bailing out and of the immediate choice he had to make. On one side he had a burning wheat field, set on fire by his burning plane. On the other side was a mob of pitch fork wielding civilians. He immediately chose to turn himself over to a nearby contingent of Wehrmacht soldiers and preclude any possibilities of escape or needless mayhem.

Don also commented on the fact that, "Never once, thanks to the expertise, knowledge, commitment, and concern of the ground personnel, was it necessary for me to abort a mission due to any failure of the aircraft. What a privilege to have been a part of such a team."

*****

Orders were received assigning 2nd Lt. Richard L. Bopp and 2nd Lt. Fernandez to 334 Squadron.

1st Lt. Donald J Patchen 336 Squadron bailed out near Hanover Germany when his a/c was hit by a rocket. Weckbacher collection.

Major Heene received a letter from Mrs. Allen F. Bunte, stating that she had received a card from her husband Lt. Allen Bunte. He stated that he was a POW in Germany, and that he was all right except for a few scratches. Lt. Bunte was reported MIA 5 April 44.

T-1735 All Group back but Lt. Patchen, Becky 37. Squadron reports he bailed out over Hanover; Lt. Callahan, Cobweb 50, landed at Martltesham, and Lt. Jennings, Caboose 49, landed at North Weald.

20 May - A Free-Lance was flown in conjunction with Bombers, Target: Liege. No e/a were seen, but intense, accurate, heavy flak caught Major McFarlane and damaged both wings of his plane.

Major Heene addressed all available enlisted men in the hangar at 1430 hours. He explained further particulars of the new Station Defense plan. A quota of 60 has been set to receive comprehensive Infantry training for a "Flying Squad." The men were to be picked from volunteers on their leadership and marksmanship abilities. They were to be the last to be called for detached service. It was most unusual to get this type of training in the Air Corps.

Orders were received promoting 1st Lt. Howard D. Hively to Captain as of 15 May.

Capt. Nicholas Megura and Maj. James Goodson were awarded the **Distinguished Service Cross.**

Oak Leaf Clusters to the Distinguished Flying Cross were awarded to:

1st Lt. Gerald E. Montgomery
Capt. Winslow M. Sobanski

T-1240 Lt. Simpson in WD-U went off the R/W at South Norle, nosed-up and settled-back on his wheels again. Prop is damaged. Pilot OK.

T-1702 VF-M Lt. Shilke, in landing scraped a wing. Plane righted itself OK. Passed info to 336 Sq. and Capt. Toy.

21 May - Orders were received promoting 1st Lt. Winslow M. Sobanski to Captain, effective 13 May 1944.

Mission: Chattanooga No.1. Railroads, Tugs, and Warehouses were attacked, as well as an unidentified A/D.

Results of Engagement: Five e/a were destroyed, ten locomotives were damaged, and miscellaneous trucks, tugs, warehouses, and a radar station were damaged. Those taking part in the destruction were: Capts. Sobanski, Megura, and Joyce, Lts. Fraser, Hills, Sharp, Hofer, Hewatt, Seims, Speer, Kolter, Monroe, Hardy, and Gillette, and Major McPharlin. Lts. Speer and Siems each destroyed two e/a, and Lts. Hewatt and Hofer shared one.

Lt. Harris spun while in clouds. He jettisoned his canopy, but finally got his kite under control and came home.

The 336 had a field day, toting up a score of nine locomotives, plus trucks, goods trains, barges, and various targets of opportunity. Capts. Millikan and Bennett, and Lts. Higgins, Lane, Smith, Young, Grounds, LaJeunesse, Van Wyk, Netting, Johnson, and Harris all participated in the shootout.

Battle Damage: QP-B (Lt. Speer) 20 or 37 mm hole through starboard wing, about 3 feet from end of wing.

T-1609 All Group back except Lt. Hunt, Caboose 56, WD-G. No news on him. (Subsequently reported KIA).

22 May - Mission: Free Lance and Escort, Target: Kiel. The 334 and 335 Squadrons escorted while 336 engaged ten Me 109s. Three 334 a/c separated from the Squadron and sighted 30 plus FW 190s. They prevented an attack on the Bombers, but they did not score due to mechanical trouble.

Casualties: Captain Megura with his Section; Capt. Joyce, and Lts. Kolter and Hewatt, along with a number of P-38s, attacked three Me 109s. In the melee, Capt. Megura's plane was hit, and he headed for Sweden, where he was interned. Megura and an unknown P-38 pilot Destroyed one Me 109. Capt. Millikan and Lt. Hofer each claimed one Me 109 Destroyed.

A report was received from the Confirmation of Victory Credits Board confirming seven e/a Destroyed from 21 Mar through 5 April by the following Pilots:

Captains Van Epps, Megura, and Montgomery, and Lts. Rafalovich, Wynn, and Monroe.

T-1608 All Group returned except Cobweb 60, Capt. Megura. (He was interned in Sweden)

23 May - Uneventful Escort Mission to Chaumont & Troyes.

T-1215 All Group returned except Lt. Allen, who landed at Lashenden. Intelligence notified and gun crews stood down.

24 May - Penetration Support, Target: Berlin. Major Goodson's Group sighted 40+ e/a and engaged them from 35,000 feet to the deck. Two B-17s were hit by flak over the target area. They exploded and knocked down three others; no chutes were seen. A red-nosed P-51 was seen to overshoot a Me 109 at 32,000 feet, which then raked the P-51 with cannon fire. The P-51 was last seen going down in smoke.

Captains Hively and Millikan, and Lts. Gillette, Lang, Hofer, Fraser, Jones, Russel, and Speer combined to destroy ten e/a.

Combat Reports: "I was flying Cobweb White 3 and had rendezvoused with bombers when 30 plus bandits at 35,000 feet were sighted coming in at 12 o'clock to us. We had climbed up to 30,000 feet when I sighted four Me 109s coming in below us. I attacked, but lost sight of them in the haze. I pulled up and sighted three FW 190s attacking a B-17 that was returning. We bounced them, and I started shooting. We were trying to scare them off, but they didn't seem to see me. Finally I closed on one, getting strikes. The aircraft started smoking, the hood was jettisoned, and the Pilot bailed. The other two broke up to the left.

I then pulled up and saw Lt. Fraser, my wing man, behind the other two FW 190s. One of them made a split "S" with Lt. Fraser following. I then broke into the leader, preventing him from firing at Lt. Fraser. He did a split "S," and I followed at 14,000 feet. I got a few scattered hits. At 10,000 feet, below the clouds, I got more strikes in a tight turn. He pulled sharply up into a cloud and jettisoned his hood. I did not see the pilot bail out, but the a/c crashed in a field burning. It's ammo exploded at intervals. I took a picture of this."

Ralph K. Hofer 2nd Lt., Air Corps.

*****

"We sighted about 20 Me 109s and FW 190s at 30,000 feet, 12 o'clock to the Bombers and 5,000 feet above us. I was flying Green 3, and our target was six Me 109s which were in a gentle turn to the left. We climbed and joined their orbit. We got fairly close to them and started firing before they broke. Only the two we fired on broke.

Lt. Frank E. Speer 334 Squadron, in escape kit picture. These pictures were carried by all Pilots for use to make fake identity papers if shot down and picked up by friendly forces. Speer, an Ace, was hit by flak on 29 May 44 while strafing Macfitz A/D with Ralph Hofer. He evaded capture for over a week before he was caught and assigned to Stalag Luft III. He eventually escaped, and with a friend, captured 24 German soldiers and turned them over to Allied forces. Speer collection.

I got strikes on the first burst, and the e/a split S'd with me on his tail. He went straight down skidding; rolling; and he took violent evasive action. I kept firing short bursts. Pieces were coming off him all the time, two of which damaged my plane slightly. We went through some contrails. I was directly above him going straight down when he seemed to hit compressibility. His plane was shuddering violently. I had to put down 20 degrees of flaps to keep from overrunning him. I was indicating above 500 mph. The e/a started to pull out, and doing the same, I blacked out. When I came to, he was diving again, and I saw his canopy come off as he bailed out. The kite was last seen going straight down at about 9,000 feet, doing at least 500 mph."

Frank E. Speer 2nd Lt., Air Corps.

*****

"I was flying Caboose Red 3 as we climbed to reach Me 109s above and in front of us. Two Me 109s attacked us from 6 o'clock high. We broke into them. When I released my drop tanks, my port tank hung up by the front holder. I went into a spin, and the 109s

1st Lt. James W. Russel 335 Squadron on 11 Sept 44, was hit by a 20 mm round which exploded in his cockpit and wounded him. He crash-landed and was captured to become a POW. A F Museum collection.

followed me down. I leveled off, and the 109s went into a cloud. I joined another Mustang that was in a Luftberry with a Me 109. The 109 broke down streaming light brown smoke, and the Mustang started climbing. The e/a immediately pulled out of the dive and started back up. I jumped him and started firing. On the 2nd and 3rd bursts, I observed strikes underneath the fuselage. Oil from the e/a covered my windscreen, cutting out my forward visibility. I closed to dead astern and started firing when I could feel his prop wash. We were in a steep spiral from 22,000 feet to 6,000 feet when the 109 fell off on one wing and headed straight down streaming glycol and black smoke. I followed him to 2,000 feet where he went into a cloud. We were in a vertical dive, and my IAS was 450 mph. I pulled out just above the deck and returned home. I claimed this a/c Destroyed."

James Russel, Jr. 1st Lt., Air Corps.

*****

A second Mission, Glide Bombing of a railroad bridge at Beaumont-sur-Oise, produced undetermined damage.

T-1436 All Group returned except Caboose 49, Lt. Jennings. (Jennings was reported KIA).

25 May - The Group received "Confirmation of Victory Credits Board Report No.59," confirming claims from 21 March to 10 April: 22 e/a Destroyed, and much miscellaneous damage inflicted to both e/a and equipment.

The destroyed were the result of the efforts of Lts. France, Markel, Monroe, Seims, Hofer, Hills, Biel, McGrattan, Kenyon and Howe; Capts. Sobanski, Care, Montgomery, and Megura; and Col. Blakeslee.

Major Goodson led a mission to Chaumont, France. Goodson, Bennet, and McDill destroyed five e/a in the Strasbourg area. Bennet and McDill both scored doubles.

T-1143 All Group returned except Becky 35, Capt. Bennet, and Becky 60, Lt. McDill. Intelligence notified. (Both became POWs).

26 May - Night flying practice only.

27 May - Capt. Charles F. Howse was assigned to 334 Squadron. 1st Lt. Herbert J. Blanchfield was promoted to Captain.

Mission: Penetration, Target, and Withdrawal Support, Target Karlsruhe: No e/a were seen, but three Pilots claimed damage to ground targets.

T-1530 Group all down except Caboose 63 (Shapleigh). No information.

Lt. Shapleigh, from El Paso Texas, was flying with 335 Squadron. His plane developed engine trouble near Wassigny, France, and he was forced to bail out. He ran for cover in a nearby woods and stayed hidden there all day. Later he started moving, and about 2200 he came upon two men plowing a field. He waited until one of the men left, and then, with his French/English phrase book in hand, he approached the French farmer. He told the farmer what had happened and asked him for assistance. The Frenchman willingly offered to help him and directed him to a "safe house."

Lt. Eliot H. Shapleigh 335 Squadron bailed out over France because of engine trouble on 27 May 44. He was picked up by the French Underground and hidden in a secret room in a private home until the area was overrun by American Forces who repatriated him. 4th Group picture.

Just before dawn, a Frenchman named Closset arrived and presented himself to be Shapleigh's guide through the French Underground. For the next ten days, Shapleigh and Closset were constant companions as they stealthily moved from house to house. They arrived at the home of Clossets' sister and brother-in-law, Albert and Jose Baillant, in Vallee' Multre. The pair agreed to hide Eliot until it was safe for the Underground to move him. They constructed a false wall in the baby's room concealing a small alcove. It contained only a bed. Here he was to stay.

Their plans were upset as D-Day approached, and the Underground members became occupied with other activities. Each night, Eliot moved into his room to sleep. The false wall was moved into place, and the baby's crib was moved into place in front of the wall. Here he lived for four months, fearing all the time for his life and wondering if he would ever get home. In June, Paris was liberated. By September, the areas surrounding Shapleigh's hideout were also overrun by the Americans. Soon after the Americans arrived, Shapleigh approached a group of them, told them his story, and asked for help. At first they did not believe him, but he convinced them that he really was an American soldier from El Paso, Texas, and was allowed to leave.

*****

28 May - Major Goodson led the Group on a Penetration, Target, and Withdrawal Support. Mission: Ruhland. Twenty plus Me 109s and FW 190s attacked the bombers short of the target. The 334 Squadron was closest and bounced the e/a from 30,000 feet and broke up the attack. Capt. Sobanski; Major McPharlin; and Lts. Hofer, Siems, Kolter, Lang, and Kenyon claimed eight Me 109s Destroyed.

Lt. Hofer, in QP-L, had his rudder damaged by a 20mm explosive shell.

Lt. Bopp was separated from the Group. He asked for the Group's location, but was not heard from again.

Lt. Kenyon saw Lt. Hewatt receive strikes on his plane from a Me 109. Hewatt bailed out shortly before his plane blew up. (Bopp and Hewatt both became POWs).

The **Distinguished Flying Cross** was awarded to 2nd Lt. Shelton W. Monroe

T-1245 Flying Control at North Weald called to report that Lt. Grove in VF-T belly-landed there just a few minutes before. Apparently something had gone wrong with his plane, and he was returning from operations. Those concerned notified. Lt. Grove had his face hit, but injuries are not thought to be serious.

T-1312 Lt. Lines, Caboose 52, in WD-J, landed at Woodbridge at 1301 with coolant trouble.

T-1412 Caboose 52 landed from Woodbridge.

T-1600 Lt. Higgins, Becky 43, in VF-A, landed at Metfield with coolant system and radio U/S. Operations has nothing to send down for him at present so Lt. Higgins is standing by. He cannot fly the ship back before repairs are made.

T-1753 All Group back except Lt. Hewatt, Cobweb 52 in QP-Y, and Lt. Bopp, Cobweb 53 in QP-H, and the two at North Weald and Metfield. No reports on two unaccounted for.

29 May - Col. Blakeslee led a Withdrawal Support to Poznan, Poland. The Group rendezvoused with three CWS of B-17s flying at 21/22,000 feet northwest of Poznan. Bombers were escorted until 1545 hours. Lts. Hofer and Speer attacked a grass airdrome northeast of Stargard, Germany, believed to have been Mackfitz. Ten camouflaged HE 177s were dispersed around the edge of the field. Hofer and Speer Destroyed seven in four passes. There was light flak of moderate intensity; disposition unknown. Lt. Speer's a/c was hit by flak at about 1400 hours, and he crash-landed near the A/D, northeast of Stargard, Germany. He was heard to say over the R/T that he was O.K.

Near Gabbert, one Me 109 crashed when its tail section came off while evading attack by Lt. Snell.

Captain Robert C. Church 335 Squadron CO, 9 Aug 44, shown in his RCAF uniform prior to joining the USAAC and assignment to 335 Squadron. He completed his tour and returned to the States 30 Sept.44. Church photo.

The 336 attacked and destroyed two Me 410s at Prutznow. The 14 a/c then made one pass each at Dievenaw Seaplane Base. The Base had 14 twin-engine and four single-engine planes at anchor, and 1 FW 200 on a landing strip. Two seaplanes were destroyed and 12 damaged. Light flak of moderate intensity was encountered from buildings running east to west.

Casualties: 2nd Lt. Frank E. Speer, MIA.

Battle Damage: QP-R Lt. Steppe—Leading edge of starboard wing was hit by flak. Plane Cat. "A".

Results: Fifteen e/a were claimed Destroyed by Lts. Hofer, Speer, Snell, Kolter, and Church; Captain Mc Grattan; and Major McPharlin. A total of twelve were damaged by the Group. Col. Blakeslee Destroyed a Me 410, and Lts. Emerson and Netting shared in the destruction of an Me 410. In addition several e/a were damaged by 336 Squadron.

T-0258 Purple alert - Got up!!! Rough, ain't it?? Concerned notified.

T-0300 Red alert - Concerned notified.

T-0345 All clear - Concerned notified.

T-1734 All Group down except Lt. Speer, who crash-landed over Germany, and Lt. Perkins who landed at Thorpe Abbotts.

Combat reports: "I was flying Caboose Blue Leader when we dove on five Jerries attacking the lead box of the 2nd Combat Wing. I saw a Me 109 fire at the bombers then climb up on the other side. I opened up everything and went after him. He started to orbit; he attempted to position himself for another attack. He saw me coming and started to wrack it in. I wracked it in, also. About halfway through his turn, he suddenly reversed his turn and dove straight down. As I was not in position, I followed him but did not fire. He jettisoned his canopy, but I did not see him bail out or see a chute. At about 4,000 feet, we were both still going straight down at about 450 MPH, so I started to pull out gradually. I saw his A/C go straight into the sea about a half mile SW of Nysted."

Robert Church 1st Lt., Air Corps.

*****

"Leading 335 Squadron, I saw five e/a going in an easterly direction along the Ehmarn Belt, heading for a box of bombers. I dove on them and got within firing range just as they opened up on the bombers. One Jerry split S'd as I came in firing at the Me 109 on the extreme right of the five. I did not observe the results of the attack as I tried to avoid running into the bombers.

I went under the bombers and climbed slightly on their far side, turning to come back for another attack. As I started to follow a Me 109, I had to turn into another e/a coming at me from 9 o'clock. Immediately, I was behind a FW 190 who dove for the deck, and I

followed. I gained rapidly, flying at about 100 feet from the deck. I fired a short burst at the 190, seeing hits. I immediately fired a longer burst, seeing more hits. As he started into a right turn, I fired again and saw more hits. He turned over on his side and back, and went into the deck. He crashed amidst a big explosion and flames."

Bernard McGrattan Captain, Air Corps.

*****

"I was leading Becky Blue Section when two Bogies passed under us from nine o'clock. As soon as we determined that they were Bandits, we turned hard to starboard and opened up. The Me 410s headed for the bombers. Col. Blakeslee's Section chased them line astern. They turned starboard, and my section dropped tanks and cut them off. One of the 410s split-S'd for the deck, and I continued after the other. I closed rapidly taking several deflection shots and then closed line astern. I got several strikes which set his starboard engine on fire. I then pulled up to one side expecting him to explode or go into the deck as he was in a steep spiral. At that time, Lt. Netting made several passes at the Me 410 and watched it crashland. Lt. Netting had also made a pass at the 410 before I set it on fire. We formed-up and made a pass on several Seaplanes on a lake, but I had only one gun operating. I don't think I did much damage to the Do-18. I claim one Me 410 Destroyed, shared with Lt. Netting, and one Do-18 Damaged."

Donald R. Emerson 1st Lt., AC.

*****

"I was flying Col. Blakeslee's #2 over the bombers when we sighted two Bandits at 9 o'clock about 2,000 feet below us. We turned to come in astern of them and dropped our tanks, closing rapidly. After firing at the bombers, one e/a split-S'd, and we went after the other one. We engaged at about 5,000 feet, and I made several passes, observing strikes. After one of these passes, I saw Lt. Emerson set the e/a starboard engine on fire. He was still running away, so I closed and clobbered him some more. He crashed, burning badly. Col. Blakeslee called saying he got the other one. I joined him just as he was clobbering the underside of the e/a from dead astern, setting him on fire. I moved in and got a good burst at him. He crashed in flames, setting the woods on fire.

We then attacked a seaplane base with Col. Blakeslee hitting one Do 18, and I hit two with good bursts. I claim one Me 410 Destroyed, shared with Lt. Emerson, and two Do 18s Damaged. I also confirm one Me 410 Destroyed by Col. Blakeslee."

Conrad Netting 2nd Lt., AC.

*****

Narrative: Frank Speer recalls: "Hofer and I came across the airdrome on the deck. There was no lack of targets, so we shot at whatever was in front of us. My plane was hit by light flak on the first pass as I Destroyed two He 177s. The engine immediately started to lose power. A second pass in the opposite direction confirmed four planes burning, and I attracted a like amount of flak as I clobbered a third and fourth e/a. When I came to the end of the field, the airspeed was falling rapidly, and the engine came to a dead stop. No efforts would revive it.

Being too low to bail out, I had no choice but to set it down. There was only a very small field available between a village and a woods. It was very close to the airfield we had just shot up. I barely had enough speed to get over the trees at the edge of the Village, and I had to set it down quickly, almost in a stall. With the wheels up, the air scoop brought the plane to an abrupt stop, just short of the woods. I immediately called and said I was down safely. With a mob running towards me from the village, I took off into the woods, completely forgetting to destroy my radio.

I ran into the woods, away from the mob, about 100 yards; dumped my chute and dinghy; and ran at 90 degrees to my right for another 100 yards or so. I came to a small stream heading to my right back towards the Village. I ran in the stream towards the Village. When I came to the clearing next to the Village, I crawled into a clump of bushes and hid for several hours while the towns people searched for me in the direction in which they had last seen me fleeing. At dusk, they came back to the Village and eventually went to bed. After it was dark, when everything was quiet, including the numerous dogs, I crawled out of the bushes and headed northwest in the general direction of Denmark, my first destination on my planned course to Sweden."

*****

30 May - Effective 25 May the following Officers were assigned:

Capt. William F. Headrick
2nd Lt. Timothy J. Cronin
2nd Lt. David K. Needham

Mission: Major Goodson led a Free-Lance Sweep, Withdrawal Support, Targets: Various. In the Genthin area, 30-40 FW 190s and Me 109s were seen at 25,000 feet. They were covered by 20-25 FW 190s and Me 109s at 30,000 feet. The Group engaged the bottom e/a and were bounced by the top e/a. Combat ensued from 34,000 feet to the deck along the Elbe River. Lts. Sharp, Scott, Hofer, Jones, and LeJeunesse claimed eight Me 109s Destroyed. Flak at Wittenburg got one Mustang, which tumbled in flames to the deck.

Combat Reports: "I became separated in the engagement with 40 plus e/a. I dove to the deck and forced a FW 190 to crash-land southwest of Brandenburg. I was then joined by Lt. F.C. Jones of Caboose Squadron. From 6,000 feet, I observed four e/a landing in trail on an A/D to my left. There were 15 plus FW 190s on the Oschersleben A/D as we attacked. We made about five passes when

we were joined by Lt. Hofer. Since we were receiving no flak, we made three or four more passes.

On my first pass, one of the four FW 190s, located at the runway intersection, caught on fire and burned. I then set another FW 190 on fire on the south side of the field and damaged others that would not burn."

Thomas Sharp 2nd Lt., Air Corps.

*****

"I joined Lt. Sharp on the attack on the A/D. On my second pass, I hit one e/a that caught on fire and burned, giving off a large column of smoke. Several passes later, I hit another one that burst into flame. This one was later finished off by Lt. Hofer, who left it burning fiercely. I hit two others, but later discovered one that was lying on its back at the end of the runway."

F.C. Jones Lt., Air Corps.

*****

"I dove on the A/D that was already under attack by two P-51s. On my first pass, I Destroyed a FW 190 in the NE corner. On my second pass, I set one of those at the runway intersection on fire. I fired at several others scattered about the field, finishing off one started by Lt. Jones. I was surprised at not receiving any flak."

R.K. Hofer 2nd Lt., Air Corps.

*****

Casualties: 2nd Lt. Mark Kolter MIA. Lt. Kolter was last seen by Lt. Steppe, Lt. Kolter's #2, in the engagement SW of Brandenburg at about 1115 hours. At that time, Lt. Kolter said there was a Jerry

Major Willard W. Millikan, acting 336 Squadron CO 13 April 44 was an Ace with 15 e/a Destroyed before he bailed out near Wittenburg, Germany 30 May 44. His P-51 was disabled in a mid-air collision with Lt. Young while they were dodging enemy flak. Weckbacher collection.

on his tail. Red 4, who was following, said "No, it is Red 4." Lt. Kolter broke abruptly down to the deck and was lost in the haze. At 1355 hours, Lt. Kolter was heard to call for a homing. He was answered a number of times, but apparently was not receiving.

Capt. Millikan and Lt. Young were MIA. (Kolter was KIA, and Millikan and Young became POWs).

T-1000 Big explosion north of us. Doc Matyner called and said two a/c collided near the Towers. We sent out one crash truck and one ambulance. Later found out it was not an a/c, but that a British ammunition dump at Little Chesterfield had exploded.

T-1400 Group all down except Becky 51 and 62 who are unaccounted for. Cobweb 57 has not landed as yet, but he was heard on "A" Channel. His receiver was out, and he could not receive us.

T-1505 Cobweb 50, Lt. Callahan, airborne on local flight called in and said he was going to make an emergency landing on Airdrome beneath him, should he drop wing tanks? Told him yes, and to call us after landing.

T-1530 Lt. Callahan called and said he had landed OK and that he was at Paddington—Wants his Crew Chief to call him back.

T-1600 Have tried several times to call Lt. Callahan and have had no success. Apparently he gave us the wrong telephone number. Am waiting for him to call back.

T-1730 Have no information about Becky 51, 62, and Cobweb 57.

31 May - Mission: Free Lance and General Support, Targets: Various. The mission became scrambled, and Lt. Hofer split off and strafed an A/D, destroying 3 of 15 plus Bu 181s.

Lt. Patteeuw was heard on Channel "C"—"Look at that little friend go by in flames—Is that a little friend? I just clobbered him."

"A" flight was airborne at 1310 hours for an air-sea rescue search for Lt. Hofer, who had not been heard from since 950 hours. He returned to Debden at 1430 hours, but the party continued to search for Capt. McElroy and Lt. Homuth of 335 Squadron. The search party was unable to locate them and returned to base at 1535 hours. (It was later learned that Homuth was KIA and that McElroy was a POW).

T-1045 Lt. Callahan called in and said he was at Tuddenham. Wanted to talk to Capt. Gabrielson. Van Eck on the telephone "Paddington"?? Sometimes I wonder.

T-1245 All group back except Lt. Hofer, Cobweb 43 in QP-L, who was heard saying he was returning to base shortly after 1000 hours. No word from him since. Lt. Homuth, Caboose 34 in WD-G, also not back and no word on them. Lt. Lang, Cobweb 63 in QP-Z, landed at Marstan and will return shortly.

T-1300 Four Cobweb a/c are going out over the Channel to see if they can spot Lt. Hofer. Ops B says for them to stay on H and go over to B if they see anything. They will stay out as long as there is gas if they don't find him.

T-1420 Ops B called. They have Lt. Hofer on Channel B. He's OK. Squadron and Intelligence called and notified.

T-1428 Lt. Hofer landed OK. Spotters to continue looking for two Caboose boys.

T-1650 Crew Chief on Lt. Callahan's plane called from Tuddenham. Asked that Capt. Gabrielson be told to send the Fairchild down as Lt. Callahan is ready to return with the a/c. Capt Gabrielson's Office notified. Lt. Callahan landed at 1643. Fairchild airborne at 1706 to get Crew Chief.

7

We Turn On the Heat

1 June 1944 - All available personnel attended a training film on louse control in the station cinema at 0800 hours; all available Pilots saw the film at 1100 hours.

All available Pilots attended a map reading lecture given by Capt. Meade in the briefing room at 1700 hours. This was an orientation on the use of grid maps and pin-pointing observations on them while on future missions.

2 June - Major Blanding led a Type 16 Control mission to Paris area. No e/a action occurred.

This was the first operational mission with "G" suits.

T-1148 Becky 34, in VF-B, came in to land, bounced, and tipped far over on left wing; he made good recovery with no damage to ship and went around again. Landed OK at 1151. Later found out he scraped his wing tip slightly.

T-1149 Becky 36, in VF-H, had brakes lock on landing. Kept plane well under control and went off to left of runway and stopped between runway and 335 dispersal. Squadron informed. Apparently no damage to plane except blown tire.

3 June - All available Pilots met in the briefing room to hear Lt. Fred Glover, of the 336th fighter Squadron, tell of his recent experiences in getting out of France after being shot down late in April.

Col. James A. Clark, who had just returned from several weeks in the States, told of the ration and travel situation on the home front. He answered many questions concerning the conditions there.

4 June - Six EM were promoted as follows:
To Tech Sgt S/Sgt Marvi B. Odle
To Staff Sgt Sgt Robert G. Cretney, Sgt Carl E. Lang, Sgt Joseph P. Langlois
To Sgt Cpl Mario M. Ranelli Cpl Edward Shipkowski

Sgt. Robert A. Boyd was assigned to RAF Station Southend-on-Sea for a four-day course on instruction in maintenance of the K-14 Gun Sight.

Col. Clark led an Area Sweep in cojunction with heavies bombing military installations at Cap Gris Nez. There was no flak or e/a involved. Major Blanding then led an uneventful Withdrawal Support mission to Bourges.

T-1145 Someone has a transmitter open. Believe it's an a/c in Cobweb section as he was heard to say "Hello, Mac. I can't see you." The "Mac" is probably Major McPharlin-Red 1. The transmitter stayed on after that.

T-1237 Cobweb Red 4, Lt. Allen in QP-K, landed. He is the one with the open transmitter as Homer got his bearing coming in.

T-2010 FCO Castle Camp called to report that a Mustang had crashed at 1945 on Latchley's Farm about two miles SE of Castle Camp. It's on the Hempstead Road between Steeple Bumpstead and Helions Bumpstead. Their crash ambulance and the fire truck from Haverhill have gone to the scene. They will call us back as soon as they get any more information.

T-2015 Squadron called to report that Lt. Dupree, Becky 51, had seen Lt. Kakerback, Becky 45, dive into the deck and explode in VF-B: Capt. Carlsaskas? was notified. Capt. Toy has information on location. MO is being notified and MPs are sending guards out with Capt. Toy. Col. Blakeslee, Col. Clark, and Major Goodson can't be located at present. Castle Camp notified that a/c is ours. They will call us as soon as their ambulance returns. Capt. Toy notified.

(Lt. Kakerback was reported KIA).

T-2145 Police Saffron Waldon called to report that a Fighter a/c had crashed one mile west of Audley End. It could be ours, as

Lt. Ingals, Becky 60, in VF-P is up and supposed to stay within sight of the field, but he's an hour overdue. Notified Intelligence and Operations. Duty MO is getting an ambulance to go as police at Saffron thought it would be a good idea.

T-2150 Ajax called to report that Lt. Ingalls had landed at Sudbury. He got lost while returning to base. All concerned notified, but ambulance went to Audley End anyway because police wanted help.

T-2315 A/c that crashed near Audley End is from Duxford. Pilot injured but apparently not serious. Lt. Ingall's? body is not at our dispensary.

5 June - Col. Clark led a Type 16 Control mission to Lille area. They observed enemy activities but took no action. The Group did, however, report on seeing a large convoy in the patrol area.

Capt. Hively led the Group to attack the enemy convoys observed by Col. Clark's mission. Bombs were dropped on the convoys with fair results. Additional sightings were observed. The 336 and 335 Squadrons provided cover escort for the dive bombers of 334.

A P-51 showing the new "Invasion Stripes."

The 335 Squadron received an assignment of new Pilots.

They are: 1st Lt. Kolbe and 2nd Lts. Berry, Diamond, Harris, Little, and McCall, "a nice bunch of fellows."

T-1530 Group all down—Group Ops said not to let anyone go up for practice flying as maintenance wants to work on the planes.

T-1700 Sgt. Melsha washed the windows!! - Cheers!

At 1645 hours all available Pilots were called to the station cinema for a showing of a secret film concerning the proper bombing technique to be used on special targets.

As soon as all planes had returned from the day's missions, all planes were grounded. Shortly thereafter, Capt. Moore, engineering chief, ordered all mechanics to report to the hangar at 1730 hours. No one knew why.

An order had been received at 1500 hours to paint all planes with 18-inch bands as follows: five bands on each wing and five on the fuselage; alternating white and black. All operational planes were ready by 2400 hours. A comment was made that the same thing was done on the night preceding the Dieppe Raid. The armorers put in a night's work as they distributed two bombs alongside each kite. The night defense squads were put on guard all night.

That evening, Capt. Ezzell was Duty Intelligence Officer when, shortly after 2000 hours, Col. Blakeslee entered the office and announced that the invasion for which we have all waited so many months was under way. Preparations should immediately be made for our initial part. For security reasons, no one on the post was permitted to leave or to make any phone calls off the station, and all incoming calls were routed through Major Baldwin's Group Intelligence phone.

All Intelligence, Operations, and Weather Officers were summoned, and the general plan was explained. Work began immediately on the necessary plotting and map work for our show. At 2300

Lt. Charles W. DuPree on his first training flight with 336 Squadron witnessed one of his flight members dive into the deck and explode while over England. Konsler collection.

hours, all operational Pilots were briefed by Col. Blakeslee on the general invasion plan. The plan indicated that some missions would be flown by only one or two squadrons instead of always using the full Group.

Narrative: Osce R. Jones:" During the two weeks preceding the invasion, duties at the 4th Group were carried out in an atmosphere of intense expectancy. Many types of training, including night flying, dive bombing, and very precise exercises in navigation were performed. We knew the 'Big Show' wasn't far off.

In the morning we were called on a short escort show, but due to bad weather conditions the bombers were called back. On this show, we had seen a large convoy of Jerry trucks and tanks that covered about 10 miles of road. The Col. called Wing and asked for permission to take a few ships over and to raise a little hell with Jerry. At about 1400 hours eight kites loaded with 1,000 pounds of bombs took off to see what could be done to alter the situation. They obtained good results, but due to the size of the convoy, eight ships hardly scratched the surface of this mass of equipment. Without wasting time, they came back expecting to get the whole Group (48 ships) and go back and do the job up, but good. This is where the big hint came of the nearness of the invasion. Upon landing, they found that all the ships in the Group had been grounded and were in the hangars for something.

This sort of thing was pretty rare in our Group, so I decided to go take a look. My Crew Chief was the first man I saw there, so I asked him what was up. Taking me to the rear of the large building, he showed me my kite with its new war paint. It was a very striking sight, five alternating stripes of black and white around the fuselage, each wing, and the tail assembly. I then realized that something was definitely coming off. The painting job was to be finished by midnight at all costs; thus, giving the mechanics a little over eight hours to paint 16 ships. Everything came off as scheduled despite the short notice.

I was in the Club Tuesday night and, as usual, hit the hay about 2130. At about 2300 an orderly came in and told me that all Pilots were to report to the briefing room immediately. "This is it" was the first thing that entered my mind. Upon reaching the intelligence shack, this was confirmed. The usual map was covered with quite a few smaller maps, with boats, naval and army, and different sectors of the French coast laid out for each Fighter Group to cover. There were a few other maps of other details.

Col. Blakeslee was there, dressed in his flying clothes. When all was quiet, he came out with what we all expected. *"This is it, boys."* Briefing went on for nearly an hour, covering everything in the most minute detail. We were to take off at 0330 and go to the sector assigned to us and patrol until 0930 in the morning. We then saw that all our training had not been in vain. The weather wasn't what you'd call ideal; as a matter of fact, it was pretty sorry. Ceiling was about 3,000 feet, with an overcast of scud up to about 6,000.

I had expected to do a bit of night flying, but not night-cloud flying! The take-off was uneventful, but the beauty of it struck me.

1st Lt. Osce Jones (l) 335 Squadron was hit by flak over France and became a POW 7 June 1944. Capt. Ted E. Lines (r) 335 Squadron stands in front of his "Thunderbird." Lines finished his tour as an Ace with 10 victories to his credit. USAAF Picture

The sky was lit by flares for the bombers to form on, and for the red, green, and white lights of the fighters. Everywhere you looked, moving lights could be seen. It was now that I realized the tremendous effort that was being put forth to protect the landing parties, and protected they were."

*****

6 June - Col. Blakeslee led 334 and 335 Fighter Squadrons on a patrol east of Rouen at 0325 to 0940 hours. For the day's operations each Squadron was to operate individually, and there was not expected to be a total Group show. No e/a were seen, but Lt. Hofer went down and strafed two locomotives. At 0705 probably firing one of the first shots of the invasion. He incurred a flak hit in his wing tank.

Col. Clark led 336 on an uneventful first mission.

Casualties: 2nd Lt. Thomas Fraser, MIA. He was last seen entering clouds at 0430 hours. He was given a vector on "B" channel at 0642 hours, but did not acknowledge. He was never reported thereafter.

THE "BIG SHOW" IS ON "D-DAY"

T-0955 Group (334 and 335) all down except Cobweb 39, Lt. Fraser - Ops B says they had him on "B" channel and gave him one vector (340). Heard no more of him—Thought maybe he might have landed at Manston, so I called Manston. He wasn't there.

T-1125 334 Squadron airborne. One aircraft dropped a bomb while taxiing out—Everything OK. Call signs are "Horseback," "Cobweb."

T-1417 334 Squadron all back except Lt. Siems, Cobweb 56, in QP-O. He landed at New Romney. Reports that he has engine trouble. Capt. Markel going down to pick him up.

T-1504 All 335 Squadron returned and down OK.

T-1612 All 336 Squadron returned except Lt. Fredericks in VF-H, Becky 36, and Lt. Lejeunesse in VF-X, Becky 58. Squadron reports that Lt. Fredericks had landed in France. No report on Lt. Lejeunesse. Intelligence notified.

T-2010 Cobweb 31 called that he is landing at an advance base. He doesn't know where, but will call us when he has pancaked. Passed information to Squadron and Intelligence.

T-2030 Ajax called (Lt. Barnaby, Combat Ops) reporting that Lt. Snell, Cobweb 31 in QP-U, landed at Benson. He has mag trouble and reports that they can fix it. He will return in the morning. Informed Capt. Toy and Squadron.

T-2253 Col. Blakeslee, Horseback in WD-C, landed from operations. He made a good landing and rolled about 1,000 yards down the R/W. His wheels collapsed and his plane settled down on the R/W. Crash truck, ambulance, and wrecker were at scene immediately. Col. Blakeslee was uninjured.

T-2345 Seven A/C still unaccounted for: Major Sobanski, QP-J; Major McPharlin, 6N-Z; Lt. Steppe, QP-M; Capt. McGrattan, WD-D; Lt.Ross, WD-K; Lt. Walter Smith, WD-H; and Lt. Garby, WD-E. Report was that the four 335 Squadron a/c were jumped by a large number of Jerries and probably shot down. Major Sobanski reported to have bailed out. Major McPharlin had magneto trouble and turned back. No further word on him.

Captain Hively led the Squadron on a bombing mission with poor results. Further activity resulted in Lts. Simon, Fernandez, Scott, Monroe, and Siems destroying four FW 190s and damaging two donkey engines.

Lt. Siems' plane was hit by 20 mm. shells on the cowling and crankcase; his spark plug head was shot up; his front coolant and crankcase emptied. He landed at New Romney at 1345 hours. The

1st Lt. Grover C. Seims, Jr. 334 Squadron was severely wounded over Italy on a mission of the second leg of the Russia shuttle run. Believed to be dead, he was placed in the morgue but he managed to attract attention with a slight movement. He was rushed back to the hospital and revived. He was taken off flight duty and returned to the States 14 Sept 1944. Grover was an Ace with 7 plus e/a to his credit. Seims collection.

plane needed an engine change—Cat. AC. Capt. Markel ferried Lt. Siems back to base.

Col. Blakeslee led 334 and 335 Fighter Squadrons on a Patrol in the vicinity of Dreux at 1825 hours. Lt. Hofer, leading a section including McGrattan, who had finished his tour but wanted to fly one more mission in the big event, joined 335 Squadron on an attack on a 20-truck convoy northwest of Evreux. Fifteen plus FW 190s and Me 109s bounced them. Lt. Hofer had to take violent evasive action in order to get away, and he returned to base alone. Of Blue Section, only Hofer escaped.

Major Goodson led 336 on a Free Lance. Lt. LeJeunesse and Lt. Fredericks were hit by flak and bailed out over "no man's land." Trains, trucks, and bridges were attacked.

Casualties: Major Michael G. H. McPharlin (on DS with our Squadron from 339th Fighter Group) MIA. At about 2100 hours, the local controller heard Maj. McPharlin tell Maj. Sobanski that his left mag was out and his motor rough. He reported that he was turning back. Lt. Steppe filled in for him. Nothing further was heard from Maj. McPharlin.

Major Sobanski was heard to ask his #2, (Lt. Steppe) to come up and look his kite over as he had run into some wires on a train beat-up. At 2030 hours, Mike reported on the R/T that he was beating up another train. At 2035 hours, #2, presumably Lt. Steppe, was heard to say, "Watch those behind you, White Leader." This was ten minutes before 15 plus e/a bounced Lt. Hofer and Blue Section, 335 Fighter Squadron, in the area northwest of Evreaux. Nothing further was heard from Major Sobanski or Lt. Steppe.

Major Winslow M. Sobanski, MIA.

2nd Lt. Edward J. Steppe, MIA.

(Fredericks evaded and returned, Fraser and Lejeunesse became POWs, and Sobanski, McPharlin, Steppe, McGrattan, Ross, Smith, and Garbey were KIA).

The following Officers were assigned, effective 2 June.

2nd Lts. Clarence L. Boretsky

Carl F. Brown

Leon J. Cole Jr.

Robert A. Dickmeyer

Harry B. Noon

T/Sgt Raymond J. Clark was assigned to RAF Station Farnsborough, Hants, to pursue a course in K-14 Gun Sight Maintenance.

Narrative: At about 0700 hours, with all personnel glued to radios, the BBC announced that the German Overseas News Agency came through with the story that Allied landings had taken place in the Seine Estuary and, more specifically, Normandy. The spearhead of the invasion had been paratroop forces. This, of course, had to be accepted with reservation, it being the enemy's report.

At 1000 hours, the radio news mentioned that the Allied Supreme Headquarters had officially announced that landings did take place in the early hours of the morning. D-Day had finally arrived. About the same time, a teletype came in stating that 716 troop carrier planes had operated successfully with the loss of only 15 men.

Having seen the events with their own eyes, returning Pilots confirmed all reports we had heard.

After this show, the Pilots went to Mess for breakfast. In the meantime, Squadron Supply brought out some beds and blankets so that Pilots, in their spare moments, could catch up on a little sleep. Thermos jugs of coffee were also provided.

The Pilots did get a couple of hours of relaxation, but they were called to briefing at 1130 hours. Each Squadron was to go on a separate dive-bombing show. Two Sections were to carry bombs, and the third Section was to escort them. On this second show of D-Day the bombs were to be dropped on targets of opportunity. A marshaling yard and a bridge were bombed by 335 Squadron with good results.

After returning, the Pilots had another moment of relaxation prior to lunch and preparation for another mission. This mission took care of a radar station. They attacked a large convoy which, unfortunately, had some 20 mm flak guns, and they knew how to use them. The Squadron also shot up some R/R cars and locomotives. Blue Section, of 335 Squadron, had not returned by midnight, so it was assumed that they had been bounced by e/a. They had reported 15 FW 190s in the area. It was a serious loss to have these four experienced men missing. They were Capt. McGrattan, and Lt's. Smith, Ross, and Garbey.

At 0130 on the 7th, the Group was finally free to go to bed.

Crew Chief "Sy" Koenig commented, "The most devastating experience for a Crew Chief is the loss of 'His Pilot.' When you've worked with a Pilot for several months, it can be heartbreaking. Captain McGrattan was a real friend, a buddy, and a partner. He

had completed his tour plus an extension and was waiting for a transfer back to the States. When D-Day arrived, he asked to fly, and he flew on the second and third missions. I lost a dear, dear friend on that third mission!"

Grover Siems recalls: "I was assigned to fly on Mission #1. We were to protect the Battleship *Arizona* that was shelling targets inland for support of the invasion forces. We took off at approximately 0230 in a drizzling rain, climbed out among roughly 2,000 other kites and, fortunately, other than seeing exhaust flames, we didn't see or hit anyone.

It was quite a sight to watch the invasion forces coming across the Channel and to see the Battleship fire a broadside, slowly roll away, come back, and fire again. At our altitude, we could watch the rounds in flight and see the impact and explosion, although they were 15 odd miles away.

Later that same day, on Mission #2, I picked up a Me 109 and managed to do him in. As I crossed over a part of Paris, I received a hit in the right side of the engine and cooler. I managed to climb to 6,000 feet by the middle of the Channel, and I headed toward England. There was some fire and some oil on the windscreen, but with full rich fuel control I was able to keep it running until I saw the English coast.

I sure didn't want to ditch after losing some friends that way. When the engine quit, I was able to make a dead stick landing into a coastal field pasture. There was no real problem. I got the wheels down at the right time and made a reasonably good landing. They were able to truck the kite back to Debden and get it airworthy again. The Britishers were nice to me with food and drink, but I never saw them again. I got picked up by a vehicle and taken back to the 4th. It turned out that I had caught a 20 mm in the right bank valve cover and one cooler. The combination was right to allow my return without losing the engine."

Osce Jones: "We joined formation under the overcast and then started up through it. Not a hard task, but things had to be done just right or someone would get hurt. We broke out at 6,000 feet, and the Group reformed. Above the clouds there was a full moon; almost as bright as day. We turned out our lights and headed for France. In the middle of the Channel, I could plainly see the flashes of the big naval guns, but all else was covered and concealed by clouds.

The clouds covered everything at dawn, and they continued to do so the rest of the day. It was a very uneventful day for me even though I did fly two shows. I got in about 10 hours of flying time over France. Half of our Group was in our sector every hour of the day, and those that did venture below the clouds found only a few trains to shoot up. That night, the sixth, I really did get a bit of heavy sleep. I guess the tension of the day and ten hours in the cockpit had taken its share of my endurance."

G.I.Gillette: "I started on Ops the ninth of May in 334 Squadron, with only a couple of Pilots over the necessary 16. We maintained a heavy flying load so that by today I felt like an old-timer. Yesterday, on the first mission, we saw a convoy of trucks. We came back to load up with bombs and returned to work them over. We came back after dark, and found we had to get our planes painted with stripes that night.

We were up at 0300 today, and patrolled for twelve hours over the invasion area. By now, I was really impressed by Col Blakeslee. He was out to fight a war and to win that war. He had a way to do it, and the way to do it was always his way. It was proving successful, and I could feel all the other guys were really behind him. I was, too.

There were a lot of things going on as the days went by. The pressure kept building up. Although you didn't see yourself changing, you did see changes taking place in others. The Flight Surgeon kept a good eye on us and let us know when to ease off for a couple of days. You just had some liquor every night or generally beer and went to the lounge and let off some steam. Then you went to bed at a decent time and got some needed sleep, so you would be ready for the next mission."

Lt. Joseph Higgins: "Our mission was to keep the Luftwaffe planes from getting through to the landing beaches. On our crossing of the 100 miles of sea between England and France, we could see thousands of ships making the crossing in waves. These ships would be arriving all day long and landing wave after wave. It was indeed an extraordinary sight to behold.

After five hours of patrolling, we returned to Debden. We refueled, loaded two 500 pound bombs, and returned to Normandy. We bombed and strafed truck convoys. After more patrolling, we returned to Debden. The last planes landed at 2340 hours, 20 hours and 20 minutes after the first planes took off.

We lost ten planes on D-Day: seven of the Pilots were killed; two bailed out and became POWs; and one bailed out and evaded, returning to Allied lines."

Narrative: Staff Sgt. Earnest K. Workman: "I was a DF Homer operator. Our building was an eight-sided building off the base. Upon leaving the back gate going to Saffron Walden, the building was located on the right side of the road on the sharp curve about one-half mile from the gate. It appeared to be a farmer's silo. Part of the time we had a mobile DF stationed across the road from the back gate.

At the base all of us were awakened at 0430 on the 6th. We had been expecting D-Day for a long time. THIS WAS IT!

I was on the first shift with two other men. We were under radio silence for a long time after the Group took off. I was in the chair to operate the homing device. Right in front of me was a handle similar to an automobile steering wheel, attached horizontally to a shaft rising upward to a directional antenna. On the shaft, just above the handle, was a round disc. Above this disc was another disc with a 360 degree scale and an arrow located just over it which would point to the degree to be given to the Pilot in order to fly home. The radio signal comes in on two sides of the 360 degree disc. When the signal comes in, the operator pushes down on the other disc. If the signal becomes louder, it indicates a false bearing. If it becomes

dimmer, you have the correct bearing. The signals would be 180 degrees apart.

When Col. Blakeslee called for a homing, I gave the Captain in the Tower the bearing, noting to myself it was not what I thought it should be. The Captain stated to me that he had the same opinion. Blakeslee acknowledged and asked me to check again. While he was talking, I checked and it was only a few degrees from the first bearing. We asked him to give us other transmissions until he found a familiar landmark.

During these few minutes, I took a long look at my past because if I were wrong, I wouldn't have a future. When a Colonel questions a Staff Sergeant, that can happen.

Actually, the Group had been in a bad storm and had been blown off course while flying cover for the ships and bombers doing their job in the invasion of Normandy. As a consequence, their inbound course was several degrees off the anticipated course.

I had never met Blakeslee, but the way he led our Group, he certainly had my respect. We heard him tell the Captain to get all the names of the Homer Operators so he could give them a commendation for their performance.

The following Commendation addressed to me and 16 other operators, appeared in my hometown newspaper:"

"You and the other men in your Section have helped to return over 275 aircraft safely to this base. I speak for myself and every Pilot on the field when I say 'Damn good show.' I appreciate your work and know it has been difficult."

7 June - There was no mission this morning, so the Pilots had an opportunity to catch up on some badly needed sleep. Orders were received, effective 1 June, promoting Winslow M. Sobanski (MIA 6 June) from Captain to Major.

Three new Pilots were assigned to 335 Squadron, bringing their strength up to 33. They are Lts. Bowyer, Glynn, and Wadsworth.

At 1800 hours, Col. Blakeslee led a Fighter bombing mission to Pennes Area, armed with 500 pound bombs. A M/Y (marshaling yard), a factory, and a bridge were bombed with poor results. Capt. Hively had slight flak damage.

Major Goodson led 336 on a bombing mission with good results. Major Goodson was hit by flak and crash-landed at Marston. His kite was wiped out.

Casualties: Lt. Osce Jones was hit by flak, making it necessary to crash-land. He was seen to climb out of the plane uninjured and run for a nearby woods.

F/O Pierini and Lt. K.D. Smith collided in the air shortly after T/O. Pierini bailed out and Smith is NYR. (Smith was killed in the crash after the collision).

T-1130 Becky 51 had trouble landing. He made several approaches, but came in too high and too hot. Capt. Carlson talked to him over the R/T. After two more trips, he landed at 1142. Nothing wrong with the ship apparently.

T-1515 Col. Clatinoff passed us a message that Lt. Perini crashed near North Weald.

T-1600 Ops B called us about Lt. Pierini. Didn't know anything about Smith.

T-1640 Have called Chipping Omgar and North Weald. Lt. Perini is at North Weald. He bailed out of his plane. Lt. Smith crashed with his plane, which exploded and is still burning, so that they couldn't get to body yet. Capt. Matyner will contact Capt. Toy and arrange for somebody to go down.

T-1805 All Group returned except Lt. Pierini and Lt. Smith, K.B., who collided; Lt. Jones O.R., who crashed in France; and Major Goodson, who crash-landed at Bognor.

T-2035 Lt. Snell, Cobweb 31, landed from Benson. Captain Toy notified.

T-2036 AT-6 back from Marston with Major Goodson.

T-2045 Cessna back from North Weald with Lt. Pierini. Capt. Blackburn went to get him in the ambulance.

Narrative: Osce Jones recalls: "On the morning of 7 June, there was an early show. Not being on this one, I slept till about ten o'clock.

Lt. Donald J. Pierini 336 Squadron on one of his first combat missions collided with Lt. K.D. Smith while taking off and climbing through clouds. He parachuted near Debden. Konsler collection.

I knew I'd be on the one in the afternoon, so this was a good chance to catch up on my rest. We were engaged in ground strafing and dive bombing. The lineup was put on the board, and I was asked if I wanted to go on the show. Liking ground work better than aerial, I was eager to make this one, so I was listed to fly on Col. Blakeslee's wing. The Group was going intact to Loudeac. They then were to split up into three individual Squadrons, each taking a railroad north to the sea. Loudeac is in the center of the Brest Penninsula, and has three railroads leading north. The 335 was going due north on the center road.

We flew around for awhile and 336 Squadron bombed a few small bridges with no opposition. With us it was a little different. The clouds, about eight tenths, were too low to allow dive bombing. So we resorted to glide bombing. The cloud base was about 3,000 feet. As we approached Quintine, directly in front of us rose an umbrella of 20 mm flak that was thick as the devil. The Col. had Dean Hill and me on his wings. When he saw this, he called and told us this was our target, "get the R/R station and tracks." He also told the rest of the squadron to fly clear of the flak area.

Now, glide bombing lacks the advantages of dive bombing in a big way. You can't obtain the speed of the approach or get away, and you afford a better target for a longer time to the flak guns. However, this was the only avenue of approach left to us. I'll have to admit that when the Col. started on his bomb run, I was plenty scared. But there Hill and I stuck, right on his wing, as we went into the target at about 350.

I put my sight on the all important rail station and opened up with my four fifties. Just before I released my bombs, I felt a sickening thud in the nose of my ship and saw my glycol come pouring out. As the target passed under my nose, I released my bombs, and in panic, jettisoned my canopy. Pulling up, I saw that the Col. and Hill had gotten through alright, but I knew I'd have to bail out soon.

At this time, glycol was streaming back into the cockpit and into my eyes. I unbuckled my safety belt, took off my helmet, and prepared to leave my ship. I looked over the side and noticed the ground was flooded with Germans. I figured escape from there was next to impossible, so I settled down a bit. Had I flown south into southern France, chances were I'd have gotten out alright, but I took up on a heading to take me back home.

At this time I was flying about 700 feet from the ground and couldn't see any of the rest of the fellows anywhere around. I did notice that my ship was still running alright and was not beginning to get hot yet. A slight hope of getting home entered my mind, so I put my safety belt back on; retrieved my helmet from the floor; and started praying.

Another ship from the 335th passed at this time, and from the letters I recognized Brock. I called him and told him that "I'd Had it," and I asked him to escort me home. This he did, or I should say, to 'the end of the line,' for me. After about five minutes of flying, I noticed that my coolant temperature was getting a little high, and this didn't help my hopes of getting back. I was still flying a bit too low to bail out, so I resigned myself to making a forced landing when it became necessary.

My coolant temperature continued to rise. Finally, it passed the red line, and then it went off the dial. I was about ten miles south of St. Malo when the engine became pretty rough and started to steam. I saw a small cleared field below that couldn't have been more than a hundred yards wide and twice as long. This is where I headed. I called Brock and told him that I was going to set her down, and I told him to set her on fire as soon as I was clear.

I guess God was at the controls with me then. When I had dropped flaps and was on my approach leg, my air speed had dropped to eighty, and I was entirely too low. I threw the throttle wide open, and by the grace of God, I cleared the trees, or almost cleared the trees, at the edge of the field. I settled down, wheels up, in the middle of the field. I didn't slide fifty feet, and in this short field, I was only fifty feet from the far end. The trees that I clipped had lost their uppermost branches to my prop and wings. I don't know what kept me from nosing over when I hit them, but I came out unscratched.

We had always been told that in a case like this, get away from the wreck as soon and as far as possible. This I proceeded to do, but I got no farther than fifty yards when I heard Brock's guns barking. As I turned, I saw the ship on fire.

On all shows we carried a parachute, dinghy, and an escape kit. After about a hundred yards of running, I realized that I still had on my parachute, dinghy, and flying clothes, so I sat down and removed these. I was in the country and figured that the Germans couldn't be far off, but I had to get rid of this equipment.

Finding a levee that resembled a ditch levee at home, I sat in a corner of a field and took off all these impediments except my jacket. Thinking that the levee was as good a place as any for my parachute and dinghy, I threw the stuff over the hill. Later in the afternoon, I found that the levee was the side of a road, and I had thrown my gear in the most obvious place possible.

This left me in GI clothes, a worn flying jacket, with my escape kit, and a large hunting knife. Now, according to the best authorities, the best thing to do in a case like this is to find a good place to hide and stay put for two days till Jerry finished his search for you, so this I attempted to do.

I ran for a mile or so going southeast. I spotted a large orchard which was covered with weeds about two feet tall. It was now about four o'clock, and darkness didn't fall for another seven hours. I planned to hide in the middle of this field till I could take a good look around.

As far as I know, I was the only man lost on that show other than the two that had collided in the clouds over England. I found out later that one had parachuted to safety, but the other was killed in the crash that followed. In the morning show, McGrattan had taken a Section of four out, and none of them had been heard from since. Hill also was missing; they think he spun-out in a cloud over France somewhere.

To get back to the story, I went to a place in this weed field and covered, as best I could, the path I left in the grass. I dug myself a semi fox-hole. Using my hunting knife, I made a hole about four feet long, a foot deep and a foot and a half wide. Here I took out my escape kit. I found a couple of compasses, the maps, and my rubber water bag. Knowing my approximate position, I started making plans for a long walk to Spain."

Osce subsequently made contact with some French civilians who fed and sheltered him for a few days. Unfortunately, he was betrayed by one of them, captured by the Germans, and became a POW for the duration of the war.

8 June - The day started with a full station air-raid alert at 0015 hours; the all-clear sounded at 0052 hours.

Col. Clark led an uneventful Bomber Support mission to the Rennes Area at 0555 hours.

Col. Blakeslee led a Fighter Bombing mission to the vicinity north and east of Le Mans, armed with 500-pound bombs, at 1250 hours. Lts. Siems, Sharp, Hardy, and Callahan, and Capt. Joyce attacked a M/Y. They destroyed about 50 percent of the rolling stock, severed a main double track in three places, and damaged five sidings. Lts. Lang, Noon, Boretsky, and Fernandez attacked two bridges with good results. The planes of Lts. Scott and Allen collided in the vicinity of Le Mans at about 1430 hours.

Casualties: 2nd Lt. Eacott G. Allen, MIA

2nd Lt. James F. Scott, MIA

2nd Lt. Boretsky was flying Blue 2 to Lt. Scott in the vicinity east of Le Mans at 2,500 feet. At 1430 hours, Lt. Scott contacted Col. Blakeslee and received permission to bomb a road bridge on their port side. He saw Lt. Scott make a sharp diving turn to port towards the bridge. Lt. Allen apparently did not see Lt. Scott turn or could not turn out of the way quickly enough, and the two ships collided. Lt. Scott's tail was severed from the plane, and it went tumbling downward. Lt. Allen's plane continued forward at about a 30 degree glide with the prop wind-milling. Lt. Boretsky, while coming out of his turn, saw one chute. He does not think it could have been Lt. Scott.

T-1630 Group all back except Cobweb 30 and 32, Lt. Scott and Lt. Allen. R/T silence lifted on A channel.

T-1830 Cobweb Blue Section up on local formation flying lost Cobweb 39 (Blue 2), all landed except him. Cannot contact him on A. Asked Ops B to call him on other channels.

T-2033 Major Goodson instructed all Becky planes to return to base and land. No others up except Cobweb 34, Lt. Byrd. Have tried to contact him several times but got no answer.

T-2100 Ops B called and said Lt. Byrd, Cobweb 34 in QP-D, crashed near Leiston. Had very little information on it. Next, Leiston called. Crash was near Blax Hall. When Leiston's ambulance and crash truck arrived, the body was already gone. Plane apparently had exploded in the air. Ajax also called and gave about the same information. Later on, Framlingham called. The Pilot's body is at Framlingham base hospital. Framlingham has put a guard on the plane. They also thought plane exploded in air. Pilot's parachute was found unopened. All concerned have been notified, except Col. Swan and Major McCullough. We have been unable to locate them, but Lt. Boggiano is going to try to find them and tell them.

Lt. Byrd, in QP-D, was flying a local formation flight as #2 to Capt. Hively. He was seen to pull up. Repeated calls from flying control were not acknowledged, indicating his R/T may have been u/s.

The local controller received a phone call from an A/D at Leiston, saying that a red-nosed P-51 had crashed nearby at 1810 hours. Personnel who witnessed the accident stated that they heard a plane coming down as though in a steep dive and that the wreckage covered a large area, bearing out the statement that the plane exploded before reaching the ground. They reported the Pilot killed, and his body removed to a hospital at Framlingham. (Scott and Byrd were killed, and Allen evaded and returned later).

9 June - Effective 1 June, Benjamin Q. Ezzell is promoted from 1st Lt. to Captain. He is also designated Unit Censor (additional duty).

The Distinguished Flying Cross was awarded to 2nd Lt. Joseph L. Lang

An **Oak Leaf Cluster to the Distinguished Flying Cross** was awarded to:

2nd Lt. Ralph K. Hofer
Capt. William B. Smith
The following Officers were assigned:
2nd Lt. James T Byrd, Jr.
2nd Lt. Arthur C. Cwiklinski
1st Lt. Herbert VanderVate, Jr.
1st Lt. Earl C. Walsh
Captain Howard D. Hively is hereby appointed 334 Squadron Commander.

10 June - Col. Clark led a Group mission: Bomber Support to Morlaix at 0550 hours. Col. Clark, and Lts. Hills, Hofer, Dickmeyer, Fernandez, Sharp, Cole, Hardy, Monroe, Lane, Emerson, and Gillette combined to damage three locomotives and several boxcars, and to destroy an armored car and two gas trucks.

Lt. Conrad Netting hit trees near Evreaux and is listed as MIA.

Lt. Frank Caple landed somewhere on the French coast and is listed as MIA.

T-0725 Lt. Lang, Cobweb 63, in QP-Z, landed at Chipping Ongar with engine trouble.

T-1755 Ops B reported that Lt. Russell, Caboose 61, in WD-T, was making an emergency landing at Steeple Morden.

T-0800 Steeple Morden called that Lt. Russell landed OK.

T-1122 All Group back except two above (Russel and Lang) and Lt. Netting, Becky 61 in VF-S. No contact with him. Squadron reports one of their a/c was seen to go down.

Ten officers and twelve enlisted men stood at "Attention" at the Main Gate at 1125 hours and saluted in turn as the ambulance carrying the remains of 2nd Lt. James T. Byrd, Jr., passed slowly through the formation. The service was held in the Cambridge Cemetery at 1500 hours.

Col. Blakeslee led a mission: Indirect Support Type 16 Control; Rouen-Paris Area at 1245 hours. Capts. Hively, Headrick, and Joyce, and Lts. Boretsky, Sharp, Kenyon, Gillette, Callahan, Hills, Simon, Hardy, and Needham collectively strafed and damaged two locomotives, several box cars, and numerous motor targets.

T-1700 Group all returned except Lt. Caple, who crash-landed at LeTouquet according to Colgate. (He became a POW and Netting was KIA).

Major Goodson led a Fighter Bombing Mission with 250 lb. bombs. At 1835 they bombed a previously bombed M/Y at Argentan with very good results. They damaged 40 plus box cars and several locomotives. Some bombs were reported to have exploded before hitting the ground.

11 June - Col. Blakeslee led a Fighter Bomber attack, with 250 lb. bombs, to Bernay Area. Bombing and strafing destroyed 20 plus rail cars, six vehicles, and a R.R. bridge. Captain Joyce and Lts. Brown, Siems, Hofer, Monroe, Dickmeyer, Callahan, and Cole, took part in this destruction.

Lt. Fernandez landed Beachy Head. The prop of his plane was hit by a 30 calibre bullet. He stayed at this station overnight.

T-1032 All Group back except Lt. Fernandez. Ops B thinks he landed at Chailey. Am trying to check on that now.

T-1115 Chailey says no Mustangs have landed there. Ops B called a few minutes later and said Lt. Fernandez landed at Deanland. Has a damaged prop but they can fix it. He will return here. Captain Toy notified.

Col. Clark led a second Fighter Bombing attack near Villedieu-les-Poeles where they bombed and strafed a convoy of 70 plus trucks near Vire. They destroyed 37 trucks and cars in the engagement. This was accomplished by Capt. Hively, and Lts. Boretsky, Siems, Noon, Hofer, Dickmeyer, Sharp, Kenyon, and Cole.

Casualties: Lt. Ralph K. Hofer reported to have landed on Allied Beachhead.

Lt. Leon J. Cole, Jr. MIA

Lt. Harry B. Noon MIA
(Both were KIA).

Narrative: Lt. Hofer - At about 1330 hours, Lt. Hofer's oil system was damaged by small calibre fire. Hofer knew he would be unable to bring his plane home, so he set course for one of the landing strips that the Allies had built on the Beachhead. He reported on the R/T, but it is not known whether he landed wheels up or down because his landing was not witnessed by anyone in the Group. Lt. Hofer thereby earned himself the distinction of being the first man of the 4th Fighter Group to land on the Allied Beachhead.

Lt. Cole - At about 1330 hours, Capt. Hedrick noticed 2nd Lt. Leon J. Cole, Jr., hit the ground in his plane while strafing ground targets. Lt. Cole was able to gain a little altitude, but his plane was pouring black smoke. Capt. Hedrick reduced his speed with the intention of escorting Lt. Cole home when he noticed a bright flash behind him. While orbitting to investigate the flash, he could not locate Lt. Cole, but saw something burning at the edge of a creek. He flew low over the fire. It was his opinion that Lt. Cole's plane had exploded in the air and finally settled to the earth on the edge of the creek.

Lt. Noon: At about 1330 hours, northeast of Villedieu-les-Poeles, France, Lt. Siems saw Lt. Harry B. Noon hit some trees while attacking ground targets. After hitting the trees, his ship flicked several times; turned over on its back; hit the ground; skidded a short distance; and exploded. The ship was carrying two 250 lb. bombs at the time. Lt. Siems made two passes over the wreck to take pictures of it.

T-1530 All down except Cobweb 43, Lt. Hofer, who, according to the Squadron, landed on beach. Also Cobweb 51, Lt. Noon, and Cobweb 52, Lt. Cole - The Squadron also says one other Cobweb a/c was seen going into the deck. Still one unaccounted for.

T-1900 Lt. Fernandez called again. Told him what Capt. Toy said, "No one available." Fernandez said he was hit through the prop, and he thought some glycol leaked out. Thought he might need a new prop. Otherwise OK.

T-2130 Saffron Walden operator passed us a message that Lt. Fernandez will come up in jeep in the morning.

12 June - Lt. Fernandez, who landed at Deanland, 11 June 1944, returned to base in a jeep at 1400 hours.

Lt. Hofer, the first Pilot from this Group to make use of an emergency landing strip on the Allied beachhead near Grandcamp, France, returned today. He was flown from the strip to Grove, Berks, where he was picked up by Capt. Markel and flown back to base.

He had quite an interesting experience having had his oil system damaged by small calibre fire while strafing near Vire, France. The resultant loss of oil made it necessary for him to land. At 1410

Lt. Ralph Kidd Hofer # 78, 334 Squadron awes the onlookers and Lt. Ezzell, in doorway. Ralph was a swashbuckling Ace with 30 plus credits. He was aggressive and unpredictable. He was KIA near Budapest when he encountered overwhelming odds. Lt. Ezzell was duty Intelligence Officer when Col. Blakeslee announced the invasion. He coordinated security, map work, etc for the invasion. He was also Unit Censor. Air Force collection.

hours 11 June, he made a wheels down landing on the emergency strip. Shortly after landing, he was introduced to General Ralph Royce, of the 9th Air Force, who tried to arrange air transportation back for Lt. Hofer and several other stranded Pilots. Due to weather conditions, it was impossible.

Lt. Hofer and some others were given rifles, helmets, and a jeep. They took a tour up to the front lines about ten miles from the shore. The area had been heavily mined by the Germans, but paths had been cleared by Allied sappers. After a substantial supper, a medical officer prepared a concoction of alcohol and grapefruit for the visitors, which contributed greatly to a good sleep. Lt. Hofer slept in a large hospital tent and reported all was quiet for the night. He witnessed no enemy air activity while there, but the Allied navies kept up a lively fire directed at heavy German installations inshore.

Being a souvenir collector from way back, Lt. Hofer returned with a very smelly Jerry helmet, a canteen, and a German edition of Mein Kampf which was somewhat overdue at a library in the Reich.

When he returned, Lt. Hofer had the pleasure of recounting his experience to Mr. Robert A. Lovett, Assistant Secretary of War for Air, General Kepner of Eighth Fighter Command, and General Auton of the 65 Fighter Wing, all of whom were visiting our field at the time.

T-1117 Lt. Chapman in "VF-Q" landing from a local formation flight bounced and stalled out. His left wing just missed the ground. As he made the recovery, his prop hit the R/W. The plane rolled on down towards the intersection and stopped - Pilot Ok. Plane not damaged badly except bent prop - All concerned notified.

T-1615 Lt. Hofer back from the beachhead. AT-6 went to Grove to get him. No report on his a/c QP-L. Squadron had two QP-L ships.

T-1727 A/c that Lt. Fernandez landed at Deanland returned to base. Lt. Fernandez came back this morning. It's also QP-L.

13 June - At about 1500 hours, Capt. Hively, the Squadron C.O., called all Pilots together. He explained to them that he wanted them to go to their planes at once where the crew chief and armorer would explain to them in detail how to refuel and rearm their ships and how to pull daily inspections.

After this demonstration, a team of four was selected from each flight, and a contest was held to determine which could rearm quickest. The "B" flight team finished first, but they had more mistakes than the "A" flight team, so the contest was considered a tie. The prize, a bottle of whiskey put up by Capt. Hively, was split among the eight pilots.

Such extraordinary procedure naturally gave rise to many questions and appeared to substantiate the current rumor that this Group

Captain Joe Patteeuw of 336 Squadron completed a tour on 10 Nov 1944. He is shown with his Crew Chief Sgt Garrison. Charles Konsler Collection

was soon to be employed on long range bomber escort shuttle flights. The location of the other terminal was a matter of conjecture, but Russia seemed to be favored over Italy. "We shall see."

Col. Blakeslee led the Group on a mission of Indirect Support of B-26s over a target east of Dombront. A convoy was sighted near Pretteville and strafed. They Destroyed nine trucks and damaged three. Those who participated were Lts. Hofer, Sharp, Hardy, Needham, Brown, and Gillette. Meanwhile, Red Section of 336, led by Lt. Patteeuw, destroyed five trucks in a convoy.

14 June - The **Distinguished Flying Cross** was awarded to:
2nd Lt. Howard N. Moulton
2nd Lt. Leonard Pierce
An **Oak Leaf Cluster to the Distinguished Flying Cross** was awarded to:
Captain Herbert J. Blanchfield

T-1700 Lt. Campbell in T/Bolt 6258 blew two tires while landing at Boxted - They are fixing the tires, and he will come back - "I Hope."

15 June -The following Officers were assigned:
1st Lt. Leonard P. Werner
2nd Lts. Norman W. Achen
James W. Ayers
Lynd J. Cox
C. G. Howard
Jack D. Mc Fadden
Victor R. T. Rentschler
John J. Scally

Cpl Ralph H. Thomson was assigned to Station 520 to pursue a one-week course in Bomb Reconnaissance.

Major Donald R. Carlson was designated Squadron Operations Officer.

Major Goodson led a Penetration, Target, and Withdrawal Support mission to Nantes. No e/a were sighted.

The secret plans that were underway for the special activities of this Group made necessary the restriction to the post of all military personnel until further notice. While these plans had not been revealed to all, those who were to be directly affected were advised. Those Pilots and EM who were to make the special trip were briefed by Col. Blakeslee this afternoon.

The briefing disclosed that 17 planes from each Squadron of this Group and 17 from the 352 Fighter Group, all led by Col. Blakeslee, were to escort a number of heavy bombers to American bases in Russia from which points they would carry out some missions in conjunction with the Russians.

Shortly after 1800 hours, Major Baldwin of Group Intelligence and W/O Nassef of Group Engineering, accompanied by 33 EM, left by truck for various heavy bomber stations from which points they were to take off.

The following 11 men from 334 Squadron were specially selected for the trip because of their technical knowledge and abilities. Upon them would rest complete responsibility for the maintenance of the 17 planes from 334 Squadron which were to make the trip.

M/Sgt Riddle (In Charge)	Engineering
T/Sgt Kehrer	
T/Sgt Wall	
S/Sgt Allen	
S/Sgt Andra	
S/Sgt Fox	
S/Sgt Kosmoski	
S/Sgt Waydak	(All) Engineering
T/Sgt Ramey	Armament
Cpl Roen	Aramament
M/Sgt Coady	Communications

The Group Intelligence Office this afternoon was the scene of great activity as complete files of European maps were prepared by intelligence officers and clerks. Work continued until nearly midnight when word was received that take-off was postponed for 24 hours.

T-1100 Operations brought over a teletype saying that the Alert A/C will continue to stand-by at their dispersals, but will not taxi up to watch office as they have been doing mornings and nights.

16 June - Trip postponed.

T-1900 Sgt. Bell called from Operations to advise that Operations order 86 regarding Alert A/C has been canceled. Squadrons have been notified.

17 June - Eleven of the EM scheduled for the trip returned.

Ira E. Grounds and Joseph Higgins are promoted from 2nd Lt. to 1st Lt.

T-1600 Major Goodson is going to Cranwell and may not be returning until late. Says he may need a homing about eleven o'clock.

T-1630 Major Goodson called from Cranwell. He says that he has blown a tail wheel tire. The AT-6 with Lt. Emerson is going up to fix it.

T-2345 I&R stood down and crews released. We are getting "Pistol Packing Mama" loud and clear over Channel "A." It just started. I&R doesn't know where it's coming from. Neither does the Tower.

T-0010 Mystery is solved! Music coming from Communications.

18 June - After a Squadron Balboa, Lts. Brioc and Morse, while waiting for photograph material of the Russian Mission, shot several hundred feet of 35 mm film, portraying the life of a Fighter Pilot. This film was taken for our Squadron record.

Col. Blakeslee led a Fighter Sweep in the area of Combourg where 334 flew top cover, while 335 and 336 beat up a horse drawn convoy.

T-1325 Capt. Helbig called asking us to drain all the wing tanks from Lt. Bodney's Mustang - We are starting the job. The 334 is sending their truck to help as they want the job done right away.

T-2228 Caboose 45, Lt. Bowyer, in WD-O landed after we had homed him. He asked for an emergency landing. He was given permission to land immediately. He made a good landing and asked for an ambulance to meet him. He taxied up by the watch office and an ambulance met him. The Pilot was helped out of the plane as he had a bullet wound in his arm. The duty MO and another ambulance was sent up immediately.

T-2300 Becky 34, Lt. Pierini, in UF-D nosed over near the intersection after landing. It was too dark to see just what happened, but he may have braked it too much or a brake could have locked. The R/W was soon clear, and the Group continued to land.

T-2315 Becky 60, Lt. Ingalls, in VF-P, crashed on landing. I had given him permission to land at 2305, but Cobweb leader told him to stay clear while Cobweb Squadron landed. Nothing was said about shortage of gasoline, so Cobweb Squadron landed. Becky 60 called in about 2313 and said that he had only 5 gallons left in each tank so I told him to land immediately. However, he couldn't complete his circuit and came in north to south. He came in very high, and I told him to drop all his flaps. He touched down near the south end and continued on through the fence, across the road, and past the blister area. He ended up in an open field. The crash crew and ambulance were there immediately. The pilot was OK. Some of our crash crew men stayed with the plane until I contacted the guard house. They are sending men out to guard it the remainder of the night.

T-2320 Caboose 44, Lt. Godwin, in WD-H, nosed over after landing. He made a good landing and rolled up near the east end. He started to turn off the runway, and the a/c went up on its nose and then settled back on its tail. He must have used too much brake as the plane had practically stopped rolling. The crash crew and ambulance were there. The pilot was OK. The runway was soon clear.

T-2330 The Group is all back except Becky 62, Lt. Arnold; Caboose 36, Lt. Little; and Caboose 64, Lt. Glynn. The latter was seen to bail out, and the others probably landed on the beach. (Arnold was KIA, Little became a POW, and Glynn evaded).

19 June - Capt. Hively led the group on a Bomber Escort mission which was aborted.

Major Donald R. Carlson was assigned effective this date.

T-0800 A/C returning with full drop tanks are to land on long R/W per Col. Blakeslee's orders.

T-0815 A/C are not to cross the new balloon area below 8,000 feet even though the balloons are lower. They will be fired on by A/A if they do. Present give references on WQ 8372, WQ 8577, WR 0790, WR 0991, WR 1281, WR 0479.

T-1012 All Group back except Lt. Hill, Caboose 58, in WD-F. Lt. Lines advises that Hill was flying #2 to him. Lines lost him in a cloud over France and couldn't contact him after that. He may have spun in. Those concerned notified. (Hill was KIA).

T-2210 P-51D-413534 - A new delivery from Warton, pilot Lt. Lohr came through a red flare and made a belly-landing on the R/W, flaps down and wheels up. He got right out of the a/c. Crash crew and ambulance were immediately at the scene. Duty MO was called and came right down. Pilot is OK. Called Capt. Toy and Intelligence. Couldn't locate Col. Swan. Pilot stated in the watch office that he had his head down in the cockpit checking and didn't see the flare. When he gave it the throttle, it was too late. The landing gear handle was in the up position when the pilot got out of the plane. Called Warta and reported to operations at Ferry Command.

20 June - Col. Clark led a Penetration, Target, and Withdrawal Support mission to Politz.

Insufficient time was allowed to get planes operational for this mission. Consequently, several planes did not catch up to the Group. Fighting occurred in the air, and an airdrome was attacked. Lts. Dickmeyer, Monroe, Gillette, Malmsten, Cwiklinski, and Capt. Joyce claimed e/a Destroyed in the air. Lt. Gillette Destroyed a JU-88 on the ground. Capt. Stanford and F/O Godwin, of 335, shared the destruction of a Me 210. Lt. Emerson observed a FW 190 pilot bail out without being hit. Jones, Clark, Cooley, Shilke, Glass, and Harris added six more destroyed, bringing the total to 15 for the day. Major Goodson was hit by flak at Neubrandenburg A/D. He crash-landed and walked slowly away from the kite.

Combat Report: "I was flying Red 3 near Politz when we sighted about 50 T/E e/a at 3 o'clock low to us. We dropped tanks and dove to attack. As I dove, a Me 109 made a pass at me from overhead. As I turned into him, he made a 90 degree deflection shot and hit my starboard wing tank with a 20 mm. As he passed beneath me, I

Lt. George W. Cooley 335 Squadron completed his tour 20 Nov 1944. After successfully bailing out near Liege Belgium on 11 Sept 1944, he returned to his Squadron on 15 Sept.

reversed my turn and started to close on him. I gave him a two-second burst at 30 degrees deflection at about 200 yards, and he went into a diving turn. I noticed pieces of canopy or cowling flying off.

At this point, a P-51 crossed beneath me with a Me 109 on his tail. I broke right. Catching the e/a in my sight, I gave him a short burst and continued to fire as I followed him. I observed strikes around his wing root and cockpit. I broke off and started climbing back up to rejoin our formation. I saw a fully opened chute below me, but I did not actually see either of the Jerry Pilots bail out. I claim two Me 109s Damaged."

George W. Cooley 2nd Lt. Air Corps

(It was subsequently verified by camera film that the first Pilot attacked had actually bailed out, and Cooley was given a confirmed Destroyed.)

*****

"I was flying Caboose Red Leader when we dove to attack 50 plus Me 210s. When we reached their level, we found they had 12 plus Me 109s as cover about 1,000 feet above. I came up behind four of them flying line abreast. I took a burst at the first from dead astern but saw no hits. As I came closer, I tried a small deflection on the second one but could not hit him. I pulled over to number three, but could not hit him, either; the same on number four. I kept my speed up so I could pull up since I was alone. They broke after I fired on number four and went in four different directions. I picked out one that was making a climbing turn and fired, but was not hitting him at first so I pulled more deflection. I hit him in the engine and around the wingroot on the right side. A huge column of smoke came out, almost obscuring the plane. The Pilot jettisoned his canopy, rolled his plane over, and bailed out. His chute opened."

Frank Jones Captain, Air Corps.

*****

"I was flying Caboose Blue 2 when a Me 210 came through the formation. I gave chase with Capt. Sanford close behind. The 210 went through a box of bombers without doing any damage. I closed on him and fired observing strikes in the cockpit area, wings, and engine. I broke away as glycol streamed from the starboard side, and Capt. Stanford closed in. I observed many strikes in the cockpit area as Capt. Stanford broke away and I closed again. The Pilot had released his canopy, and his starboard engine was in flames. He attempted to crash-land, but flicked over at about 100 feet and went in inverted. The a/c exploded and burned.

I claim this Me 210 Destroyed, shared with Capt. Stanford."

Lester Godwin F/O, Air Corps.

*****

T-1230 Group all back except Becky 30, Major Goodson reported to have landed on the beach, and Caboose 55, Lt. Harris, who is unaccounted for. Caboose 67, Lt. Cooley landed at Leiston. (Both Harris and Goodson became POWs).

T-1248 Caboose 38, Lt. Ceglarski, in WD-V, up on a local flight came in for a landing. His approach was too low and his undercarriage caught in the fence. He came on in and made a good landing. Wire is wrapped around wheels and air scoop. The right tire blew out, and the air scoop is damaged. Pilot OK. All concerned notified.

T-1515 Smoke was seen coming from around the gun post near 334 dispersal.

The nine EM who returned from their bomber base 17 June left again from this base at 1400 hours.

This evening the field order was finally received to proceed with the big and the long awaited escort shuttle mission to Russia.

All evening and through the night up until take off time there was considerable excitement and much work involved in preparing final course maps for this history making event. The Group Intelli-gence Office was the scene of action, and all Officers and Enlisted personnel of the Group and Squadron Intelligence departments were on hand. A Signal Corps moving picture unit was present setting up equipment so that the briefing might be recorded on celluloid.

As the hour grew late, coffee and sandwiches from the Officers' Mess stiffened drooping eyelids and weary knees and enabled the work to continue.

As is normal, there had been rumors galore about this impending event. They began to take on reality when several days before, the Medics began inoculating Pilots and certain Crew Chiefs with Typhus and other exotic shots.

Hofer, the boxing champ who thought it was sport to attack flak towers and slip off alone on private missions over enemy territory, refused to take his shots.

Blakeslee gave it to Hofer where it hurt most. He made Hofer fly #4 position where there was little chance to bounce the Jerries, and he also barred Hofer from participating in the upcoming secret mission. Blakeslee then barred him from the bar for two weeks.

At this point, Virginia Irwin, a personable reporter, arrived to do a feature story on Hofer, "The last of the screwball Pilots." Hofer, unable to escort her into the bar, suggested that she quench her thirst with the other boys, to which she agreed, promising to return in a "Couple of pints." After she returned and interviewed him, Hofer finally had enough. He went to Deacon Hively, the Squadron CO, and promised to take his shots if they would allow him to resume his bar privileges and to go on the secret mission.

21 June - Col. Blakeslee led the Group on the long awaited and historic Escort Shuttle Mission to American bases in Russia. Bomber target: Ruhland. Pilots were not to return for an indefinite time.

T-0030 Purple Alert - Wing called that enemy plot is nearing base and should call this a Red Alert. CQ at Hq and defense switchboard notified. Q Site also notified.

T-0045 Plots turning south toward London.

T-0107 All clear.

T-1015 Ops B say that "Spouse" is in effect now instead of "Fickle."

T-1645 Big explosion west of Wing disposal in line with Watch Office. Cloud of smoke covered west end of the field. Crash truck and Ambulance sent - Called Fire Dept., Duty MO, and Defense Board. Little Walden called and offered to send us help if we needed it.

T-1655 Found out it's a Chemical Warfare Demonstration. We surely should be warned in advance of things like this!! Capt. Brillan and Major Booth said they would see about it.

Supplement: From 21 June to 5 July, 49 Pilots of the 4th Group and 16 Pilots of the 352nd Group plus 33 EM from the 4th were on a shuttle mission from England to Russia to Italy to England. During this period, there were no direct communications from this Group to Debden. Consequently, entries in the narrative, under the heading SUPP:, between 21 June and 5 July, have been added upon the return of the Group from this mission.

At the beginning of this mission, Nazi attention was diverted by sending 1,000 bombers over Berlin. Three 16-plane Squadrons from the 4th Group and one from the 352nd were to provide escort for 104 heavy bombers that were to hit German targets between England and Russia. Combining forces this way was all for "show." It was to show the Germans who ruled the sky, and to show the Germans we could hit them at random from three different sides at once.

Only 48 of the 4th's 125 qualified Pilots were chosen for this special mission. To service the Mustangs at foreign bases, crew chiefs and mechanics were chosen to go along. They flew as gunners on the B-17s. Major "Deacon" Hively, 334 Squadron CO, remarked, "that of the 125 guys available, 126 were chomping at the bit to risk their lives on this damned difficult and dangerous do."

On the first leg of the shuttle, the Huns attacked the bombers and Goodson's crew chief, Bob Gilbert, was forced to bail out. He was to spend over a month fighting the Germans with Polish/Russian guerrillas before making it back to Debden. Pilot Frank Sibbett was killed when his P-51 was hit by flak.

The Group took off at 0805 hours and, despite solid cloud cover half way to Berlin, Col. Blakeslee led the Group to the R/V at Lezno, Poland, on time at 1113 hours with three Combat Wings of B-17s of the 3rd Bomb Division. Shortly thereafter, near Siedlce, Poland, the Fighters dropped their wing tanks to intercept 25 Me 109s making a head-on attack on the Bombers. The 4th Group claimed two Destroyed and three Damaged. The score could have been higher, but the Group could not pursue due to the necessity to conserve gas.

Although the Fighters were running low on gas, they were able to escort the Bombers beyond the Russian front lines. Due to excellent navigation on the part of Col. Blakeslee, they arrived at Piryatin, their designated Russian base. The actual escort distance of 580 miles was the longest on record. They landed safely at 1450 hours after being airborne seven hours and fifteen minutes. Lt. Hofer was the only one missing. He had been off on a show of his own and had been forced to land at Kiev due to insufficient fuel. A teletype was received at Debden trying to confirm the markings on Kid Hofer's kite in order to confirm that he was indeed a U.S. Pilot.

The Bombers, with the 4th Group ground crews aboard, landed at other bases.

The accomodations in Russia were crude, but their hosts were cordial, and vodka was plentiful.

Following interrogation, refreshments, and assignment to tents, sleep was in order. The Germans, however, did not cooperate, and the resultant ack ack (anti aircraft fire) woke everyone, and the slit trenches filled rapidly. Deacon Hively, on a call of nature, was summarily interrupted, and Grover Siems, unable to unzip his sleeping bag, hopped about as in a sack race. He was trying to reach the nearest slit trench, as Lt. Simon, clad only in shorts, shouted for his steel helmet.

Narrative: Grover Siems relates, "We had a mission briefing and were told that we were to escort some bombers to Russia. It was a shock, but we were eager because we wanted to be part of something that big even if we had no idea of how it would end. After weather delays, we took off. I was flying number three to Squadron Commander Deacon Hively as he liked my keen eyesight. Everyone had been ready for a week, and we were very excited.

There was much concern over baggage and the briefing on what we were to experience upon arrival in Russia. Baggage had to contain a set of class A's, toilet paper, and soap. These items were not readily available in Russia.

The first part of the trip was routine even though we had extra kites. This changed when we got to Frankfurt. Since there were so many of us, the Germans anticipated we were going to bomb hell out of them. They put up all the smoke they had and a lot of very accurate flak. It didn't look like it would be possible to fly through the wall of smoke and flak, but we managed it with very little damage. Unfortunately, I got a close burst that killed the engine, put some holes in the skin, and bounced me around somewhat. I became very excited, and called Deacon to advise him that I would be bailing out. After losing ten years of my growth, the engine caught and we continued on to Russia. As we passed through the last of the flak curtain, Horseback, Col. Blakeslee, came on the R/T to tell us that we shouldn't see any more flak for quite a while—he hoped.

As we passed through Poland, we met a very impressive formation of yellow-nosed Me 109s. We outnumbered them ten to one, so we had no problems.

Seven and one half hours after leaving England, we were landing at a grass field at Piryatin. There were so many flares of different colors that it looked more like the 4th of July than just signal flares. Most of us required physical help to get out of the cockpit; our legs just wouldn't work properly. There were some Americans and some American equipment, Jeeps and what not, that had preceded us, so it wasn't too bad. They had tents ready so we got set up.

After eating and talking, we sacked out in our sleeping bags, only to be awakened at 1130 hours by the God awful sound of anti-aircraft fire. As we regained our senses, we saw chandelier flares hanging over the whole area. It seemed like every Russian had a gun and was trying to put out the flares before they disclosed too much. My sleeping bag zipper jammed, and I did a great potato sack race to a slit trench. Some were sorry that they had previously used the slit trenches as latrines. Although frightened and shook up, we didn't suffer any damage. They did, however, do a job on the bomber fields, and we lost some kites.

Subsequently, we found out that a Ju 88 with high altitude capability had followed us and knew where we had landed. The Russian P-39s, sent to intercept, were unable to reach that altitude."

"Mike"(Gilbert W.) Hunt recalls: "About 1500 hours, we were rolled out of bed and with little ceremony we were briefed and made ready to take off. The timing could have been a lot better. I had successfully defended my un-official title as champion beer/ ale/stout drinker of the Squadron (if not the Group) several times before, but I managed to outdo myself last night, up until about an hour and a half before the wake-up call. There hadn't seemed to be anything special in the offing, and the boys were in the mood for a real "slosh-up." The briefing revealed that we were to escort bombers 2200 miles over enemy territory and into Russia where shuttle-bombing bases had been set up for us. Even without a flight computer, I knew this was going to be a very long day, especially considering the meager creature comforts provided by a P-51 cockpit. I'm sure my buddies had the same apprehension, but with the excitement of being on such a historic mission, it became secondary.

It seems time and experience had demonstrated that, for some combination of physical and psychological factors, I found it nearly impossible to use the relief tube (pee-tube to the Pilots). This is a sort of funnel and tubing arrangement tucked under the seat designed to help equalize the flying range of the P-51 and its Pilot. (They added wing tanks to the P-51 but did nothing to increase bladder size.)

I couldn't help but remember an engineering evaluation flight on which I had identified this unique problem. I was to fly for two hours at each of three high altitudes to observe engine performance using a new 100 octane that was starting to be furnished. After about three hours into that mission, I had begun to feel mild bladder pressure. I thought, I don't have a wingman so I don't need to be concerned about him having to try to fly formation 15 feet away from me as my flight becomes erratic while trying to maneuver the necessary components into position for consumation of the desired objective. It ought to be a piece of cake this time. With that mental pep-talk, and those low stress conditions, unbelievably, I still was unable to achieve even the slightest relief. Facing a stressful seven hour mission, knowing all these things, and after a multiple pint intake, I contemplated the flight with the utmost of apprehension.

The mission sounded boring during the briefing, but it turned out to be anything but. We escorted a diversionary Group of bombers over Berlin and then diverted toward Poland with the rest of the Shuttle Group. Somewhere south of Poznan, some FW 190s showed up. They, apparently, did not expect fighter escort and decided not to hang around. So, we continued on our way to the general area of Kiev in the Ukraine. After the first three hours in the air, I was feeling major discomfort and attempts to use the relief tube had been miserable failures. Somewhere over Poland, the discomfort

escalated into pain. By the time our welcoming escort of Russian P-39s appeared, I felt I was on the point of explosion.

When we arrived at the A/D at Piryatin, we found the runway to be made of perforated metal strips that had been made some months earlier in anticipation of our arrival. During the spring, lush grass had grown up through the holes in the metal matting. The first P-51s to land had turned the runway into a skating rink of slick green grass. Somehow, I managed to fight off a skidding ground-loop and stop at a designated parking spot. With a single thought in mind, I burst out of the restraint straps, slammed open the canopy, and bounded to the leading edge of the wing before the prop stopped turning. I tore through zippers and layers of flying clothes and soon had the objective well in hand.

Immediately, blessed relief was established, but I suddenly became aware that there was a figure in front of me, in a military brace and performing a right hand salute. The uniform was Russian, as was the salute. Protocol slipped my mind, but it seemed proper that I return the salute with my right hand; this, unfortunately, was occupied in a very urgent task. Accordingly, without losing eye contact, I changed hands and straightened up as much as possible and then produced the casual gesture we Pilots normally pass as a right hand salute. There we stood until the final act played out; he on the ground looking up and me on the wing looking down, until the beer came to an end and the salutes were finally dropped. Thus the age-old greeting of military men finally came to an end and the war could now go on. I'll always remember that long, long salute.

The Russian Lt. waxed eloquent by pointing upward and saying, "Boom Boom." At my equally eloquent reply, "No Boom Boom," he led me around to the other side of the plane and pointed out the missing exhaust deflectors that he assumed had been blown off by flak. I was stumped in trying to find a way to tell him these had a way of coming off all by themselves from time to time.

That night we had an extremely noisy air-attack with more apparent danger of being killed by mis-directed Russian AA fire coming through the tops of our sleeping tents than from enemy planes. Worst of all was the smell of some of the fellows when they returned from the slit trenches. After the raid, they vowed never again to use them as latrines."

Lt. Joseph Higgins: "We were airborne at Debden at 0755 hours, heading for Piryatin, in the Russian Ukraine. Seven hours and 20 minutes later, Col. Don, with great enthusiasm, announced over the R/T, 'There she is boys, and we're right on time.'

After landing, my recollection was that I had never been so thirsty in my life. Blakeslee was whisked off immediately, not to be seen again for several days. It was surprising to see the Russians: their uniforms, boots, the women; big women who seemed to make up 90 percent of the troops who maintained the A/D.

The first night, we slept on cots in four-man tents. In the middle of the night, we were awakened by gunfire. I sat upright, and the

1st Lt. Gilbert W. "Mike" Hunt 336 Squadron with his Crew Chief Don Groomer in his P-51 B "Judy." Konsler collection.

tent was bright with light from the sky. A voice shouted, 'I don't know about you, but I'm getting out of here.' We immediately headed for the slit trenches, but found them not only full but overflowing. We took scant cover behind a wooden communications pole. The sky was full of flares which the Russians were trying to shoot out. As the flares fell lower, so did the gunfire, until the bullets were hitting the tents in which we were supposed to be sleeping. That night, the Germans destroyed about one-half of the bombers at Poltava.

The next day, we moved to an A/D near Kharkov. The soldiers at this field were Mongolians, about seven feet tall, accompanied by boy soldiers of 12 and 14 years of age. The boys' rifles, with bayonets, far exceeded their height. Our request to visit a nearby town was greeted with the statement that if we set foot out of camp, we would be shot. This was an indication of the "Cold War" to come.

We were billeted in a former hospital, which among other things had a distinctive feature, a 40 holer outhouse and a common bed, two feet high, six feet long, and 75 feet wide. It consisted of wood slats and straw and slept 25 Pilots.

Our evening meal was unique to say the least. We each received a flat dead fish, in all its scales, fins, and glory; with one eye looking up at us. In order not to offend our hosts, we individually found methods by which we disposed of the offering, but I saw no one actually eating the fish.

On the 26th, we flew a mission to Drohobycz, Poland, and continued on to Italy. We landed at Lucera, near Foggia. I soon discovered that my brother was stationed at Sterparone, about 20 miles away. He was a Navigator on a B-17 and was greatly surprised when I walked in on him and his crew. I was extremely grateful for the opportunity to see him, for two weeks later, he was killed on a raid to Memmingen, Germany.

On 2 July, we went on a mission to Budapest, Hungary. After leaving the bombers, we attacked the A/D at Budapest. Our plan was interrupted by an attack by 75 Me 109s from above. Due to wing tank malfunctions, we could only muster about 30 planes out of 48 to fend off the attack. Never-the-less, we had a nine to five advantage in kills in the huge fight which followed. I shared with Don Emerson in the downing of one of the Huns.

On the 5th of July, we escorted bombers over the Beziers, France area, and then proceeded on to Debden."

*****

Eleven pilots who had not gone on the Russian Mission were briefed by Col. Clark on various formations and tactics. This was primarily for the many new and inexperienced Pilots. Major Carlson will be in charge of this training program. The 335 Fighter Squadron Pilots will be divided between 334 and 336 Squadrons for this training program. The 335 Pilots assigned to 334 Squadron are:

Lts. B. Diamond
E. N. McCall
J. N. Peters
G. W. Cooley
R. G. Fischer
C. F. Holska
S. V. Wadsworth

The bomber that was to have taken S/Sgt Andra to Russia was hit by another bomber while warming up in the revetment. Sgt. Andra could not be transferred to another bomber in time to go on this Mission. He returned to Debden with his and Capt. Hively's baggage. Due to this unfortunate accident, our Commanding Officer is without baggage, except for a tunic and rumpled spare trousers that were picked up a few minutes before the Squadron took off for Russia.

22 June - The following Officers were promoted as of 10 June:2nd Lt. to 1st Lt.

James F. Callahan
Joseph P. Fernandez
James F. Scott
Grover Siems., Jr.

The following Officers were assigned as of 15 June:

2nd Lt. Dean E. Lange
2nd Lt. Kenneth J. Rudkin

Reuters Radio News carried the following report:

"Mustang Fighters of United States Eighth Air Force escorted American heavies whole way to Russia in first Russia-Britain shuttle raid it was disclosed here today. It was probably the longest fighter escort mission ever undertaken."

Moscow: "Industrial objectives southeast of Berlin were today named as target of first shuttle bombing raid from Britain to Russia," says Soviet News Agency. "Devastating blow was struck at appointed target," said Colonel in command of American bombers which carried out a raid on his arrival at Russian Airbase. "Shuttle raids place any given point in Germany or her satellite countries within reach of Allied air forces," he said.

Supp: There was no operational activity, but the fighters were split up into three sections and dispersed to other fields for safety. The 334 Squadron and 1/3 of 336 Squadron were assigned to Chugiev, east of Kharkov. It was a grass Stormovick fighter base, and our Pilots were welcomed with much Russian conversation and many salutes. This was followed by much true Russian hospitality, including food and drink. They were taken to an old hospital which had been converted into a barracks, assigned beds, and given an opportunity to wash up. They then repaired to the banquet hall where they were royally feted with constant music and gallons of vodka, which they drank out of water glasses.

The Russian General in command of the Air Army at Stalingrad invited the CO, Deacon Hively, and his aide, Capt. Bill Hedrick, to visit him. The Russians were extremely congenial and many toasts were drunk to Roosevelt and Stalin with vodka, stadka, and wine. More food was presented. Chesterfields and Luckies were exchanged for double king-sized Russian brands. The General and the "Deacon" exchanged short-snorters, and in a magnanimous gesture "Deacon" presented his hand-tooled western belt with a silver buckle to the General. The General responded with the presentation to "Deacon" of his belt with a huge square brass buckle emblazoned with the sickle and hammer insignia.

Narrative: Grover Siems - "We took off for Chuquiev at about 1900. It was approximately 200 miles away, and it was thought to be safer from German attack. It was a grass field with a large building, a former hospital, where we were to stay. When we arrived, we were met by a goodly number of inquisitive Russians, none of whom could speak English, and we had no one who could speak Russian. They ushered us into a sleeping area which was about 40 x 80 feet with a sloping six foot bench along each wall. At the bottom of the bench was a foot board so you wouldn't slide off. The bathroom was outside, about 40 x 10 feet with a plank every foot with a four foot fence around the entire thing for privacy.

They had a banquet for us; raw fish and donkey stew, which didn't exactly appeal to us. However, there was a waitress behind every few people with an unending supply of Vodka, clear or pink, which was served in six or eight ounce water glasses. Many toasts were drunk, and after each it was bottoms up. Deacon was doing quite well with the ranking Russian, protecting our honor, but most of us were stoned.

About midnight, they took us off to bed, and we really needed it. There was a layer of straw, covered with a canvas and straw pillows on which we slept rather well.

In the morning, the party started again with an accordion and a trumpet for music, both very good. They brought in soldiers of both sexes who danced with us and with each other. Men danced with men as readily as with the women. It continued from 0830 to 2000 hours without stopping, and they never seemed to tire. Since we had no musicians in our group, the best we could do was some of our bar room songs.

Prior to the party, they had taken us to a barber, who was six or seven feet tall at least with big shoulders and dressed only in pants. He shaved us and trimmed our hair. He scared us to death, but did a great job with about four strokes of his straight razor, after shaving our bar of soap from which he made a lather."

Lt. Gillette: "Last night the Germans must have followed the bombers in, and sometime after midnight, a pathfinder dropped a flare that hung in the sky for an extended period while the Germans made a traffic pattern around the field. Their bombing and strafing destroyed possibly 20 bombers and damaged several Mustangs. The next day, we drove around the field and saw smoldering lumps where engines had been. We had to assess the damage in order to decide the strength available for our next mission."

23 June - Capt. Laraby and Major Carlson, Acting CO, continued intensive training of the new Pilots.

Captain William Hedrick 334 was aide to 334 Squadron CO Deacon Hively on the Russian shuttle. Konsler collection.

T-1500 Nothing happened.

T-1502 Local flying (Nothing happened)

T-1800 Nothing is going to happen—don't worry!

Supp: Rain and mud precluded operational flying, but the Russian hospitality continued with music, singing, dancing, and food for the entire day.

24 June - The following order was received from Brigadier General Francis H. Griswold: By order of the Secretary of War: G. C. Marshall Chief of Staff.

"The 4TH FIGHTER GROUP, VIII FIGHTER COMMAND, Army Air Forces, United states Army, is cited for outstanding performance of duty and extraordinary heroism in action during the period 5 March, 1944 to 24 April, 1944. During this period, the 4th Fighter Group displayed determination, aggressiveness, and will to seek out and engage the enemy, destroyed one hundred eighty nine (189) enemy airplanes, probably destroyed nine (9), and damaged forty-one (41),in the air, and destroyed one hundred thirty-four (134) enemy airplanes, probably destroyed six (6), and damaged ninety-nine (99) on the ground.

This Group suffered (44) casualties, including pilots killed in action, missing in action, and prisoners of war. On 21 March, 1944, a day in which no operations were scheduled, knowing of a concentration of enemy aircraft in the Bordeaux area of France which had been detrimental to Military operations, the 4th Fighter Group requested permission to attack this target and voluntarily executed an attack in a determined effort to seek out and destroy the enemy air force. On this sweep the Group destroyed twelve (12) enemy airplanes in the air, nine (9) on the ground, and damaged four (4) on the ground.

(7) of their pilots failed to return from the mission. The daring and skill displayed by the group in this voluntary venture inflicted irreparable damage to hangars, airdrome buildings, wagons, and airdrome soldier personnel in addition to the enemy airplanes destroyed. On 8 April, 1944, the 4th Fighter Group, in its continued aggressiveness and determination to free the skies of enemy aircraft, destroyed thirty-one (31) enemy airplanes and damaged six (6) in the air: and destroyed one (1) enemy airplane and damaged four (4) on the ground, thus breaking the record for the largest number of enemy airplanes destroyed in the air in a single day by any one Group of the VIII Fighter Command. The extraordinary heroism, gallantry, determination, and esprit de corps in overcoming unusually difficult and hazardous conditions reflect highest credit upon this organization and the Army Air Forces."

T-2200 Ops B report that "Flabby" is effective.
The three plans are:
Spouse: Dealing mostly with ack/ack
Flabby: Dealing mostly with a/c who are in pursuit of e/a

Fickle: Combination of the above two
Supp: The Squadron returned to Piryatin where wing tanks were installed and then returned to Chugiev in the afternoon. At 1900 hours, Capt. Joyce and Lts. Monroe, Gillette, and Simon were scrambled against an enemy photo recon mission, but returned after 2 hours and fifteen minutes without making contact.

Narrative: One of the Pilots had taxied into a slit trench; he didn't do much damage, but with no heavy equipment, recovery of the plane seemed remote. The senior Russian Officer made it known that at 0800 today, we would get it out. Grover Siems was assigned to show where they could lift, and lift they did. At his command, about 60 of them picked the kite up and set it down on firm ground. It could then be given routine maintenance and await the installation of a new prop.

Grover continues: "There were P-39s at Piryatin which had been scrambled several times. We were not allowed to scramble; there was a guard on each kite, and nothing would interfere with their orders. The kites were there; they were camouflaged, and there they stayed. Four of us borrowed a jeep and started off to see the sights. We didn't get very far when we heard a loud command 'STOY.' Not knowing what it meant, we continued until a loud report and a bullet through the windshield convinced us we shouldn't proceed. I guess the cold war had started, but no one told us."

25 June - No activity.

T-2230 Diver plane crashed 8 miles south of Saffron Walden.
Supp: The planes returned to Piryatin where the mechanics pulled inspections and serviced them preparatory to the second leg of their trip - to Italy.

26 June - A training session was conducted by Col. Clark for all pilots.

T-1700 Capt. Mead, Intelligence, called. Signal has just been received advising that all information received regarding pilotless planes is to be treated as Secret.

Supp: Col. Blakeslee led the Group on a Penetration, Target, and Withdrawal Support mission to Drohobycz, Poland, where the previously escorted Bombers bombed an oil refinery with excellent results. The 15th Air Force Mustangs, based in Italy, were sighted, and like ours had red noses, but unlike ours, the fuselages and tails were garishly painted in many colors. At 1850 hours, the Group broke escort at the Yugoslavian coast and flew across the Adriatic, landing at Lucrera, near Foggia, Italy; thus ending an uneventful 1100 mile mission.

The 15th Air Force Group provided an enthusiastic welcome, and after a good feed, assigned the Pilots to tents equipped with army cots, which was a welcome change from the Russian board pallets. They then joined in consuming plentiful supplies of Champagne. Fraternization continued into the wee hours.

Narrative: G.I. Gillette- "We departed for Italy with six hours and 15 minutes of mission and six hours and 45 minutes of fuel. The glass tubes on my wing tanks broke on takeoff. When I found they wouldn't draw, I aborted and went back to the field and landed. They made repairs immediately, but I was unable to catch up with the Group, so I and four others who had aborted stayed. We all had to move to another field and await personal permission from Stalin to take off again."

27 June - Sgt Leslie E. Kucera was ordered to AAF Station 520 to attend a one-week Bomb Reconnaissance course.

An **Oak Leaf Cluster to the Distinguished Flying Cross** was awarded to:

1st Lt. Robert Hills
1st Lt. Shelton W. Monroe
Captain Howard D. Hively
2nd Lt. Ralph K. Hofer
Captain Gerald E. Montgomery

One hundred nine EM reported with basic weapon to the rifle range in groups of ten for familiarization firing of their weapon.

Supp: The fighters were again dispersed to three different fields, with 334 ending up at Lesina, home of the 325th fighter Group, the leading Group in the Mediterranean Theatre. This Group had done the original Italy to Russia shuttle mission.

At Lesina, the accommodations were good and the congenial hosts provided jeeps and cars for the use of the 4th. Unlike the 4th, here the Squadrons have individual messes and Officers' Clubs. The bar stock consisted primarily of cognac, gin, and poor Italian vino.

28 June - Ninety EM reported with basic weapon to the rifle range in groups of ten for familiarization firing of their weapon.

Col. Clark led the remaining 11 aircraft on base on a mission: Penetration, Target, and Withdrawal Support, to Saarbrucken. This force flew as a Squadron with the balance of the 352nd Fighter Group. This necessitated changing all crystals in the radios to the frequency of the 352nd. Special call signs were used. No action was encountered until, upon returning to the English coast, the group was fired on by the British defense batteries near Naze. Firing ceased when pilots lowered their wheels.

T-0555 There are 11 a/c going on this show. Col. Clark will go as, "Tiffin Leader." Pilots from 336 Sq. flying VF a/c will use their own individual call signs with "Tiffin." We will have no R/T contact with any of our a/c on "A." Bodney will do all homing to them, and Tiffin boys will come home from there on their own or C or D Channel if emergency. D will be Walcat - "Mohair."

T-1105 Darky call from a B-24. Answered him and he wanted to land—short of fuel. He landed OK. He was from operations Pinetree, 2nd Bomb Division. His home station were all notified.

The number of the aircraft is 129397 - Pilot's name is Lt. Reed, and his home station is Rackheath. We have no 100-octane gas here. He doesn't want 150 octane, so I have called Little Walden, and they will send some "100" over. They said it may be a couple of hours as they have about six B-17s to refuel first. The weather is getting worse, so his home station advises him to check with them before returning. They know he won't be able to take off for a couple of hours. Officers and men have been sent down to eat.

T-2115 Pilotless plane crashed — Defense Board notified.
Supp: After being based in England so long, swimming and sunshine were novelties, and the most was made of the opportunity to enjoy them in the blue Adriatic.

29 June - Col. Clark led the Group on a Penetration, Target, and Withdrawal Support mission to Leipzig. No enemy aircraft were seen.
Supp: Lts. Hofer, Gillette, Callahan, and Lane took off from Russia to rejoin the Group in Italy. They had been unable to accom-

1st Lt. Charles H. Shilke 336 Squadron with Crew Chief S/Sgt John Ganofsky in front of P-51 Black Lace. Weckbacher collection.

pany the Group due to troubles with their a/c and had flown to the airfield at Poltava, Russia, to assemble for an independent flight to Italy. Lts. Gillette and Lane landed safely near Foggia, Italy.

While over the Mediterranean, Lt. Hofer ran low on fuel and reported the fact over the R/T, indicating he would soon have to bail out. A flight of British Spitfires then escorted him to a safe landing at Malta. Lt. Callahan exhausted his gas supply and was forced to crash-land on the beach at Sampieri, Sicily. Being uninjured, he was taken by a British Army truck to Catania.

Capt. Hively took off for Sardinia to visit his brother in the U.S. Army, whom he had not seen in over three years. His prop began throwing oil badly, and he was forced to land at a small field covered with wrecked German planes. Since he could not get repairs there, he flew to a nearby P-47 field near Rome where the work was completed.

Narrative: G.I. Gillette - "We had waited two days for permission to take off for Italy. When it finally came, we had to give our planes a complete preflight since we had not been allowed to go near them. We were given an hour to get ready, so I teamed up with Joe Lang. He was to do all the preflight on both our planes while I went to get all the info I could on the route to Italy—wind, weather, course, etc. Hofer was still with us, but he did not leave with us.

When Hofer was finally airborne, we talked on the R/T. I found Hofer was flying a route possibly 30 degrees south of the course that Joe and I were flying. I told him he was on the wrong course, but I was unable to convince him. Joe and I finally arrived in Italy, and Hofer ended up in Sicily or Malta."

Lts. Joseph Higgins, George Logan, and Charles Shilke, classmates in Aviation Cadets, were awarded Oak Leaf Clusters to the Air Medal.

30 June - An **Oak Leaf Cluster to the Distinguished Flying Cross** was awarded to:

1st Lt. Hipolitus T. Biel
1st Lt. Alexander Rafalovich
Capt. Victor J. France (Posthumously)

T-1845 Lt. Howard, Tiffin 35, called from Marham. He was flying at the Wash and had coolant trouble . R/T also went out. He made an emergency landing at Marham, which is under construction. Couldn't locate Capt. Toy. Capt. Gabrielson is checking and will let us know what to tell Howard. Howard will call back at 1905 and let us know situation regarding AT-6 landing there if mechanic can gas up that a/c, WO-E. Nearest airdrome completely serviceable is Downham Market.

T-1930 AT-6 with Lt. Wiggin took off for Markham to pick up Lt. Howard. The P-51 will remain overnight, and they will put it in a hangar up there.

T-2133 AT-6 lands from Markham - Lt. Howard came back in it. His a/c does not need any coolant, but they will probably have to take a battery as the one in the a/c is down.

Supp: Lt. Hofer, having refueled at Malta and having been briefed by the British on how to get to Foggia, took off and flew to Catania to see Lt. Callahan. Lt. Callahan being planeless, he then continued on alone to Foggia, this time arriving safely at his destination.

Lt. Callahan was flown by British Air Transport to Algiers and then to Rabat, French Morocco, to await transportation back to England.

Capt. Hively, with Lt. Siems, again took off for Sardinia to try to see his brother. They landed at a tiny A/D at Alghero and then proceeded on a hectic 50 mile jeep ride over tortuous routes to his brother's station, where the reunion was finally accomplished. After a three-hour reunion, they retraced their route back to Lesina.

Narrative: Grover Siems- "We had spent several days swimming, laying around, and watching the natives blowing up mines

Lt. Pierce L. Wiggin 336 Squadron with Crew members. Konsler collection.

that had washed ashore. I drank my share of 24-hour old cognac, like the others. I had also traded my 45 for a Navy issue 38, which I thought would be better than the 45 and a lot easier to carry in the shoulder holster. It seems a case of them had been "found" on a wharf.

Deacon had located his brother, whom he hadn't seen for many months. He was stationed on the top of a mountain at a radar station in Sardinia. He obtained permission for Deacon and me to visit him. We flew across Italy, over Rome, and across the water to Sardinia. We landed at a small field at the foot of the mountains. We were met by some American soldiers who wanted to know what the hell we were doing there since they had just secured the field the day before and hadn't, as yet, cleared the mines.

Deacon's brother arrived shortly with a jeep. On the way up the mountains, some guerrillas appeared, but when they found us well armed, they backed off. During this encounter, I pulled my trusty new 38 and fired at one. The bullet landed about ten feet in front of the jeep; bad ammo. Fortunately, there was a Thompson sub-machine gun by the seat which they found very convincing.

Upon arrival in town, we were met by all the town fathers; it seems Deacon's brother was well known and liked. There was a small banquet and much wine toasting, ending with a tour of the wine cellar beneath the church. There were many barrels, two rows of 500 gallons each. We tried quite a few. We took M-1s out to the edge of the cliff and proceeded to snipe at people in the valley, range 1,000 yards to over a mile. You can guess at the results. After a nice visit, we said our good-bys, and headed down the mountain to our kites. We discussed how to get airborne in such a short distance. We enlisted some locals to hold down our tails till we could

The reverse side of a "Russia Shuttle" ID card - The front displayed a photo of the bearer with his name and serial number. Bob Church photo

rev up to max power. It worked well, and we got off and returned to Italy."

*****

Monthly Strength Report:

334 Squadron	Officers 50	Enlisted Men 240
335 Squadron	Officers 53	Enlisted Men 245
336 Squadron	Officers 51	Enlisted Men 246

8

The Boys Come Home to Debden

1 July 1944 - All available Pilots attended a lecture by Capt. Mead, of Group Intelligence, outlining the value of and need for accuracy in reporting visual intelligence.

T-0225 Diver reported 7 miles south of here. Crashed instantly - Defense Board notified.

T-2030 Lt. Howard in WD-E landed from Marham. Generator is u/s, and there are dents in the leading edge and aileron of the left wing where it hit a stake at Marham.

T-2045 P-38 Pilot Capt. Vanderhoh is staying here overnight. There is a bombsight in the a/c. MP posted to keep everyone away.
Supp: There were no operations so the R&R continued.

2 July - Supp: In conjunction with a 15th AF attack on Budapest, Hungary, Col. Blakeslee led 45 P-51s on take-off at 0740 hours. The mission: Fighter Sweep in advance of bombers. At Budapest, they encountered 75 to 80 Me 109s. Combat ranged down to 10,000 feet over Budapest with very agressive Huns. Our fighters claimed eight Destroyed and one Damaged.

Capt. Stanford and Lts. Hofer, Norris, and Sharp did not return from this mission. It is believed that Lt. Hofer bailed out or crash-landed in Yugoslavia. Lt. Sharp was last seen near Budapest, having difficulty releasing his wing tanks (Norris and Stanford became POWs and Hofer and Sharp were KIA).

Of the e/a destroyed, three are credited to Capt. Hively. After shooting down his first Me 109, his canopy was hit by a 20 mm shell, and he sustained facial injuries near his right eye. Although handicapped by impaired vision, he persisted in his attacks and chalked up two more kills before returning and being hospitalized. While Capt. Hively was attacking one Hun, he was in turn attacked by another. Lt. Siems, who was above picking out a target for himself, saw that his CO was being attacked. With disregard for his own safety, he dove on the attacking German and destroyed him,

thereby saving Capt. Hively's life. Capt. Hedrick claimed one Jerry destroyed and one damaged, while Capt. Frank Jones and Col. Blakeslee each destoyed a 109. Capt. Joe Higgins and Lt. Don Emerson shared a 109.

Later in the battle, Lt. Siems was severely wounded in the shoulder, neck, and chin by fire from an e/a and was forced to return to Italy. He landed at an A/D near Foggia. He was so weak from loss

Captain Chuck P. Mead, Intelligence, was in charge of making all the maps for the 4th, including evaluation of visual intelligence. Zigler collection.

of blood that he could not open his canopy to get out of his plane. The A/D personnel ignored his plight until he managed to kick on his gun switch and fired his guns. Help came immediately, and he was taken to a hospital near Foggia where he remained in serious condition.

Narrative: Grover Siems, Jr. - "When I finally got their attention, they hauled me into the hospital and examined me. I was so weak from loss of blood that I could not move, although I was still able to see and hear. They decided I was dead. They covered me with a sheet and put me in the morgue. I couldn't move or speak to let anyone know what a mistake they were making.

When I heard someone come in, I concentrated with all my might and was able to move the first finger of my right hand slightly. A very surprised orderly wheeled me back to a room where they gave me a blood transfusion. I lost it then. Some time later I came to, and I discovered that a beautiful blond lady was sitting by my side holding my hand. It turned out to be 'Madeline Carrol,' who was volunteering while her husband was operating a PT boat back and forth to Hungary in support of the resistance. I thought, if this is heaven, it's OK by me.

They still didn't think I was going to make it, so they had awarded me the **Purple Heart**, posthumously, while I was unconscious.

After I had recovered considerably, I was presented with a 'Statement of Charges' for $55,000 for my kite, which had disappeared. I was fortunate enough to have met a Pilot who had access to a C-47, and we went up to search Air Dromes for my plane. I was lucky enough to find it within two hours. A Colonel from the 15th Air Force had adopted it. Since he had not repainted it, it was easy to spot from the air with its red nose and invasion stripes. There wasn't another one like it in all of Italy.

He signed for it without argument, and I was off the hook. I would have been paying for it forever with my pay."

*****

Narrative: (Reported after returning to Allied control) George Stanford recalled - "The 'Kid' (Hofer) died because he played the part of a good wingman. Let me go back first of all to tell you how it all came about.

Just prior to the Russian Shuttle Mission, the Kid had left the Group upon returning from a mission over Europe. As a reprimand, he was not allowed to accompany 334 Squadron on the Shuttle Mission. I was a flight commander in 335, and we had a shortage of Pilots. He came to me and asked me to take him with us. I agreed to take him as my wingman.

The Group got into a fight over Poland on the way to Russia, and the Kid and I got separated. He ended up landing at a Russian airfield near Kiev rather than at Poltava where the Group went. I think he had a rather bad time at Kiev, because the Russians were

so suspicious of Americans and didn't like our flying around their country. However, he eventually did join us in Poltava.

When we finally headed back to England after having done some missions out of Russia, we landed at Foggia in Italy hoping to go on to England the next day. However, the weather in England was so bad that we couldn't do this. Some of us were staying with the Commanding General of the Fighter Forces in the 15th Air Force at his villa on the Adriatic. At dinner he mentioned that they would be short handed for the next day's mission over Budapest since the black group, having just changed over from P-47s to P-51s, needed additional practice flying.

We pursuaded the General to let the 4th go on the mission with the 15th, and as can be expected, when you volunteer, you generally 'get it.'

Lum, 335's Squadron Commander, had a cold and bad ears that day, so I was leading the Squadron with the Kid as my wingman. Somehow I had gotten into an argument with the crew chief assigned to me in Russia. As a result, he must have sabotaged me by fixing it so my wing tanks wouldn't drop. After we passed Budapest

1st Lt. George I. Stanford Jr. was downed near Budapest on 2 July 1944 when he threw a rod in his engine and crash-landed. He was leading 335 Squadron with "Kid" Hofer on his wing. This was the mission on which Hofer was KIA. George is shown with his Crew Chief Sgt Keefhover. (Konsler collection)

going east, we spotted a gaggle of about 50 Me 109s. As we took chase, I couldn't drop my tanks.

Stupidly, I kept on instead of aborting. I had to draw too much power to keep up with Blakeslee, and all of a sudden, I threw a rod. I lost all power, and my wind-screen was covered with oil.

I yelled for my buddy Capt. Frank Jones to take over the Squadron. I pulled up out of the planes behind me and onto my back. I put the plane into a spin so no Me 109s would follow me down hoping to knock off a cripple. The Kid must have pulled out of formation in order to protect me. When I finally realized that the jig was up for me, I pulled the plane out of the spin; found it to be on fire; got up in my seat to jump; and realized that, being in the hills, I had only about 300 feet of altitude. Consequently, I had to crash-land in a wheat field.

The Kid must have been watching all this. After I had gotten out of the fire and was sitting in the field taking off my boots and chute, he must have buzzed me to see if I was alright, not looking behind him. There right on his tail was a Me 109, pouring lead into the Kid. The Kid was obviously too busy looking for me to realize

what was happening, for he took no evasive action and was probably fatally hit soon thereafter.

The thing I remember most about those moments was the loud noise the German's guns made, firing only 50 feet above my head. As you know, enclosed in a cockpit, we really didn't hear our guns when we fired them.

So this is how the Kid died. It is hard to figure why he 'got it' instead of me. I have surrendered to the Lord. As a result, I have been born-again and been baptized with the Holy Spirit, but I still have much to do for the Lord to make up for his having taken that great Kid. The Kid died being the best, most loyal wingman possible."

Combat Report: - "I was leading a Section of six 336 Fighter Squadron Pilots. We were flying north from the target after a Group of Me 109s which had been reported at the base of the clouds. I sighted a Me 109 flying with some Mustangs as if he were part of their Section. I pulled in line astern of him and gave chase, but closed very slowly as my engine would not pull more than 40" of Mercury (Without my knowledge, the air intake was set in unrammed filtered air).

When I finally got within reasonable range, Lt. Higgins was also in position to fire. I got numerous strikes on the fuselage and cockpit of the 109, which then pulled up in a steep climb. I stalled out and started to spin. When I recovered, the Me 109 was spiraling down. I followed him down because I was not sure if he was out of control or not. At this time, I saw pieces of the wing come off, and the 109 continued to spiral into the deck. I saw no one bail out of the e/a. I claim one Me 109 Destroyed, shared with Lt. Higgins." - Donald R. Emerson, 1st Lt. Air Corps

*****

3 July - Orders were received promoting the following to the grades indicated:

Sgt Harvey D. Kuykendall - To be Staff Sergeant
Cpl Robert H. Riggle - To be Sergeant

T-0925 Diver reported 15 miles SE of here - Crashed instantly. Defense Board notified.

T-2200 FLABBY.

T-2300 Darky call from B-26. He wanted to know his position; gave him Debden.

Supp: The Group provided Penetration, Target, and Withdrawal Support for a bomber attack on marshaling yards at Arad, Yugoslavia. The 1,000 mile Mission was completed without mishap.

*****

Captain Frank C. Jones 335 Squadron with his lucky Teddy bear. On 8 Aug 1944, returning from an escort mission against a ship convoy, he downed a Ju 88 before, it appears, he tried to parachute. He did not surface. This was to be his last mission prior to being married in ten days, and taking a 30 day leave. He was an Ace with 10 1/2 Destroyed. Konsler collection.

1st Lt. Orrin C. "Ossie" Snell 334 Squadron was an ex-RAF Pilot. He was grounded 4 July for medical reasons. Konsler collection.

4 July - Orders were received confirming the following promotions:

2nd Lt. to 1st Lt. - Willard G. Gillette

2nd Lt. to 1st Lt. - Jack T. Simon

Sgt Jerome J. Byrge is to report to No. 21 School of Technical Training Warrington, Lancashire, for a course of instruction in Packard Merlin Engines.

1st Lt. Orrin C. Snell was taken off Ops pending action of the Central Medical Board.

Col. Clark led the Group on a Penetration, Target, and Withdrawal Support mission to Gien and Sully-sur-Loire. No e/a were encountered, and the cloud cover of 9/10ths was not conducive to any ground Ops.

T-0530 FICKLE.

T-1145 If Col. Clark and section take off to chase Buzz Bombs, they will take off on our regular H. Colgate will control them on H until they arrive at patrol area. Then they will take them over on D.

T-2025 Lt. Cronin, Tiffin 32, landed in QP-I. He called for an emergency landing as he had trouble with his tail. Top of rudder was loose when he landed. Pilot states that he came up under a B-24 while flying near the Wash and hit the top of the rudder on the belly of the B-24 just back of the cockpit. He doesn't think that the B-24 was seriously damaged as he says he just ticked it. Unable to contact Major Edwards, but notified Capt. Toy. Lt. Cronin thought the B-24 had vertical red markings on vertical stabilizers, which would make it in 34th Group if that is correct. Major Edwards called at 2015, and he knows about it now.

Supp: No operations were conducted as planes and equipment were readied for the proposed 5 July return to England and it's not-so-nice weather. Captain Hively talked his way out of the hospital in order to be able to make the final leg of the shuttle with his Squadron.

Since all EM were restricted to the post, a special program was arranged to celebrate the Fourth of July "At Home."

1500 hours - Cinema showing of "Journey into Fear."

1800 hours - Soft-ball game. Officers vs GIs.

Players wear boxing gloves.

The GIs won by the score of 21 to 5.

1800 hours - Carnival booths opened. Each Squadron had a booth where the familiar call, "Step right this way Ladies and Gentlemen, the best show on the Midway" resounded over the field as GI barkers vied to attract customers. Beer, Coca Cola, hot dogs, and tomatoes were plentiful. In no time, the area looked like a miniature Coney Island. Guests could attend the carnival, and several GIs were on hand with their wives and children—just another reminder that we have been here since 1942.

2045 hours - Second showing of "Journey into Fear."

2045 hours - Movie show "Rationing" with Wallace Beery, in the Red Cross Aeroclub.

The Special Service Bulletin ended the account of the day's activities with the following paragraph - "The Station Athletic and Recreation Fund, due to the carnival, was enriched by 76 Pounds, 6 Shillings, 4 Pence. The booth operated by Cpl. Blaney of Maj. Mitchell's organization was tops in the financial take, gathering over 34 Pounds. Major Heen's outfit had the most attractive booth resembling those seen at home. All the credit for a successful 4th goes to the GIs of the station."

5 July - Orders were received promoting:

Thomas S. Sharp from 2nd Lt. to 1st Lt.

David K Needham from 2nd Lt. to 1st Lt.

Col. Clark led a Penetration, Target, and Withdrawal Support MEW Control Mission to Le Culot. No e/a seen.

T-0445 SPOUSE.

T-0900 FICKLE.

T-1500 Intelligence and Ops B say that our Group will be coming back about 1600 hours today.

T-1630 All back except the following:

Lt. Siems	QP-O - Hospital in Italy
Lt. Boretsky	QP-M - Started but returned to Italy
Lt. Sharp	QP-D - Missing in action
Lt. Callahan	QP-R - OK, is coming back by boat
Lt. Hofer	QP-X - Missing in action
Lt. Berry	WD-M - Started but returned to Italy
Capt. Stanford	WD-K - Missing in action
Lt. Sibbett	WD-X - Missing in action
Lt. Grounds	VF-O - Started but returned to Italy
Lt. Lane	VF-S - Hospital in Italy
Lt. Norris	VF-A - Missing in action
Lt. Russel	Came back a couple days ago

Lt. Simpson Must have lost his aircraft because he flew a strange ship in. The letters were BH-L. He landed at Red Hill before coming back.

Only six of the Bodney a/c landed here. Three others started, but aborted and returned to Italy.

The following are still out:

Major Jackson	J- Presumed to be in Italy
Howell	V- Missing in action
Brashear	K- Russia
Gremarex	W- Russia
Whinneim	K- Italy
Williams	K- Started but returned to Italy
Major Andrews	A- Missing in action
Northrop	N- Started but returned to Italy
Bastrom	S- Started but returned to Italy
Hiller	H- Russia

Note- The diary margin indicates " This is not Official"

Supp: Col. Chester L. Sluder, CO of the 325 Fighter group, presented Capt. Hively with the Purple Heart for wounds received on the Budapest Mission 2 July. The award, in the name of the Commanding General, Mediterranean Theatre of Operations, read as follows:

"Hively, Howard D., Captain, Air Corps, Army of the United States, for wounds received in action against an armed enemy while participating in a fighter sweep mission to Budapest, Hungary, on 2 July 1944. Capt. Hively, as Squadron leader, led his flight to 30,000 feet to engage approximately 40 Me 109s. A direct hit on the canopy of Capt. Hively's plane by a 20 mm shell caused severe lacerations of the right side of his head. Although partially blinded, Capt. Hively continued to engage the enemy and destroyed three Me 109s in the ensuing battle. He then courageously flew his crippled plane back to his base and landed without furthur damage to the aircraft. His act reflects great credit upon himself and the Army Air Forces."

Chester L. Sluder
Lt. Col., Air Corps
Commanding

Col. Blakeslee led the Group from Salinas A/D on a shuttle escort of bombers on a bombing mission to the marshaling yards at Beziers, France, and then on to Debden. The mission was without incident and all planes arrived safely in England.

Much excitement greeted the Pilots upon their return laden with souvenirs and stories. After indulging in the offerings of the Mess and catching up on their mail, free beer enlivened the recounting of their tales, which became taller as the evening wore on.

Lt. Callahan left Rabat today on a British Air Transport bound for England.

The returning ground personnel confirmed that S/Sgt Gilbert had the misfortune of bailing out over Germany on the way to Russia. The bomber in which he was acting as a waist gunner was hit by flak. Six of the crew bailed out, after which the plane was able to continue on to Russia.

6 July - Orders were received promoting: Herbert D. Kneeland from 2nd Lt. to 1st Lt.

Supp: Nine P-51s, including those who aborted yesterday and late arrivals from Russia, took off from Madna A/D, Italy and returned to Debden, England without incident.

Lt. Callahan arrived in Lyneham and was to be picked up by Major Carlson in the AT-6.

T-1030 Lt. Callahan is down at Lyneham. Major Carlson in AT-6 went down after him.

T-1100 Doing Amendments when Angus leader called in for a homing—checked with Ops B—Finally Intelligence says nine other a/c returning from Italy. They say they should have told us. (Why didn't they?)

T-1230 The nine a/c that landed are:

Boretsky QP-M
Berry MX-O
Lane 69
Grounds VF-J
Jackson J
Whinneim W
Williams K
Northrop N
Bastrom S

T-1800 Four different times this afternoon there have been transmissions on A channel that are not our a/c. Bodney says they are not theirs either, and Ops B reports that Colgate is not on our A this afternoon. Homer can't get a bearing because the signals are too weak, but they are coming in here R5 S3.

Supp: Summary - Of the 65 Fighters which took off for Russia 21 June, 52, (41 of the 4th), returned to England. Five 4th Group

Pilots and planes are missing from all operations. One 4th Group P-51 was transferred to the Eastern Command in Russia; one, Lt. Siem's plane, was transferred to the 15th AF in Italy; one crash-landed in Sicily; and two were missing. The tour covered some 6,000 miles and ten countries and resulted in total claims of 15 Destroyed and four Damaged. The operational time totaled 29 hours and 15 minutes.

The EM assigned to the mission, after much delay at bomber bases, had taken the place of gunners on several of the bombers. Although fully equipped with oxygen masks, electrically heated flying suits, and flak suits, many had mixed emotions since many had never been on an aerial flight, and none had ever been on a combat mission. However, they boarded the B-17s which then carried them across the breadth of Hitler's Europe and set them down in less than 12 hours in a part of Russia only recently recaptured from the Nazis.

T/Sgt Ramey was particularly impressed by the amount of information they received at briefing, down to the most minute details. Don Allen, with his artistic viewpoint, claimed the clouds beneath them looked like a world of snow, and Paul Riddle concurred in this thought. As an additional "treat," the boys saw other bombers bombing Berlin and drawing flak, which they said really looked thick enough to walk on.

Tension grew as their bombers slowly flew straight and level on their bomb run over the target. They were much relieved when the "Bombs Away" sounded, and the bombers began to again pick up speed. Their confidence was greatly enhanced when our red-nosed Mustangs appeared at R/V. Shortly thereafter, the Huns attacked, and our boys got a chance to try their skill at the 50 calibre guns. Cpl. Roen recounts seeing a Jerry knock out two engines on a Fort, but two 51s, who were on his tail, made sure he would never bother another bomber. All reported that the red-nosed boys were in there pitching.

Don Allen's ship ran out of gas over Russia and was forced to land in a grain field. The ship landed safely with no one injured and no damage to the plane. Paul Riddle also was sweating out the fuel supply, and it looked like they might not make it to Russia. Several other ships also dropped out of formation, but Don's Pilot coaxed the ship into a small field and was happy to find the greeting committee was made up of tommy-gun-bearing Russians.

The Russians, aloof at first, became very friendly upon finding that our crew was American and had just bombed German targets. It turned out that they had landed at Kiev Airport, the best in the area. This was a break because they had to stay there about five days during which time they were banqueted and entertained continuously. Back at Piryatin, which had been their destination, the rest of the group had given up hope for Paul by the time he finally joined them.

After all our fighters had left for Italy, several of the bombers, which were ready for flight, took off to follow ATC routes through Persia and Egypt and then to Casablanca and home. The lone ex-ception to this routing was by Don Allen who, through a misunderstanding, went on to Italy with his bomber and then back to England with it. He was the only one of the boys to make the entire shuttle mission. The rest took the trip in a leisurely fashion through Teheran, Cairo, Tripoli, Algiers, and Casablanca. They had the opportunity to collect many souvenirs and see such sights as the Sphinx, the Pyramids, and tombs of the ancient Egyptian rulers. Glen Roen enjoyed the trip, but remarked, "The more I travel, the more I realize what a grand place the U.S. is."

During this trip, they had to perform the usual inspections and even make some engine changes. They missed the help of the eager and willing Russian mechanics who aided them back at Piryatin.

T/Sgt Ramey found Teheran and Cairo to be quite modern cities with good stores and many American products, including automobiles. After all the time spent in England, none of them could get used to the lighted street lights, shop windows, and cars with bright lights. In the native markets, they learned how to haggle over prices, which was the only way to obtain reasonable prices.

Paul Riddle's bomber pilot gave him a real Cook's Tour with the navigator pointing out Bagdad, Palestine, Jerusalem, the Dead Sea, and the Suez Canal. They flew low and circled over many places of interest.

The bombers straggled into England from the 6 July to 10 July. Without exception, our mechanics were glad to get back. They wouldn't have missed the trip for anything, but agreed that once was enough.

7 July - The **Distinguished Flying Cross** was awarded to:
1st Lt. Herbert P. Kenyon

Lt. Monroe led the Group on a Penetration, Target and Withdrawal Support mission to Aschersleben - Bernburg.

Results of the engagement: Green Section led an attack on 70 single engine e/a threatening the bombers near Nordhausen. Capt. Joyce got his first Me 109 and Lt. Gillette also got a Me 109. Lt. Monroe chased a tricky FW 190 to the deck, getting a few strikes. Lt. Walsh damaged a Me 109. About 75 twin engined e/a approached the bombers but did not attack. Capt. Joyce shot his second Hun of the day shortly thereafter. Lt. Hardy rejoined the bombers and bounced 14 Me 109s, Destroying two and Damaging one. Lt. Gillette attacked several Me 109s in the Blankenburg area, Destroying one and Damaging two. Lt. McFadden completed Capt. Joyce's second victory just as the Hun was bailing out. Lt. Scally was not seen after the first attack as it was believed that he joined up with the 335th Squadron. He claimed one Me 410 Destroyed. Lt. Goodwyn of 335, Destroyed an Me 109. Lt. Chapman destroyed a FW 190.

Casualties: 2nd Lt. John J. Scally MIA. (Scally was later reported as a POW).

Seventy s/e e/a were engaged near Nordhausen. Lt. Scally was not seen after this engagement by our Squadron. Lt. Charles Evans, 335, reported seeing a P-51 collide with a Me 410. Lt. Evans reports: "When we were about 25 minutes from the target, twin-engined e/a were called in below us. We were flying at about 24,000 feet, and the e/a were at about 21,000 feet. There were about 30 of them, and I saw six plus Me 109s above the twin-engined e/a. The enemy was behind and to the starboard and going in the same direction as our bombers. I started down on the e/a from high and behind. Another P-51 came in behind the twin-engined e/a as I was going down. His port wing hit the starboard wing of the twin-engined e/a. The P-51 immediately began spinning with one wing gone, and the e/a started a flat spin to the starboard. I did not see the color of the nose of the P-51, nor did I see any parachutes."

*****

Capt. Ezzell phoned the P-51 Groups that took part in this mission. None of their Pilots were involved in this type of accident. The statement from Lt. Evans is with reference to an accident he witnessed involving a P-51. It is therefore believed that this ship was flown by Lt. Scally.

Combat Report: John W. Goodwyn - "Flying Caboose Squadron Leader at 20,000 feet, I spotted 30 plus t/e e/a about to attack the B-24s. As I dove on them, I saw six Me 109s above them as cover. I climbed in behind them and fired on one, and missed at about 400 yards and 20 degrees deflection. I closed behind and beneath him. I lifted my nose and fired with a half radii lead. I saw no strikes. I pulled back slowly, lessening my lead, and noticed many strikes along the underside of the engine, cockpit, and the

wing roots. The e/a immediately started streaming coolant, and the fuselage combat tank exploded, setting the plane on fire. It started spinning down trailing coolant, smoke, and fire.

I pulled up and saw the Pilot open his chute. I then looked for other e/a, but finding none and having lost my Squadron, I saw two P-51s chasing a Me 109 on the deck and went down to join them. The lead man was firing continuously until the e/a crashed and was demolished. The 51 letters were OS-Y. I confirm a Me 109 Destroyed by him and claim one Me 109 Destroyed by myself."

John W. Goodwyn 1st Lt. A.C.

*****

T-0700 Group airborne, Col. Clark came back, took off again, then landed. Major Blanding taking over.

T-0705 Two a/c were reported to have collided in air. Called Little Walden, Ridgewell, Wratting Common—Combined the information and here's the dope—two Forts collided, one landed and some of the crew of the other bailed out. Crash is two miles NE of Haverhill. Intelligence and Col. Clark notified.

T-0945 Crash truck back from crash. It was two B-17s. Our crash truck and ambulance were the first ones at the scene of one of them. They picked up two bodies. Sgt and two men left there to guard ammunition, etc., until regular guards take over.

T-0947 Operations called to report that Lt. Pierini had landed at Sudbury and asked us to get the dope. Called Sudbury and talked to Pierini. He landed there at about 0910. His R/T is out, and he has a flat tail wheel. We will send one down to him. He's in VF-H.

T-1010 Tempsford F.C. called to report Lt. Hagan in VF-U landed there because of weather. He will come back to us shortly. Notified Squadron.

T-1157 All Group back but Lt. Gillette, Cobweb 55, who landed at Bury St. Edmonds at 1150 with hydraulic trouble and short of gas; Lt. Walsh , Cobweb 66, who landed at Wytan with u/s R/T; Lt. Scally, Cobweb 32, in QP-E, who is unaccounted for. Gillette is coming back wheels down, and Walsh should be here soon. Those concerned notified.

T-1200 There were fifteen homings this morning, all with a transmitter open which made it difficult. It was probably one of three a/c QP-P, VF-S, or VF-N, as it stopped after they were down. Asked Squadron to check.

8 July - Orders confirmed Major Donald R. Carson as Operations Officer.

Captain John W. Goodwin was assigned to 335 Squadron 20 February 1944. He was one of the first U.S. trained pilots to join the 4th Group. He became Squadron Operations Officer prior to completing his tour 30 Sept. 1944. Konsler collection.

S/Sgt. Harvey D. Kuykendall has been reclassified from Cook to Mess Sergeant.

All available Pilots attended an aircraft recognition test in the briefing room.

Eight a/c were airborne on a Balboa.

T-0330 Buzz Bomb coming—Called Defense Board—Crashed near North Weald—Q site off.

T-0400 Buzz Bomb—same as 0330.

9 July - Col. Clark led a Penetration, Target, and Withdrawal Support mission to Saumur and Tours. No e/a were seen.

Major Heene addressed all EM in the hangar. He said we could not write about the Russian Mission in our letters back home, but that it could be discussed in camp. He then suggested that we go through our personal belongings and discard the items we do not need. He then inspected the I.D. tags of all men present.

The buzz-bomb alert was sounded at 1137 hours; the all-clear at 1147 hours.

The buzz-bomb alert was sounded at 2105 hours; the all clear at 2109 hours. Another was sounded at 2117 hours; the all clear at 2122 hours.

T-0900 Group returning.

T-0915 Caboose 62, Lt. Kolbe, landed at Ipswich, he's OK and is returning.

T-0940 Cobweb 66, Lt. Walsh, had a flat tail wheel, landed OK, and turned off clear of R/W.

T-1130 Ops B reports that a Buzz Bomb is 30 to 40 miles south of base, headed this way—notified Defense Board and they blew the siren? Ops B reported it had crashed before the siren had stopped.

T-1420 Ops B reports Buzz Bomb 20 miles south. Called Defense Board. Just as I hung up Ops B called to report it had crashed. Called Defense Board right back.

10 July - Orders were received from Headquarters European Theatre of Operations mandating that all ground personnel will attend weekly, one-hour Discussion Groups. These Groups were scheduled to be conducted by Sgts Ettner, Kirby, Meyer, Underwood, and Schumacher.

11 July - Col. Clark led a Penetration, Target, and Withdrawal Support mission to Munich. No e/a seen.

T-1700 All a/c back except Caboose 69 Lt. Hanrahan in WD-N. T and R truck thought they heard him call Everett for landing

instructions; but I have called Woodbridge and he isn't there. Lt. Lang and Lt. Werner landed at Andrews Field but have returned to base. (Hanrahan became a POW)

12 July - The Victory Credits Board confirmed the following credits for 19 May 44:

Major McPharlin, one Me 109 Destroyed, shared with Lt. Scott.

Major McPharlin, one Me 109 Damaged.

Col. Clark led the Group on a Penetration, Target, and Withdrawal Support mission to Munich. The usual flak was encountered but no e/a seen.

T-1445 Lt. Schnider from Langford Lodge in C-47 scraped his right wing on a tree beside 334 Hangar and put a hole through the aileron skin. His station is sending someone down to make repairs. He came here for ferry Pilots and was leaving for Shipdam.

T-1649 All Group back but two who are down at advanced base short of gas. They are Lt. Fowler, Caboose 49, in WD-Y at Southend and Lt. Achen, Cobweb 39, in QP-A at Downham Market. Both willl return as soon as they have gassed up. All notified.

13 July - Major Blanding led the Group on a Penetration, Target, and Withdrawal Support mission to Munich. The Group encountered unusually heavy barrage type flak at the target, but no e/a were seen.

T-0805 Our relay a/c are flying on the GOLD Sector.

T-0900 Wormingford called to report that Capt. Van Wyr in VF-X landed there with no R/T. He will return shortly. He is airborne back to us at 0925, here at 0935.

T-0905 Ops B reports that Capt. Mc Farlane in VF-F landed at Marston.

T-1317 Group returned to base. All OK except Maj. Edwards (Bailed Out). (Later he was reported as a POW).

Col. Blakeslee and Capt. Hively returned from London following a week's convalescence.

All Pilots attended a meeting in the briefing room at 1630 hours, conducted by Col. Blakeslee and Lt. Col. Clark. The policy was laid down governing the new operational training unit (OTU) to be established for our many newly-arrived Pilots. To keep the other Pilots in line, it was stated that any of those not meeting the basic requirements of operational flying would do time in the OTU. Discipline is to be tightened. For example, any Pilot not saluting Col. Blakeslee would be automatically grounded for two weeks. Accidents of any category are much more expensive than Pilots and will not be tolerated. The theme of the meeting expressed the intentions to rebuild this Group to its former status as the best outfit in the world.

A group of new pilots arrived swelling the ranks of 335 Squadron. They are: 1st Lt. Rosensen, 2nd Lts. Dahlen, Mabie, Green, Groseclose, Lindsay, and F/O Poage.

Don "Snuffy" Smith arrived back in the Group today and was assigned as Group Operations Officer. He thought it was too dangerous flying student pilots in OTU in Florida, so he had asked to be returned to the ETO.

14 July - Col. Clark led the Group on a Penetration, Target, and Withdrawal Support mission to: Special Target No. 10 southwest of Grenoble.

Near Bourges, the bombers started letting down until they were under 1,000 feet over the target area. Curiosity aroused by the unusual tactics of our "Big Friends" was soon satisfied when many containers were dropped by colored parachutes on a high plateau in this area. Many persons were seen to immediately gather these items up and wave their thanks to the bombers and fighters. This was apparently an airborne supply to partisans who will engage the Nazis in this area. We do not know the nature of the items dropped.

Lt William R. Groseclose 335 Squadron was apparently shot down on 11 Sept 1944 when the Group was jumped by 30 plus Me 109s. The Group lost 5 Pilots that day. Konsler collection.

During a wide swing, we observed a large power station being constructed in a deep gorge northeast of Grenoble. No flak was observed during the entire mission, and no e/a were seen.

T-0610 SPOUSE.

T-0615 Lt. Morgan in VF-K taxied into Lt. Shilke in VF-J on the grass at the east end of the field as the Group was forming to take off. K's prop chewed a hole in J's left wing. Lt. Shilke took off right away in VF-M. Wrecker removed the aircraft after the group was airborne. All concerned were here except Col. Swan and the photographer, and it was too early to get them.

T-1223 All Group down except Cobweb 41, Major Carlson. He landed at Palebrook.

15 July - Two Victory Credits Board Reports confirmed 37 e/a Destroyed in April and part of May by 334 Squadron. Capt. Hively and Lt. Lang each scored five, and Lts. Blanchfield, and Siems, and Capt. Megura each had triples. Eleven other Pilots scored doubles and singles for the period. In addition, there were many other e/a damaged as well as various trains and miscellaneous equipment destroyed and damaged.

Capt. Gerald Brown was assigned as Squadron Ops O.

Selected personnel met and were required to fill out a questionnaire from VIII Fighter Command, regarding their attitudes toward proceeding to the Pacific Theatre after the European War has ended. Most of the questions were multiple choice and were to be unsigned, so it was anticipated that an honest consensus would be obtained.

Questions were asked about age, length of overseas service, marital status, disposition of the enemy upon cessation of combat, comparison of conditions in the two theatres, and probable length of the war in each theatre. It also asked if service in the Pacific were desired, would it be preferable to go directly from the ETO or via a leave in the States. The results were to be published upon completion of the tabulation. Each Squadron was represented by three Administrative Officers, five Pilots, and fifteen Enlisted Men. The other Group organizations were represented on a pro-rata basis.

Sixteen 334 a/c flew a Squadron Balboa.

T-1545 Right after Cobweb 43 transmitted for his third bearing of a homing, a transmitter remained open. It stayed that way until 1557 when Cobweb 43 in QP-X had landed and taxiied to Dispersal. I talked to the Pilot, Lt. Wells. He said he never received any more transmissions, but he says his green light remained on. Asked Squadron to check his radio. I am sure it was his a/c.

T-1900 Mrs. Willis from Steeple Bumstead called to report that an a/c crashed between Steeple Bumstead and Cornish Hill

End. Passed this information to Castle Camp. They think it was a Mosquito from Hunsdar. Lt. Shilke was flying at the time and circled it along with several other a/c. He thought it was a Mosquito. He says it's a mile north of the east end of Great Saysford.

16 July - The following article appeared in today's *Sunday Express*. It referred to Pilot Capt. Wilkinson, who made his last operational flight with our group on 13 March 1943. On a local flight on 27 April 1943, Capt., then Lt., Wilkinson bailed out due to a collision with another aircraft, and in jumping, pulled the ripcord too soon, causing serious back injuries and ripping panels of his chute. On 17 May 1943, he was transferred from our Squadron to 2nd Evacuation Hospital.

"While Thunderbolts flew overhead and soldiers stood at attention, a hatless English girl on the parade ground of a U.S. Eighth Air Force fighter station yesterday received the second and third highest Military medals, awarded posthumously to her American husband for gallantry in action. It was the first time that an English girl has had this honour."

She was Mrs. Freda A. Wilkinson, widow of Capt. James W. Wilkinson, from Pennsylvania.

Brigadier General M. Woodbury gave her the **Distinguished Service Cross** (second highest U.S. medal), the **Silver Star** (third highest), and the fourth **Oak Leaf Cluster to the D.F.C.**

Captain Wilkinson, six-foot two, broad and dashing, went to Canada in 1939 and joined up as a gunner. He was already known in New York as a crack polo player and newspaperman.

He fought with the Canadian artillery in France and became a Captain. In 1941 he transferred to the RAF as a fighter pilot. In January 1943 he went to the American Eagle Group and later to the U.S. Eighth Air Force.

As a fighter pilot, he Destroyed eight enemy aircraft in combat (two on the ground) and Damaged 15 others. Altogether he flew in 103 combat missions."

Said Mrs. Wilkinson "Although my husband was such a splendid fighter pilot, he was normally quite a peaceful and idealistic person. He believed that we were in the right. That was why he joined the Canadians so early in the war. In order to do this, he forged a birth certificate which said that he was born in England."

"We met 18 months ago at a dance. We married at the beginning of the year and lived in an old world cottage near his station. Just before he was killed, he said to me, 'War gave us each other, so we owe quite a lot to it.' He loved England and the English people and planned to stay here and write after the war. He had already written quite a number of sketches. I hope to publish them one day. I have no definite plans for the future, but when the war is over, I hope to go to America and meet my husband's people."

"There was a time when Captain Wilkinson's flying days were over. He was bailing out, his parachute split and he fractured his spine. Six months later he was flying again, with an ambition to be in the fight on D-day. Two days before, he crashed into a hill-side."

*****

Col. Blakeslee led a Penetration, Target, and Withdrawal mission to Munich. They met intense accurate heavy flak at Stuttgart, Munich, and Freiburg. No e/a were seen.

T-1544 Capt. Bird took off in Oxford 579 against a red light without a clearance. His home station is Matching, but I don't know if he is going back there or not. No message sent.

Our commanding Officer, Captain Hively, addressed all officers and enlisted men of our Squadron (334). He said that it has been noticed and commented upon by the Station Commander that discipline and military courtesy on this station is below par.

"Effective immediately, all military courtesies will be observed at all times. Disrespect and negligence in these matters will be the occasion for immediate disciplinary action.

This squadron has never relinquished its lead in anything and can boast of the best record in the ETO. We will maintain this superior performance in all matters. We can and will be exemplary in all our actions." Concluding, Capt. Hively said he was proud of his Squadron, the leading Squadron in the Group that has more "firsts" than any Group in the ETO. "Ours was the first Fighter Group in the Eighth Air Force; the first Fighter Group to escort bombers over Berlin; the first to get 500; then 600 e/a destroyed. The other Squadrons look to us for leadership. We have done a swell job and bigger things are yet to come."

17 July - A Nisson hut in Abbotts Farm (334 Dispersal area) was chosen as headquarters for OTU training. Capt. Markel was to be in charge, assisted by Lt. Fernandez. New Pilots assigned to our Group were to train with OTU until it was felt that they were qualified to fly operationally. The Fighter Squadron was to keep 17 planes for operations and all other planes were available for OTU.

Captain Alfred Markel 334 Squadron was placed in charge of OTU training for newly assigned pilots 17 July 1944. His task was to train and qualify new pilots for operational flying. He was later assigned to 4th Headquarters Squadron. Konsler collection.

Lt. Fernandez did a little scrounging this morning for their dispersal. Our Squadron Intelligence sent him away happy with an armful of papers, magazines, and books.

Col. Clark led a General Target Area Support and Ground Strafing mission to Auxerre Area. Col. Clark led a Section to strafe 20 plus R/R cars while the remaining Sections tackled goods cars at St. Pierre until a terrific explosion occurred. The concussion was felt by others in the Group several miles away. It is presumed that an ammunition train was destroyed. The Group then reformed and attacked armored vehicles on rail cars south of Cosne with good results.

Lt. Fernandez received a letter today from Mrs. Richard L. Bopp, stating that she has been advised by the War Department that her husband, 2nd Lt. R.L. Bopp, was a prisoner of war. Lt. Bopp was listed MIA after an operational mission with our squadron on 28 May 1944.

Major Blanding led the Group on a Penetration, Target, and Withdrawal Support under type 16 control Mission. No e/a were contacted.

Lts. VanderVate and Gillette were involved in a taxiing accident on takeoff. Their statements follow:

By Lt. VanderVate in QP-F - "I was flying Red 3 in Cobweb Squadron. We were waiting in take-off position when White Leader taxied back to Dispersal and told Blue Section to lead. Blue Section pulled out on the runway and took off. Red Section then pulled onto the runway. As there was no flagman, I turned at a slight angle to the runway to see that Red 1 and 2 were at proper distance before taking off myself. Just as Red 1 and 2 were about to leave the ground, I signaled my Number 4 man and gave it the throttle. At this moment, I saw in my rear-view mirror another airplane extremely close to my tail. In another second he had collided with me. I had no rudder control after that, but got my aircraft off the runway to the right and cut the switch."

*****

By Lt. Gillette in QP-B - "I was flying Cobweb Green Leader. White Leader returned to the line calling Blue Leader to take over. Blue Section took off, leading Cobweb Squadron. Red Section followed, and I waited on the runway, seeing White Leader return in another kite. I called Lt. Monroe to go ahead and I would follow. I had watched Red Leader take off, and then I called to Lt. Monroe to take off ahead of me. He waved me to go ahead. As there was no flagman, I looked to see if Red 4 was on the runway and, seeing no airplane, gave it the throttle to take off. As soon as I moved forward I saw Red 3 and 4 just starting to move. I could not stop, so I tried to turn left to miss him. My right wing hit Red 3's rudder and up the fuselage. I taxiied off the right side of the runway, cut my switches, and got out of the aircraft."

*****

Fortunately, neither Pilot was injured. However, Lt. VanderVate's plane is not repairable, but Lt. Gillette's plane is repairable by the 45th Service Squadron.

T-1945 Group airborne. At approximately 1943 hours, Lt Gillette hit Lt. VanderVate while taxiing. The right wing of Lt. Gillette's plane hit the tail of Lt. VanderVate's plane and climbed all the way to the cockpit. The prop of Lt. Gillette's plane, QP-F, also chewed up the left wing of the other plane. Lt. VanderVate's plane, QP-B, was completely demolished. Lt. Gillette's plane has damaged right wing and prop.

T-2230 Group all returned, except Becky 44, Lt. Chapman, who landed at Horham. He will remain overnight and return in the morning.

18 July - Orders were received for Capt. Cecil H. Blackburn and 1st. Lt. Orrin C. Snell to report to Station 101 with the Central Medical Board.

1st. Lt. James F. Callahan was ordered to report to AAF Station 563.

The following Officers were assigned to Station F-356:
2nd Lts. Henry E. Clifton, Jr.
Lewis F. Wells
Edward J. Wozniak
Thomas A. Underwood
William K. Whalen

An **Oak Leaf Cluster to the Distinguished Flying Cross** is awarded to
1st Lt. Joseph L. Lang
Capt. Nicholas Megura

Col. Blakeslee led a Penetration, Target, and Withdrawal Support mission to Kiel. No e/a seen. Mission uneventful.

T-1715 F.C. Bovington called to advise us that a C-87, Pilot Major Kimm, call sign JAMKNIFE T, would be airborne to us tommorow morning at 1100. Will have at least two Major Generals on board. They will call us again in morning when airborne— Couldn't contact operations, but notified Intelligence. (Capt. Meade)

19 July - Major Blanding led a Penetration, Target, and Withdrawal Support mission to Munich. Near Munich, Captain Joyce and Lt. Hardy attacked two e/a with no claims.

Elsewhere, 10 to 15 Me 109s attacked in twos and threes. In the ensuing combat, Lt. Simpson and Lt. Grove Destroyed one, and Lt. Grounds claimed two e/a Destroyed.

Lt. Simpson reported that Lt. Dahlen had bailed out and that he, himself, was over Switzerland with a glycol leak. Another report had it that Lt. Dahlen's kite had blown up, but we would like to believe the first report. (Dahlen was KIA, and Simpson was interned)

Capt. Hedrick was shot at by two blue-nosed P-51s over Lake Wurm.

The morning briefing was quite detailed since it was attended by Major General G. A. Salinas and Captain R. Gaxaiola of the Mexican Air Force. They were accompanied by Major General Guy Henry, Brigadier General William Hall, Brigadier General Griswold, Brigadier General Jesse Auton, and Lt. Col. Godfrey McHugh. Col. Blakeslee, Capt. Leverock, Capt. Conrad, and Lt. Swope conducted the various aspects of the briefing.

T-1100 I called Bovington F.C. to see about the C-87. They said it was just taxiing out to take off then. I asked if there were any VIPs aboard. They said "No, the plans have been changed and the Generals should already be here." They want us to call them when the C-87 is about ready to take off.

T-1255 All Group back except Lt. Simpson, Caboose 59 in WD-V; Lt. Dahlen, Caboose 58 in WO-E; and Lt. Cox, Cobweb 52 in QP-P. Lt. Cox called in for a fix at 1210, but we could not make him receive. He did not call again.

20 July - The Victory Credits Board confirmed one Me 109 was Destroyed 20 June by Lt. Dickmeyer.

Major Blanding led a Penetration, Target, and Withdrawal Support mission to Dessau, Kothen, and Leipzig. This was Capt. Henwick's first mission with 334 Squadron. He is from the South African Air Force and attached to the Group to get experience in P-51s.

Various targets were hit by the bombers with apparent good results. Intense flak was encountered at all major flak centers, some reaching as high as 35,000 feet.

T-1420 Group all back except Cobweb 63, who was reported to have landed elsewhere, and Caboose 44, Lt.Godwin, who bailed out near Antwerp. (Godwin successfully evaded capture and returned).

T-1455 Cobweb 63 lands from Manston.

Captain Howard D. Hively was appointed to the Aircraft Accident Board as of 18 July. Capt. Hively was also appointed to the "Awards and Decorations Board."

21 July - Col. Clark led a Penetration, Target, and Withdrawal Support mission to Munich. Heavy cloud cover appeared to have resulted in the bomber formations being split up and quite disorganized, but bombing appeared to have been successful.

T-1052 Ops B say they have Col. Clark on B channel. He is in trouble, and there's a possibility that he may have to ditch. They have a boat near him.

1st Lt. Edward Hernandez 336 Squadron completed his tour 8 March 1945 and left the Group.

T-1100 Ops B says that Col. Clark is 13 miles from Manston. They think he will make it OK.

T-1105 A crash northwest of here. Called Duxford, and they think it is a P-51 or P-47. It is three miles south of them, and they are taking care of it.

T-1115 Col. Clark called in on R/T and wants someone to pick him up at BlueFrock (Manston). Ops B called a few minutes later and said he had landed at Manston. Someone is flying down after him. All concerned notified.

T-1150 Snetherton Heath called and said two of our Mustangs had landed there: Lt. Ingalls in VF-O, and Lt. Hernandez in VF-Y. They were both up on local flights. Will return to us immediately.

T-1800 New IHZ is operative up to 10,000 - Homing bearings between 300 degrees and 360 degrees - (all the way in to Chelmsford at one point) is effective tomorrow morning at 0600. Notified Intelligence and Homer. Pilots should be told at briefing, as it includes country between here and Manston and Bradwell Bay. Red Snowflake rocket fired from the ground are to warn a/c they are headed for Diver Balloon Area. Major Baldwin has the signal on this and will advise Pilots at briefing tomorrow.

Group Intelligence received an ETO Machine Records Unit Report stating the following Pilots were prisoners of war:

Capt. Duane W. Beeson reported MIA 5 April 44

Capt. David A. Van Epps reported MIA 9 April 44

1st Lt. Vernon A. Burroughs reported MIA 9 May 44.

All summer there has been an inter-unit softball competition for officers on the field, and our (334) Squadron has not faired so well, (Our EM team, however, leads the field in their league). Very little interest could be aroused in the Squadron; therefore, our showing on the field was poor. As a result, we came up to date with three games won and eleven lost. Whereas 336th Fighter Squadron was leading the league with twelve won and five lost. We beat them once, which was practically phenomenal. They were so thoroughly convinced that it was a fluke, they challenged us to a special game at 1930 hours.

About 1500 hours, Captain Benjamin of the 336th Fighter Squadron phoned Lt. Ashcroft. He stated that his Pilots had about 25 Pounds to bet on the game and were inviting us to back our team with the coin of the realm. Such a challenge couldn't be ignored, and our boys quickly scraped up 41 Pounds in a show of confidence which amazed the 336 Squadron boys, and they gleefully covered it. Our confidence was considerably bolstered by the fact that "Doc" Achen, our pitcher, put up five Pounds himself.

By game-time, word had spread over the field that this was to be a "grudge" game, and all and sundry were on hand to witness this epochal event. More money was put up, and by the time the 'ump' called 'Play Ball!,' there was in the neighborhood of 120 Pounds ($480.00) wagered, which ain't hay, even when figured in Pounds.

The 334 line-up called for "Doc" Achen in the pitcher's box; "Pop" Werner catching; "Gabe" Gabrilson, on first; "Bob Kenyon, at second; "Gerry" Brown, at third; "G.I." Gillette, at short. The brilliant outfield was composed of Clarence Boretsky in left field; "Dick" Dickmeyer, centre; Lynd Cox, right field; and "Penrod" Hills, in short field.

The game was hotly contested with that sterling 334th aggregation scoring three runs in the second inning, which was topped by the enemy with four runs in the third. Things were plenty tight when the last inning came up with the score six to six and the crowd going crazy. We chalked up four more runs in our half of the inning. That was more than our competitors could do, so we came out on top ten to six.

The losers paid off, cash on the barrel head. The ecstatic winners repaired to the bar in the Mess for a bit of convivial rejoicing and to spend some of their well-gotten gains. The vanquished team, still not satisfied, wants another game on 1 August, and they shall have it.

Had we had this hot team earlier in the season, 334 might well be in the upper brackets of the league by now, instead of the cellar position. With the season not yet over, this outfit should certainly wind up in a better position.

22 July - Combat films of the Russian-Italian mission, June 21 to July 5, were shown to all available Pilots.

Col. Blakeslee led the Group on an Escort mission for B-17s dropping leaflets on Bremen, Hamburg, and Kiel. No e/a were seen.

Shortly after take-off Lts. Gillette and Brown collided in the air. Their reports follow:

Lt. Gillette: "I dropped a tank on taxiing out to the runway to take off. I stopped at 335 Squadron Dispersal and they put another one on, and I took off as Blue 3 late. My wingman, Lt. Ayers, took off with me. I flew around with my wingman below the clouds as it looked to me as though my Section was joining up with me. They

Captain Carl F. Brown of 334 Squadron later became Squadron CO. (Konsler collection)

1st Lt. James Ayers of 334 Squadron became an Ace with 8 e/a Destroyed. He was with the Group until the end of the war.(Konsler collection)

did. I straightened out and started to climb 170-180 mph. I noticed a motion out the left side of my cockpit, and my #3 man fell below me. Next, someone swished up by the side of my kite and felt very close or actually hit. I climbed up through the overcast and heard someone call on the radio that he had had a collision. I returned to base and landed. My aircraft was damaged on left side of fuselage in front of the tail about the star." Lt. Gillette down Debden at 1655 hours.

*****

Lt. Brown: "I started to climb up through the overcast. We went into the overcast, and my airspeed was down to 150 mph. My artificial horizon indicated I was in a steep bank to the left. Afraid I would spin in with so much weight, I leveled out and saw the leader disappear above me. I was flying straight and level according to my instruments and letting down when another ship came down and hit my right wing tip. As I leveled out he disappeared, crossing under the nose of my ship and below. I continued my let-down and broke out of the overcast a little north of Bishop Stortford, going

south. I turned 180 degrees and returned to the field. I landed on the north-south runway." Lt. Brown down Debden at 1640 hours.

*****

Landing at 1735 hours, Lt. Cox made the following report:-"I aborted from this mission because of a broken fuel line on my right drop tank. I began my let-down through the overcast at about 6,000 feet. My gyro instruments were uncaged and set for level flight. Before taking off, I was warned that the gyro horizon would tilt slightly to the right. This, however, was not the indication on the instrument before letting down. At about 4,000 feet, the gyro horizon indicated that I was turning to the left. I immediately staightened the ship out. This happened several times, but each time the gyro horizon was indicating a turn to the left, and the directional gyro indicated a turn to the right. During this time, my verticle speed began building up, but before I could switch to needle and ball, I found myself inverted. I attempted to roll the ship over. I broke out of the overcast at about 3,000 feet in an almost verticle dive. I pulled back on the stick, causing a high-speed stall. I broke the stall and again pulled back on the stick. The ship flicked, but I managed to straigten it out. Upon landing, I found that the drop tanks had been torn off, causing damage to the flaps, undersurface of the wings, and tail."

*****

Lt. Ayers landed at Charlton Hawthorne. His report follows: "I took off from this field, and my engine conked out a couple of times on the way to the target. The ship wouldn't go past 27,300 feet. I got mixed up in some flak and started back. The engine conked a couple of times coming back. I came through the overcast when I thought I should. I saw I was lost, and the ceiling being so low, I started to land at an airport. I landed long and started to go around. The engine conked, and I went through a fence and turned over in a potato patch." Lt. Ayers crashed at 2130 hours. The plane Cat. "E."

*****

T-1625 Group airborne.

T-1630 Smoke seen about 5 miles NW of drome—Definitely a crash. Reported by Cobweb leader and Maj. Adriance. Dispatched Crash tenders, Ambulance, and guards. Not positive it is one of ours.

T-1650 Baltisham called that it may be one of ours. Crash positioned at Little Bury Green about 3 miles west of Saffron.

T-1800 Details of crash not yet ascertained except that the ship is definitely ours—WD-A Lt. Kingham—His body is at the station morgue.

T-1910 Lt. Gillette, Cobweb 55, in QP-Z, landed at 1650; Lt. Brown, Cobweb 53, in QP-R, landed at 1657. Both a/c are damaged. Pilots report that they were in a mid-air collision shortly after takeoff while flying in clouds. They do not know if they hit each other or if someone else flew into them. Apparently this collision happened at the same time as Lt. Kingham spun in in WD-A. Lt. Cox, Cobweb 52, in QP-X, landed at 1132 from the show. He reports that his gyro tumbled, and he found himself flying upside down. He came out of it so quickly his wing tanks were torn off, damaging the wings on his a/c.

T-2105 Lt. Cox called that Lt. Ayers (Cobweb 57) had landed at Charlton Hawthorne and had flipped over on his back. Pilot unhurt. Gp Ops and Sq notified. Told Ayers to remain overnight.

23 July -
T-1743 An Oxford, AP-468, from Steeple Morden, Pilot Maj. Dewitt, crashed on take-off. His right motor cut out, and he swerved off to the right. He just missed a P-51, QP- that was parked on the hard-stand. He dented the wing on the P-51 and crashed into the trees. Both wings of the Oxford are washed out and other minor damages. All concerned notified—Nobody hurt.

T-1840 Steeple Morden will send transportation over for the passengers of the Oxford.

T-2100 Capt. Hively took off; evidently for local flying. Contacted him on the standby. He beat up the "jernt" for a few minutes and then landed OK - Ho! Hum!

24 July - Sgt. Eugene R. Baim was ordered to report to Sta. 101 on D.S. for 45 days.
1st Lt. Joseph P. Fernandez was ordered to report to Det "B," 65th Ftr. Wing, Sta F-150, on T.D.
S/Sgt Charles H. Schroeder was ordered to report to AAF Sta. 470 to attend a three-day course on the operation and maintenance of oil purifier.
Col. Blakeslee led the Group on an Airdrome Strafing mission to Lechfeld A/D. 10/10ths cloud cover over the target prevented the Group from strafing. They then found a hole in the overcast and attacked a power station at Weingarten, which they badly damaged. They then split into sections and attacked targets of opportunity near Lake Constance. The Group did much damage to railway trains and equipment.

T-0945 Group Airborne.

T-1506 All Group back but Lt. Davis, Caboose 68., in VD-B who is at Yearlton. He will return shortly. He landed at 1633 here OK.

25 July - All personnel attended a British training film on camouflage.

T-0325 Buzz Bomb 10 miles north of base headed this way. Defense Board notified. Some say he went over the airfield. Others saw it crash about 3 to 4 miles west of here.

T-0949 Ops B called to report a friendly Ju-88 in the vicinity of Wiltering between 1000 and 1100. We are to advise all our a/c that may be around there. Have a six a/c Balboa airborne. Controller says to tell them on the R/T. Has been done.

T-1430 Lt. Callahan called from Kings Cliff saying he had pranged the Fairchild there. Capt. Gabrilson is with him. Nobody "hoit." All concerned notified.

26 July - The 334 Squadron flew a two hour Balboa.
A buzz-bomb alert was sounded at 1426 hours; the all-clear at 1431 hours.

27 July - There was a clothing and equipment inspection for EM requiring the display and checking of all clothing, etc., for quantity and identification markings.
Captain Charles F. Howse was detailed as a class "A" Finance Officer for the purpose of making payments of July payrolls. He also was designated to verify cash in the hands of Major Issac Q. Rayburn.
Six new Pilots joined 335 Squadron: 2nd Lts. Boren, Conley, Cooper, Peterson, Rinebolt, and Vozzy.

T-1425 Caboose Red leader called Red 4, Caboose 31, to find out where he was. No reply. He disappeared from the formation north of Cambridge. Balboa landed at 1441 without him. The 335 is concerned about him, so I called Ops B to see if they had him in D. Also checked with FCLO at 12 Group. No one knows about him.

T-1535 Caboose 31 landed OK. Apparently, his radio went out and he got lost. Squadron reports he didn't land anywhere else.

28 July - Captain Van Wyck led the Group on a Penetration, Target, and Withdrawal Support mission to Merseburg. No e/a were seen, only intense heavy flak.
Captain Hively dropped a wing tank taking off in QP-J, but returned and took off again in QP-W. Being unable to catch up with our group, he joined up with the 355th Fighter Group. Six e/a be-

lieved to be the new Me 209s were attacked by that Group near R/V, and Capt. Hively claimed an Me 209 Probably Destroyed.

T-1300 Group all back.

T-1515 Col. Clark gave permission for Capt. Godfrey to beat up the field.

T-1530 Col. Clark called to have Godfrey cease - Hmmmm!

29 July - Col. Blakeslee led the Group on a Penetration, Target, and Withdrawal Support mission to Merseburg. Although vectored around by controller, the Group was unable to find bombers, and with the undercast, there was no option but to return to base. No e/a were seen.

At 1030 hours an alert was sounded for a Station Defense Drill. Members of the Team reported to their respective stations. The all-clear was sounded at 1055 hours.

Lts. Church and Goodwyn are now new Captains, Congratulations!

T-0600 Briefing; 0707, Press; 0713, Take off 0731, Set course. Return at 1227 from the Northeast. Group will be under Greyfriars Control. Dwarfbeam is call sign.

T-1000 Ops B informed us that the Group was coming back early. Also possibly some other a/c diverted to us—Homer set up on C Channel.

T-1030 Ops B informed us that Group is on its way back and that no other a/c would be diverted to us. Homer changed back to A.

30 July - The 334 was airborne for a Squadron Balboa.

Captain Howard D. Hively was appointed to the Officers Mess Council and is to report to 28 Grovenor Square, London, on TD for further inst.

The following Officers were assigned:
1st Lt. Ralph H. Buchanan
2nd Lt. Jerome E. Jahnke

T-1048 A-20 #709 (Kelly Pilot) landed here from operations. He was in Little Waldens circuit when one of his motors cut out, so he joined our circuit and landed south to north. Both motors were running when he landed, but he was short of gas. Little Walden has been notified and is sending some gas over for him.

T-1400 A C-64 called on 6440 saying the Pilot was Lt. Ryder. He is from Backgammon (Walttisham) and going to Dosage (Heston). Called Wattisham and told F.C. there. They say ship was supposed to go to Mont Farm. Called them back to check on this and now they say he was cleared to us. Called Hestan at 1530 to

make sure he got there. He did and went to Bovingdon—No longer any concern for us, but I called Wattisham and told them the story.

31 July - Col. Blakeslee led the Group on a Penetration, Target, and Withdrawal Support mission to Munich. The Group covered the bombers, leaving them as briefed. At this time, a large explosion was seen. When the escort was finished, the group dropped down to attack a small A/D near Heilbronn on which were parked four FW 200s and several other a/c. They dropped their wing tanks but were unable to set the woods on fire. They then returned to base.

T-1130 Urinal in enlisted mens' latrine stopped up—called Clerk of Works.

In accordance with instructions from Hq., 8th AF, relative to including in the unit history more information on problems of administration within the unit, it will henceforth be the policy in this history to record at the end of each month any such problems that have arisen during the month.

"During the months of June and July, morale of both Officers and EM has shown a decided drop from previous levels. Contributing factors were: the letdown following the invasion buildup when it was found that our part in the invasion was very small and did not bring the protracted extra activity that had been expected. This Squadron and the entire Station posted extra guards and prepared special defense plans in anticipation of possible aerial or paratroop invasion during this time. Failure of any action materializing along these lines left all with pent-up energy. This contributed to lowering morale.

Then, about two weeks after the invasion, our Group went on the Russia-Italy-England mission and there resulted some 15 days with practically no operational activity. Subsequent to the return of the Group from that mission, we went back to a routine that existed prior to the invasion. In addition, because the German Air Force has provided but little competition, there have been few claims registered by the Group. This all seems to add up to a general feeling that if we're not doing any good here, why don't we go somewhere else - even another theatre.

Nearly ten percent of the Squadron strength has been in the ETO for about twenty-four months and approximately seventy-five percent for twenty months with the balance having been overseas for lesser periods. Neither Officers nor EM have any rotation scheme to look forward to. Those who have tried to transfer to units where they believed they would see more action have been unsuccessful and have the feeling that they cannot get out of the unit. It is believed that if there was a rotation scheme instituted which could be looked forward to at the end of some specified period of duty in the theatre and that if the restrictions on transfers were relaxed within reason, the morale of all concerned would be appreciably raised.

One of the outstanding administrative headaches are the many details outside of the unit for which the Squadron is called upon to supply men. In a unit of highly trained men such as we are in a fighter Squadron, it is essential to operations that these men be available for their primary duties at all times. It is difficult to maintain operating efficiency when, as was the case this month, it was necessary to detail an extra man for duty in the Officers' Mess or furnish 19 men one day per week for training with a Mobile Striking Force in addition to the ten men previously furnished for this activity, making a total of 29 men for one day per week. This month, additional men were required for duty with the M.P. company for defense purposes. The Squadron has been called on to furnish two men daily for a road building detail and two more daily for a salvage detail.

To further complicate the situation, Army Orientation Talks were started this month, and it has been necessary to select NCOs and train them as leaders for the discussions. The difficulty arose in trying to coordinate the discussion hours with regular and extra duties and still not conflict with operational requirements. The discussions, however, are considered beneficial and valuable to the Squadron.

Complicating the pilot personnel problem is the fact that the Squadron is carrying in its strength six Officers who are not available for duty. Captains W.B. Smith and Gerald Montgomery and Lt. D.W. Howe left for the United States over two months ago and have not returned. Captain Nicholas Megura left for the states the 16th of this month. Lt. Grover Siems is hospitalized in Italy for an indeterminate length of time, and Lt. Joseph Fernandez is on D.S. to the 65th Fighter wing."

Battle Honors - Citation of units - 29 July 1944

As authorized by Executive Order No. 9396, superseding No. 9075, 20 June 1944, as approved by the Commanding General, Eighth Air Force, is confirmed in the name of the President of the United States as public evidence of deserved honor and distinction.

By order of the Secretary of War:

G.C. Marshall, Chief of Staff.

Monthly Consolidated Strength Report:

334 Squadron	Officers 56	Enlisted Men 245
335 Squadron	Officers 60	Enlisted Men 249
336 Squadron	Officers 55	Enlisted Men 248

9

Back to Routine

1 August 1944 - Major Hively led a Penetration, Target, and Withdrawal Support mission to the Paris area. Although the mission was uneventful, several problems arose on take-off and form-up.

On take-off, Lt. Cronin skidded to a stop at the end of the runway for a very close call. Mechanical problems prevented him from taking off.

On form-up, Lt. Green's glycol caught on fire at about 4,000 feet. He dropped tanks and bailed out; his chute opened at 400 feet. His aircraft crashed near a small village ten miles south of the field. These two accidents gave our boys a bad start on this mission.

The rendezvous was accomplished, and the Controller gave the Group several vectors, none of which proved fruitful.

Upon landing, Lt. Rentschler ground-looped, springing the starboard landing gear and damaging the tip of his starboard wing, Plane Cat "AC."

Note: Wing Commander Wickham flew our QP-Z in a section composed of Colonel Blakeslee, Captain Godfrey, and Lt. Glover. They flew below the Group looking for enemy aircraft. Their mission was uneventful.

At 0900 hours, the first group of 30 enlisted men reported to the gym to have their gas masks checked. The Officer's masks had been checked at CWS headquarters at 0630 hours.

T-1340 - Group airborne - Lt. Cronin in QP-O did not get off. His brakes apparently locked just as he was gathering speed. He came to a stop at the end of the R/W. Both tires blew and both wheels were worn down.

T-1430 - Group operations called and said Lt. Green in WD-H had bailed out. He called them from a phone at Camp Hixham, which is a British Army Camp at Allenby, which is 6 miles northwest of Bishop Stortford. The A/C also crashed near Albury. Pilot

OK - "Stanstead" are taking the necessary action and furnishing a guard for the a/c. All concerned notified. Major Smith is going down to look it over. Telephone number is "Puckeridge 125."

T-1655 - Lt Daily and Lt. Berry in WD-M and WD-K landed at Holme. Both had R/T trouble.

T-1715 - Lt. Rentschler, Cobweb 69, in QP-Y landed from operations. He made a good landing and taxied to the east end of the R/W. About 25 yards from the end of the R/W his aircraft got out of control and started to ground loop to the left. As he went off the R/W his right tire blew out, swinging him around. His right landing gear buckled in and his right wing tip hit the ground. No one was hurt, and the aircraft pulled off the R/W.

T-1740 - Lt. Dugan, Becky 50, landed from operations in VF-V. He made a good landing, but both brakes locked. He came straight down the middle of the R/W and stopped just west of the intersection. A/C landing were told to go around.

T-1746 - Becky 50 is off the R/W and a/c are landing again. His a/c has a nicked prop where it hit the R/W when brakes locked.

T-1750 - Lt. Grove, Becky 54, called from Snaith. He landed there in VF-Z at 1712 with his electrical system US and no compass. Otherwise he and his a/c are OK. Reported this to Group operations. Major Smith says to tell Grove to stay there all night and to check to see what a/c needs. They will send for him tomorrow if they can't fix the trouble there.

T-1810 - Talked to Grove at Snaith and passed message to him. Operations said we will call him in the morning to check progress made before sending up. Grove will call us if he doesn't hear. Generator is US and battery is dead.

T-1812 - Lt. Berry landed from Holmes. Lt. Daily is not with him. Lt Berry said they got separated in some bad weather.

T-1840 - Called Holmes and reported non-arrival of Lt. Daily to them. They have heard nothing. Checking with FCLO 12 Group. No news.

T-1850 - Lt. Daily landed from Holmes. His R/T still US.

T-1900 - R/T silence lifted on "C"and"D." Group all back but Lt. Grove and Lt. Green who bailed out near Stanstead.

2 August - Orders were received promoting Preston B. Hardy from 2nd Lt. to 1st Lt.

Capt. Gerald Brown was designated Squadron Operations Officer of 334 Squadron.

In the presence of 100 Officers and 200 Enlisted Men, General Auton presented awards on the parade ground at 1330 hours. Awards were presented to the following Pilots:

Two Oak Leaf Clusters for the D.F.C.
Major Hively

One Oak Leaf Cluster for the D.F.C.
Capt. Markel
D.F.C. and One Oak Leaf Cluster.
Lt. Lang
Lt. Monroe
Lt. Hills
The **Distinguished Flying Cross**
Lt. Kenyon

All available Pilots assembled in the briefing room at 1430 hours to hear Lt. R.C. Smith, of the Airborne Infantry, describe proper parachute technique. He gave many valuable tips on jumping and landing procedure, and illustrated the difference between a Fighter Pilot bailing out and a parachutist jumping with 200 pounds of equipment.

As Lt. Smith had been on the Normandy beach-head for 38 days (29 of which were spent in the front lines) he had many interesting experiences to relate and gave an illuminating talk on activities on that front.

Major Blanding led a Type 16 control and ground attack mission to the Rouen and Paris area. Dense haze prevented much ac-

Captain Francis M. "Lefty" Grove became 336 CO on 22 Sept 1945 and served until it was deactivated on 10 Nov 45, thus he was the last 336 CO in the WWII era. Konsler collection.

Captain Robert P. Kenyon 334 Squadron, C Flight CO completed his tour 25 Oct. 1944. Charles Konsler Collection

tion, but several wagons and trucks were damaged or destroyed. Intense flak was received, and Capt. Joyce received hits to the carburetor scoop and tail by 7.9 mm bullets.

T-0930 - Called Flying Control Snaith and they say Lt. Grove will be able to return in a half hour. Told them not to let him come yet. We will call them when weather breaks.

T-1030 - Called Lt. Kister and he says he will be able to paint all our trucks and trailers Friday. I told Sgt Hall. Starting early Friday morning, we will take them down. He will call us tomorrow (Thursday) to make any necessary arrangements.

T-1355 - Called Ridgewell Flying Control. Told them it is OK for relay Fortress to come over now—Ceiling 1200 feet, Viz 6 miles.

T-1420 - Lt. Grove called from Snaith. He will go to Goxhill to get 150 octane fuel and come here from there if weather is OK.

T-1555 - F.C. Goxhill called. Lt. Grove is there, still having trouble with his electrical system. They will call us when they find out what is going on.

T-1630 - Major Caudill called at 1400 and reported that the Searchlight unit near Lt. Green's crash yesterday by Stanstead had called him to report that there was no guard at the wreckage and kids were picking up ammunition. He wanted us to get Stanstead to put the guard back. Called Control there. He said he would call us back. He did, and reports that some Major from here was at the crash this morning and told the Provost marshal it was OK to remove the guard as everything worthwhile had been salvaged. I talked with Major Caudill and Major Smith. They know nothing about anyone from here removing the guard. I told Stanstead I'd call them back.

T-1710 - Called Stanstead and told them it's OK to leave the guard off per Col. Swan's order. He has just returned from there. Still don't know who gave the first order.

T-1759 - Lt. Monroe, 334 Sq. called to report that he thinks VF-F (Lt. Higgins, Becky 43) had his wheels locked when he took off. Called Major Smith and reported to him, also asked Major Smith's advice to tell Becky 43 when the Group returns and have him land on the R/W as usual.

T-2030 - Ops B called and said that they had quite a few a/c to be diverted to us as home bases along the coast were closed in. Homer is set on Channel "C."

T-2200 - After quite a few homings, we had (8) P-38s land here from Wattisham, also (26) P-47s from Martlesham. P-38 letter "7" from 436 Squadron, Pilot Lt. Hightower crashed on landing. He was very short of fuel and did not think he could make it around to the west end to come in west to east. I told him to use any R/W he wanted. He had one prop feathered and only 5 gallons of gas left, so he came in north to south. His approach was very high, and he did not touch down until he had only 300 feet of R/W left. He started to use his brakes as soon as he touched down, and after traveling the remaining 300 yards of the R/W, his right under-carriage collapsed. He continued on through the fence and across the road. The crash crew and ambulance were there immediately. The Pilot was OK: however, the plane is washed out pretty bad. (some slang) Arrangements have been made for a guard to remain with the A/C, and all concerned were notified.

T-2210 - Both Martlesham and Wattisham have been given all the information, also combat Ops and Ajax. The 26 P-47s will remain here overnight, and 4 of the P-38s will also remain here. The other 4 took off for Wattisham and have landed there OK. One of the remaining P-38s "F" has trouble with his left magneto. The two sevicable ones will take off first thing in the morning for Wattisham. Martlesham will call us when it's OK for the P-47s to return. One of their P-47s "PI-P" has a flat tail wheel.

T-2215 - All of our a/c returned from operations after many homings, except Becky 44, Lt. Chapman, in VF-A. We have no information of him. (Chapman was KIA).

3 August - Major Hively led a Penetration, Target, and Withdrawal Support mission to the Auxerres area for four CWs of B-17s. The Mission was uneventful.

T-0805 - Called Wattisham to advise that according to the Pilot "F" will be able to go back OK. Wattishamn will call us when weather there is OK for their boys to return.

T-1033 - Two P-38s, A and F, airborne to Wattisham. Y is still here. He came back from the end of the R/W. His right mag is out. Notified Wattisham and 45th S.S. They are working on it. Airborne at 1240.

T-1155 - Lt. Whitaker called from Group Communication. He said 12 Group called to tell us that an a/c will be airborne to us at 1430 from them. Call sign Lynchgate. He doesn't know where it's coming from or anything else about it.

T-1200 - Lynchgate's call sign belonging to North Coats. After looking around, they report that Group Capt. Braithwaite will be airborne to us at 1415 in Beaufighter X. I told them our weather is bad here now but is expected to be alright by then. They will check before he takes off. I gave this information to Lt. Bogianno at Group Operations. He will tell Col. Blakeslee. It seems that Blakeslee is expecting Braithwaite.

T-1435 - All Martlesham aircraft airborne to their own station.

T-1725 - Capt. Byrd took off in an Oxford without a clearance or telling us where he is going. He came here from Matching. No signal sent.

T-1811 - All Group back except Major Smith in VF-S who is reported to have bailed out south of Caen and Lt. Ceglarski, Caboose 38 in WD-K.

T-1840 - Lt. Ceglarski landed apparently OK. Squadron says his R/T went out, and he joined up with another Group.

Major "Snuffy" Smith had just returned to the Group on 13 July. Prior to today, he had only flown two missions on this tour. He had engine failure on today's mission and bailed out near Falaise, France. Later it was discovered that he was captured and assigned to Stalag Luft III for the rest of the war.

4 August - Capt. Howard D. Hively was promoted to Major.

Capt. MacFarlane led a Penetration, Target, and Withdrawal Support to Rostock. The mission was uneventful.

T-1545 - Great Dunmow called and said Lt. Conley, Caboose 69 in VF-Y, up on local flight had landed here lost, and he will return shortly.

T-1630 - Lt. Conley lands here from Great Dunmow.

The 334 Squadron Officers' volleyball team was engaged in a game with 336 Squadron. They outplayed the opposing team (336) in 3 games out of 5.

5 August - Col. Blakeslee led the Group on a Penetration, Target, and Withdrawal Support to Brunswick. The escort was without event, so Capt. Henwick and Lt. McFadden were left to escort the five Combat Wings of B-24s home while the rest of the Group split up to Free-Lance. Oil storage tanks were set on fire. A locomotive and oil cars were damaged east of Meppel.

Major Carlson and Lt. Dickmeyer saw eight Me 109s below them and dove, but could not catch them.

Capt. Godfrey got a Me 109 in aerial combat and three on the ground. He capped it off with eight locomotives.

Glover destroyed a 109.

T-1105 - Called Little Walden in regard to some smoke in their direction. They say their AFC said a Mustang crashed, and the Pilot bailed out. The location of the crash was 2 miles southeast of them near Nutts Farm at Ashdon. They have sent out their crash truck and ambulance and are taking care of the crash. Saffron Walden police gave us about the same information.

T-1145 - After checking with everyone, it is believed that the P-51 belonged to Fowlmere. They say at Ops that the Pilot is at the Wing hospital in Saffron.

T-1200 - Another show is supposed to come off. Only 12 a/c are taking part. The leader's call sign is "Amber," and the Pilots' call signs are "Ronnie"- Due back at 1430.

T-1353 - AFC called to report that Cobweb 62 in QP-S had a flat tire when he took off. Can't contact him on R/T. He probably has it turned off as there is R/T silence. Reported it to Sq. and Group Operations. AFC & crash crew will be on the lookout for him.

T-1451 - Second Show "Ronnie" boys all back OK.

T-1550 - QP-S, Lt. Whalen, landed with a flat left tire. AFC gave him a red light and made him go around as his R/T was off. He turned it on the second time around, and we told him the trouble. He made a hell of a good landing, keeping the the weight on his right wheel until he was practically stopped. Corp. Dill was AFC on duty at the time. He did a good job in spotting that tire.

T-1715 - QP-W landed from Manston where it has been since 21 July.

T-2200 - C-64 asked for QDM to Stanstead. Gave him 210 degrees for ten miles; acknowledged.

T-2215 - A civilian called up from the gas dump in Saffron and said one of their gas trucks had tipped over between here and Thaxsted. He wanted to know if we would syphon the gas out. I got Day and Schaeffer and they went out with our gas bowser.

6 August - Capt. Gerald Brown was designated CO during the temporary absence of Major Howard Hively.

Cpl Floyd K. Oman was promoted to Sergeant.

Major Blanding led the Group on a Penetration, Target, and Withdrawal Support to Berlin. Upon take-off, Lt. Lange's canopy came loose. Upon landing, in the low overcast, he started to drop due to low speed from full wing tanks. He hit the throttle, but the engine did not catch until he hit the runway and bounced, at which time the torque caught the plane and threw it on its left wing, which will have to be replaced.

R/V was accomplished as scheduled and Bomber boxes separated to go to different targets. "Bombs Away" resulted in many explosions in the south, southeast, and southwest sections of Berlin. At Brandenburg, many large fires were seen, and one B-17 went down in flames. Four very large oil fires were seen at Hamburg. One B-17 was seen to ditch out at sea.

The Free-Lance Section resulted in Lt. Lang and Lt. Malmsten destroying eight tank cars and damaging three locomotives and many goods cars. Capt. Otey Glass destroyed two Ju 52s, while Capt. Godfrey and Lts. Glover and Patteeuw each destroyed one e/a.

Major Carlson and Lts. Hardy, Wells, Callahan, Clifton, and Werner performed air-sea rescue flights.

This afternoon, 50 men from the station attended a Salvation Army "Drumhead" service at nearby Dunmow. Lt. Eugene M. Kennedy of the 335 Fighter Squadron was in charge of the formation.

Professor Dobbie, a Texan, who is at present a lecturer at Cambridge University, addressed the assemblage and the balance of the service was given over to singing and prayer. It is the policy, in this theatre, to have American soldiers attend British functions to further Anglo-American relations.

T-0830 - Three grills on E/W R/W were broken last night. We are placing them on N-S R/W just south of intersection. Called clerk of Works, but only the duty Electrician is on duty and he doesn't know if they have any spares or not; They should be checked again before S to N R/W is used.

T-0940 -Lt. Lange, Cobweb 70, in QP-B landed. He had taken off at 0923 for operations. He stalled out about 12-15 feet above the R/W and came straight down, probably springing the undercarriage, and bounded about 6 feet in the air. Apparently the Pilot gave it full throttle, pulling the left wing down. It hit the ground (left wing tip) and the aircraft settled back on its wheels heading toward 335 dispersal. It came to a stop to the left of the parking space for Col. Blakeslee's a/c.

T-1000 - Called Capt. Gabrielson about loose paper and cardboard around 334 blister hangar. It's blowing out on the R/W. He will see that it is taken care of.

T-1210 - Ops B reports that a Mustang crashed and blew up about 1035 approx. 10 miles NW of Duxford. They don't know whose ship it is as it's practically all destroyed. Am checking.

T-1220 - FCLO 12 Group called regarding crash. He has report that it's one of ours. He got his information from F.C. Bourn. Am checking with them.

T-1240 - Have definite information via Steeple Morden and FCLO 12 Group that Mustang is from Fowlmere. Pilot was Lt.

Tonge. He did not get out. Have notified those concerned—Ops B, etc. It crashed at Hasling Fields near Trumpington (4-5 miles SW of Cambridge).

T-1533 - All Group returned OK except Capt. Godfrey, who landed at Beccles because of battle damage and slight personal injuries. The AT-6 is going to fetch him back-All concerned notified

7 August - Our CO received a letter, dated 28 July 1944, from Lt. Thomas Fraser's family, stating that they had been advised through the International Red Cross that their son was a prisoner of war. Lt. Fraser was reported MIA 6 Jun 44.

The field was closed in by fog, canceling the scheduled morning mission.

Col. Blakeslee led a Strafing mission to the Dijon, Chaumont, St. Dizier area. The Sections split up with each Section attacking in a different area and all Sections had strafing of locomotives, cars, and wagons. Lt. Malmsten and Lt. Whalen, flying together, near Dijon, received intense, heavy, accurate flak. Lt Malmsten made a port turn and Lt. Whalen made a starboard turn and beyond that point, Lt. Whalen did not see or hear from Lt. Malmsten again. He continued home alone, strafing water towers and a lorry.

Narrative - Lt. Whalen reported: "Lt. Malmsten and I were flying along a railroad track from Chalon-sur-Saone in a northerly direction. We had finished strafing an engine down the track from what I think was the town of Dijon, France. Very soon after this, we topped a hill and were over the town of Dijon. The flak both light and heavy was very thick. The last I saw of Lt. Malmsten was when he broke port, and I broke starboard."

Captain Donald M. Malmsten (*3rd from left*) 334 Squadron was hit by flak and crash-landed. Although suffering burns and wounds, he evaded for a month and returned to Debden 12 September. He was an Ace with 10 1/2 planes Destroyed. Sherman collection.

T-1905 - Six A/C airborne for Air Sea Rescue.

T-1915 - Cobweb 62 also having trouble with his under-carriage, and after getting them down, he couldn't get his flaps down either. He landed OK, but used all the R/W and part of the open field at the west end.

8 August - Again the morning mission was canceled as the field was closed in by fog.

Major Blanding led an afternoon mission to escort 30 RAF Beaufighters to attack a convoy off the Norwegian Coast. The escort was performed at 300 to 500 feet, and the attack on 14 merchant vessels took place near Varhaug. The Beaufighters attacked with torpedoes and four ships were seen to be sinking, three smoking, and one listing badly. One Beaufighter with one engine afire was seen to hit the water.

Blue section stayed with the Beaufighters as escort, and the rest of the Group proceeded north to the vicinity of Sola A/D, and finding no e/a to attack, turned southeast to the vicinity of Kvinesdal. They still found nothing to attack, and they went to an A/D north of Kristiansand with no targets sighted. They continued to search in vain for enemy targets without success. Heading home, they sighted a convoy of nine ships headed northwest due south of Vestbygd about 15 miles off the coast.

Capt. Jones of 335 strafed a Ju 88, setting it on fire.

He left Norway O.K., but later over the North Sea, he ditched his canopy and his plane hit the water. His parachute was seen floating on the water. Apparently he did not get out. This was to be his last mission, and he was to marry in ten days and have a thirty-day furlough in England to honeymoon. (He was KIA)

Casualty: 2nd Lt. Thomas A. Underwood MIA. At 1455 hours, just after the Beaufighters attacked convoy, Lt. Underwood reported on R/T that he would have to bail out over the water off the Norwegian coast, not far from the target, as his engine was on fire. His conversation was almost unintelligible as it appeared that his radio was out of order. The cause of his trouble is not believed due to enemy action. (Underwood became a POW).

Lt Fischer was heard to say he was hit by flak and he was heading for Sweden, nothing else was heard from him. (He was KIA)

Major Blanding was hit by flak, and flying glass from his canopy severely injured him on the side of his head. He tore a piece of cloth from his trousers to bind up the wound. He appeared to lapse into semi-conciousness at times, and his flying became erratic. Lts. Berry and Kolbe, who were flying with him, guided him to Acklington Airdrome, near Scotland, where he was hospitalized. Although he lost a lot of blood—his plane was covered with it—he remained conscious.

Captain Robert H. Wehrman 336 Squadron was wounded in Feb 1944 but came back to earn the DFC prior to leaving the Group on 30 Oct 1944. Konsler Collection

*****

Lt. Wadsworth was hit by flak and lost his coolant. He was seen to crash. No parachute was seen. (Later it was learned that he was a POW).

Results - Fifty-one locomotives were damaged along with 87 goods cars, box cars, and oil cars, with all Pilots having fired their guns.

T-0700 - Closed in tight - Viz; 20 yards, R/W W-E

T-1820 - Becky 62, Lt. Wehrman, had a lot of trouble getting his wheels down and after he got them down, he couldn't get his flaps down - finally landed OK without them.

T-1900 - Group all back except Caboose 65, Lt. Wadsworth, who was reported to have asked for a course to Switzerland from the target area. Also Cobweb 59, Lt. Malmsten, and Cobweb 62, Lt. Whalen, of whom we have no information.

T-1215 - Group airborne—Heard explosion and saw lots of black smoke just to the south of the Airdrome—sent one crash truck and ambulance out to investigate.

T-1245 - Crash crew came back with nothing to report.

T-1250 - Col. Blakeslees' call sign will be Masca for the show.

T-1630 - Becky 58 called for a homing. The Homer is not receiving. They are changing their receiver. Ops B got a bearing for him on D Channel and passed it on A as Becky 58 can't receive on D.

T-1700 - F.C. Acklington called to report Major Blanding in WD-G landed there at 1650. He is injured and at their hospital. They do not know the extent of his injuries, but they will call us back. Lt. Kolbe, Caboose 62, and Lt. Bury, Caboose 56, escorted Blanding there and will return shortly. Reported to Intelligence, Group Operations and Squadron.

T-1808 - Acklington called again to report that Major Blanding was reported by their MO to have a fractured skull and superficial injuries. They say his condition is serious but not expected to be fatal. They say he made a "Wizard" landing considering his condition. Reported this to the same as at 1700. Capt. Restivo is checking. Lt. Kolbe and Lt. Bury are airborne back here at 1807. They landed back here at 1906.

T-1816 - Wood Hall called to report that Lt. Lines and Lt. Holske landed there in WD-D and WD-M. They were short of gas and will return shortly. Here at 1955.

T-1831 - All Group back but five listed above and three others:- Lt. Underwood, Cobweb 32, in QP-C, Capt. Jones, Caboose 57 in WD-P (Sq. reports he was seen to disappear in the water in his a/c.) and Lt. Fisher, Caboose 54, in WD-N. Capt. Croxta says he had a report he had been shot up and was trying to make land but he knows nothing more. All concerned notified.

The **DFC or Oak Leaf Cluster to the DFC** was awarded to:
Maj. James Goodson
Capt. Robert Hobert
Lt. Donald Patchen
Lt. Warren Johnson
Lt. Ira Grounds
Lt. Joseph Patteeuw
Lt. Charles Shilke

9 August - Lt. Monroe led the Group on a Penetration, Target and Withdrawal Support mission for eleven CWs of B-24s to Stuttgart. Dodging a cloud front, the Group arrived at R/V on time but sighted no bombers, nor could they be raised on the R/T. They then followed the bombers' briefed course and found them to be bombing targets of opportunity through the cloud cover along the Rhine. The Group then escorted these bombers and about 300 B-17s to the coast where they broke off escort.

Capt's. Joyce and Hedrick attacked and damaged a locomotive and cars, but due to dense haze, it was impossible to determine damage or location. No e/a were seen.

All available Pilots were summoned to the briefing room to hear a talk by Lt. Col. Richardson of Wright Field, Ohio, on the various types of jet-propelled and rocket-propelled aircraft. He described the principles employed in their design and operation and outlined their flying characteristics as far as possible. He then gave information concerning the newer models of the P-51 aircraft that are now in the experimental stages.

Col. Blakeslee led the group on a Dive Bombing attack on Communication targets in Chalons-sur-Marne, Chaumont area. All planes armed with 250-lb GP bombs. Nearing the target area, the three Squadrons diverged to attack separate targets.

Fifteen locomotives were damaged and 35 goods-wagons, plus miscellaneous cars, trucks, and ground installations were damaged or destroyed. The bombs were dropped on a R/R tunnel, a M/Y, a highway bridge, and a factory at Vitry with fair results.

Lt. Ayers, in QP-F, landed at Manston, having suffered a hit by a 40 mm shell and 30 calibre bullets which damaged his prop and starboard wing. The engine and prop will have to be changed and the wing patched.

T-0850 - Press; 0856. Take off; 0914. Set Course; Due Back at 1341 from the ESE. Col. Blakeslee may leave the Group after rendezvous. If so, Lt. Monroe, Cobweb 61, will be Horseback.

T-0853 - Horseback took off 3 minutes early. Rest of Group followed him. Capt. Meade, Intelligence called to instruct us to tell Horseback to set course at 0914. All of Horseback first three times are three minutes early. Horseback acknowledged 0914 OK.

T-0903 - Group airborne. It looked like Lt. Dugan, Becky 50, in VF-V had a locked left brake on takeoff. He should be warned when landing.

T-0905 - Flt. Lt. Tinsley, Station C.O. at Great Sanford, called to report that a tail fin from an American bomber was found on their field this morning. I reported this to controller at Wing. No color markings on it. Has a Lot No. 43-23177-4.

T-1125 - Army 951—Y for Yohe called Darkie. He could transmit but couldn't receive. He came over the field and wanted to land. Controls shot up and no brakes. AFC gave him a green light and Yohe acknowledged it. Apparently he got his receiver fixed because he came over the field again instead of landing after being in the approach and asked for a QDM to a base with a longer R/W.

Passed him 280 degrees, 10 miles to Nuthampstead. He acknowledged OK. Called Nuthampstead on phone and told them.

T-1155 - F.C. Nuthampstead called to report Yohe landed there on their 2,000 yd R/W. He ground-looped at the end, otherwise OK. It's a good thing he got his receiver fixed!

T-1250 - Talked to Acklington F.C. about AT-6 bringing a Pilot up to fly Major Blanding's ship back. They think an Engineering Officer should come to look at it first. I told Lt. Boggiano.

T-1300 - Group Operations called to tell us that per order of Col. Blakeslee, Lt. Williams was to spend a week with the AFC from 0800 to 1700 hours daily with a half hour out for lunch.

T-1310 - Lt. Hermansley in VF-N has an oil leak at Woodbridge per Ops B. They can't fix it there. We are to call them and let them know when and what we are going to do about it. Lt. Boggiano is checking and will call us back.

T-1645 - Dive bombing mission—3 hrs 15 minutes maximum duration—Will probably be coming back scattered—RW E-W.

T-2029 - Manston called, Lt. Ayers, Cobweb 57, QP-F, landed there. His a/c was shot up. Holes in prop and right wing. Manston can repair it in 3 or 4 days. Lt Ayers will call back about 0900 tomorrow morning to see when they will come for him. Reported this to Lt. Boggiano and 334 Sq.

10 August - Major Hively led the Group on an Area and Withdrawal Support to Sens and St. Florentine. The escort mission was uneventful, but one section strafed ground targets damaging several including 11 locomotives.

T-0530 - Called Officers Mess for Lt. McFadden who is to flight check Col. Blakeslee's ship per orders of Capt. Gabrielson. Weather is good now and supposed to be OK. A/c is to get an hour's test when it goes up.

T-0600 - Lt. McFadden at dispersal OK but crew chief found something wrong with the Colonel's ship, so it will be a half hour or more before it goes up.

T-0914 - All Group airborne okay. Becky 68, Lt Patterson, did not get off on his first attempt. While taxiing back to starting point, he hit a stop sign at the west end on the perimeter crossover. He was told about it on the R/T after being airborne, and he acknowledged that he understood and elected to go on regardless.

T-1100 - Becky 34, F/O Pierini landed at Manston and will be coming back as soon as repairs are made.

T-1620 - Gave a QDM to a B-17 Rathmore "M" for Mike to Leicester—318 degrees for 74 miles.

T-1630 - VF-H (Lt. Pierini's a/c) will have to stay at Manston for repairs for a couple of days.

T-1800 - Lt. Ayers is back from Manston. His a/c QP-F is still there. Lt. Pierini is also still there.

T-2200 - All local flying back except Cobweb 70, Lt Lange - He landed at Alconbury to find out his position and burst his rear tire taking off. He will stay overnight. All concerned notified. He could have asked for homing.

11 August - Capt. Van Wyck led a Penetration, Target and Withdrawal Support mission to Coulommiers Airdrome.

Lt. Needham developed an extremely rough engine and was forced to land on one of the landing strips near the Normandy beachhead. Lt. Gillette covered him in his landing. Later, Lt. Gillette was airborne in QP-B on a test flight. The plane seemed to be alright, and at 21,000 feet he started to dive. At about 425 mph the right ammo cover came off, next the left one came off. The plane then went out of control. He looked back and saw that the tail appeared to have gone so he bailed out, landing safely about one mile from Haverhill.

T-0930 - AT-6 Capt. Markel airborne to Alconbury with tailwheel for Lt. Lange's Mustang QP-Y.

T-1435 - All Group landed except Cobweb 60 Lt. Needham who might have landed at Beachhead.

T-1630 - Grove Op'ns called that Lt. Needham had landed at airfield A-2 at 1330 on Beachhead. Pilot OK. Engine trouble. Will proceed back to base when repaired. Col. Swan wants us to send gas truck to Fairlop near N. Weald to gas up a P-51 OK for Cpl. Day and Cpl. Dicksen to go.

T-1955 - Lt. Gillette who went up at 1907 in QP-B called from Haverhill, telephone 147. He had bailed out just a few minutes before when his a/c started to go to pieces in a dive. He's Ok except for a few bruises. He doesn't want the ambulance to come for him as the MP's are with him now and they will bring him in. His a/c is a couple of miles or so Southwest of Haverhill. Reported crash to Group Operations. Duty MO and Col. Swan.

T-2015 - Castle Camp is sending a guard out to the crash. Grid referred WM127619. It is north of Steeple Bumpstead on the Haverhill road. Lt. Gillette landed in the cricket ground in Haverhill. Castle Camp would appreciate having the guard removed as soon as possible in the morning.

T-2145 - F.C. Castle Camp called to advise that Lt. Gillette is at Ridgewell, and Ridgewell is providing the guard for the crash. The a/c did not explode. Apparently the tail came off in the air before Gillette bailed out.

T-2150 - Talked to F.C. Ridgewell. Crash was at Copy Hall Farm. Grid reference 1162. Haverhill police can direct anyone to it. Their guards, Ridgewell's, are on it. Lt. Gillette on his way here. Their medics report him O.K.

12 August - Capt. Brown led the Group on a Penetration, Target, and Withdrawal Support for B-24s to Mourmelon and Le Grand. Control vectored 334 Squadron to Charleroi to attack ten box cars loaded with buzz bombs, but they were unable to find them. They turned, and Lts. Wells and Callahan attacked goods and flak cars at Blanc Misseron, damaging ten.

Lt. Hardy, leading Green Section, spotted a M/Y with round-house with 27 locomotives. Only two had steam up, and it is presumed that the rest, being rusty and having no coal in the tenders, were there for repairs from previous strafing missions. They shot

Lt. Harry N. Hagan 336 Squadron was an Ace with five e/a Destroyed. He survived an encounter with a tree in Jan 45 to finish his tour in May 45. Konsler collection.

up 15 of them for good measure and damaged two more on the way back to base.

Effective this date, the following Officers were assigned:
2nd Lt. William B. Hoelscher
2nd Lt. Arthur J. Senecal

Major Howard D. Hively was designated Deputy Station CO and Deputy 4th Fighter Group CO, during the temporary absence of Col. James A. Clark, Jr. Major Leon M. Blanding, relieved, is hereby confirmed and made record. Major Donald R. Carlson was released from the 334th fighter Squadron and assigned to Headquarters, 4th Fighter Group.

Capt. Brown led the 334 Squadron, armed with 500 lb. G.P. bombs, on a Dive-bombing mission to the Chalons-Troyes-St. Dizier area. They arrived in the wrong area and shot up several locomotives and flat cars, receiving moderate, accurate flak from 88s on the flat cars. They then headed in the direction of Chalons, dropping bombs on targets of opportunity with generally poor results. Lt. Walsh, however, bombed a highway bridge over railroad tracks with good results. Lt. Boretsky, Lt. Achen, and Lt. Howard destroyed miscellaneous staff cars and trucks.

Lt. Jahnke bailed out near Bradwell Bay, he relates: "I took off on a dive-bombing show. I developed at maximum 2,800 rpm; a good reason to come back, but didn't. I joined the Squadron at 8,000 feet, and climbed to angels ten, then my engine conked. It caught again, etc. I told "Cobweb" White Leader I was going home. I fooled with my kite for about 1,000 feet. White smoke then gushed out of the left and right stacks, also from the firewall into the cockpit. I could hardly see; jettisoned the canopy; could not find the radio plug; then I tore off helmet and safety belt. I half crouched on seat; popped stick; and bailed out at 9,000 feet at 1600 hours. I went 45 degrees to longitudinal axis on right side; somersaulted twice and pulled rip-cord; landed in a hayfield ten miles west of Bradwell Bay. I was assisted by a RAF radar outfit whose station was not far off. I asked to be taken to my plane, which crashed a mile from me in a pasture. Bombs went off with crash; plane was reduced to nothing. Big hole five yards deep and three yards in diameter. Stationed a guard due to live ammo. Civilians were very considerate. Was taken to Bradwell Bay A/D. Was picked up there by Debden A/C. Arrived base 2000 hours."

T-0737 - Group airborne OK.

T-1030 - Lt. Hagen, Becky 53, landed from operations in VF-Y. He bounced when he hit the R/W, apparently used too much throttle, and his left wing hit the grass along side the R/W. Pilot made a good recovery and came to a stop by 335 Dispersal where Col. Blakeslee's a/c is usually parked. Wing tip appears to be all that is damaged.

T-1220 - Capt. Hecht, Controller at Wing, called, Colgate is going to do a lot of checking on "A" Channel for the next couple of hours. He suggests that any of our local a/c use "C" Channel for local control.

T-1530 - All Group airborne OK. Becky 62, Lt. Wehrman called for emergency landing. He came in OK, taxied back to end and took off again.

T-1745 - Cobweb 72, Lt. Jahnke, bailed out over England near Latchingdon. He's OK. AT-6 will pick him up at Bradwell when Lt. Glover brings it back.

T-1830 - Caboose 70 landed at Sudbury OK. Will come on home when gassed up.

T-1920 - Cobweb 47, QP-O, landed at Framlingham OK. Will come home when gassed up.

T-2100 - All aircraft down from show or accounted for.

T-2330 - Cranfield called that Lt. (Muham?) was down there with a bad radio and would be coming back to us in the morning. We have no such guy unless it might be Lt. Needham. (It is Lt. Needham.)

13 August - Capt. Van Wyck led the Group on a Dive-bombing and Strafing mission to Beavais-Compiegne-Paris area. All planes were armed with 500-lb G.P. bombs. The Group split up into Sections covering a large area. They bombed and strafed railway equipment damaging or destroying 17 locomotives, 74 various railcars, bridges, and other communication structures.

Lt. Needham, who was forced to land in Normandy 11 August 1944 reports as follows: "On 11 Aug 44 the Group was flying bomber escort for B-24s who were to bomb targets around the Paris area. I

Capt. Neil Van Wyk "Dutch" fought in both 335 and 336 Squadrons. He "hailed" from Patterson N.J. and served in the 4th from Oct 1943 to Feb 1945. Konsler collection.

was #3 in Cobweb Red Section. Just after the target, my engine began to vibrate very badly, so I headed for the beach-head in Normandy with Red 1 and 2 as escort. Upon reaching the beach-head, I picked out a landing strip at Circqueville (A-2) around which P-51s were dispersed, and I landed. I was taken immediately to the Service Squadron on the field and they finally decided to change the engine and accomplished the change the following day—12 August. That night I returned to England and landed at Cranfield, an RAF base, for the night. I returned to my own base the following morning—13 August."

Capt. Van Wyck led the group on a Dive Bombing and Strafing mission, armed with 500-lb G.P. bombs, to the Mantes-Gassicourt-Etampes-Chartres-Dreux area. They encountered heavy, accurate flak, but managed to effectively bomb and strafe, destroying or damaging ten locos, over 100 various cars, a bridge, and a couple of R/R tunnels.

Capt. Goodwyn, strafing, flew too low and hit the top of a tree and brought back a piece of a branch as a souvenir.

F/O Poage was presumed lost, but in reality, he made an emergency landing on a strip in France, due to an overheating engine. He remarked, upon returning, that where he landed, they considered "K" rations a treat.

A third show was flown to halt transportation in an area west of Paris by dive-bombing.

Lt. Boren, while strafing, was killed when he hit a tree and ripped off a wing.

T-1235 - All aircraft on second show airborne - duration 2 hrs 36 min.

T-1530 - Group all back except Caboose 45, Lt. Poage of whom we have no information. R/T silence lifted on Channel A.

T-1645 - Caboose 45, Lt Poage lands here from France. He landed at "A7."

T-1719 - Becky Leader, Lt. Gimbel, Becky 66, in VF-X dropped the bomb from his left wing on take-off. It damaged his flaps on that wing. R/W cleared immediately and ordinance officer called to handle the bomb.

T-1721 - Colgate's vectoring Becky 66 to the Channel to drop his other bomb before landing. He's on "D." In the future if any shows take off with bombs, Capt. Lanning, Group Armament Officer, is to be called in advance and he's to have a man report to the tower and be here in case of trouble with bombs on take off. If Captain Lanning can't be reached, call Station Ordinance. Capt. Lanning was here today but took no action. His presence was not known.

Capt. Edward L. Gimbel 336 Squadron crashed in Belgium 1 Mar 1945 and was hospitalized. On 16 April, he was downed by flak and became a POW. Konsler collection.

T-1830 - Lt. Gimbel landed OK. Left wing appears slightly damaged.

T-1840 - Caboose 37, Lt. Rosenson, landing with bombs still on. Told him to standby. Called Capt. Orenshaw, and he says to tell him it is OK to land even though Pilot has already tried to release them before returning. Told Lt. Rosenson he could either land or go over to D and have Colgate vector him to a place to drop them.

T-1846 - Caboose 37 landed. Both bombs dropped off as he touched down in spite of the fact he made a very nice landing. The straps hung on and dragged both bombs along the R/W for a hundred yards or so. Capt. Orenshaw coming to get the bombs. Quite an afternoon !

T-2037 - All Group landed OK except Caboose 59, Lt. Boren who is supposed to have crashed. (He hit a tree while strafing, tearing off a wing. He was KIA)

14 August - Donald M. Malmsten was promoted from 2nd Lt. to 1st. Lt.

Capt. Thomas Joyce was assigned Flt. Comdr "A" Flight, relieving 1st. Lt. Shelton W. Monroe, 334 Squadron.

1st Lt. Robert P. Kenyon was Assigned Flight Comdr "D" Flight.

1st Lt. Preston B. Hardy was Assigned Flight Comdr "C" Flight.

Capt. Van Wyck led a Penetration, Target and Withdrawal Support mission to Lyons A/D. The escort was uneventful, passing near Geneva, Switzerland. No e/a were seen. Lt Lang escorted a B-24 home while Lt. Brown escorted a B-17 out the enemy coast.

15 August - Capt. Emerson led a Penetration, Target and Withdrawal Support mission to Zwischenahn. The bombing was accurate; moderate, inacurate flak was encountered.

Blue Section beat up ground targets, damaging or destroying five locos and 21 goods wagons. Thirteen boats were observed at Borkum and two convoys—ten small craft each going north off Northeast Polder.

Lt Achen followed Lt. VanderVate on a beatup of a dummy airdrome near Lake Zwischenahn. A few minutes later it was heard on the R/T that he had crash-landed and was O.K.

Combat films (July 24, 28, Aug 1 and 2) were shown to all available Pilots.

2nd Lt. Norman W. Achen was reported MIA near Lake Zwischenahn, Holland. Lt. VanderVate reports; "I was flying a two-ship Section in the vicinity of Zwischenahn Lake. Lt. Achen was flying on my wing. After making a pass on the deck to inspect what I believed to be, and was, a dummy airdrome, I pulled up and climbed sharply. I drew no flak on this pass. I looked around for Lt Achen who had been slightly behind me on the pass, but could not locate him. I flew west for several minutes, climbing and looking for Lt. Achen. I saw an aircraft flying approximately southwest towards the target, and then believed it may have been Lt. Achen. He did not join up when I rocked my wings. I continued to climb west, and in about five minutes, I heard Lt. Achen call and say that he had made a crash-landing. I answered him and repeated what he had said and he replied and confirmed that he had made a crash-landing. He was on the ground at the time and must have been safe. I wished him luck and signed off."

T-1430 - Group all back except Caboose 37, Lt. Acken—reported to have crashed-landed in Germany. (He was a POW).

T-1946 - Becky 38, 45, and 37 in VF-B,G,&F airborne to Hethel. They will not come back until tomorrow.

16 August - Capt. Van Wyck led the Group on a Penetration, Target and Withdrawal Support mission to Dessau. The 336 Squadron reported seeing 40 plus e/a. Ira Grounds Destroyed one Me 109.

Major Fred L. Heene was assigned to Rollestone camp, Salisbury, Wiltshire, to attend Senior Gas Officers Course.

Capt. Kanaga was assigned to Group effective this date. The following awards were authorized effective 10 Aug:

3rd Oak Leaf Cluster to the Distinguished Flying Cross
Lt. Biel
Capt. Sobanski

4th Oak Leaf Cluster to the Distinguished Flying Cross
Lt. Hofer

6th Oak Leaf Cluster to the Distinguished Flying Cross
Capt. Beeson

Oak Leaf Clusters to the Air Medal
Lt. Sharp
Lt. Barden
Lt. Fraser
Lt. Kolter
Lt. Scott
Lt. Speer

17 August - Capt. Van Wyck led the Group on a Penetration, Target and Withdrawal Support to B-24s to Les Foulons. 10/10ths clouds covered the target and subsequent stooging over the beachhead resulted in no actions. (Apparently several high ranking officers were aboard the B-24s as there were about 100 Mustangs escorting the ten bombers.)

Captains Smith and Montgomery and Lt. Howe, who left for the States, 24 May 1944 on leave, were greeted with "Welcome Home" this afternoon at the "Times Square" dispersal, by Pilots and crews.

"Looking out of our Dispersal window today, we saw a very good example of Anglo-American cooperation. A farmer was gathering up his bundles of wheat, assisted by a number of crew chiefs, assistant crew chiefs, and armorers who had finished a hard days' work on their planes. The weather looked a little uncertain, so their help was doubly welcome."

T-0845 - Group airborne—The crash crew reported that the brake locked on the right wheel of Becky 50 in VF-V - I do not know if the Pilot is aware of it or not.

T-1630 - Lt. Grove in VF-T landed at Hethal with coolant trouble. They fixed it all right there, but now he has a flat tail wheel tire. Lt. Patteeuw is going to Bodney. He will take the assembly over to him.

T-1828 - VF-T back here from Hethal OK.

18 August - Sgts Goodrich, Ebling, Kucera, Schlezes, and Shmidt, and Cpls Mrock and Shea were assigned to Sta F-369, to carry out instructions of CG, 65 Fighter Wing.

Lts. Creamer and Anderson were asgnd to 335 Squadron.

"By GO 67, 1 August 1944, an Air Medal is awarded to the following EM for exceptionally meritorious achievement in aerial flight while participating in the longest escort mission and shuttle raid in the history of VIII Fighter Command. The ground personnel necessary for the crewing of planes and the carrying out of operations engaged long, arduous, and dangerous flights over enemy territory subject to attack from anti-aircraft artillery and hostile aircraft. This devotion to duty and disregard of personal safety reflect great credit on themselves and the Armed Forces of the United States."

M/Sgt Gerhardt H. Betz	S/Sgt Glesner H. Weckbacher
M/Sgt Warren G. Adams	S/Sgt John E. Wilson
M/Sgt Elwood L. Briel	Sgt George W. Ashton
M/Sgt Lawrence H. Krants	Sgt Albert A. Burnham
M/Sgt Dorn I. Painter	Cpl Ellsworth C. Schaldach
M/Sgt Joseph D. Coady	S/Sgt Donald E. Allen
M/Sgt Paul F. Riddle	S/Sgt Paul G. Fox
T/Sgt Howard C. Kehrer	S/Sgt Milton A. Kosmoski
T/Sgt Wilbur V. Ramey	S/Sgt Joseph S. Waydak
T/Sgt Chester C. Wall	Cpl Glen K. Roen

By GO 70, Hq. VIII Fighter Command, 6 Aug 44.

The **Distinguished Flying Cross** is awarded to Lt. Grover C. Siems.

Captain Donald D. Perkins completed his tour on 4 Nov 1944. He was CO of D Flight, 335 Squadron. Konsler collection.

An **Oak Leaf Cluster to the Distinguished Flying Cross** is awarded to the following officers:

Capt. Howard D. Hively
1st Lt. David W. Howe
1st Lt. Joseph L. Lang
1st Lt. Shelton W. Monroe

An **Air Medal and/or Oak Leaf Cluster to the Air Medal** is awarded to the following officers:

Captain William F. Hedrick
2nd Lt. Clarence L. Boretsky
2nd Lt. Robert A. Dickmeyer
1st Lt. David K. Needham
1st Lt. Jack T. Simon
1st Lt. Willard G. Gillette
2nd Lt. Preston B. Hardy
Captain Thomas E. Joyce
2nd Lt. Donald M. Malmsten

Col. Blakeslee led an Area Support for Fighter-Bombers to the Beauvais area. Mission was uneventful and no e/a were seen.

Captain Mc Farlane led the Group on a Dive Bombing and Strafing mission to Beauvais-Chantilly-Pontoise area, armed with 500-lb. G.P. bombs. They attacked two tunnels and a M/Y with poor to good results. During the attacks, Capt. Joyce's plane was hit by flak, and Lt. Lange was bounced before dropping his bombs. The Group was bounced by 50 plus Me 109s near Beauvais.

Casualties:

Captain Thomas E. JoyceNYR
2nd Lt. Arthur C. Cwiklinski MIA
2nd Lt. C. G. Howard MIA
2nd Lt. Dean E. Lang MIA
1st Lt. Rosenson MIA
2nd Lt. Conley MIA
2nd Lt. Cooper MIA
2nd Lt. Smith MIA
2nd Lt. Dailey MIA
Captain Glass MIA

(Captain Joyce landed in France and returned; two others, Glass and Cwiklinsky, became evaders; one, Lange, was captured, and six, Dailey, Cooper, Conley, Rosenson, Smith, and Howard, were killed).

Results:

Lt. Hardy	1 Me 109 Destroyed
Lt. Whalen	1 Me 109 Destroyed
Lt. Cwiklinski	2 Me 109 Destroyed
Lt. Iden	1 Me 109 Destroyed
Lt. Perkins	1 Me 109 Destroyed
Lt. Diamond	1 Me 109 Destroyed

Reports: Lt. Clifton - "We were on a dive-bombing mission in the Beauvais-Paris area. I was flying White Two to Cobweb Leader, Capt. Joyce. The target he chose to bomb was a railway tunnel just to the north of Meru. Myself and the rest of the Section stayed up while he went in to drop his bombs. He immediately encountered a heavy concentration of light flak, but continued on to drop the bombs. Upon pulling up, he R/T'd and said he was pretty badly shot up. I could see that his starboard wing was in bad shape; about 18 inches or two feet of it was sticking up at a right angle to the rest of it. We took up a heading of west, trying to make our own lines. After flying for a while, the ship seemed to be in better shape than first thought, so we switched over to channel "C" and got a fix from "Snackbar." We were directed to a landing strip on the coast (A-1 Normandy). Upon reaching the field, Capt. Joyce put his wheels down and landed the ship O.K."

*****

Lt. Gillette - "I was flying Cobweb Blue Leader with Lt. D.E. Lange, who was my No. 2, in Beauvais area. We had been top cover (4,000 feet) for Cobweb Squadron for about 35 or 40 minutes when I started looking around for a target. Six Me 109s came down from 4 o'clock high (5,000 feet). I circled, doing two turns, when they decided to attack either our Section or the one below us (Becky Blue). I looked back and saw strikes all over Lt. Lange's kite 1,000 feet below me. I saw his kite going down and then a chute opened. Later I saw a chute lying on the ground in a field near some woods. The time was 1935 hours and south and west of Beauvais about five or ten miles."

*****

Lt. Hardy - "I was leading Cobweb Red Section at 500 feet just south of Beauvais on a strafing deal. We were bounced by 15 plus Me 109s and broke left. Lt. Cwiklinski and Lt. Howard were my #3 and #4. In the ensuing fight, I saw two parachutes which I think were both my Pilots, although one could possibly have been a Hun that was clobbered at the same time. I had shot one Me 109 off the tail of one P-51 and Lt. Whalen shot one off my tail. The action had worked its way to the west outskirts of Beauvais about 1930 hours."

*****

T-1205 - Briefing; 1224, Press; 1230, Take off, no set Course, time. This is a rush job! Duration 3-4 hours. Will be coming back from southeast.

T-1228 - Caboose White 2 said he was coming to land. Told him there were a/c on the R/W. Asked his trouble. Horseback told him to land at Great Sanford. White 2 said OK. He thought he could make it. Couldn't get Great Sanford on the phone to tell them.

T-1240 - Great Sanford hasn't seen any of our aircraft. White 2 may have been the one who called Horseback at 1237 and said he was OK and catching up to him.

T-1554 - All Group back OK except Caboose 44, Lt. Vozzy. No word from him. Caboose White 2 OK.

T-1655 - Lt. Vozzy landed OK. Had landed on the beachhead.

T-2049 - All group back to base except 10 or 11 (rough show). Lt Green, Caboose 70 landed on beachhead. May be more there.

T-2057 - Lt. Green landed. He says that Capt. Joyce is on beachhead. Plane shot up. No news of other 9 still unaccounted for.

A new development had the Enlisted Men buzzing. An order from Headquarters requested the names of 20% of the Enlisted Men who were most eligible to be transferred back to the States for furlough. A point system was being established.

19 August - There was a buzz-bomb alert at 1455 hours; the all clear at 1500 hours.

Capt. Joyce, who landed due to battle damage at A-1 Landing Strip in Normandy, 18 Aug 44, returned to base today and reported as follows: "I landed at Strip A-1 about 2010 hours, 18 Aug 44. A P-47 Group was operating off this strip. I was interrogated by their Intelligence Officer. I talked with their Service Squadron. They were very indefinite as to how long it would take to repair the wing (2 days to 2 weeks). I went to A-2 Strip in a jeep. This was a C-47 Troop-Carrier strip. I stayed in Transient Officers' billets overnight. Their Security Officer made up the necessary orders so that I could leave on a C-47 at 0930 hours. I landed in England at Grave about 1100 hours. Capt. Markel ferried me back to the base in an AT-6. We arrived about 1900 hours."

2nd Lt. William J. Dvorak assigned, effective this date.

S/Sgt Eber G. Haning left our 334 Squadron today to return to the United States under the emergency provisions of W.D. Circular No.58, 1943. Gary had been a Crew Chief in 334 from Nov 42, when he first crewed Steve Pisanos' Spitfire. He turned over his duties to his able assistant George Russel.

T-1145 - Atcham called to tell us that Capt. Van Wyck had not yet arrived. Took off from here at 1028.

T-1235 - Called Atcham. They have no word of Capt. Van Wyck and have started overtime action.

T-1310 - Becky 80, Capt. Van Wyck, called in on R/T for a homing. Notified Atcham immediately but as they have already taken over-due action, I also notified D.C. Ops (Temple Bar 5411)

Van Wyck had landed at High Cliff about 1200 hours. High Cliff says they notified Atcham. Atcham says they didn't.

T-1327 - Capt. Van Wyck lands at base.

T-1400 - Capt. Joyce called from Grove. He is there now and wants some-one to come after him.

T-1416 - Capt. Markel airborne in AT-6 to pick up Capt. Joyce, also going to Hendon and Membury.

T-1450 - Ops B reports buzz-bomb 15 south of base headed this way. Defense Board notified.

T-1453 - Siren blew.

T-1504 - All clear.

T-1515 - Lay called from Q site and says one of the glim lamps doesn't work, and #1 motor is still out. Reported this to Mr. Testi. He says he will take necessary action.

T-1530 - Channel C is u/s as Sgt Dewitt has been working on it. Ops B notified.

T-1800 - Channel C standby shut down. We have nothing up with VHF. Controller at Op's says OK.

20 August - Weather bad no operations.

21 August - Weather bad no flying.
1st Lt. Orrin C. Snell to report o/a 21 Aug 44 to AAF Sta. 101, to appear before the Central Medical Board.
Capt. Alfred H. Markel assigned to Hq., 4th Fighter Group.

22 August - Weather still bad no flying.
General Auton presented awards to the following Pilots:
Oak Leaf Cluster to the Distinguished Flying Cross
Capt. Montgomery
Capt. Smith

Lt. Allen, who was reported MIA from the second mission on 8 June 1944, returned to base today and reported as follows: "While on a Fighter-Bombing mission, 8 June 44, I collided over the target (Le Mans, France) with Lt. Scott. We were at about 500 feet. I did not see Lt. Scott's or my plane crash, nor did I see Lt. Scott bail out. The collision killed my engine. Being over a village, I had to leave the ship quickly. No difficulty was met in bailing, although I left the ship in straight and level flight. Being only a few hundred feet off the ground, I landed very soon after the chute opened, sliding

Lt. James F. Scott 334 Squadron was killed instantly when his plane dove into the ground after the tail was cut off in a collision with Lt. Allen near LeMans Fr. He is pictured with crew chief Gary Hanning. Konsler Collection.

off a house top. The chute prevented a hard hit. There were Frenchmen in the yard who hid my chute and flying clothes after a few minutes' arguing.

I walked down behind a few houses, then out into the street, slowly leaving town. I only walked about a half-mile because of bad bruises. Then I hid in a grain field for several hours. I approached a farmhouse as advised in previous Evasion and Escape lectures. At this place I received clothes and started out the next morning after a good night's sleep and breakfast. After this, I traveled by day on small roads and cart roads, stopping only for food and sleep or when my legs were too sore to walk. After a week of being on my own an organization contacted me and everything was planned from then on. I think dog tags are the most help, with knowledge of French, or a phrase book, running second. I was very glad to get back to England."

*****

T-1500 - Reception on "A" Channel is very bad. Too much distortion, sounds very hollow as if someone was talking through a barrel. Have been using stand-by. Channel "C" is the same way. They have used 3 or 4 different receivers at Lenards End, but it doesn't make any difference. Sgt. Dewitt thinks it may be because everything is hooked up in 'parallel' instead of 'series.' He will be up tomorrow morning to check it.

24 August - Col. Blakeslee led the Group on a Penetration and Target Support for the 1st Task Force of 96 B-24s to Misburg and Target and withdrawal Support for 2nd Task Force of six CWs of B-17s from Merseburg. The object was the bombing of the jet plane centers. The Group rendezvoused with the B-24s and escorted them over the target, which they bombed with good results. They then proceeded to Merseburg where they escorted the B-17s through

Captain Ted E. Lines (r) 335 Squadron completed his tour as an Ace on 30 Nov 1944 with ten kills. Konsler photo.

their bomb run and then to the coast. While escorting some straggling B-24s, Lt. Line's Section sighted two Me 109s. They attacked, and Lt. Lines claims two 109s Destroyed.

Godfrey destroyed four Ju-88s, but was hit by flak and crash-landed. He had a total of 36 planes to his credit. He was reported to have become a POW. Pierce Wiggin destroyed one, and Melvin Dickey got three.

Combat report:

Ted Lines- "I was leading Blue Section on the Starboard side of the bombers when I spotted 2 Me 109s several thousand feet below. I called my Section to let them know I was going down after them. I dropped my tanks and headed down. When I was at about 5,000 feet, the 109s split up, so I took the nearest one expecting my #2 to take the other, but I did not realize my R/T was out. I was closing fast, so I started firing out of range and the 109 did a split S and dove into the ground, exploding on impact.

As I looked around for the second 109, I was getting intense light flak from the ground, so I started climbing in a port orbit. When I reached 12,000 feet, I spotted the second 109 and dove on him. I was closing fast and again started firing out of range. The 109 started a slow port turn and the pilot started to bail out, but we were right on the deck. When he opened his chute, it caught on the tail, and I saw the Pilot and his a/c crash into the ground. The plane broke into a thousand pieces on impact, and the Pilot was still hanging on to the tail when it crashed. Again I was receiving intense light flak from the ground.

Ted E. Lines 1st Lt. Air Corps.

*****

All enlisted men met in the hangar where Major Heene announced that furloughs are again authorized for the Group, but that this information was not to be discussed outside the Group.

Capt. Howe then stressed the importance of all personnel investing as much as possible in war bonds. The Group had already subscribed 100 percent of its quota, but a goal of 150 percent was suggested.

A super collosal variety show, headlined "This Ain't The Army," with an all GI cast, sponsored by the Post's American Red Cross Club (entire script and original lyrics by Sgt. Leonard Anker) made its premier performance in the cinema at 2015 hours. The GIs started to que up about 1930 in the rain, and by showtime the house was packed. The show went over big, to the credit of those who made the show possible. By the time the show was over, it already had two offers for repeat performances outside the field.

Sgt Leonard Anker was Master of Ceremonies, and Bennie "Dad" Schroeder, Director of the "Flying Eagles" band, was the Musical Director. Three of the musical organization come from 334 Squadron; "Dad" Schroeder, "Kirk" Kirkpatrick, and Bill Brong. Four of the 17 members of the cast were from 334; Maynard Bartels, in four scenes, Pete Abbott, in one scene, Lou Tartaro, in one scene, and Howard Crosset, a surprise crooner, who cut loose with some mighty fine singing, some of it done in convincing black-face.

T-0900 - Having trouble with Channel "A." Sgt Dewitt and Capt. Conrad both here. Using stand-by.

T-1100 - Channel "A" is working a little better now.

T-1400 - Colgate calling Caboose 70, Lt. Green. They had him in ASR but apparently lost contact with him. He was with the R/T Relay. They think he bailed out.

T-1415 - Sgt. Anderson from DF Station Duxford called. They are picking up an open transmitter at about 159 megacycles. Have been getting it off and on for the past week. It isn't one of the Channels, but they get it when they hand tune their set. They say it is in one direction. Gave the information to Capt. Conrad, and he will call Sgt. Anderson at Duxford. Ext. 214.

T-1453 - Group all back but Capt. Godfrey, Becky 44, who's reported to have landed in Germany and Lt. Green who's reported to have definitely bailed out. He was flying WD-E. Approximate

position WJ04—about 70 mileseast of Lowestoft. Bailed at about 1329.

T-1454 - Lt. Vestal from 9th Weather Recon. Sq. landed for an operational mission in a P-51. Letter 80-0. His generators out. Home station is Matching. He aborted from his mission and lost his #2 man. Had trouble getting 9th Air Force on phone so passed information to Flying Control at Matching, and Pilot talked to his Squadron. 45th will fix his a/c.

T-1515 - Lt. Vestal's Squadron called back to tell him the weather there is bad and we should check before he takes off.

T-1535 - Called F.C. at Farnborough to tell them that Major Trippett would not be coming to them. He had told them he was going there in a C-64. Had to relay the message through RAD 11 Group, but they said they understood it OK.

T-1701 - Called F.C. Matching again. Lt. Vestal ready to take off. Control Officer said OK. Our weather 2 miles viz and 3,000' ceiling. He took off at 1702.

T-1735 - Lt. Vistal's weather Squadron called. Connection very bad. Message had to be relayed. They report Lt. Vistal down at some other base. Want to know who gave him permission to come home. Told them F.C. Officer at Matching. Research shows that Lt. Vistal landed at Stanstead OK. The control jeep started leading him in, and the a/c ran into the jeep. Pilot was uninjured. Prop. bent!

T-1840 - Op's controller says Ok for Gen. Auton to return if their weatherman says. It's Ok now. Called Deanland and told them. They said he would be airborne right away. I told them he should check the weather enroute!

25 August - Capt. Brown led the Group on a Penetration, Target and Withdrawal Support to Schwerin. Six e/a were sighted. One Section dove, but was unable to engage. The 336 Squadron attacked eleven Me 109s. Lts. Grounds, Logan, and Hagan destroyed three.

Casualties: 2nd Lt. Kenneth J. Rudkin, MIA. Lt. Werner, who last saw Lt. Rudkin, made the following statement: "On the 25th of Aug 44, while on a bomber escort mission to Northern Germany, Lt. Rudkin, flying my wing as Blue 4, failed to return. While over the target area, bandits were reported, whereupon our section dropped tanks and proceeded to dive on an unidentified e/a at about 10,000 feet. We were at 20,000 feet. While diving, a white-nosed radial engine aircraft made a pass at Lt. Rudkin who was behind and slightly to port of me. I saw the unidentified aircraft coming in high from about 8 o'clock. I broke into him and made him break off the attack. As he went underneath me, I recognized it as a P-47, whereupon Lt. Rudkin and I proceeded to take off in the direction of our Group.

It was then that heavy flak started to come up. I broke up and to the right; Lt. Rudkin, down to the left. After I was out of range of the flak, I called Lt. Rudkin and received no reply, but I can't say if he answered or not. My radio could possibly have been out, for shortly after that, I could hear nothing. The time we started flak evasion maneuvers was about 1230 hours; the altitude 20,000 feet; and it was in the vicinity of Lubeck, Germany." (Rudkin became a POW).

Lt. Glover led the group on a Penetration, Target and Withdrawal Support to Liege. The mission was uneventful, but the bombing produced good results.

With members of the unit modeling, a mobile intelligence unit put on a humorous lecture and demonstration of German military uniforms, insignia, and weapons. They also explained the construction and operation of German mines, mortars, and light weapons.

T-1400 - Dispatched Crash Truck and Ambulance to B-26 crash SW of field near Newport.

T-1612 - All Group back except Cobweb 71, Lt. Rudkin. No word. He and Cobweb 51 were bounced by P-47s.

T-1630 - Crash MV back from B-26 crash. Need a wrecker to extricate bodies. B-26 belongs to Stanstead, and they know about it—Complete washout. All concerned notified. Guards posted.

T-1645 - By order of Col. Clatinoff, no food will be brought to crash crews. Henceforth all meals will be consumed at the mess hall.

26 August - Lts. Gillette, Hills, and Terry and T/Sgt Walter Kiefer were ordered to various stations to carry out instructions of CO.

Capt. Brown led the Group on a Penetration, Target, and Withdral Support to Rheine. No e/a were seen.

T-0600 - 336 Sq. called asking why the runway lights weren't lighted for takeoff. This is the first we knew of anybody going anyplace. Viz. 300 yards or less, ceiling OK. Apparently an ASR mission.

T-0610 - After phoning Intelligence, 335 Sq. and ASR at Wing, I learned that four of our a/c are to meet a Warick over the field right away to go on an ASR mission. Still dark and weather very bad. Ops B is trying to find a field nearby where our boys can land if they have trouble.

T-0620 - Capt. Graff, ASR at Wing called to advise that Steeple Morden is open. The Warick is over the field and is standing by for our a/c. Capt. Graff says he talked with Lt. McCall here this morning at 0530 and he told him weather OK.

T-0635 - 3 a/c airborne - The 4th Lt. Vozzy in WD-J had coolant trouble and did not go . Viz-200 yards at the most. Really about 50 yards.

T-0645 - Capt. Graff at Wing advises that arrangements were made with Group Operations last night for the flight. No one told us, and Capt. Croxtar at Intelligence said he didn't know about it either.

T-0815 - Called Controller at Wing that we are closed in tight here in case one of ASR a/c has to return.

T-1110 - One of our aircraft (found to be Cobweb 32, Capt. Kanaga) asked permission to drop tanks. He sounded very urgent. He did so on the field and then proceeded to land the wrong direction. No damage.

T-1430 - All planes returned to base from Op's. R/T Piss Poor—Right you are lad!

T-1700 - Q Site reports strange object found by farmer. Cannot locate ordinance Officer. Think it might be bomb fuse or incendiary.

27 August - Col. Blakeslee led the Group on a Penetration, Target, and Withdrawal Support to Oranienburg and Basdorf. Vinegrove 3/1 reported they were turning back due to a solid front to 26.000 feet just inland. No e/a were encountered, but further convoy activity was observed.

T-1216 - Group airborne.

T-1400 - Our old "A" Channel receiver is hooked up. Works much better. "C" Channel is still the same.

T-1636 - Group all back but R/T relay and Caboose Green Section on ASR. They are OK.

T-1845 - R/T reception much better—Using our old receiver!

T-1958 - Two Mosquitos landed from Walton.

T-2000 - 7 Tempests landed from West Molling. Will stay overnight.

28 August - A War Department training film "Articles of War" was shown to all available EM. All EM will be required to attend one of the showings.

Col. Blakeslee led the group on a Strafing mission to the Strasbourg area. Weather prevented the Group from going beyond

Sarrebourg, and the Group landed at Manston due to low visibility at Debden. They returned later in the day to Debden.

Results: 56 goods wagons Destroyed

22 locomotives Damaged

13 trucks Destroyed or Damaged

1 factory and 1 oil tank Damaged

Battle Damage: Lt. Brown (QP-T) has a small flak hole in leading edge of starboard wing.

Casualties: 1st Lt. Herbert VanderVate, Jr., MIA. Major Carlson, Group Operations Officer, reported as follows: "I was flying in #4 position; Lt. VanderVate was flying in #3 position; both of us in Blue Section of the lead Sq. We reached the target area near Sarrebourg. At approximately 0845 hours, we descended to about 1,000 feet and changed to trail formation for the purpose of strafing a truck convoy. I was directly behind Lt. VanderVate on the first pass made on the trucks, but was out of the pattern after firing. I lost contact with him and joined the first Section I saw, which was White Section. I did not see Lt. VanderVate after this first attack on the trucks."

*****

Capt. McKennon bailed out near Niederbronn, having been hit by flak. He was seen to land near some trees.

Major Thompson and Capt. Schlegel are missing, and no one can account for them, so they are classed as NYR.

Those Pilots who were available assembled to hear S/Sgt Robert Gilbert of the 336th relate his experiences beginning with 5 June 1944 when he parachuted from a B-17 on the England to Russia shuttle. He was Major Goodson's crew chief and was one of the 33 mechanics of this Group who went on this mission, to service our aircraft. Over Poland the B-17 in which S/Sgt Gilbert was assigned as a gunner; was disabled, and he and six others chuted. After landing, they joined a Polish guerilla band and for 36 days constantly fought German patrols and larger units. Eventually they got through to the Russian front lines where the guerillas delivered the Americans to the Russians, who arranged their passage back to England.

*****

Today the first three of the Enlisted Men chosen to go home, left the Station. They are M/Sgt Gilbreath, T/Sgt Boucher, and S/Sgt Corn.

T-0700 - Group airborne.

T-1000 - Weather bad. Part of Group Landing here. Others landing at forward base as follows: 21 at Marston. All OK except Lt. Corbett in VF-E. He hit a tree and damaged both wings, air scoop, etc. It will take several days to repair the a/c. Landing at forward base are:

Lt. Holske	Woodbridge
Lt. Ceglarski	Woodbridge
Lt. Russel	Gosfield
Lt. Lindsey	Gosfield
Lt. Poage	Liston
Lt. Shilke	Wormingford
Lt. Hoenickel	Wormingford
Lt. Young	Wormingford

T-1230 - Five of our a/c are not accounted for from operations: Capt. McKennon, Caboose 32, in Wd-A- Reported to have bailed out in Germany.

Capt. Schlegel, Caboose 37, in WD-O

Major Thompson, Caboose 36, in WD-F

Lt. VanderVate, Cobweb 36, in QP-K

Lt. Harris, Becky 63, in VF-Q - Thought to be at Manston, but Manston says "No"!

(McKennon and Thomson evaded, and Harris, VanderVate and Schlegel were KIA).

T-1430 - All a/c that landed at advanced bases are back here except VF-G at Wormingford (Will be there a couple of days) and VF-E at Manston.

Captain Albert L. Schlegel 335 Squadron was KIA near Strasburgh France. He was an Ace with 15 e/a Destroyed and was the Squadron Operations Officer. Charles Konsler Collection

T-1700 - Angus 53 called Speedboat for landing instructions on "A." He came in loud and clear. Speedboat didn't answer him, but I did. He said he was sorry he had the wrong frequency. Reported this to Group Communications. Sgt DeWitt.

T-1810 - Lt. Corbett back from Manston in AT-6. A/c still there (VF-E). He says they are going to salvage it. He hit a tree strafing in Germany.

29 August - S/Sgt Charles M. Carwell left for the States as the first of 334 Squadron to return on the new rotation plan.

T-1145 - Col. Clatanoff has given permission for the crash crew to use the weapons carrier to go to the Mess Hall to eat when there is flying going on at meal times. He will notify the M.P.s so they will know about it being parked there.

T-1635 - Op's B called to report Caboose 71 had called D for a fix. He was right over London very near the Balloon Barrage. They steered him away, but want him to know he shouldn't be there on a local. It's Lt. Iden. I'll tell him.

T-1715 - Hq Fwd Bomb Division called to report that Becky 37 has landed at Biecles with engine trouble. They don't know the extent. Group Operations and Sq. notified.

T-1730 - Talked to Becky 37, Lt. Dickey. He will determine the extent of the trouble and call back. A/c is VF-F.

T-1850 - Lt. Glover decided they would not try to get Lt. Dickey back tonight. Lt Boggiano is familiar with all details. The a/c needs a thermostat valve. The 336 Sq. has the valve. There's glycol available at Beicles according to Lt. Dickey.

30 August - Combat films of August 11 and 12 were shown to all available Pilots.

T-1009 - Group airborne. Only 335 Sq. on show: A Ramrod Escort to Pas de Calais. No e/a encountered.

T-1250 - All Group back OK.

31 August - The 335 Squadron flew a short escort mission to the Pas de Calais area. The bombers were not sighted and there was no action.

Sixteen aircraft of 334 were airborne on a Squadron Balboa. Commendation:

1. The following crew chiefs of the 334 and 336 Fighter Squadrons were commended for having crewed airplanes, which have completed over sixty non-abortive missions or 185 operational hours:

S/Sgt Willard W. Wahl- 79 missions
S/Sgt Vincent J. Andra - 61 missions
S/Sgt Dale L. Hall- 69missions
S/Sgt Roderic S. Lonier - 62 missions

2. Reports of this nature are most gratifying to receive and indicate, upon the part of the crew chiefs concerned, a devotion to duty and technical skill and knowledge above the average, which reflects great credit upon them.

3. It is desired that they be commended for the very real contribution they have made to the highly creditable record of your Group.
/s/ Jesse Auton
Brigadier General, U.S.A.
Commanding.

Effective this date, 1st Lt. Orrin C. Snell and Capt. William Gabrilson are assigned to Hq. 4th Fighter Group.

T-1700 - Clerk of Works report #1 motor OK now, and #2 will work if they continue to use it as they have.

T-1800 - Beaufighter from Cranfield will remain overnight. Administration:

"The past month has seen improvement in Squadron morale. This has been most notable on the part of the EM due to the start of the rotation policy, with the first group of them leaving for the zone of the interior.

A big factor also was the return of furloughs and 48-hour pass privileges. All men, with few exceptions, seem to be utilizing this privilege at the first opportunity.

This month six EM, formerly on special duty with the 1063rd MP Co., were returned to the unit for duty, which has made them happier and also lengthened the duty roster, making everyone happier.

This month requests were made to the unit for volunteers for farm help. Although this is not a detail, it became increasingly difficult to obtain volunteers for it. By the close of the month it became to be looked upon much the same as an additional detail would be.

For the first time in the history of the unit, enlisted men were returned to the Zone of the Interior on the basis of applications submitted. S/Sgt Eber G. Haning and Pvt Floyd Fuller submitted applications under emergency provisions, and both felt the Army did have some consideration for an individual when their applications were approved.

This month, Squadron Headquarters has been exceptionally busy. All men had to be contacted to determine whether they wanted election ballots for the coming general election. The 5th War Bond Drive was also in progress this month, and all men responded warmly in the purchase of bonds to achieve the quotas set for us. We reached well over 150% of that quota. This also placed an added heavy burden on Squadron Headquarters, but all men worked extra hard to make it a success.

Transfer of two of the Sq. Administrative Officers without replacements has placed an added amount of extra work on the remaining Officers. However, so far they have been able to cope with it.

Monthly Consolidated Strength Report

334 Squadron   Officers 49   Enlisted Men 245
335 Squadron   Officers 50   Enlisted Men 247

The Assessed Enemy Casualty Report USAAF confirmed the following claims for the period 1 April thru 17 June:

Aircraft Destroyed 85

Aircraft Damaged 50

Plus Miscellaneous locomotives, cars, barges, factories, towers, hangars, etc.

The following Officers posted aircraft Destroyed, of various types:

Col. Blakeslee	1
Lt. Col. Peterson	1
Lt. Col. Clark	1
Maj. Cohen	1
Maj. McPharlin	1/2
Capt. Hively	4
Capt. Sobanski	2-1/3
Capt. Beeson	2-1/3
Capt. Care	2
Capt. Montgomery	8-1/2
Capt. Howe	1
Capt. Markel	1
Capt. Smith	4-1/2
Capt. Schlegel	1/2
Capt. Megura	5-5/6
Lts. France	2-2/3
Wynn	2
Bunte	1
Biel	6-5/6
Carr	1-1/2
Pierce	1-5/6
Blanchfield	3-1/3
Moulton	1
Hofer	5-1/2
Monroe	4-5/6
Siems	2-5/6
Hills	3
Howe	3
Lang	5-1/3
Malmsten	1
Kenyon	2
Riley	1/2
Barden	1/2
Scott	1/2
Fiedler	1/3

10

New Records

1 Sept 1944 - Capt. Brown led the group on an escort mission for three CWs of B-24s to Haguenau. After the bombers aborted, the Group went hunting, and Col. Kinnard, Capt. Montgomery, and Lt. Werner destroyed four e/a. Later, near Lens, the Group sighted the Germans, apparently demolishing an A/D's runways with land mines.

The 334 Squadron was led by Capt. Joyce on a support mission to Holland. It appeared that the B-24s dropped leaflets, and later a new type of bomb since the explosions made great flashes which were different from those previously observed.

Blakeslee was placed on leave for the States, and Jim Clark became acting CO.

2 Sept - Capt. David Moore was assigned to 334 Squadron, and 1st Lt. Herbert Kneeland was assigned to 336.

Major Heene held an informal meeting in the hangar. He covered a new furlough policy, and the point system for rotation of Enlisted Men, setting priorities for rotation to the States.

3 Sept - Lt. Steve Pisanos, who was reported MIA 5 Mar 44, returned to Debden. He regaled his many listeners with stories of his crash-landing near Le Havre and his subsequent experiences. Returning from the mission, he experienced engine trouble and decided to bail out. He stepped out on the wing, but his dinghy strap had caught in the cockpit. He was unable to jump. He was unable to get back into the plane. He was forced to remain standing on the wing, from which position he manipulated the controls to crash-land. Steve bellied it in nicely, but as he hit the ground, he was thrown off the wing and landed some fifty feet away. He broke his shoulder. Such a landing was a remarkable feat, and Steve owes his life to his expert handling.

Lt. Pisanos attempted to fire his plane, but he was receiving rifle fire from some eager Jerries. He took off for a nearby woods and eluded them. For security reasons, not much of the ensuing story could be told, but he managed to get medical attention and to get to Paris, where he stayed until liberated by the advancing American Armies. While in Paris, he allied himself with the Maquis, who were harassing the Germans, and he had some extremely close encounters with them. He threw a hand grenade which separated a German Officer from his uniform and helmet. Steve appropriated the helmet as a souvenir, bringing it back with him.

*****

The past few days have seen considerable local flying, and on all local flights, the newest type of compressed air "G" suits were used. They seemed to be much more practical, and comfortable, as well. The old type water-filled suits were never used operationally.

The 335 Squadron had the addition of four new Pilots: 2nd Lts. Bancroft, Effner, Lewis, and Willruth.

5 Sept -The **Purple Heart** was awarded to 2nd Lt. Eacott Allen for wounds received as a result of enemy action on 8 June 44.

On a Bomber Escort mission to Karlsruhe, led by Lt. Glover, there were no e/a seen. However, an unusual incident occurred. Capt. Gerald Brown, NYR, flying Cobweb White 3 at 21,000 feet near Arras, began to trail white smoke and lose altitude. He immediately dropped his wing tanks and took up a course of 270 degrees. His wingman followed him down. At 10,000 feet, Brown jettisoned his canopy, pulled up, and rolled over, but did not get out. He went into a spin, recovered, pulled up again, rolled over, and bailed out. His chute opened at approximately 5,000 feet, and his plane went into a vertical dive, exploding on impact in a field below. As his wingman passed over him on the deck, Brown was standing by his chute waving.

Indicative of the spirits of the Pilots is the fact that when Capt. Brown announced over the R/T that his intention was to bail out, some wag asked, "*Are you taking your Section with you?*" Bailing out is not looked upon as a very serious affair by those who are not contemplating the jump.

1st Lt. Oscar F. LeJeunesse was shot down on D Day by flak and he bailed out over enemy territory. As a POW, he escaped and returned on 5 September. He was transferred to Mitchell Field, NY. Charles Konsler Collection

The **Distinguished Flying Cross** was awarded to:
1st Lt. Preston B. Hardy
1st Lt. Willard G. Gillette
Captain Thomas Joyce
An **Oak Leaf Cluster to the Distinguished Flying Cross** was awarded to
Captain Gerald Brown
1st Lt. Shelton W. Monroe

6 Sept - 2nd Lt. Raymond Dyer and 2nd Lt. Morton Savage were assigned to 334 Squadron.

Capt. Gerald Brown, who bailed out yesterday over France, returned today after having been toasted with Champagne for being the first American into the village of Bucquoy. He returned to England by C-47.

The 336 Squadron sent four a/c, flown by Lts. Dickmeyer, Wozniak, Warner, and Mc Fadden, to Northolt for briefing on a special escort mission. The mission was uneventful.

7 Sept - The following Officers were promoted as indicated:
1st Lt. to Capt. Shelton W. Monroe
2nd Lt. to 1st Lt. Clarence L. Boretsky
2nd Lt. to 1st Lt. Robert A. Dickmeyer

1st Lt. Spiros N. Pisanos was ordered to report to Headquarters Commander, European Theatre of Operations, USA, for temporary duty, and upon completion, to Headquarters U.S. Strategic Air Forces in Europe, reporting to the Director of Intelligence for temporary duty not to exceed 30 days.

Major Heene today received a letter from Mrs. Jean Halbrook, Lt. Ralph Hofer's wife, stating that she had been informed that her husband had been killed in action over Hungary. However, no official notification has yet been received by the Squadron concerning Lt. Hofer, who was listed MIA as of 2 July 1944.

Capt. Joyce, while on pass in London, met Lt. Malmsten, who was reported MIA 7 Aug 44. Malmstem should be returning to the Squadron soon.

Due to rain the past couple of days, the Pilots are catching up on their poker time. Lt. Rinebolt has been taking the worst licking!

8 Sept - An uneventful Support mission was led by Lt. Glover to Mannheim.

Lts. Walsh and Buchanan, while on pass in London, met Lt. Cwiklinski, who was reported MIA 18 Aug 44.

F/Os Olin A. Kiser and Charles E. Konsler joined 335 Squadron today.

9 Sept - Capt. Brown led an uneventful Support mission to Mainz.

Col. Kinnard led a Dive Bombing Mission to Schouwen Island. They dive-bombed three large boats with twenty-two 250-lb. G.P. bombs with no hits, but strafing set all three on fire. They were forced to beach.

1st Lt. Earl C. Walsh bailed out over the English Channel. He was picked up by an Air Sea Rescue launch and returned to England.

Lt. Cwiklinski, reported MIA 18 Aug 44, returned to base. He reported as follows: "Flying at 1,000 feet, I lost power. The cockpit filled with smoke, so I jettisoned the canopy and prepared to crash-land. I left my chute and dinghy in the burning plane and hid my helmet and Mae West in an oat stack. Looking for a place to hide, I saw some farmers beckoning to me. I approached them, and they hid me in a wagon under some oats. They outfitted me with civilian clothes and moved me to a farm about five miles away. From there I rode a bike about five miles to Etrepagny, where I stayed in the mayor's home. On 29 Aug the town was liberated by the English. The next day I looked at my plane, which was completely destroyed. On 2 Sept, I left and reached England on 5 Sept."

*****

S/Sgt Grimm, of 335 Squadron was awarded a Bronze Star for meritorious conduct in his work as Crew Chief for extended availability of his kite for missions without a single abort.

10 Sept - On a Support mission for B-24s to Ulm, the Group, led by Capt. Brown, heard a R/T from Lt. Lines that there were seven Me 109s in the vicinity of Strasbourg. Lt. Lines, of 334, attacked and Destroyed three of these 109s by himself. He, then, topped it off with a Ju 88 Destroyed.

F/O Poage is NYR from 335 Squadron.

Capt. John C. Fitch has joined 335 Squadron.

Combat Report: "As the result of engine trouble, I was flying alone trying to catch up with the Group. As I approached Strasbourg, I saw seven Me 109s pass beneath me. They were flying as a Group of four, and a considerable distance behind them a Group of three, one of which was smoking. I called the Squadron leader and asked for help. I then attacked the rear section, concentrating on the one that was smoking. I fired from 600 yards down to 100 yards, at which point he went straight into the deck and exploded.

I then picked on the one to the left and got him in a port turn. He also went into the deck and exploded. Meantime, two of the e/a got on my tail and started firing. As we orbited, I saw what I thought were six FW 190s closing on the Huns on my tail; they turned out to be P-47s and got the Me 109s off my tail. I then went after the third 109 of the original formation and followed him across an A/D where they really threw the flak at me. The Hun then made a very short port-turn and tried to land, but he didn't quite make it; he crashed with one of his wings flying off through the air.

My R/T was out and I could not contact my Squadron, so I started climbing and headed for home. I spotted a JU 88 at about 2,000 feet and dove after him, getting strikes along the port side of the fuselage. As I overshot, I pulled-up and observed three chutes come out as the JU 88 hit the ground and exploded."

Ted E. Lines 1st Lt. Air Corps

*****

The **Distinguished Flying Cross** was awarded to
1st Lt. Donald M. Malmsten

Lt. Walsh, NYR 9 Sept 44, returned to base, and reported: "I was flying Cobweb Red 3 on a dive-bombing mission, 9 Sept. My engine was running rough, but I thought I could safely drop my bombs on the target and return OK. I dropped my bombs on the first pass and called my wingman to come home with me. When I reached 9,000 feet, my engine cut out, and I called Air-Sea Rescue. I turned my ship up, got out on the wing, and stepped off. I opened my chute at about 4,000 feet. At about 1,000 feet, I unbuckled all straps and slipped into the water with no trouble. I had no trouble getting into my dinghy. In about 40 minutes, a Walrus arrived and

tried several times to pick me up from the rough water. He ran over me twice, and I do not remember much after that until the Walrus started to sink. I got out of the Walrus and remember nothing until I woke up on an Air-Sea ship some time later. We docked at Felixstowe, and I was moved to sick bay at Martlesham. I returned to base 10 Sept at 1830 hours."

*****

Lt. Joseph Higgins: "As we crossed into England on the return from this mission, my Wingman, Bob White, slipped his P-51 in close and motioned that his R/T was inoperative and that he was going to land at the airfield below us. Ten minutes later, I landed at Debden, taxied in, and parked my plane. I was greeted by my crew chief 'Weck' Weckbacher. As he climbed onto the wing, he said, 'Bob White is dead; he spun in and crashed at Boxsted. 'This was a bad day'."

*****

11 Sept - Col. Focht of the 2nd Armored Division reported that 2nd Lt. Harry B. Noon was killed today when he hit a tree while strafing a road near Morigny. He is buried in the Morigny Cemetery, France.

Major Heene announced that all line personnel no longer need to carry their rifles to work.

Col. Kinnard led the Group on an escort to Halle.

Capt. Montgomery saw an e/a near Bad Frankenhausen. While chasing it, he saw ten e/a attempting to land at Plotzkau. He Destroyed one Me 109. The Pilot bailed out at 2,000 feet.

Lt. Werner caused a Me 109 to spin in and explode. He later Damaged a FW 190 with a 60 degree deflection shot, using the new K-14 computing sight.

Col. Kinnard Destroyed a Me 410 on Limburg A/D and later Destroyed a Me 109 about to land at Wernigerode.

Lts. Peterson, Peters, and Rinebolt mixed it up with some Me 109s. Rinebolt Destroyed one, and Peters reported a Probable. Lt. Cooley got two FW 190s, Lt. DuPree and F÷O Pierini each added two more, while Lts. Dugan, Joiner, Grove, Ingalis, and Patterson each scored one.

The total for the day was 14 Destroyed.

Lt. Cooley bailed out and landed in a tree near Paris.

We have no report of Lts. Russel, Groseclose, and Iden, who are believed to have landed in France or Belgium. (Patterson and Iden were KIA, and Ingalls, Russel, and Groseclose became POWs).

Combat Report: "Flying #2 in Red Section, I saw about 50 plus e/a off to our right, three or four thousand feet below us. As we started to turn to port, I saw eight Me 109s about 10,000 feet above us. In clearing my tail, I observed an e/a coming up below me, and I immediately broke left. I came up behind an e/a and started firing. The sun, however, obliterated the gunsight reticule, and I observed

Lt. Richard Rinebolt 335 Squadron (3rd from left, rear) from Montana, poses with Squadron Pilots (from Left) Lt. Robert Stallings, Lt. Wilbur Eaton, and Capt. John Fitch, and (front) Capt. William George and Lt. Enoch Jungling. Konsler collection.

no strikes. He dove away into the clouds. I climbed and joined another Mustang as he clobbered a 109. A 109 came in from my left, and I broke into him and dropped flaps to get behind him. He dove, and I began to fire, observing strikes on his right wing root. He pulled up and then started down with smoke streaming from his right wing. His canopy came off, and I saw a chute open. However, I kept an eye on my tail, and I did not see the plane crash. I pulled up and joined another P-51 and headed home."

Richard Rinebolt 2nd Lt. Air Corps

*****

The following is copied from a combat report filed by 1st Lt. James Russell, Jr., 29 June 1945, while at Camp "Lucky Strike," Le Havre, France. It was submitted as a claim for one FW 190 and two Me 109s Destroyed.

"I was leading 335 Squadron when Green Section called in Bandits (FW 190s) at nine o'clock low. As the Group pulled in between the Bandits and the bombers, I saw a bunch of Me 109s coming in high and started climbing to meet them. They came through us and joined the 190s. Two P-51s went down with them. I followed and made a head-on attack on a 190 that was on the tail of a P-51. I got strikes on the engine and wing roots, and he blew up.

I climbed and turned onto the tail of a Me 109, observing strikes underneath the cockpit and engine. The wheels came down, and it started smoking just as the Pilot bailed out. I skidded over to the port side of another Me 109 and gave him a long burst from dead astern, getting strikes on the wing roots and engine. Smoke started pouring from the ship and flames engulfed the front of the cockpit.

I tried to turn into a FW 190 that was firing at me from about 10 o'clock, but a 20 mm shell exploded in my cockpit, cutting my head in two places. Blood got in my eyes, so I couldn't see. When I cleared my eyes, I discovered I had been hit in the coolant system and oil lines. I dove into some low clouds and headed for home. I

flew as long as my ship would fly. I was afraid to bail because one chute strap had been cut. Near Fulda, the engine froze and started to burn, so I crash-landed in a field. I got about 150 feet from my kite and passed out. I was picked up by a forest ranger about 10 minutes later."

*****

F/O Poage returned from Amiens, France, where he had landed on a bombed field with engine trouble yesterday.

12 Sept - Capt. Brown led the Group on a Support mission to Brux/Most. Two enemy jets were seen near the bombers at different times, immediately followed by flak, leading us to believe they were directing the flak. Near Frankfurt, 336 Squadron reported 14 e/a, which 334 Red Section bounced from 26,000 feet. Lt. Dickmeyer Destroyed one FW 190 that exploded in Weisbaden. He then attacked another 190 which had been attacked by Lt. Hustwit of 336 Squadron. The Pilot bailed out. The claim is shared.

The 336 again got into the shooting, and brought the total kills for the day to nine. Lt. Lane Destroyed two with Lts. Chandler, Hustwit, Quist, and Hunt each claiming one. Lts. Davis and Evans combined to Destroy one.

Capt. Thomas Joyce is MIA, and Lt. Dickmeyer reports as follows: "I was flying Red 3, when Red 2 called in a plane to his right. Red Leader, Capt. Joyce, told him to go get it and he would cover. Then eight FW 190s came in at 4 o'clock above me. As I climbed, I saw Capt. Joyce following Red 2 towards Darmstadt. If he does not return, I believe it will be from flak, not e/a." (Capt. Joyce and Lt. Lane both became POWs).

*****

A Section of 335 attacked four Me 109s with several Pilots firing, but the credit goes to Lts. Davis and Evans.

Lt. Robert A. Dickmeyer 334 Squadron poses with Crew Chief George Russel. Konsler Collection.

Lt. Malmsten, reported MIA, 7 Aug 44 returned today. Malmsten reported that he had been wounded, but that he had met friendly Frenchmen who helped him evade until he returned to Allied Territory.

Two years ago today, the three Eagle Squadrons of the RAF swapped their Blue uniforms for the OD of the USAAF. The *Stars and Stripes*, 15 Sept, summarizes as follows:

P-51 GROUP TOPS FIGHTER OUTFITS

"Destroying 11 parked Nazi planes on an airfield in Germany on Wednesday, the Mustang Group commanded by Lt. Col. Donald M. Blakeslee, of Fairport Harbor, Ohio, who is now in the U.S., nosed ahead of the Thunderbolt group headed by Lt. Col. David Schilling of traverse City, Mich., as the high-scoring unit in the 8th fighter command."

"The Blakeslee outfit, which celebrated its second anniversary, 12 Sept, by shooting down eight enemy aircraft, has held the lead from April 10 until last week when Schilling's Group copped the No. 1 spot. Since then the P-51 Group has destroyed 24 German planes for a total of 687, while the P-47 outfit scored five victories for a total of 684."

"USAAF headquarters said that through an error, the Schilling Group was credited 10 Sept with a total of 700 enemy planes destroyed. This figure has since been revised."

The Field Day was the major event of the day. Each unit of the Group had athletic teams on the field. For the second consecutive year, the 335th Squadron won the team trophy. Later, the 335 football team won the finals for the title by beating the 336 Squadron 6-0.

Brigadier General Edward Anderson, the 4th Group's first CO, presented awards to some of the Pilots.

The **Silver Star** was awarded to Lt. Col. James A. Clark

Air Medals and/or Oak Leaf Clusters to the Air Medal were awarded to:

Lts. Preston B. Hardy, David W. Howe, David K. Needham, Grover C. Siems, Earl C. Walsh, Timothy J. Cronin, and Jack D. McFadden

In a brief address, General Anderson expressed that he has "A warm spot in his heart for this Station and Group and is proud of the record and the reputation this Group has made for itself."

A USO show was presented at the Station Cinema, and the Flying Eagles played for a dance at the Red Cross Aeroclub. Later, S/Sgt Les Watson, 335 Squadron's Field Day Ace with 24 points in the day's athletic events, and a WAAF sliced a birthday cake with two candles.

At the dance, Field Day prizes of cigarettes, trophies, and medals were awarded to the Champions by Capt. Gerald Brown.

The Aeroclub was well decorated with cartoons by S/Sgt Don Allen and a picture display by the photo lab and PR office, depicting highlights of the Group's two-year history.

13 Sept - On a mission to Ulm, led by Col. Kinnard, Blue Section strafed an A/D. They received intense flak as they strafed 25 plus planes (some were dummies). Capt. Smith destroyed one UI TE e/a and damaged another. In the process, he received 20 mm fire in the engine and cockpit, and he crashed in flames. He was killed instantly. Lt. Gillette damaged a FW 200.

The 335 Squadron was the star for the day, strafing two A/Ds. F/O Poage got three; Lt. Diamond three; Lt. Eaton one; Lt. Ceglarski two; and Col. Kinnard two, for a total of 11 Destroyed.

Combat Report: "I was flying Caboose Red 3, as top cover over Gelchsheim A/D, as Col. Kinnard led his Section on strafing passes to check out and destroy any flak batteries. He made three passes and called for us to attack. We went down from East to West firing on several dispersed aircraft. On the first pass, I set an e/a ablaze. It blew up as I passed over it.

We made another pass from the same direction, and I observed strikes behind the engine of the second plane. It blew up in front of me. On the third pass, I got strikes behind the engine of another plane, which blew up before me. After this last pass, we orbited the field and counted eleven planes burning with possibly two planes left untouched. We then set course for home.

I claim three e/a Destroyed, biplanes which I believe to be Hs 123s."

Charles E. Poage, Jr., Flight Officer.

*****

15 Sept - F/Os Charles W. Harre and Kenneth E. Foster were assigned to 334 Squadron.

The **Purple Heart** was awarded to Spiros Pisanos for wounds received by enemy action on 5 Mar 44.

Lt. Malmsten reported: "On 7 Aug, we went on a strafing mission SE of Paris to try and destroy locomotives, as well as boxcars believed to contain buzz-bombs. I was leading Green Section. We clobbered a couple of locos and received some intense light and heavy flak near Dijon. I became separated from my Wingman. I started out alone looking for more trains and, subsequently, blew up three when I came upon some trucks. I clobbered one, and as I pulled up, my engine started to smoke and it sounded like a hay bailer.

I was at 150 feet and could only keep it running for about two minutes before it caught fire. I crash-landed in a beet field and got out as quick as I could since the cockpit was full of flames. I discarded my equipment, took off across the fields about 3/4 of a mile, and crawled into a ditch filled with weeds. Here I discovered that I was burned on the cheek and nose. I walked at night and for three days before the underground picked me up. They turned me over to the Maquis, where I spent a pleasant four weeks fishing, eating wild strawberries, etc. I returned to London on 5 Sept and then back to my Squadron."

*****

Lt. Cooley, missing since 11 Sept, returned today. He had bailed out so near the front lines that the area had only been taken hours before.

17 Sept - Yesterday a buzz-bomb hit near the water tower in Saffron Walden, injuring several people.

At 0300 hours, all watches were put back an hour, so we now are operating on British daylight saving time instead of double British summer time.

The Group, led by Col. Kinnard, went on a sweep in support of the second assault on Hitler's fortress Europe. Thousands of paratroopers and hundreds of gliders landed in the Arnhem and Eindhoven area.

A few Pilots of the 335th Squadron were bounced by 15 FW 190s near Bucholt, but they shot down six e/a and damaged one for the loss of two.

Capt. Norley got on the tail of one FW 190 and destroyed it. Lt. Lines got three FW 190s, which puts him at seven e/a destroyed in two missions. Lt. Davis destroyed one FW 190 and a possible second one.

Lts. Holske and Vozzy failed to return with no one having any information other than a report that a Red-nosed Mustang was seen to go down in flames. (Holske became a POW and Vozzy was KIA).

Combat Report: "I was leading Caboose Blue Section in the area of Bucholt, Germany, when we were bounced from behind and above by 15 FW 190s. My Wingman hollered for me to break as I was trying to discard my right external wing tank. When I broke, I was head-on to five FW 190s and immediately started firing, causing one FW 190 to burst into flames. I turned starboard, still trying to drop my tank, as two FWs came under me, heading in the same direction as I was. I got on the tail of the one nearest me and started firing, and the Pilot bailed out. At this point, a 190 closed on my tail and fired at me, hitting me in the tail and wing. My tank finally came off, and I was able to maneuver onto the tail of the 190 that had been firing at me. After three orbits, he broke for the deck with me right on his tail. I fired from 500 yards down to about 100 yards and saw strikes on his engine, canopy, fuselage, wings, and tail. He burst into flames and went into the ground and exploded. I claim three FW 190s Destroyed."

Ted E. Lines 1st Lt. Air Corps

*****

"I was leading Caboose Squadron when Caboose Blue Section was bounced by 15 plus e/a from 6 o'clock high. Caboose Blue 3 called for a break, but it was too late for one of the Sections, either 2 or 4 was already going down in flames. The bandits had been flying at the base of a layer of haze and with their light grey color were very difficult to see.

I dropped my tanks. In a port break, I met an a/c head-on firing at me. These were supposedly Me 109s, and this one, with an inline engine, looked like an e/a. I fired a short burst at long range. I then noticed two FW 190s on his tail, the closest one firing, and getting strikes as it became apparent that the plane I fired on was a P-51. I broke up, coming down on the tail of the FW 190 as he broke off his attack and turned to port. I dropped 20 degrees of flaps and turned with him, the other 190 being attacked by my Wingman. I fired. The 190 rolled and started to split-S, but leveled out and started to climb. I fired again with no results. He leveled off and did some skidding evasion efforts as I closed firing and skidding past him. He dove to port, allowing me to drop back on his tail. I fired, getting many strikes on his wings and fuselage. He flicked over on his back. The canopy and some pieces flew off, and he went into a verticle dive, crashing into a farm yard where the plane blew up.

I climbed up, found my Wingman, assembled the Squadron over Wesel, and completed our mission."

Louis H. Norley, Capt. Air Corps.

*****

S/Sgt Dale L. Hall 334 Squadron at work on a P-47. Notice the pitting of the Propeller. Zigler Collection

An **Oak Leaf Cluster to the Distinguished Flying Cross** was awarded to 1st Lt. Joseph L. Lang

Air Medals and/or Oak Leaf Clusters were awarded to 18 of the 334 Pilots.

A **Bronze Star** was awarded to:

S/Sgts Vincent J. Andra, Dale L. Hall, Roderic S. Lonier, Willard W. Wahl, and M/Sgt Paul F. Riddle

All for meritorious conduct

The street lights in camp were lit tonight for the first time in over five years.

19 Sept - 2nd Lt. Thomas E. Fraser, reported MIA 6 June 44, is a prisoner of war of record.

The 335 Squadron has had four Lts. promoted to 1st. Lt.: Lts. Berry, Miles, Evans, and McCall.

20 Sept - 1st Lts. James F. Callahan, Robert L. Hills, David K. Needham, Grover C.Siems, and Jack T. Simon are relieved from duty with this organization and assigned to 70th Replacement Depot to await return to the Z of I.

The **Silver Star** was awarded to Captain Shelton W. Monroe

2nd Lt. Andrew C. Lacey and 2nd Lt. Robert S. Voyles were assigned to 334 Squadron.

Captain Robert L. Hills 334 Squadron was an ex-RAF pilot. He completed his tour in the USAAF 4th Group on 14 September 1944. He had been CO of "D" flight. Konsler Collection

22 Sept - The **Distinguished Flying Cross** was awarded to:

Lt. Joseph Higgins

Lt. James Lane

Lt. George Logan

23 Sept - On an Area support to the Allied Airborne Army, led by Lt. Col. Kinnard, what appeared to be a rocket projectile was observed to go vertically into the air from a site near Cologne, leaving an unbroken contrail to its full height.

Lt. "Doc" Achen, reported missing on 15 Aug 44, was reported to be a prisoner of war. His brother phoned this information from Goxhill today.

The following officers were assigned to 334 Squadron: 1st Lt. Carl G. Payne, 1st Lt. Donald L. Bennett, and 2nd Lt. Carmeno J. Delnero.

25 Sept - On a bomber escort to Coblenz, near Frankenberg, White and Green Sections shot up a locomotive and six passenger cars filled with German soldiers. Other vehicles, including a beer truck, were also destroyed.

Warren Williams of 336 Destroyed a Ju 88 for the only score for the day.

Capt. Roy Henwick is MIA.

The Red Raiders (335th football team) opened their season by trouncing the QM team 36-6 late this afternoon. They were sparked by "Doc" Alexopoulos. They had control of the ball most of the game.

27 Sept - Major Gerald Brown led the Group to Kassel in escort of B-24s. Lt. Senecal, who was a spare, destroyed one Me 109. The 336 got in a few licks with 100 bandits attacking the bombers. They ended with four for the day by MacFarlane, Smith, and DuPree.

A **Silver Oak Leaf Cluster to the Distinguished Flying Cross** was awarded to Captain Nicholas Megura

28 Sept - On an Escort to Magdeburg, 60 plus FW 190s attacked the bombers from low and 7 o'clock. Green Section and P-38s attacked, knocking down two before they split S'd and evaded. Lt. Howe Destroyed one.

Capt. Henwick, reported MIA 25 Sept, returned to base today. He had been strafing and lost his Section. His radio was U/S and his compass inoperative. He eventually made his way to Castel Jaloux, where he ran out of gas. He made a forced landing. He was immediately picked up by the Maquis and FFI.

They were very excited about using his 50 calibres for mopping up Germans. After much wine, cognac, and champagne, they drove him to Bordeaux. After much more drinking and talking, he finally arrived in Paris for more of the same partying. Eventually, he was provided with transport to England, arriving 28 Sept.

*****

30 Sept - Yesterday's *Stars and Stripes* carried an article lauding the 4th Fighter Group for receiving a Presidential Citation for outstanding performance of duty and extraordinary heroism in action. It also stated they have Destroyed 701 e/a. On 8 April 44 they Destroyed 31 planes in the air, breaking the VIII Fighter Command record for one day's kill. The record still stands.

More Enlisted Men left on rotation to the States.

The Assessed Enemy Casualty Report USAAF listed 334 Squadron Confirmed Claims 19 May 44 to 30 May 44—34 e/a Destroyed, 11 Damaged, plus misc. locos, trucks, etc., Destroyed claims were:

Hofer - 8 1/2

Speer - 6

Lang - 4 1/2

Siems - 3

Mc Pharlin - 2

Kolter - 2

Howe, Hively, Gillette, Fraser, Sobanski, Kenyon, and Snell, 1 each

Hewatt and Megura, 1/2 each

The 335 Squadron added Capt. W.C. Anderson and Lts. Henderson, Jungling, Stallings, and Tyler to the roster.

Lts. Lines and Perkins were promoted to Captain. "Congratulations!"

The Red Raiders won again! They beat the 24th "Brewers" in a hard fought game, 6-0.

Monthly consolidated Strength Report 30 Sept

334 Squadron	Officers 51	Enlisted Men 240
335 Squadron	Officers 51	Enlisted Men 247
336 Squadron	Officers 54	Enlisted Men 238

2 Oct 1944 - Joseph L. Lang was promoted from 1st Lt. to Captain.

Capt. Thomas R. Bell and 1st Lt. Fred E. Farrington were assigned to 334 Squadron.

Major Brown led a support mission to Hamm.

A P-51, believed to be Lt. Logan of 336, was seen spiraling down in the target area. His airspeed was reported to be 600 plus at 5,000 feet. (He was KIA).

Before takeoff, Capt. Ezzell, Squadron Intelligence Officer, recalled that on 2 Oct 1942 the Squadron got its first claims when Col. Clark (then 1st Lt.) Destroyed a FW 190. In 1943, Major Beeson (then 2nd Lt.) Destroyed a FW 190.

Today the 334th put up 20 aircraft, 4 more than usual, and there were no aborts. Unfortunately, today the Huns did not show up.

Gen. Auton read the Presidential Citation (Previously awarded) for the 4th Fighter Group and pinned the decoration on Lt. Col. Kinnard as a token presentation to the Group.

He then awarded the **Distinguished Flying Cross** to:

Lt. Gillette

Capt. Perkins

Capt. Read

Lt. Cooley and Capt. Lines were commended for their accomplishment of each destroying three e/a during one mission.

S/Sgt Schultz was given the Air Medal for his participation in the shuttle raid to Russia in July.

Auton then presented the Bronze Star to S/Sgts Vincent G. Andra, Roderic S. Lonier, Willard W. Wahl, and Grimm of 335.

4 Oct - The 335 Squadron held a party starting with beer at the Sergeants' Mess. Later there was a dance with girls from neighboring airdromes. Following the dance, all were served coffee, punch, food, and a big cake. Music was provided by the Flying Eagles."

A casualty report was received from Maurice Bolle of Merard par Bury (Oise), stating that he witnessed the crash of a U.S. fighter plane on 18 Aug. By means of dogtags and an identification tag, he identified the dead pilot as Leo Dailey. He had been wounded in several places.

Bolle assisted at Dailey's formal burial ceremony and requested the address of Dailey's next of kin in order to send pictures of the ceremony.

5 Oct - Col. Kinnard led a Support mission to Paderborn. No e/a were seen. Lt. Malmsten led his Green Section on a strafing mission against trains, disabling five locomotives and damaging many cars. In the vicinity of Nauen, three Sections left escort to chase eight Me 109s, which they were unable to catch. Meanwhile, Green Section jumped Me 109s attacking the last box of bombers. Lt. Werner chased one in a dive, indicating 600 mph. As the 109 attempted to turn port, his wings came off. Thanks to the new "G" suit, Lt. Werner did not black out in this maneuver. He then attacked a FW 190. His Wingman, Lt. Farrington, saw strikes on the e/a as he broke off the chase in the western suburbs of Berlin. During this attack, Lt. Werner's oxygen mask hose burst. Upon landing, it was discovered that a .303 bullet went through his cockpit from right to left, severing his hose. The e/a was later confirmed Destroyed.

A British jet propelled "Meteor" buzzed the drome and landed to the great interest of all on the base.

Forty-seven aircraft of the 354th Fighter Group landed here from their base at St. Dizier, France. They are to fly with us until further notice. It has placed an unexpected work load on our crews. They worked till after midnight to service these extra planes so they would be available for combat.

The **Distinguished Flying Cross** was awarded to:

1st Lt. James F. Scott

1st Lt. Thomas S. Sharp

2nd Lt. Frank E. Speer

An **Oak Leaf Cluster and a Silver Oak Leaf Cluster to the Distinguished Flying Cross** was awarded to 1st Lt. Ralph K. Hofer

6 Oct - Capt. McKennon led the Group on an escort to Berlin. Just before R/V, Lts. McCall and Lewis sighted a Me 410 north of the Hague. They chased it and brought it down, with two chutes observed. Other encounters saw Leonard Werner and Joseph Joiner each Destroy a Me 109.

Combat Reports: "I was flying Caboose Red 1 when I sighted a Me 410 above us. My Section started to climb after the e/a. At about 300 yards, I took a short burst and observed strikes. The right engine started to smoke, and he dropped his tanks as I started to fire again. He broke into my wingman, Lt. Lewis, who followed him through a diving turn, firing as he went. Lewis broke off, and I took another shot at him. Two chutes opened, and the plane crashed into the sea. I claim one Me 410 Destroyed - shared with Lt. Lewis.

I used the Gyro Gun Sight and am confidant that it was to my advantage."

Elmer N. McCall 2nd Lt. Air Corps.

*****

Fifty strange Mustangs appeared on the field today. They are from the 353rd and 354th Squadrons and will be flying with us.

7 Oct - Col. Kinnard led the Group on a Support mission to Magdeburg. The mission was uneventful, and no e/a were seen.

F/O Kenneth Foster is MIA. Lt. Rentschler reported as follows: "I was flying wing to Red 3, F/O. Foster. He peeled off from 20,000 feet at 1030 hours and said he was going home. He was streaming white smoke out of both sides of his kite. He rolled over and bailed out. Just as he rolled, the kite blew up. I did see him fall out, but lost sight of him in the smoke and flames of the explosion. I saw where the kite hit the water, but no trace of Red 3. The location was 57 miles east of Lieston.

Two air-sea rescue kites joined me in the search about an hour later. When I left, at 1320 hours, they were still there and were to be relieved by two more craft."

*****

9 Oct - Word was received that F/O Foster was picked up this morning by an ASR launch.

Major Brown led the Group to Giessen. The show was uneventful. There was heavy cloud cover, but an opening in the clouds gave Capt. Lines a glimpse of two Me 109s taking off from a field below. He dove on them and shot down both of them.

Combat Report: "Near Gedern, Germany, I developed engine trouble and started for home. As I descended, my engine started running better. I came upon a fresh clearing with six Me 109s sitting there with their engines running. One was just taking off, so I

attacked him and hit him just as he was putting up his wheels. He started to turn, crashed, and exploded. I turned and came back, attacking the one on the starboard side of the runway about to take off. I got strikes on the fuselage and engine area, and he flamed and exploded. He was still burning as I left the area. The flak was too intense to make another pass, so I called my Squadron, not realizing my R/T was out, and headed for home."

Ted Lines Capt. Air Corps

*****

10 Oct - All Pilots attended a meeting with Gen. Auton, who presented a Fighter Pilot Creed, based on interviews with a number of Aces. The text follows:

65TH FIGHTER WING

"Fighter Pilot Creed"

"I RESOLVE THAT I WILL"

1. Know my airplane perfectly.

I will know in detail the mechanical workings of every part.

I will know every flying characteristic, both good and not so good.

I will know every new development that may affect my airplane.

I will know the limits of stress and power of my airplane and engine.

2. Know my enemy airplanes thoroughly.

I will know their flying characteristics, speed, armor, and armament in comparison to my airplane.

I will recognize each of them at the first glance.

3. Be a superior gunner.

I will know my guns and sights completely.

I will practice firing and sighting at every opportunity, with every weapon available.

I will make every shot an aimed shot.

I will take enough lead to center every shot in the target.

I will never waste ammunition back of effective firing range.

4. Be an outstanding pilot.

I will always maintain combat formation teamwork.

I will keep myself in perfect physical condition.

I will use my radio sparingly and confidently.

I will develop my flying technique to perfection in every maneuver.

I will out-fly every other pilot in smoothness, judgement, and skill.

5. Have the will to fight.

I will seek out the enemy always.

I will never be deceived by enemy tricks

I will see the enemy before being seen.

I will close quickly on the enemy, destroy him, and break away fast.

I certify that _____ is eligible to sign this creed by his ability as a Fighter Pilot.

Jesse Auton

Brigadier General, U.S.A.

Commanding

11 Oct - David W. Howe was promoted from 1st Lt. to Captain.

The following were promoted from 2nd Lt. to 1st Lt.: Henry E. Clifton Jr., Jerome E. Jahnke, Lewis F. Wells, and Edward J. Wozniak.

12 Oct - On a support mission to Salzbergen, led by Capt. Norley, White and Green Sections of 334 Squadron went down to strafe. They damaged boats, locomotives, and trucks, and they destroyed 2 oil storage tanks. In the process, Lt. Dyer's plane was hit by MG bullets causing a bad glycol leak, and Lt. Wozniak hit a tree, damaging both wings, which will have to be replaced.

Yesterday the 355 Squadron returned to their base in France after having flown 2 missions with us.

All ground personnel continued their required participation in discussion groups covering subjects from Socialized Medicine to America's Post-War Foreign Policy.

A 334 Squadron party was held, starting stag, with beer at the Sergeants' Mess and then moving to the Red Cross for dancing with music by the "Flying Yanks" and attractive girls from the surrounding villages. At 2200 hours, a buffet was served with pineapple ice cream, sandwiches, cookies, and coffee in the Sergeants' Mess.

A great evening was had by all and ended with the band playing "*The Star Spangled Banner*" and "*God Save the King.*"

13 Oct - Fourteen of 334 A/C were airborne on a Balboa. Lt. Dyer bailed out on this flight. His account is as follows: "Lt. Wozniak

Capt. Joseph L. Lang 334 was a double Ace with 11 plus e/a to his credit. He crashed and was killed in a dogfight with ten Me 109s. His last R/T was "this is Lang, I am down below clouds with ten 109s, I got two. I don't know where I am and I need help."

and I had been rat-racing when I developed a run-a-way prop - 3500 RPMs. I called for a homing. When the coolant started streaming out of the engine, I realized I couldn't make it, and I looked for a field to land. The oil pressure went down to zero, and the bearings started to pound. White smoke was coming from both banks, and it was getting hot and smoky in the cockpit. I got down to 3500 feet, and I knew I had to get out.

I jettisoned the canopy, loosened my oxygen tube, and released my safety belt. I trimmed it full forward, holding back on the stick, and stood on the seat releasing the stick. I popped out of the cockpit and pulled the ripcord as the kite went straight in. I had forgotten to loosen my R/T cord and G-suit plug when I left the kite. The G-suit came loose, but the R/T cord pulled off my helmet and oxygen mask. I landed softly near a couple of trees. Three civilians stopped, picked me up, and took me to Chedburgh, a nearby RAF base, where I was soon picked up in the AT-6 and brought back to Debden. The date, *Friday the 13th Oct 44.*"

*****

14 Oct -

An **Oak Leaf Cluster to the Distinguished Flying Cross** was awarded to

1st Lt. Willard G.Gillette

1st Lt. Robert P. Kenyon

Col. Kinnard led the Group on an Escort mission to Kaiserslautern. The mission was uneventful except for the following account by Lt. Jahnke. "I was flying wing to Blue 1, Capt. Lang. About 1145 hours, Capt. Lang told Lt. Cox, Blue 3 to take over the Section. Capt. Lang then peeled off. Thinking he was aborting, we thought no more of it. At about 1310 hours, Capt. Lang called, saying 'This is Lang. I am down below the clouds with ten Me 109s....I got two. I don't know where I am and I need help.' We could not contact him thereafter." (Lang was KIA).

Assessed Enemy Casualty Report confirmed the following 39 e/a Destroyed, from 29 May 44 through 11 Sept 44:

Lt. Hofer	5 1/2
Lt. Gillette	3 1/4
Capt. Hively	3
Capt. Joyce	2 1/2
Lt. Cwiklinski	2 1/2

Lts. Scott, Sharp, Monroe, Siems, Hardy, and Lt. Col. Kinnard, 2 each

Lt. Pisanos, Capt. Montgomery, Lt. Dickmeyer,

Lt. Malmsten, Lt. Lang, Capt. Hedrick, Lt. Scally,

Lt. Whalen, and Lt. Werner, 1 each

Lt. Simon and Lt. Fernandez, 1/2 each

Lt. Shilke 1/4

The **Distinguished Flying Cross** was awarded to:
Capt. William F. Hedrick
1st Lt. Robert A. Dickmeyer
An **Oak Leaf Cluster to the Distinguished Flying Cross** was awarded to:
Capt. William B. Smith
Capt. Howard D. Hively

20 Oct -

The **Distinguished Service Cross** was awarded to Captain Howard D. Hively

"For extraordinary heroism in action against the enemy, 2 July 1944, in the area of Budapest, Hungary. Capt. Hively, with 2 other members of his Squadron, attacked over 40 enemy fighters. He climbed to attack, destroying one e/a even though one was on his tail. His canopy was shot off, wounding him, but he engaged ten more fighters, destroying one. He then pursued a third, scoring hits and forcing the pilot to bail out. The heroism, perseverence, and skill displayed by Capt. Hively on this occasion reflects highest credit upon himself and the Armed Forces of the United States."

Capt. Benjamin Q. Ezzell was ordered to report to London to attend the Monthly Escape Meeting - "1 1/2 hours of B.S."

Official confirmation was received that Capt. Joseph L. Lang, reported NYR 14 Oct 44, was killed in action.

At 1520 hours on 14 Oct 44, Capt. Lang was seen to crash 4 miles SE of Eurville-sur-Marne, France. His body was removed from the burning wreckage by personnel of the 405th Fighter Group. Reason for crash unknown.

22 Oct - Capt. Mc Kennon led the Group on an Escort to Hamm. When the escort was completed, 334 Squadron, White Section went strafing in the area of Groningen, where they shot up steamboats, barges, and gas works at villages at RQ 0110 and RQ 1510.

Meanwhile, 335 Squadron strafed and disabled ten locomotives and a barge.

26 Oct - A mission to Minden, led by Col. Blakeslee, was uneventful. However, Capt. Lines, flying spare while trying to catch up with his Squadron, was attacked by six FW 190s. They fought from 25,000 feet down to 6,000 feet. Capt. Lines managed to destroy two of them. During the combat, a Me 163 jet made two passes at Capt. Lines but registered no hits. The jet left the area and was soon out of sight. Unfortunately, upon returning to base, Capt. Lines taxiied into the revetment, damaging his left wing. It turns out his brakes were faulty.

As Lt. Peterson taxied past the dispersal, he hit the back of a truck with his left wing.

Combat Report: "I was having engine trouble and could not keep up with my Squadron. Suddenly I was attacked by six FW 190s, putting my right external tank on fire. I went into a spin and

recovered at about 8,000 feet. My wing tanks were now gone and my elevators were damaged, so I headed for the overcast with the FWs still after me. I came out of the clouds. Three were still above me, and three were behind me. I again entered the clouds. I began to maneuver onto the tail of one of the two still carrying drop tanks. When I started firing, I immediately saw strikes on his engine, fuselage, and drop tank. He blew up right in front of me. I turned onto the other one with a drop tank and fired, hitting him hard. He started to burn furiously and went straight down.

During this time, I was being fired upon by the three FW 190s from above, and a Me 163 made two passes at me. Since my engine was still acting up, I entered the clouds and steered for home."

Ted Lines Captain, Air Corps

*****

27 Oct - Orders were received to remove the red stripe from the vertical stabilizer of all our planes and to then paint the entire rudder a red color for 334 Sq., white for 335, and blue for 336.. This work was finished today.

30 Oct - Blakeslee led a support to Hamburg. The 334 Squadron sent up six Sections. This was the first time we had sent up as many as 28 planes. Unfortunately, no e/a were seen.

Upon returning from the mission, news was received that Col. Zemke, CO of the 56th Group, was downed. Blakeslee was immediately grounded to keep him from possibly sharing the same fate.

Lt. Jennings joined 335 Squadron, bringing their total of Pilots to 43.

31 Oct - The following Officers, having completed their tour of duty, were removed from duty to return to the ZOI:
1st Lt. Willard G. Gillette
1st Lt. Robert P. Kenyon
Monthly Consolidated Strength Report

334 Squadron	Officers 52	Enlisted Men 240
335 Squadron	Officers 54	Enlisted Men 246

1 Nov 1944 - Lt. Col. Kinnard assumed command of the Group, replacing Col. Blakeslee.

A siege of early morning fog has been disturbing the activities of the Group, but the fog usually lifts by noon, enabling our Pilots to go on at least one mission for the day.

Both Major Hively and Capt. Monroe, having completed their tours and returned to the States for R and R, returned to base today.

The following named 2nd Lts. were assigned to 334 Squadron: John Childs, Kenneth Helfrecht, Walter Hughes, Michael Kennedy, and Benjamin Griffin.

2 Nov - William Dvorak, Raymond Dyer, Morton Savage, and William Hoelscher were promoted from 2nd Lt. to 1st Lt.

Capt. Glover led a sweep in the Brunswick, Magdeburg, area. Five Me 163s were seen, and 335 and 336 Squadrons engaged them; each Squadron shot down one. These were the first jets claimed by our Group.

There were about 15 Me 109s with the Me 163s. Capt. Norley and Capt. Glover Destroyed a Me 163, and Lts. Brock and Kolbe each Destroyed a Me 109.

Lt. Senecal and F/O Foster damaged four locomotives.

Combat Report: "We had sighted jets going up thru the haze to attack the bombers and waited for them to come back down. I sighted one at 6 o'clock, a Me 163, and immediately dropped my tanks and advanced to full boost and revs. I set my gyro sight for 30 feet and maximum range. I had no trouble putting the dot on the jet, but at 1,000 yards I was out of range, so I followed the jet down. He started pulling away from me, so I fired a few short bursts hoping to make him turn. The jet started to level off and make a port turn with his speed dropping considerably.

I closed rapidly. Using the K-14 sight for the first time, I did get a couple of strikes on his tail, firing from 280 yards to 50 yards. With my speed at 450, I was unable to turn with him and I overshot. I pulled up and got on his tail again. As I closed on him the second time, he used his blower for a couple of seconds and then cut it off.

2nd Lt. Earl A. Quist 336 Squadron had his combat flying career cut short on 8 November 1944 when he failed to return from an escort mission to Germany. He became a POW. Glesner Wechbacher Collection.

At 400 yards, I again got strikes on his tail. He rolled over and went straight down from 8,000 feet with fire coming from his port side and exhaust. He crashed in a small village and exploded."

Louis H. Norley Capt., Air Corps

*****

"I was flying Caboose Blue Leader when we saw and Destroyed a Me 163. As I pulled away, I saw a Me 109 at one o'clock and attacked. He dove for the deck, and I opened fire at extreme range using the K-14 gun sight. He started streaming glycol. I continued firing up to about 100 feet behind him with pieces of his plane flying off and striking my plane. Just before I broke off, the whole rear underside of the fuselage blew out and broke into flames. As I passed and turned back, the Pilot was struggling to get out. He jumped with his chute opening immediately."

John E. Kolbe 1st Lt., Air Corps

*****

"Flying Caboose Red 3, I saw an aircraft several thousand feet below me. As I was closing from above and astern, I discovered it to be a Me 109. I fired a short burst and observed strikes on the tail surfaces. The Pilot jettisoned his canopy, rolled over, and bailed out. I claim one Me 109 Destroyed."

Charles Brock 1st Lt., Air Corps

*****

5 Nov - Major Carlson led a Support mission to Karlsruhe. After the support was concluded, the Group strafed misc. targets with 334 Squadron damaging 3 locomotives, goods cars, trucks, and warehouses, and 335 damaging 6 locomotives and their cars.

Lt. Anderson is NYR. He was heard to say over the R/T, that he was bailing out. However, he was not seen to do so. (He became a POW).

6 Nov - On a support mission to Minden, led by Col. Kinnard, 334 Squadron attacked two Me 109s that were attacking a P-51, believed to be Lt. Childs. Lt. Mc Fadden took on one e/a, whose Pilot bailed out north of the Rheine/Salzbergen A/D, and Lt. Van Chandler attacked one e/a which landed and crashed into a revetment. Lt. Dickmeyer damaged an e/a attempting to land, but it evaded into the clouds.

Casualties: 1st Lt. Earl Walsh and 2nd Lt. John Childs NYR. (Walsh became à POW and Childs was KIA)

Combat Reports: Captain Montgomery - "I was flying Cobweb Leader near Rheine. I heard Cobweb Purple 2, Lt. Childs, call that he had a FW 190 on his tail and wanted his leader to get him off. Later, I spotted two Me 109s at about 7,000 feet firing on a red-nosed Mustang. Cobweb Purple 2 called again, "I have a FW 190 on my tail, what will I do?" I dove to assist, but the Mustang was taking no evasive action and was shot down before I could help him. He rolled over and went straight in, smoking. The Pilot never bailed out. Purple Leader, Lt. Walsh, is also missing in action. Since there was a small explosion and fire in the vicinity just prior to our dive, I assumed that Purple Leader was shot down first, and the plane we saw shot down was Purple Two."

*****

Lt. Mead, 336 Squadron, was killed on a local flight. He appeared to have bailed out too low.

All available Pilots attended a lecture on what to say and what not to say if captured by Jerry.

8 Nov - The 335 Squadron was divided into two groups, 4A and 4B. The 4A Group escorted bombers and then let down to strafe, damaging 7 locomotives before heading for home. The 4B Group escorted bombers, also, but then it returned to base with no action reported.

Earl Quist failed to return and was later reported as having been captured.

9 Nov - Capt. Montgomery led the Group on a Support to Saarbrucken. After leaving the bombers, the Group went on a strafing mission near Neufchateau. The 334 Squadron shot up 14 locomotives, numerous goods wagons, oil cars, trucks, etc., and 335 Squadron damaged five locomotives and assorted cars and wagons.

Hellcat "75" monopolized "C" Channel. "Chatty Bastard!"

With appropriate ceremony, General Auton presented Awards on the Parade Ground.

The **Silver Star** - Captain Monroe

The **Distinguished Service Cross** - Major Hively

The **Distinguished Flying Cross** - Captain Hedrick

11 Nov - The topic of this week's discussion group was—"What to do with Germany?"

An uneventful Support was flown to Gladbeck. No e/a were seen, but a V-2 was observed climbing through the clouds to 50,000 plus feet.

15 Nov - 54 a/c took off in a Group Balboa to practice a glide bombing mission. Capt. Monroe returned to make a spectacular wheels-up landing.

His Account: "I was leading Cobweb Section. I started my dive from 10,000 feet, airspeed 160 MPH, prop pitch forward and throttle at 15 to 20 inches. As I started recovery at 4,000 feet, my windscreen clouded over. Thinking it had iced up, I completed my recovery on my #3. When my entire canopy became white, I opened the canopy

far enough to see my coolant was popping off. I opened the coolant doors manually. I was fighting with my canopy, which was sliding free, and trying to keep my plane level by airspeed and turn and bank indicator alone. Sparks began to fly in the cockpit, and I could see flames from my engine. I jettisoned the canopy and cut switches. With my altitude at 50 feet, I saw the field in front of me. There was a plane taking off west to east. Too low to bail, I made a sharp starboard turn and crash-landed on the left side of the west to east runway."

*****

18 Nov -

A **2nd Oak Leaf Cluster to the Distinguished Flying Cross** was awarded to 1st Lt. Spiros N. Pisanos

The Group, led by Lt. Col. Kinnard, conducted a Strafing mission to Leipheim Airdrome, Germany. The 335 and 336 Squadrons made two passes to attempt to take out the flak defenses. The 334 then attacked the drome, making four passes.

Lts. Eaton and Kolbe, and Capt. Anderson, of 335, each Destroyed a Me 262. Capt. Fitch and Lt. Creamer combined to Destroy a Me 262. Majors Hively and Ackerly each destroyed a Me 262, as did Lt. Payne. Meanwhile, F/O Harre and Lt. Brown each added two 262s. Lts. Grove and Pierini accounted for one each, and Capt. Emerson, of 336, clobbered a 109. Several other Me 262s were damaged. The JPs are much more difficult to set on fire. On several occasions, repeated passes were made on the same a/c, which burst into flame and then went out each time.

Narrative: "I was flying Caboose Green 3, strafing Leipheim A/D. I spotted three Me 262s and fired on one, which caught on fire. I also got hits on the one next to it. As I crossed over the second plane, it exploded and I flew through the mud and debris of the explosion. My windscreen was completely covered with mud, so I couldn't make another pass, but I saw two of the three Me 262s burning. I claim these two Me 262s Destroyed.

Wilbur B. Eaton 1st Lt., Air Corps

*****

20 Nov - Major Hively led a Support mission to Coblenz area. Layers of clouds at different levels prevented execution of the mission.

Casualties: 1st Lt. Leonard Werner and 1st Lt. Donald Bennett, NYR. (Werner was KIA and Bennett became a POW).

Lt. Hoelscher was flying Cobweb Blue 3 to Lt. Werner, Blue 1. Lt. Bennett was Blue 2, and Lt. Cox was Blue 4. They tried to climb over a layer of clouds between 14,000 and 27,000 feet. Hoelscher was unable to keep up and lost sight of Werner. He then went on instruments to the top at 27,000 feet. When Hoelscher last saw Lt. Bennett, he was flying close formation to Werner.

On a previous mission with Werner, Hoelscher had gone through a high layer of clouds, and Lt. Werner's compass froze and his gyro went u/s, which may account for what happened to him today.

21 Nov - This morning the GIs rolled out of their sacks at 0600 hours, which at this time of year was the middle of the night. The path to the Mess Hall looked like a swarm of fireflies with all the flashlights flickering around in the dark.

An early Support to Merseburg, led by Capt. Glover, saw the Group encounter bombers scattered due to heavy cloud formations. Sections operated independently, escorting what big friends they could find and also strafing ground targets south of the target area. Several vertical contrails were observed, as well as a T/E J/P e/a.

Strafing resulted in the damaging of 12 locomotives and several army vehicles.

Lt. Kolbe spotted a lone Me 109, which he immediately destroyed.

Glover got three Me 109s, and Douglas Groshong got two.

2nd Lt. Carmen Delnero was NYR. Lt. Malmsten reported that he was flying Cobweb Red Leader and Delnero was Red 3. While strafing a train, Delnero called in a Me 109 at 7 o'clock. Red Leader turned into the 7 o'clock position. He saw a plane firing and getting strikes, but it was raining and snowing so hard that he couldn't identify one from the other. The plane blew up and crashed from about 500 feet, completely disintegrating. Lt. Voyles, Cobweb Red 2, confirms the report. (Delnero was KIA)

*****

George Klaus was hit by flak and was believed to have been captured. (He was confirmed to be a POW).

Combat Report: "I was flying Blue Leader. At about 3,500 feet, I sighted a S.E. a/c and went after him. He made a port turn and went into the clouds. I followed and could see him occasionally through breaks in the lower part of the clouds. When I had identified him as an e/a, I slowed down and fired at him from behind. I immediately got strikes around the cockpit and wing roots. He pulled into a vertical climb and I lost him in the thick clouds. When I could no longer see him, I feared collision. I dropped below the overcast and made an orbit, at which time I saw a fire and wreakage of a plane. I made a picture of it. I believe he spun out of the cloud and crashed. I claim this e/a Destroyed.

I used the K-14 Gun Sight and believe it to be a distinct advantage in all types of shooting."

John E. Kolbe 1st Lt., Air Corps.

*****

Word was received that 2nd Lt. John Scally, reported NYR 7 July 1944, and 2nd Lt. Norman Achen, reported NYR 15 August 1944, are officially prisoners of war.

Lt. Col. Claiborne H. Kinnard, Jr. came to the 4th Group 8 September 1944 from the 15th Air Force. A much decorated Ace, he had 25 e/a Destroyed. He became Group and Station CO 3 November and left for the 335 FG 29 November 1944. He was succeeded as 4th CO on 7 December by Lt. Col. Harry J. Dayhuff. **Charles Konsler Collection**

The *Stars and Stripes* today bore a headline which caused vigorous discussions in the mess, latrines, and barracks, by both Officers and EM alike. It is the most devastating news since D-Day. *"NO MORE CIGARETTES!!! For noncombatants!!! Absolutely none."* A clarification is due within a few days.

23 Nov - Two years ago today, about 800 Enlisted Men and 40 administrative Officers boarded the queen Elizabeth after dark. This outfit was known as 131-A and 131-B. We believe this is the only outfit of comparable size to sail overseas unassigned. The "Lizzie" pulled out the next morning and docked in Scotland, 29 Nov 1942. They were taken ashore the next morning, where a special LMS train took them to Atcham near Shrewsbury, Shropshire, on the Welsh border.

These 600 EM, with an average of 4 months' training, plus 40 administrative officers—*"OCS alumni possessed of somewhat more eagerness than seasoning"*—came to Debden 21 Dec 42.

While some of these Officers and Enlisted Men have left us, a large portion of our present Squadron (excluding Flying Officers), left the States two years ago today. Their 2nd anniversary overseas is also Thanksgiving Day. To some this was just another Thanksgiving dinner away from home, but it meant a lot more to these men.

Without a doubt, the outstanding event of the day was an excellent turkey dinner with all the trimmings, topped off with ice cream and apple pie. This was at the EMs' Mess, but I think the menu at the Officers' Mess was very similar.

24 Nov - 1st Lt. Victor Rentschler was transferred out, and the following men were assigned to 334 Squadron: 2nd Lts. Marvin Arthur, Calvin Beason, Paul Burnett, Arthur Bowers, and F/O William Bates.

29 Nov - In the last few days, several uneventful missions were flown. Today was no exception. Weather has contributed to the problems.

Capt. Bell proudly passed a big box of cigars around the dispersal this morning before taking off on the mission. A note on the box read: "It's a boy—naturally! Poppa Bell." Thomas Rollins Bell, Jr., born 18 Nov. 1944, Victoria, Texas.

The first two graders and department heads met to make suggestions. There are more and more details and more and more planes in the Squadron. The work load is believed to be unfairly distributed. There are too many men exempt from details. There are some details that are unnecessary with a shortage of men on the line. Major Hively will examine the suggestions and has called another meeting for 4 Dec.

A **Bronze Star** was awarded to M/Sgt Herman J. Hager and to T/Sgt Raymond J. Clarke For meritorious achievement in the performance of outstanding services from 1 Dec 42 to 26 July 44.

30 Nov - Major Hively led the Group on an uneventful mission to Halle. Over the target they observed the largest explosion they had ever seen. Flames went up 3,000 feet, with a mushroom at the top towering to 10,000 feet. A black, low pall of smoke covered the countryside.

Monthly Consolidated Strength Report

334 Sq.	Officers 51	Enlisted Men 240
335 Sq.	Officers 55	Enlisted Men 246

2 Dec 1944 - On a Bomber Support to Bingen M/Y, Nuthouse control vectored the Group to South of Coblenz where they encountered 30 plus FW 190s. They were in sections of three, tucked in close. The bombers were in perfect position to be attacked. They were strung out in multi layers of clouds. Aided by the 361st Group, the e/a were dispersed. The 334 Squadron claimed one Destroyed, one Probable, and one Damaged. Lt. McFadden claimed the Destroyed.

A new educational plan was introduced to the discussion Group. The EM may take advantage of correspondence courses to further their education at the cost to each of only $2.00.

4 Dec - The Group went on an uneventful Support mission to Bebra M/Y. Major Hively led the Group again splitting into A Group and B Group, with 334 Squadron putting up 26 kites, and 335 Squadron putting up 23 kites.

The Wing has informed us that the 4th's score now stands at 748.

The first two graders and department heads met again with Major Hively. He decided that nothing could be done about the complaints that had been registered previously.

5 Dec - Group A, led by Capt. Glover, supported bombers to Hertford. Group B, led by Major Hively, supported five B-17s, two

of which were robots, to bomb Munster.

"A" was uneventful. "B" watched as the mother bombers led their "babies," separated by several thousand feet, towards their destination. The higher baby spiraled down to 1,000 feet and headed toward Diepholz A/D. It nosed-down, caught fire on hitting the ground, and exploded with a tremendous blast about a mile east of Steinfeld. The whole area was rippled by the explosion. Our aircraft felt the concussion at 14,000 feet.

The other "parent" bomber turned, and its "baby" crashed in an open field about ten miles south of Dummer Lake. It skidded 150 yards and did not explode. A request to strafe this robot was emphatically rejected by our boys.

As the bombers headed home, our boys strafed in the vicinity of Hague.

F/O Harre became lost and was engaged by a TE/JP e/a, but he came home on the deck.

Major Hively Destroyed a FW 190.

The 334 damaged nine locomotives and various trucks and barges.

Capt. McKennon, recently made CO of 335, continues to make changes around the dispersal. A new radio/record player has been purchased and is being installed. New records are being purchased. The Pilots' room renovations are continuing.

10 Dec - Except for an uneventful show yesterday, weather has kept the Group from operations since the 5th. Today the Group had an uneventful Escort mission to Bingen; however, two Pilots had mishaps of a serious nature.

2nd Lt. Robert Voyles took off behind the Group and, using 43 inches of boost, was attempting to catch up. At an altitude of 2,000 feet, his prop ran away and started vibrating badly. He cut his boost and turned towards a nearby runway. Meanwhile, he called on the R/T that he was making an emergency landing. At that point, there was an explosion, and the engine started to burn. Coolant or oil immediately covered his windscreen, and smoke filled the cockpit. By now he was at 500 feet, and his engine conked out.

"I saw I would be short of the field, so I jettisoned my canopy and locked my shoulder harness. I hadn't dropped my external tanks because of houses below. I planned to do so in a clearing at the east end of the runway. Now my only chance was to land in this clearing, so I released my tanks just as I cleared a sort of henhouse. Clearing this obstruction almost killed the rest of my flying speed, and I dropped the plane.

I must have been dazed from the crash because I remember trying twice to get out. The next thing I remember was stumbling away from the crash. I fell about 100 yards away, rolled over, and watched the wreckage burning. Two men, civilians, led me away to a house, where I was picked up by a British ambulance."

*****

The plane was completely wrecked (Cat. E). Lt. Voyles was treated for face burns and taken to a hospital in Braintree. It is expected that he will be out in about ten days.

F/O Charles Harre - "On our return flight, we were directed to an alternate field where the weather was better for landing. It was an RAF Station, Andrews Field. I landed short, but the brakes would not hold on the wet runway. I tried to ground loop, but it turned over. The plane was Cat. D."

Lts. Berry, McCall, and Kolbe have finished their tours and are awaiting transport to the ZOI.

11 Dec - Capt. Howe, on an escort mission to Hanau, found the bombers in very poor formation. The Group escorted several stragglers to friendly territory.

2nd Lt. Michael Kennedy was NYR. Capt. Thomas Bell and 1st Lt. Robert Dickmeyer reported that Kennedy, who was flying #4 to them, indicated he was heading for home. He was heading 270 degrees, towards France. They speculated that he either hit bad weather over France or he ran out of gas over the ocean if his heading was off.

12 Dec - On a follow up to yesterday's bombing of Hanau, the Group was split into two Groups, led by Major Hively and Capt. McKennon, respectively. One Section of B Group photographed three target areas and withdrew.

MEW vectored "A" Group onto bandits attacking Lancasters in the Rhur, but no e/a were encountered.

All personnel able to be absent from their duties were asked to report to the Cinema for a showing of a technicolor movie, "The Taking of Tarawa."

The Red Cross managed to get a few fresh eggs and were preparing them on toast when a buzz-bomb alert sounded and all personnel had to leave the ARC building. There was a real scramble to queue up again when the all clear sounded.

13 Dec - All available Pilots assembled in the briefing room for the new Commanding Officer, Lt. Col. Dayhuff, to introduce himself and his Deputy, Lt. Col. Oberhansly. He then announced that shortly the U.S. Standards of flight will be used instead of the British Standards currently in use.

Col. Dahuff then presented the following awards:

The **Purple Heart**

Major Hively

Lieutenant Malmsten

5th and 6th Oak Leaf Clusters to the Distinguished Flying Cross

Major Hively

2nd and 3rd Oak Leaf Clusters to the Distinguished Flying Cross

Captain Monroe

Orders were received awarding Air Medals and/or Oak Leaf Clusters to the Air Medal, to ten of the Pilots of 334 Squadron.

15 Dec - Capt. Glover led the Group on a Support to Kassel. which was uneventful with no e/a seen.

Lt. Kennedy, reported NYR 11 Dec 44, returned to base. He reported that on his flight he was having engine trouble and he could only sustain flight at reduced RPM and boost. He got a homing from Messenger and left the formation. Later he called again for a homing, but was unable to reach Legac, Ripsaw, or Messenger. He then decided to let down through weather to look for a landing field. Losing power and unable to find a field, he bellied in on a turnip patch about five miles NW of Charleville, France.

He was picked up by MPs at a Frenchman's house and was taken to Charleville, where he stayed for two days. He was then taken to various towns. He finally got a ride on a B-24 to the U.K. He returned today, surprised to find he was MIA. The MPs who originally picked him up said that they would contact Debden about his whereabouts.

*****

18 Dec - Weather conditions have kept activities at a negligible level, but today Lt. Col. Dayhuff led the Group on a Fighter Patrol to Kassel-Frankfurt area. The Group let down through 10/10ths cloud cover. In doing so, they became split up. Two Sections then encountered seven Me 109s with Lt. Clifton Destroying one. Capt. O'Donnell spotted a FW 190 on Capt. Fitch's tail and turned on him, getting strikes which caused the e/a to break off the attack. O'Donnell closed rapidly in a tight turn, getting strikes as he closed to about 50 yards and passed the e/a. The e/a did a half roll and dove with his engine smoking badly. At this point, Capt. Fitch and Lt. Stallings went after him. Lt. Stallings engaged the e/a and finished him off; the e/a plowed into the ground and exploded. O'Donnell and Stallings will share this victory. Capt. Fitch then saw four Me 109s, one of which stayed below the clouds long enough to get on Lt. Stallings' tail. Capt. O'Donnell clobbered him, and the e/a dove into the ground and burned.

Capt. O'Donnell later stated, "I used the K-14 sight and found it to be excellent for deflection shooting and superior to the reflector sight."

Lt. Stallings remarked, "I used the K-14 Gyro Gunsight. The percentage of strikes was high, and I believe it to be a definite advantage in our favor."

Capt. Hewes failed to return. He was last seen at 1430 hours at 4,000 feet near Giessen. He had not reported any trouble. (He was KIA).

Capt. Monroe, low on gas, turned toward home with his Wingman, Lt. Lacy. He received a flak hit and became separated. He was heard on the R/T to say that he was low on gas and was going to crash-land. He was believed to be in friendly territory.

Word was received that Capt. Thomas Joyce, reported NYR, 12 Sept 44 was a prisoner-of-war as of 10 Oct 44.

European Civil Affairs Division reported that 2nd Lt. C.G. Howard, reported NYR 18 Aug 44, crashed, and was buried in the Communal Cemetery of Saint Martin-le-Noend.

22 Dec - Word was received that 2nd Lt. Kenneth Rudkin, reported NYR 25 Aug and 2nd Lt. Thomas Underwood, reported NYR 8 Aug 44, are POWs.

23 Dec - Major Hively led Group "A" and Capt. Montgomery led Group "B" on a Support to Ahsweiler, south of Bonn. The show had many unusual aspects, as follows: (none of which damaged the enemy).

1. Lt. Foster taxied into Lt. Cronin's tail, damaging Cronin's tail section with his left wing and his right aileron with the propeller. Neither became airborne.

2. After take-off, Blue Section of "A" Group was unable to form up.

3. "B" Squadron joined Group "B," led by Capt. McKennon, but was unable to locate the B-24s.

4. "A" crossed in at Ostend and saw the bombers, but their combat Group had aborted so they did not rendezvous.

Capt. Calvin W. Willruth 335 Squadron, prior to becoming Asst Ops Officer and Gunnery Officer. Konsler collection.

5. Some B-26s were mistaken for e/a and were bounced, causing the Group to drop tanks.

6. MEW control vectored the group all over the target area, probably chasing other Squadrons of the Group.

7. Lt. Dvorak landed A-72, France-NYR.

8. A scarecrow was seen south of Mayen

Capt. Monroe, NYR 18 Dec 44, returned in Lt. Dickmeyer's plane. He had trouble with his wing tanks drawing on the mission. After many tries and drawing his internal tanks down, he decided to return to base with his wingman, Lt. Lacy. He was given a heading of 240 degrees by "Manager" and started to let down through the clouds. They broke out at 3,000 feet and immediately experienced flak. Monroe hit the deck, and Lacy headed for the clouds. He had only 15 gallons of gas left when he decided to land on a concrete highway, but he overshot. His engine began to cut out, so he was forced to set it down in a field with normal damage. He stayed at B-58, Brussels, where he found Lt. Dickmeyer's plane being repaired. He waited for clearance until Saturday the 23rd, and then flew it back to base.

*****

24 Dec - The 334 Squadron, led by Col. Dayhuff, escorted bombers over the target at Giessen with only two e/a engaged. 2nd Lt. Calvin Willruth spotted a Me 109 on the deck, which he dispatched for his first kill. Lt. Green got strikes on a Me 109, which evaded into the clouds.

The Group observed a U/I P-51 with no markings clobber another U/I P-51 near Oberwesal. The ship caught on fire, and the Pilot bailed.

Willruth reports: "I was flying Caboose Blue 4 at 20,000 feet. I spotted a single a/c on the deck and went down to check it with Blue 3 following me. It was a dull grey Me 109 with crosses on either wing. I fired a couple seconds burst, getting strikes. I continued to fire indicating 400-450 MPH, and I saw the 109 burst into flames. I saw the Pilot bail out with the chute opening just before he hit the ground. He bailed at about 50 feet as we were receiving a heavy barrage of light flak."

*****

George Green reports: "I was flying Caboose Blue 3 when I saw a Me 109 being chased by a P-47. I started after them with my Wingman following. As we closed, the P-47 broke away. I closed and fired. I observed strikes all over the e/a, and he flipped and spun out. That is all I saw of him. By the time I turned around, he had disappeared.

I used the K-14 Gun Sight, which was very much to my advantage."

*****

Captain George D. Green 335 Squadron is famous for his daring pig-gyback rescue of Major Pierce McKennon, his Squadron CO, in a P-51 on 18 Mar 1945. USAF collection.

Eighteen of the a/c from 334 Squadron and 24 from 335 landed at another base in Raydon, England, due to Debden being completely closed in by fog. The fog appeared so suddenly, it engulfed the Dispersal and shut down the field instantly to the Pilots about to land. The Pilots did not want to be away for Christmas, and their calls to the tower for landing instructions were actually entreaties.

As the men from 334 Dispersal stood about the iron box stove, suddenly there was an explosion. The door slapped open and fire belched out. In strode Capt. Montgomery of Littlefield, Texas. "You Bastard," they shouted. Montgomery, of course, had climbed up on the roof and dropped a dinghy flare down the chimney.

The Group landed at Rayden and the Dispersal closed. When it became evident that they could not return, due to the fog, the mess secretary dispatched four turkeys, whiskey, and cigarettes to them at Raydon..."So that's that!" The Officers' Mess was bare and lonesome with most of the Pilots at Raydon. Those left on the Station entered the bar early and left late.

Masses and Holy Communion Services were held in the Station Chapel, after which a Christmas Eve song service was held.

A buffet supper was served in the American Red Cross Aeroclub with the singing of Christmas Carols and a recording of Charles Dicken's "The Christmas Carol" enjoyed by a mixture of Officers and Enlisted Men.

25 Dec - As the line EM felt secure for a long winter's nap, knowing that they did not have to service their kites which were at Raydon, they were suddenly rousted out at 0515. They were to be in readiness to go to Raydon to service the kites or to stand by in case they returned to Debden. At 0830, they were released, since the planes were going on a mission from Raydon.

Considerable bitching ensued as some crawled back into the sack and some off to do justice to fresh eggs in the Mess Hall. All of this took place before daylight and before anyone could see the White Christmas of the frozen fog. The *London Daily Express* reported that this was the coldest day England has had in 54 years.

Lt. Col. Dayhuff phoned Capt. Ezzel at 0010 hours to send blankets, cigarettes, and money to the Pilots who landed at Raydon yesterday. Accordingly, 100 pounds, 12 cartons of cigarettes, and 200 blankets were sent by truck.

"This was the third Christmas in England for many of us, and much to our surprise, it was a white one. One of the heaviest fogs in years enveloped the field just a few minutes before our Pilots were scheduled to touch down from yesterday's mission to Germany. That is the reason for our scarlet-nosed Mustangs landing at another base and spending Christmas Eve at someone elses Officers' Mess.

During the night, the fog hung on and a cold snap drew the moisture from the air, leveling a white blanket of frost one quarter of an inch thick over the ground, trees, and buildings, with the unusual effect of a white Christmas without benefit of a snow fall."

Joe Sills commented that the frost that enveloped the base was so thick that crystals hung suspended like fog in the air. He could wave his arm and the crystals would float away like a mist. Everything was completely covered with a sparkling crystal blanket. "It was beautiful beyond belief."

Early morning services were held in the Chapel.

The Station custom of EM of the first 3 grades being entertained at the Officers' Mess didn't vary this year, and the drinks at the bar were free.

Noontime found the Enlisted Mens' Mess "kaypees" supplemented by Officers dishing out the Yule meal. That too follows an old Royal Air Force custom that has been instituted by the 4th Group, which has its early roots planted in RAF ways.

While the GI stomach began accommodating turkey, the Eaglettes, a quartet from the Station Flying Eagles band, entertained.

At 1400, GI trucks began arriving at the base, loaded down with British children from nearby communities. The annual Yule party for the Blitz Orphans began with about 250 children and almost as many GI and Officer "Daddies for the day." After a cartoon show at the Cinema, the Daddies and Kiddies retired to the Aeroclub for refreshments and a visit from Santa Claus, in the person of Sgt.

Fred Oheler. He did a very capable job of bringing cheer to the kids.

The children's eyes bulged with delight and their tummies bulged with the rare treat of ice cream and cake. Santa's gifts included all sorts of toys made on the base, sent from home, and scrounged from everywhere. Each child also received a package of candy, gum, and other goodies. It was not hard to read the delight on their faces.

The large amount of sweets contributed by all personnel came from Christmas gifts from home, and Post Exchange rations. Paper wrappings were obtained from U.S. mailed packages.

The Officers had a tasty Christmas meal, which concluded with an informal dance at the Aeroclub to the music of the Flying Eagles.

No man at Debden went hungry for lack of turkey as the Christmas dinner was superb. In addition to turkey, the trimmings included cranberry sauce, oranges, apples, and ice cream with pumpkin pie.

Back at Raydon, the war continued with Lt. Col. Dayhuff leading a Support mission to the Bonn/ Trier area. In the vicinity of St. Vith, Nuthouse reported e/a 15 miles east of Bonn. Thirty plus Me 109s and FW 190s were engaged as they tried to attack the bombers out of the sun.

Lt. Rentschler claimed one Me 109 Destroyed and one FW 190 Destroyed, shared with Lt. Hoelscher, who also claimed one Me 109 Destroyed.

Lt. Cronin claimed one FW 190 Destroyed and one FW 190 Destroyed, shared with Major McKennon of 335. Major Glover and Lt. Chandler each destroyed a FW 190, and Chandler also destroyed a Me 109.

A total of twelve e/a were destroyed. This presented a very nice Christmas present to 334 Squadron, by breaking 300 Destroyed. They also remained the highest scoring Squadron in the ETO.

Lt. Charles Poage was forced to bail out northwest of Leacher Lake due to enemy action, and his chute was seen to open. (He became a POW).

Donald Emerson was seen to head home on the deck after tackling six Me 109s single handed, destroying two of them. He failed to return to base and was later found dead in the wreckage of his plane VF-D in Belgium. He was the victim of ground fire. Donald was flying his second tour with the 4th. Donald has the unenviable distinction of being the only Pilot of the 4th Group to be lost on a Christmas Day.

Major McKennon gives this account: "I was Caboose Red Leader when Huns were reported at 12 o'clock to the bombers. Soon after this report, I spotted a S/E a/c diving straight down out of some contrails. We spotted three FW 190s at two o'clock, which we immediately engaged. There were quite a few more above us because all four of us ended up with 190s on our tails.

I yelled at Lt. Poage to break, but it was too late as the FW 190 had just finished him off. His plane went down burning, but he succeeded in bailing out.

Captain Donald R. Emerson 336 Squadron, an Ace with 7 e/a Destroyed, checking his rabbits foot. Donald had the dubious distinction of being the only 4th Group Pilot casualty on a Christmas day. He was killed in action on 25 Dec 1944 when he single-handed attacked 6 FW 190s, downing 2 before he was shot down. Konsler collection.

The FW 190 on my tail finally broke and dived to the deck. I followed and shot quite a few bursts at him, getting occasional strikes. I pulled up to clear my tail, and Lt. Cronin closed in and fired, getting numerous strikes. The Jerry pulled up, rolled over on his back, and bailed out."

*****

Lt. Rentschler had his Fairing doors shot off and his port wing tip and elevators damaged by 20 mm explosives. Capt. Bell had his elevator, rudder, and prop hit by 20 mm explosives.

Unfortunately, Debden was still fogged in and again the group had to land at Rayden where they stayed for Christmas.

26 Dec - Due to unfavorable weather, the Group could not take off on the scheduled mission, but they were able to return to Debden.

31 Dec - From the 27th until today uneventful Support missions were flown each day with no e/a engaged.

Having finished their tours, 1st Lt. Robert Dickmeyer of 334 and Lts. Evans and Peters of 335 awaited return to the ZOI.

Monthly Consolidated Strength Report

334 Squadron	Officers 49	Enlisted Men 239
335 Squadron	Officers 51	Enlisted Men 247

11

The Reunions Start

1 January 1945 - Major Glover and Major Mc Kennon led A and B Groups, respectively, on an Escort to the Stendal area. "A" Group was vectored to the Wittenburg Area and encountered approximately 15 Me 109s flying in singles and pairs below them. The 336 Squadron attacked. Claims were made as follows:

Lt. Pierini	one Me 109 Destroyed
	one Me 262 Destroyed
Lt. Young	one Me 109 Destroyed
Lt. Chandler	one Me 109 Destroyed
Lt. Kessler	shared
Lt. Wallace	one Me 109 Destroyed

Major Hively, CO of the 334th Squadron, sent a memorandum to all personnel:

"It is my sincere desire to wish all members of the Squadron a Happy New Year. The past year has been a rough one, yet a good one, for 334. We have come a long way in the past 12 months, and certainly, or at least I feel, no other bunch of guys could do it over again half as well from P-47s to P-51s, the rough shows of Berlin, and the trying days of March and April when every man on the ground and in the air was going at his best. The invasion and the Russian show were followed by the doldrums and homesickness of the summer.

I would like to thank everyone for his part in making 334 the best Squadron in the Air Force, and ask that you hold on a little longer fellows, and we'll all be home for the next one."

There were a host of activities scheduled to usher in our third New Year's Day at Debden. There was a dance at the Officers' Mess with music by the Flying Eagles band.

The new Non-Coms' Club for the first two graders was opened in the transformed Sergeants' Mess (a hold-over from the RAF days at this field). The new bar was the pride and joy of the new club.

The Airmens' Mess served a fine turkey dinner to all the GIs.

All the other ranks were taken in by the all embracing dance at the American Red Cross Aeroclub.

Sales of mild and bitter at the "Belly Tank," the EM Pub on the base, were high, but no arrests were made by the MPs for disorderly celebrations.

Lt. Dvorak, who landed at A-72 in France, 23 Dec 44, returned to base, 31 Dec 44. He told of his problems as follows: "I was returning from the mission on 23 Dec when my engine began to vibrate quite badly. I landed at A-72, a B-26 base. The mechanics there did not know much about inline engines. Since I thought that I had plug troubles, I asked them to get some for me. Many tries left me with no plugs or coolant and no prospects. On the 26th, I went to Paris hoping for a ride to Debden. However, the weather was bad, and I got tired of waiting.

I talked to an Engineering Officer. He called A-42 and got two mechanics, the plugs, coolant, and a jeep. The plugs did not help. The engine still would not start, so we got an electrician who by-passed a faulty condenser, but it then ran on only one bank. After fixing the timing it ran alright, but the weather officer wouldn't clear me till the 31st."

*****

Lt. Ben Griffin was on his first combat mission, flying as Wingman to Lt. Pierini. "We followed other 336 Pilots down to the snow-covered deck as they shot down three Me 109s, which crashed in flames. Lt. Pierini and I were climbing back out together when, at about 12,000 feet, a 109 crossed in front of me. The plane suddenly inverted, and the Pilot dropped out. His chute opened immediately about 100 yards in front of me. I had to skid violently to the right to avoid hitting him. I had concerns about his chute tangling in my prop as I passed him with no more than 15 feet between him and my left wing tip. He had his hands and arms crossed in front of his face as if he also feared a collision.

I looked in my rear-view mirror and saw that my propwash had half collapsed his chute. It immediately popped open again, and we continued our climb. At about 20,000 feet, we saw a Me 262 jet fighter in a left turn about 5,000 feet below us on our left. Pierini signaled me to follow as he dove down toward the 262. He started firing from the rear and slightly below the e/a. I immediately observed strikes on the Me 262 as Pierini broke to avoid a collision with the Hun. I had just begun to fire when there was an explosion in the Me 262 cockpit. Balls of fire, like soap bubbles about the size of softballs, floated out of the right side of the 262 cockpit. The plane flipped over to the left and dove straight down into the snow. I followed the Me 262 down to the deck—the Pilot did not eject. I rejoined Lt. Pierini at 20,000 feet and we returned to Debden."

*****

2 Jan - There was early morning excitement as a gas truck caught on fire while servicing a 334 plane. The fire was extinguished with only minor damage.

The Group took off on a Free-Lance to the Ruhr area. Major McKennon led. Nuthouse vectored the group to the Cologne area, and at that time, Lt. Senecal saw two Me 109s on the deck. Green and Red Sections dove to attack them. Lts. Senecal and Payne attacked first, followed by Lt. Rentschler. Both e/a were Destroyed. The two claims were shared among the three Pilots.

Lt. Senecal's plane was hit by flak, and he dove to 8,000 feet and set course for home with Lt. Payne on his wing. About 10 minutes later, he was forced to bail out when his a/c caught fire. His chute did not open, and he struck the ground about ten yards from his crashed plane.

6 Jan - The Group flew a support to Limburg, led by Lt. Col. Dayhuff and Major McKennon. They got off to a rough start as Lt. Jahnke, while taxiing out for takeoff, skidded on the ice and damaged Lt. Malmsten's horizontal stabilizer with his prop. The mission was uneventful in all other respects.

7 Jan - Major McKennon led a support to Achern and Buhl. The mission was uneventful, and no e/a were seen.

Yesterday was Lt. Buchholtz's first mission. Today was Lt. Cammer's first operational mission.

2nd Lt. Michael Kennedy, reported NYR, 31 Dec 44, returned today with an interesting story of his escapades. On the 31 Dec mission, he aborted due to a rough engine and inability to get full boost above 25,000 feet. On his way back, he encountered three Me 109s. He attempted to turn with them but was unable. He dove into the clouds and again headed for England. He was unable to get a homing on any Channel. He let down over what he anticipated would be England, but he saw nothing but water.

He then turned and headed for France. When he made landfall, he encountered flak, which confused him and made him believe that he was over Holland. He then flew south until he was low on

gas and bellied in on a plowed field near Rochelle. Not being sure he was in friendly territory, he hid until he heard Frenchmen speaking. They were members of the FFI and did not convince easily that he was American. They took him to a well-to-do French family's home, where they fed him and took a message for the authorities to send to Debden. He was shuttled around to try, unsuccessfully, to get a plane back to England. He finally met a B-26 Pilot who flew him back to Grove in England. From there, Captain Monroe picked him up and took him to Debden. This concluded his second unofficial visit to France. "May I never go there again."

*****

10 Jan - Word was received that the following MIA Pilots are determined dead:

334 Squadron Capt. Richard Mc Minn	15 April 43
1st Lt. Stanley Anderson	15 April 43
1st Lt. Robert Boock	18 May 43
1st Lt. John Lutz	4 May 43
2nd Lt. Leland Mac Farlane	21 May 43
335 Squadron Lt. Edward Freeburger	18 Mar 44
Lt. Robert Homuth	31 May 44
Lt. Ralph Saunders	13 Apr 44
Lt. Joseph Sullivan	24 Feb 44
Lt. Burton Wyman	29 Jan 44

Snow continued to hold up operational flying, but the pilots had some fun flying the Cub during the day. Lts. Rinebolt, Kiser, Creamer, and Lindsay took turns flying it and giving rides to some of the EM.

14 Jan - This morning, the 3rd AAF Combat Camera Unit shot news reels depicting the day, 25 Dec 44, when our Pilots of 334 Squadron passed the 300 mark of enemy aircraft destroyed. Prior to the mission on the 25th, their score was 298 5/12. Lts. Hoelscher, Rentschler, and Cronin combined for a total of 4 1/2 on Christmas Day.

Lt. Col. Jack J. Jake Oberhansly transferred from the 78 FG to become Deputy Group CO of the 4th Group 8 Dec 1944. He was well seasoned with 150 combat missions and nine victories to his credit. Zigler collection.

A shot was taken of S/Sgt. Don Allen painting the 300th swastika on the Victory Board. Then a shot was taken of Lt. Col. Oberhansly congratulating 334 Squadron CO, Major "Deacon" Hively, on behalf of the first Squadron in the ETO to pass the 300 mark. They then photographed Lts. Cronin and Rentschler chalking up three more swastikas and receiving the "300 pool" from the Deacon. Lt. Hoelscher, unfortunately, was in the "flak shack" at the time.

The films should be ready for release to the news within the week.

A Support mission to Brunswick under Major Hively proved uneventful with sightings of seven rockets, oil fires, and flak, but no e/a and no action.

Andrew Lacy was promoted from 2nd Lt. to 1st Lt.

16 Jan - Major Glover led a support to Ruhland. The 336 Squadron went strafing and beat up an A/D south of Berlin, destroying 25 e/a parked there. The 334 tried to find them, but found another A/D, believed to be Neuberg. They proceeded to clobber it instead.

334 Squadron

Lt. Ayers shared - Lt. Kennedy 1 He 177

Lt. Brown shared - Lt. Jahnke   1 Me 262

336 Squadron

Major Glover	2 FW 190
	1 Me 109
Lt. Kaul	1 FW 190
Lt. Van Chandler	3 FW 190
	1 JU 87
Capt. Carpenter	1 Me 109
Lt. Groshong	1 FW 190
Lt. Riedel	1 FW 190
Capt. Alfred	1 FW 190
Lt. Corbett	3 FW 190
Lt. Wallace	1 FW 190
Capt. Carlson	1 FW 190
	1 JU 88
Lt. Kesler	1 FW 190
Lt. McCord	1 HE 177
	1 FW 190
Capt. Joiner	4 FW 190
Lt. Hagan	1 JU 87

Lt. Van E. Chandler 336 Squadron racked up nine victories, helped by four destroyed on 16 Jan 1945. Konsler collection.

(*Left*) **Capt. Joseph H. Joyner 336 Squadron shared the stage with Lt. Chandler on 16 Jan 45 when he also destroyed four e/a bringing his total score to 8 1/2. Konsler collection.**

Capt. Bell got a hit by a 40 mm while shooting at a Ju 88. The hit knocked out all his instruments and his landing gear. He ended up in a snow field at Laon, France. He came home on a B-17 three days later.

1st Lt. Victor Rentschler was MIA. (He became a POW). Lt. Frederick Hall was killed as he tried to land his disabled plane at a forward base.

Lt. Wozniak reported that as he was breaking off from a pass at a He 111 on the A/D, he saw Lt. Rentschler jettison his canopy. He called on the R/T that he was hit. "I noticed his kite was streaming a little coolant, but when he opened his coolant scoop, it seemed to stop. We flew on a course of 270 for about 15 minutes, and his coolant started streaming again. He motioned me to move away and he bailed out, Jack-in-the-Box style. His kite hit and blew up in a woods. He came down about 100 yards to the west of the woods. He gathered up his chute and started for the woods. I waited until he got to the woods, and I noticed about 12 people heading towards the spot where he went down. I made a couple of passes at them without firing, and they ran back to the building from which they came. I then left at about 1415 hours."

*****

Due to a heavy ground fog in England, the Group landed at various advance bases in France.

S/Sgt Willard Wahl received a letter from Mr. and Mrs. Carl Beeson, dated 13 Dec 44, giving their son's address: Capt. Duane W. Beeson, U.S. Prisoner of War No. 4170, Stalag Luft No. 3; Stalag Luft No. 1, Subsidiary Camp, Germany. They said his camp is located at Rostock, Germany. They have received one card and two letters from him. He is upset that he missed the invasion and was full of praise for the way "Willie" Wahl took care of his plane.

17 Jan - Major Hively led the Group, reduced to six planes since the main force was still in France, on an uneventful Escort of bombers and planes dropping chaff.

Capt. Davis took 335's reduced force of eleven a/c on a support to Hamburg. The mission was uneventful with no e/a, but 1st Lt. Stallings had some trouble and bailed out near Lowestoft. (He was KIA).

Capt. Hall received a letter from Capt. Megura, stating that both "Tiger" Booth and "Abie" O'Regan were married.

Capt. Norley walked into the briefing sporting a new "Badge," indicating he was just promoted to Major. Lt. Davis was promoted to Captain.

Orders were received awarding The **Silver Star** to 1st Lt. Grover Siems

"For gallantry in action on a mission over enemy occupied Europe, 2 July 1944. Lt. Siems, with two other Pilots, intercepted approximately 100 Me 109s and made a bold attack with utter contempt for the overwhelming odds. He went to the assistance of a

fellow Pilot, putting himself in a precarious tactical position. Two cannon shells penetrated the cockpit, severely wounding him. The cool presence of mind and indomitable fighting spirit displayed by Lt. Siems reflect the highest credit upon himself and the Army Air Forces."

18 Jan - Major Norley took off with 12 planes to search for Lt. Stallings, who bailed out yesterday. After two hours they returned to report the dinghy (upside down) floating on the water.

Lt. Rinebolt cracked up while attempting to land here in the rough wind. The plane was a total wreck, but he received only slight wounds. He is reported doing fine in a nearby hospital.

20 Jan - Last night, four rockets fell nearby at various times between 1815 and 2300 hours. Again this morning two rockets exploded near the field at 0845 hours. Just after takeoff, another exploded uncomfortably close.

The morning Escort mission to Heilbron was uneventful.

Effective today, all personnel (enlisted and commissioned) will take a daily dose of one tablet (1/2) grain of Sulfadiazine. This is a prophylactic program to control and reduce the upper respiratory disease rate of the 8th Air Force.

21 Jan - Major Mc Kennon led "A" Group, and Capt. Joiner led "B" Group on an Area Patrol, Frankfurt to Wertheim. Green and Blue Sections of 334 joined 336 Squadron in strafing a train with 20 coal cars. Then they turned north and strafed more cars in a marshaling yard. They then shot up four dummy He 111s on a field near Geislingen and a train station at Donausworth. No e/a were seen.

Major Louis H. "Red Dog" Norley started his third tour with 550 plus combat hours. He fought in each of the three Squadrons and served as 335 CO from Aug 44 until he became 334 Squadron CO in Jan 45. He had 16 1/3 victories. Konsler collection.

"B" Group went to the deck in the vicinity of Donausworth and strafed rail targets.

One Hundred Four Air Medals and/or Oak Leaf Clusters to the AM were awarded to Pilots of the 335 Squadron this month.

28 Jan - From the 22nd to the 28th bad weather, including snowstorms, have precluded operational missions. Again today, as the Group was taking off, a sudden snow storm caused the mission to be scrubbed and those airborne to be recalled.

A two-minute silence was observed on the occasion of the third anniversary of the Eighth Air Force, in tribute to those men who have died in the war against Germany.

The Eighth Air Force set up its first headquarters in Savannah, Georgia National Armoury, and marked its third anniversary today by dispatching over 1,250 planes and 10,000 airmen to lash at oil plants, railroads, and bridges in the Reich.

The Anniversary Program started with worship services and the two-minute period of silence. During lunch, the station orchestra played dinner music in the EM Mess. In the afternoon, the Cinema presented "Desert Song" in Technicolor, followed by Benediction Services. The evening was capped with an Enlisted Mens' Dance at the Aero Club.

Eleven new Pilots, fresh from the States, have been assigned to 335 Squadron: 2nd Lts. Charles Greenlese, Paul Lucas, Robert Couse, Mack Heaton, Leslie Burgess, Robert Hawley, Leonard Otto, Henry Lee, Wade Underwood, and James Halligan, and F/O Lucian Freeman.

29 Jan - An uneventful Group Escort was flown to Hanover. 1st Lt. Andrew Lacy and F/O William Bates were ordered on TD to the Rolls Royce Co., Ltd., to pursue a four-day course on Pilot Engine Handling.

Major Hively was Assigned to Headquarters, 4th Group, and replaced with Major Norley in the 334th Squadron.

Major Glover led "B" Group on an escort mission to Koblenz. The mission was uneventful, and no e/a were seen.

Green 4, 1st Lt. Morton Savage was NYR.

30 Jan - Another snowfall—4 inches—last night kept the planes on the ground and the ground crews busy with snowplows and shovels.

Major Norley posted a memorandum to all Enlisted Men and ground Officers to read:

All small arms (carbines and Thompson sub-machine guns) and clips will be thoroughly cleaned and well oiled and turned in to Squadron Supply today.

Word was received that 2nd Lt. Robert Sherman, reported MIA 9 May 1944, is a prisoner-of-war.

Monthly Consolidated Strength Report

334 Squadron	Officers 54	Enlisted Men 238	
335 Squadron	Officers 57	Enlisted Men 245	

1 Feb 1945 - "As the dawn breaks on the second month of '45 we find our Pilots off on another mission into German territory. These shows are still new and exciting to a few of our boys, while to others they are only considered the 'Chores of another day.' Today's mission under Field Order 1575A is a Free-Lance into the Giessen area."

Major Norley led the Group on this an uneventful Free-Lance. The cloud cover became 10/10ths over the Continent, precluding any serious strafing.

Lt. Savage, reported NYR 29 Jan, returned to base. He had gone with his Section to look for an U/I a/c beneath the clouds. Instead, they saw a convoy of trucks. He had made a pass, but was too low, and he hit a tree. The force of the blow turned him over on his back, but he was able to recover and headed for Allied territory. The plane was hard to control because of the damage to the wing, and he landed at St. Trond, Belgium. The plane needed a wing change which they could not do there, so he came back by other means.

2 Feb - There was a meeting of 334 Squadron Enlisted Men in the hangar at 1500 hours, at which Capt. Jensen introduced their new Commanding Officer, Major "Red Dog" Norley. He said in effect that he would have an open door for any complaints and that they would work together as a team with harmony and understanding.

5 Feb - The weather has been keeping our planes grounded the past few days. Today mist and low clouds kept them grounded until afternoon when the weather cleared enough for some local flying.

Eight new Pilots were assigned to the 334th Squadron: 1st Lt. William O'Bryan, 2nd Lts. Philio Burney, Gordon Denson, Daniel James, Donald Lowther, Alan Skirball, William Spencer, and F/O Alvin Hand.

Capt. Monroe had been busy building an entrance to the "Narvik," the 335 dispersal. The roof is fast taking shape.

6 Feb - 1st Lt. Lynd Cox was released from duty for return to the ZI.

Group "B", led by Lt. Col. Oberhansly, flew a Support to Magdeburg. Lt. Savage aborted due to a rough engine. On the way out, he strafed a train and claims one locomotive damaged.

When the Group left escort, 335 Squadron left the rest of the Group and strafed in the area of Torgau. They claimed the following either destroyed or badly damaged: 13 locomotives, 1 passenger train, 2 goods trains, 18 box cars, 11 trucks, and 2 cars.

The 335 Squadron lost one of their best Pilots, 1st Lt. Paul Santos. He was last seen near the strafing target, but no one actually saw him get hit or spin in. (He was KIA)

Before leaving on this mission, 1st Lt. Wilbur Eaton, 335, made the statement that this show would give him enough time to complete his operational tour (270 hours), and that he would not under any circumstances take any chances by going down to strafe. However, the urge was too great, and as a result, Lt. Eaton returned to base screaming with excitement over the fact that he had killed three Jerry Officers as they were getting out of a staff car which he was strafing.

The 335 Squadron received two new Pilots, direct from the States, 2nd Lts. Kenneth Green and Robert Hunter, Jr.

Casualties: F/O William Bates, KIA. At about 1000 hours, F/O Bates, Cobweb Green 2, called Lt. Brown, Green 1, and said his engine was rough and smoking, and he was going back. That was the last they heard of him.

F/O Bates bailed out about 1017 hours, 40 miles west of Leiston. Air-Sea Rescue P-47s were with him when he hit the water. His chute opened. When he hit the water, his dinghy was about 20 feet away. He reached the dinghy and inflated it, but he was too weak to get into it. He then floated in his Mae West. A Walrus appeared, but the water was too rough to land. When a launch arrived about two hours later, he was dead when they picked him up.

Bad weather conditions forced the returning Group to set down at various forward bases in England with the Pilots returning later or on the following day.

Orders were received awarding **74 Air Medals and/or Oak Leaf Clusters to the AM**, to Pilots of the 334 Squadron.

7 Feb - Bad weather again grounded the planes.

"The Negro Engineering Squadron now on this field is doing an excellent job. They are removing the badly damaged iron-mesh 'Hard Stands' where the planes park and are replacing them with new wooden stands. Others, where the iron-mesh is still good, are being rolled up. A heavy layer of sand and straw is being laid down, and then the iron-mesh is being put back. In either case, it is a great improvement over the mud and slush as it was before. This work will be complete in a few weeks."

"To the surprise of many, the Negroes have not caused any social disturbances as was predicted when the colored boys first arrived. We are still living on the same field and eating in the same mess hall. So far, everything has been peaceful. I'm sure our relations will continue in this same good manner as I see no need for a row."

8 Feb - A guard of honor of Officers and Enlisted Men said farewell to Lt. Bates at the main gate as his body left for burial at Cambridge Cemetery.

All available Pilots attended a dinghy lecture where F/O Bates' dinghy was on display.

Lt. Col. Dayhuff said Pilots would no longer peel off under 500 feet or assimilate combat under 7,000 feet.

The new Pilots in 335 got some more training in the afternoon. Their instructor, Lt. Orval Miles, is giving them very thorough training.

Robert Voyles was promoted from 2nd Lt. to 1st Lt.

9 Feb - An uneventful mission was flown to Magdeburg.

The tail wheel on Lt. Elffner's a/c failed to retract on take-off. After several unsuccessful attempts to retract it, he attempted to land. He skidded off the runway into the mud and pranged his kite. He twisted the fuselage, bent the prop, and broke one landing gear. The whole kite was pretty well wrecked.

2nd Lt. Marvin Arthur, reported NYR 6 Feb, returned today. "I was flying Cobweb Purple 2 and developed engine trouble near the target area. I turned for France escorted by #4, Lt. Voyles. After two hours, I reached and landed at Martini with Lt. Voyles going on to England. Thirty or forty P-51s and twenty or thirty Forts and Libs also landed there; the field was jammed. After two days for engine repairs, I flew back to Debden."

*****

A new shipment of eggs and oranges came in today. In addition to candy, gum, cigarettes, first aid kits, escape kits, and surplus food kits, which we were already issuing to the operational Pilots, we were now supplying them with three fresh eggs and three oranges per week.

11 Feb - Major McKennon led the Group on a Fighter Sweep to the Kassel-Hanover area. Ten locomotives were put out of commission, one tug damaged, several boxcars destroyed, and one house was destroyed by a wing tank. Three barracks with troops were strafed. In addition, 335 Squadron set a small factory afire; strafed oil tanks, six barges, and one cow shed (courtesy of Lt. Buchholz).

Lt. Henry Kaul of 336 Squadron was killed when he hit a tree while strafing.

Due to adverse weather conditions, ten of our aircraft landed at other bases in England.

Lt. Savage landed at Wattisham at 1153 hours. He took off for Debden at 1535. He flew over Debden at 1545, but was unable to land because of ground haze. At 1550 hours, on the way back to Wattisham, his a/c struck a radio tower at Nuthampstead and crashed. He was killed instantly.

12 Feb - A Guard of Honor, composed of Enlisted Men and Officers, stood at the Main Gate at 1400 hours to pay last respects to fellow Officer, 1st Lt. Morton Savage. He was buried at Cambridge Cemetery.

13 Feb - All available EM Attended a showing of a training film "Ground Crew Safety" at the Station Cinema.

There was a practice alert at 1400 hours. All members of the Mobile Striking Force, the Commando Force, the Gas Decontamination Squad, the Reserve Platoon, and the Line Crews immediately took up their various defensive positions. A practice gas-mask drill was held in conjunction with this "Dry Run."

After release from the Alert at 1600 hours there was a formation in the Hangar for all EM. 1/Sgt Morris read a Directive from Supreme Headquarters Allied Expeditionary Force, dated 23 Jan 1945.

1. A review of the security situation has shown that a dangerous amount of information is being given to the enemy through carelessness.

2. All personnel have been instructed in security and now severe disciplinary action will be taken against any who fail to practice security.

3. The telephone monitoring services will be increased; therefore, all telephone users should bear that in mind.

4. Commanding Officers will ensure that all security offenses will be severely punished. There will be no leniency.

He also read a memorandum describing the appropriate uniform to be worn, especially in London, to cut down on the number of delinquencies.

Capt. Jensen then urged all men to take furloughs coming to them since it is possible the privilege might be curtailed.

It was also announced that in the near future, *1 Officer and 14 EM per month will be given a 30-day furlough and 21-day rest period in the States.* This applies to the entire 8th Air Force. Selection will be made on the basis of time spent overseas.

Jensen, also, suggested there may be an increase in operations in the near future, and he asked that all men fully cooperate in accomplishing the job ahead.

14 Feb - The 334 Squadron Snack Bar in the Dispersal area was officially opened this morning. Coffee, toast, and oranges were available for the Pilots. It was much appreciated, since they will not be back for lunch today.

Capt. Ezzell read the Security Directive from SHEAF to all available Pilots.

Major Norley led Group "A" on a Support to Magdeburg. Operating as Free-Lance, they dropped to the deck south of Bremen and strafed, damaging four locomotives and three switch towers. They then found a new barracks type area. They damaged three of them with wing tank fires and clobbered a 40 mm AA gun emplacement. Lt. Elffner and Capt. George strafed four command buildings.

Wing Commander Blanford of the RAF spoke in the Cinema on the part the RAF plays in the war, "RAF Fighters in Action." He has 700 Operational hours to his credit.

Orders were received naming the following Officers "Fighter Ace," having destroyed their fifth e/a.

Lt. Col. James Clark Jr.	8 Oct 43
Major Duane Beeson	8 Oct 43
Major Howard Hively	21 Mar 44
Major Henry Mills	20 Feb 44
Major Lewis Norley	8 Apr 44
Major Winslow Sobanski	25 May 44
Capt. Raymond Care	8 Apr 44
Capt. Archie Chatterley	6 Mar 44
Capt. Victor France	21 Mar 44
Capt. David Howe	18 Apr 44
Capt. Joseph Lang	30 Apr 44
Capt. Nicholas Megura	6 Mar 44
Capt. Gerald Montgomery	27 Mar 44
Capt. William Smith	11 Apr 44
Capt. Vasseure Wynn	27 Mar 44
1st Lt. Hipolitus Biel	29 Mar 44
1st Lt. Ralph Hofer	18 Mar 44
1st Lt. Spiros Pisanos	5 Mar 44
1st Lt. Grover Siems Jr.	21 May 44
1st Lt. Frank Speer	29 May 44

17 Feb - A film "The Articles of War" was shown at the Station Cinema, followed by a Sex Morality film entitled "Pick Up."

Michael Kennedy and Kenneth Helfrecht were promoted from 2nd Lt. to 1st Lt.

20 Feb - On the 19th, an uneventful escort to Meschede was flown. Due to adverse weather, the group had to land at Wattisham where they stayed overnight.

Planes took off for Wattisham to join the Group there on an Escort to Nurnberg. Due to weather conditions, the bombers aborted. The Group then went strafing in the Neumarkt-Regensburg area. A factory was set on fire with dropped belly tanks. Two locomotives were deactivated, and oil storage tanks and cars were damaged, as well as goods wagons and trucks. Joiner and Carlson each destroyed a FW 190 at low level.

Col. Everett W. Stewart 4th Headquarters Squadron came to the 4th as Group and Station CO in Feb 45. He had flown his first combat mission at Pearl Harbor 7 Dec 41. He served in a P-40 unit on Wake and Midway where he racked up 280 combat hours prior to transfer to the 335 FG where he became CO in Nov 44. He had a total of 180 missions and 10 1/2 victories by wars end. Weckbacker collection.

After strafing trains, Capt. John Fitch was hit by flak and had to bail out S/W of Neumarkt. After calling on his R/T, he was seen to bail out; hit the ground; collapse his chute; and walk away. (He became a POW).

This show completed a tour plus a 50-hour extension for Capt. Albert Davis.

An order was received designating Col. Everett W. Stewart as Commanding Officer 4th fighter Group and AAF Station F-356, effective 21 Feb 45.

21 Feb - Today, the target was Nurnberg. After leaving the Escort mission, the Squadrons went strafing, damaging 5 locomotives, 66 rail-cars, and several vehicles, including trucks.

2nd Lt. August Rabe hit a tree while strafing, damaging his kite to the extent that he had to belly in S/W of Coburg. He was seen to make a beautiful landing in an open field; walk away about 20 yards; return to the ship; get back into the cockpit; and call for Maj. Mc Kennon to destroy his kite. When he again left the kite, Maj. Mc Kennon and Lt. Cammer dropped their tanks on the plane and ignited the gas with a few squirts of 50 calibre.

*****

1st Lt. Andrew Lacy is MIA. Lt. Helfrecht reported: "Lt. Lacy was leading Blue Section as they strafed a train near Donausworth. As Lt. Lacy pulled up, he was hit by three 20 mm shells, two in his oil radiator and one in his left internal tank. He was streaming gas and oil and had no oil pressure. He immediately dropped his rpm and opened his radiators. He headed towards base, but after five minutes, his oil stopped streaming. In another five minutes his engine stopped, and he bailed out.

He waved as he was floating down to a plowed field near a woods. I lost him after he landed, so I believe he hid his chute and started to evade." (Both Lacy and Rabe became POWs).

*****

The 335 basketball team, the "Raiders," hasn't broken any records, but they are sure giving the other 12 station teams plenty of competition. After leading the "Signaleers" eleven different times, they went down to defeat in overtime 55-56 when the Signaleers were given a technical foul.

Wing Commander H. D. Villers, RAF, gave talks on Night Bombing by RAF Lancasters in the Station Cinema. It was very enlightening to those of us who know very little of this type of operation.

A Wednesday night dance was held at the Aero Club with music by a crack 16-piece band from 2nd Bomb Division.

22 Feb - Major Glover led an Escort to Peine and Hildesheim. They watched as the B-24s used a sensational new bombing tech-

nique. Swooping down from their usual level of about 25,000 feet, they smashed their targets from 9,500 feet.

After leaving escort, the Group dropped to the deck and strafed the autobahn between Brunswick and Hanover. They destroyed trucks, oil storage tanks, and a locomotive. Several Pilots found an A\D to strafe, resulting in the loss of eight planes for the Krauts. Major Glover had two, Major McFarlane one, Lt. Crawford three, and Lt. Alfred two.

Carl Brown, Jr., was promoted from 1st Lt. to Captain.

24 Feb - Yesterday, the USO show "Going to Town" was held at the Station Cinema. It was exceptionally good and was praised by both Officers and EM.

Last night, Maj. McKennon made good on his promise of "the best Squadron party we have ever had." The "Bar," located in Hut #91, near the PX, was opened at 1930 hours. The "Flying Eagles" furnished the music for dancing in the Aero Club, starting at 2000 hours. The Red Cross hostess invited 100 girls and also provided the food. The highlight of the dance was 24 "New" Land Army girls who were here for the first time. They seemed to give all the boys, especially our new Pilots, a great thrill.

The 335 received three new Pilots: 1st Lt. Robert Moe, and 2nd Lts. Howard Miller and Edward McLoughlin.

Today's target was Herford, and Major Norley led the Group in support. After leaving the uneventful support of the bombers, the Group went strafing near the Zuider Zee. This effort damaged six barges, three locomotives, and assorted goods cars. The Group also set a factory on fire with its wing tanks.

F/O Alvin Hand is MIA. Lt. Arthur reported that Horseback spotted a barge, and he peeled off to strafe it with his Flight in trail. F/O Hand followed him and pulled up to the right. "I saw Hand was in trouble and called it in as I pulled up left following the leader. Before I could locate Hand again, someone spotted the wreckage where he had bellied-in. Major Norley inspected the cockpit and declared it empty. Then, he fired on it in an unsuccessful attempt to

Capt. Kendall E. "Swede" Carlson was a double Ace with 10 1/2 e/a on his record when he became a POW. Ziegler collection.

set it on fire. I confirmed that the cockpit was empty and the location was near Emmen, Holland." (Hand became a POW).

*****

25 Feb - A Fighter Sweep to Dessau area was led by Major McKennon. In the vicinity of Nijmegen, numerous Allied Spitfires and Typhoons were observed. Four peculiar looking FW 190s came head-on below us. Several of our a/c dropped tanks to attack, but someone called out they were friends. The attack was broken off.

At Dessau, the Group started attacking targets of opportunity when Lts. Malmsten and O'Bryan found a FW 190. They destroyed it in the air.

Blue Section found an A/D near Naumburg with 60 e/a dispersed about a strip. They were camouflaged with green branches. They strafed the Drome, destroying eight and damaging three. They then climbed up and were attacked by seven Me 109s and FW 190s. Being low on gas and ammo, they evaded successfully. They landed in France to refuel and then continued on to base.

Results: Lt. Payne claimed one Me 262 and one Me 410 Destroyed, shared with Capt. Bell, who also claimed one FW 190 Destroyed; and two Me 210s Destroyed - shared with Lt. Denson. Lts. Malmsten and O'Bryan shared a 190.

Lt. Bowers claimed one FW 190, one Me 110, and one Me 410 Destroyed. In addition, seven trucks were destroyed, and five trucks and two locomotives were damaged by 334 Squadron.

The 335 Squadron hit railways and highways, Damaging four e/a, six locomotives, many rail cars, three passenger trains, and several trucks, with all Pilots taking part in the shootout.

The 336 claimed four: Lt. Corbett, Capt. Carlson, and Lt. Hileman each had one; and Lts. Morgan and Brooker shared one.

The Group ended up with a total of 13 e/a Destroyed.

Capt. Carlson was shot down on the first pass, after having destroyed one e/a. (He became a POW).

26 Feb - The Pilots were able to sleep a little later today since there was no briefing until 0900. At that time the Group led by Major Glover was directed to support B-24s over Berlin. There was little activity other than flak, and the Group left the bombers over Dummer Lake and did a little strafing on the way home.

Although no one in the Group was of aware of it, one of the B-24 Pilots on that mission was 1st Lt. James J. Scanlon. He was completing his tour of 35 missions with the 453rd Bomb Group. He had finished his flight training at Tonopah, Nevada, with his new crew, and arrived in Ireland while he was still 19 years old. He recalls, "Existing in a bomber outfit, is just that - EXISTING. The food was bad, the huts were only a step above tents, the missions were long, and you got shot at on every one. We had flak damage on 90% of our missions and crashes were numerous due to ice and/ or overloading of our aircraft.

Bomber flying was no fun and extremely dangerous, so I decided to try for fighters." Two days later, Lt. Scanlon was interviewed by Group CO Col. Stewart and transferred to the 4th on TDY for 30 days. If he proved to be OK, he was to have a permanent assignment. Scanlon was assigned to 335 Squadron and was to room with Capt. Robert Kanaga, who had transferred from the same B-24 Group as he, but had flown only a few bomber missions.

Scanlon found a brave soul to check him out in a T-6. After 2 hours and 10 landings, the Pilot turned the aircraft over to Scanlon with the admonition that, "If I wanted to kill myself it was OK with him, but he had enough and he did not intend to be killed by a Bomber Pilot."

On 6 Mar, Sgt. Edlund and Paul Lucas showed Scanlon how to start a P-51B, and told him all he needed to know, except to burn down the fuselage tank prior to pulling any maneuvers. In a subsequent 3 to 4 "G" loop, the "beast" swapped ends with him and he learned the folly of his ways. Later, while doing his normal bomber landing pattern, the Group landed under him and he thus discovered that fighters have their own unique landing program. He discovered that they did not linger in the air when it was time to land. The typical landing arrangement was for a flight of four P-51s to swoop low over the field in the direction of landing, cutting their power, dropping flaps and gear, and then climbing, while forming a single file. They then did a 360 degree turn and landed one right after the other. Each plane then rapidly dispersed to its assigned location, clearing the runway for following planes to land.

Forty-two days after his last B-24 mission, over Berlin, James Scanlon was again over Berlin, but this time he was flying a Mustang. He recalled that there were at least four other bomber associated Pilots in the 4th who had made the transition to fighters. They were: Gervais Ford (334), who had completed a tour as Co-Pilot in B-24s, George Ridler and Douglas Pederson (336), and Robert Kanaga (334), all having flown B-24s.

27 Feb - The **Bronze Star** was awarded to Staff Sergeant Raymond Mayorga for meritorious achievement in the performance of outstanding services from 15 April to 20 April 44.

Henry Clifton, Jr., is promoted from 1st Lt. to Captain.

Col. Stewart led "B" Group on a Support to Halle. After the support was completed, 335 Squadron stayed with the bombers, and 334 Squadron strafed targets of opportunity and Weimar A/D. All a/c made four to six passes each. In addition to damaging four locomotives, several box cars, and trucks, the following e/a were destroyed at Weimar A/D:

Lt. Malmsten   6
Major Montgomery
Major Glover
Lt. Kesler
Capt. Bell

Capt. Clifton	3 each
Lt. Ayers	3
shared Lt. Voyles	1
Lt. Payne	
Lt. McFadden	
Lt. Antonides	
Lt. Dickey	
Major MacFarlane	2 each
Lt. Garvin	
Lt. Harre	
Lt. Wells	
Lt. Robert Davis	
Lt. Harry Davis	
Lt. Hustwit	
Lt. Pedersen	
Lt. Crawford	1 each

These victories brought the day's total to 43 Destroyed.

1st Lt. Robert Voyles is MIA. Cobweb Red 3, Lt. Ayers reported that he made two or three passes on Weimar A/D when he saw Cobweb Red 4, Lt. Voyles, pull up streaming coolant. "He had to break to avoid being hit by a 336 Squadron plane firing in his direction. In doing so, he lost Red 4. Lt. Voyles set course for home. A few minutes later, he called saying he couldn't make it. He did not answer my call, and the last R/T contact was at 1415 hours."

Lt. Harold Crawford was also MIA. (Both Voyles and Crawford became POWs).

28 Feb - An uneventful Fighter Sweep was flown to the Weimar-Ingolstadt area. Weather prevented going to the deck.

The following letter was received from Capt. Charles Howse: "In order to perpetuate and honor the memory of the men of the 65th Fighter Wing who have given their lives in this World War II, we the living are being given the opportunity to endow a permanent memorial to their sacrifices for the years to come.

In what way could the memory of the dead be more brightly kept than in the minds and hearts of growing children? In what way could we more fittingly honor our dead than by making children happy and providing a suitable and enjoyable place for them to spend happy carefree hours? If we, the living, can keep the memories of our dead alive in the heart of youth, perhaps the knowledge of the horrors of war can be kept alive and today's children who are tomorrow's statesmen will better and more industriously work for a brighter future and more lasting peace."

The chairman of the memorial project has contacted the Mayor of Saffron Walden in regards to building a year-round playground complete with clubhouse. The idea was enthusiastically greeted both by the Mayor and City Council. The City Council, not to be outdone, voted that the city should match the American contribution and make this a truly worthwhile project, and the following plans were made:

That a 10-acre tract of land be purchased upon which tennis courts, bowling greens, cricket, and football fields could be laid out.

That a clubhouse is to be built, and that this is to be the American Memorial. This clubhouse is to be given an American name and is to have a plaque in it for all to see, stating that the clubhouse was built by contributions of the American Forces commemorating the dead of their fellow comrades.

That the town of Saffron Walden is to permanently maintain these grounds and clubhouse in the years to come.

Estimates of the cost of this project were made and the figure of 9,000 Pounds was arrived at, of which it was agreed that Saffron Walden would pay half and the 65th Fighter Wing the remainder.

There being four Fighter stations and one Headquarter in the 65th Fighter Wing, it was agreed by the Station Commanders that each Station could subscribe 1,000 Pounds, with the 65th Headquarter subscribing the remaining 500 Pounds. This would constitute 4,500 Pounds, or our half of the estimated 9,000 Pounds.

In order for as nearly an equitable donation as possible to be arrived at, the following scale is submitted for this station.

Pvt & Pfc 0-5-0	1st & 2nd Lt.1-0-0
Cpl & Sgt 0-10-0	Capt.1-10-0
1st 3 Grades 0-15-0	Field Grade 2-0-0

While this is not the maximum contribution accepted, it is believed that if each man will contribute the amount set up in his grade scale, our Squadron will fulfill its obligation to this worthwhile cause.

A Collection Table and sheet will be set up at pay call for the Enlisted Men who care to donate, and the Officers may make their contribution through the Officers' Mess.

"A memorial of this type is a chance for us to leave pleasant memories and happy thoughts in the minds of one of our Allies. It will be a monument to the sacrifices of the few, the contributions of the many, and should in a small way be an indication of the American way of life."

All available EM attended one of three showings of a film "The Battle of Russia" at the Station Cinema.

Gerald Montgomery was promoted from Captain to Major.

Monthly Consolidated Strength Report

334 Squadron	Officers 52	Enlisted Men 235
335 Squadron	Officers 56	Enlisted Men 244

1 Mar 1945 - Major Norley started March with a support run to Ingolstadt. After escort, "A" Group went on the usual strafing run, shooting up four locomotives and miscellaneous vehicles and rail cars.

This was the first operational mission for 2nd Lt. Leonard Otto and the last for 1st Lt. John Creamer, who completed a tour of 300 hours today.

4 Mar - On the 2nd and 3rd, uneventful support missions were flown to Magdeburg, led by Lt. Col. Woods and Col. Stewart, respectively. These were the 12th and 13th successive missions in as many days.

On the 3rd, 335 strafed two locomotives and a truck. At this time, Capt. George Davis apparently was hit by flak and bailed out.

Near Rotterdam, Lt. Kenneth Green, a new 335 Pilot with five missions to his credit, seemed to have trouble with his kite. He acted a bit crazy as if he had been hit himself and kept going around in circles. Lt. Cammer tried to direct him home, to no avail, and circled with him until he lost him in the clouds. We have heard nothing more of Lt. Green.

Both Green and Davis were subsequently reported as being POWs.

Today started with an air raid alert, making it seem like old times.

An Order was received awarding **Air Medals and/or Oak Leaf Clusters to the Air Medal** to 13 of the Pilots.

Major John D. McFarlane 336 was Squadron CO when shot down 12 Mar 45. He was fortunate enough to evade to Sweden. Konsler collection.

There was a Milk Run to Schwabisch Hall A/D with 10/10ths cloud cover obscuring the target.

At 2005 hours there was another air raid alert causing the Cinema patrons to leave with only 3 minutes more of the show's Grand Finale.

A year ago today, Col. Blakeslee led the 4th Fighter Group on its first escort to Berlin. His Wingman was Commanding Officer, Major Norley of 334 who then became the 2nd Fighter Pilot to see the "Big City."

6 Mar - Yesterday, escort to Hamburg made fifteen days in a row without a break. Today bad weather gave the crews a much needed chance to catch up on maintenance work.

This weeks topic of "Army Talks" was "Russia Its Historical Background." All EM will attend one of the five lectures in the following days.

Orders were received awarding eight Pilots **Oak Leaf Clusters to the Air Medal**. They were presented by General Auton who also awarded the **Bronze Star** to: M/Sgt Herman Hager, T/Sgt Raymond Clark, and S/Sgt Raymond Mayorga.

The 7th, No show - the 8th, Uneventful tour of Siegen. On the 9th, all Squadron personnel holding a driver's license were required to attend a showing of a Transportation Training film. On the 10th, an uneventful show to Paderborn and on the 11th, a similar no excitement trip to Kiel.

12 Mar - Of much concern to the Pilots is the progress of Lt. Jenk's duck farm in the little pond behind the 335 dispersal where "Philber" and his mate have a nest, now overflowing with eggs. The "Duck Farm" has been the property of Lt. Jenks for several months. He had lost sleep for a month worrying about how he could get the duck to lay enough eggs to raise some little ones, but now his headache is how he can get her to stop and start sitting on them. So far, he hasn't found the solution.

Today, "A" Group was led by Col. Stewart and "B" Group by Major Mc Farlane with the target being Swinemunde. 10/10ths cloud cover provided no opportunity to strafe or take pictures.

Group B did chase three UI/AC on top but was unable to engage them.

Major Mc Farlane of 336 Squadron was heard on the R/T saying that he was bailing out, over Fehmarn Island, Germany, due to a coolant leak. (He evaded to Sweden).

13 Mar - Major Mc Kennon took his one and only crew chief, S/Sgt Joe Sills, for a nice long ride in the pick-a-back Mustang. Later, he took Lt. Shirtell up for a ride, much to his regret, because he had to wait until his crew-chief cleaned out the kite before anyone else could go for a ride.

Later Capt. Davis took his crew chief, S/Sgt Edlund for a spin. Edlund got along fine except for blacking out after a dive.

14 Mar - Lt. Col. Woods led a Fighter Sweep over a great deal of territory with no action what-so-ever.

The taking of sulfadiazine tablets by all personnel was suspended as of this date.

15 Mar - Col. Stewart led "A" Group and Lt. Col. Woods led "B" Group to Berlin. There the "Heavies" dropped the war right into the lap of the German High Command as they bombed the German General Staff Headquarters at Zossen, near Berlin. The 4th furnished escort for this exclusive mission.

Three high flying jets were seen but not engaged.

16 Mar - Charles Harre was promoted from 2nd Lt. to 1st Lt.

17 Mar - 1st Lt. Clarence Boretsky and 1st Lt. Timothy Cronin were released from combat duty and are awaiting return to the ZI, having finished their tours.

A trip to Hanover, led by Capt. Howe, found 10/10ths cloud cover and, again, no action.

18 Mar - Capt. Howe led "B" Group on a Support to Berlin. "A" Group was led by Major Mc Kennon, 335 Squadron Commander.

After finishing the escort, Major Mc Kennon led his group over Neubrandenburg A/D where they spotted a large number of E/A.

Capt. David W. Howe 334 Squadron, an ex-RCAF Pilot, completed two tours without an abort. He was an Ace with 8 1/2 e/a to his credit. Konsler collection.

He circled several times and then went down alone to look over the set-up before starting to strafe. The Major was hit in his oil line by flak. About three miles west of Penzlin, he was forced to bail out. He and his plane landed in the same plowed field. His kite exploded.

Lt. George Green decided to go rescue him, being covered by the rest of the Squadron. Two enemy soldiers and a dog, who were heading for the Major, were discouraged by a few well placed 50 cal slugs. Mc Kennon and Green discarded all unnecessary equipment and scrambled into the "one-man" cockpit and took off from the rough, grass-covered field and headed for home.

The second outstanding feature of today's show is that Capt. Howe, of 334, completed his second operational tour with a total of 502 operational hours.

We have to thank the 334 Squadron Officers for our fifth and finest Squadron party to date. Previously our parties were held at the Sergeants' Mess and were climaxed by dancing and a buffet supper, but this one was strictly a Squadron Smoker.

A chicken dinner with cake and ice cream was served in the EM Mess. The tables were set around the perimeter of the big Nissen Hut with a lighted candle on each table. Wherever possible, the Crew Chief sat next to his Pilot. After dessert, Sgt. Meyer, the Master of Ceremonies for the evening, introduced our Commanding Officer, Major Norley. The Major reminded us that we are the highest scoring Squadron in the USAAF. He pointed out that this is due to three things: (1) the plane, (2) the crew, without whom it could not fly, and (3) the Pilot. Most of us have always thought of this sequence as reading in reverse.

Major Norley then introduced our new Station Executive Officer, Major Mitchell, who introduced our Squadron Executive Officer, Capt. Jensen. "Red" Norley then introduced our Operations Officer, Major Montgomery, who has been with us for nearly two years. "Monty" then introduced the four Flight Commanders: Lts. Mc Fadden, Hoelscher, Malmsten, and Capt. Bell. Each in turn introduced the members of his Flight.

The Wattisham band began to play and the first of ten barrels of beer was tapped. The band adjourned, and the program began. The review consisted of a singer, a sister tap dancing act, a juggler, and a pianist, and it ended with an "Artistic" dance. The balance of the evening was devoted to good fellowship.

We owe a special vote of thanks to the committee who put this great evening together.

19 Mar - A support to Ingolstadt was led by Major Norley with "A" Group, and Capt. Alfred with "B" Group. In the Frankfort area, an Me 109 was observed head-on. Major Norley engaged with the Hun who jettisoned his canopy and bailed out. Red Section was bounced by two Me 109s who managed to evade.

White smoke was rising to 15,000 feet over Donausworth. Large fires with black smoke rising to 15,000 feet over Cologne were seen on the way out.

Lt. Col. Sidney S. Woods Hq Squadron, Deputy Group CO (left) with Crew Chief R. Lonier and Armament Man R. Easley. Col. Woods was shot down on 16 April 1945 and was a POW for 13 days. He was an Ace in the Pacific in P-40s and scored an additional five victories on 22 March 1945 in a P-51. Konsler collection.

Word was received that the second highest scoring Squadron in the USAAF is the 2nd Fighter Squadron of the 56th Fighter Group. They have destroyed 311 planes, while 334 has destroyed 333 11/12.

21 Mar - Under Maj. Montgomery, the Group escorted over Hesepe A/D. Due to intense flak, the group did not strafe the A/D but went to Achmer A/D which was being strafed by the 353rd Fighter Group. When they withdrew, the 4th went to work. Lt. Malmsten claimed two Me 109s, Lt. Burney, one Me 109, and Lt. Hoelscher, one FW 190.

Capt. Albert Davis, 335 Squadron Leader, was hit by flak on his first pass over Hesepe A/D. He was heard to say "I'm bailing out." He was about two miles north of Hesepe and at only 50 feet. His chute was not seen to open. (He was KIA).

2nd Lt. Robert Cammer was last seen west of Achmer when he told Lt. Buchholz that he had been hit. He was losing his coolant and his oil pressure was 0. He said he was heading for friendly territory. (He became a POW).

The 335 claimed: Capt. O'Donnell, one Me 262 Destroyed, while Lts. Connors, Rasmussen, Buchholz and Bucher each claimed a U/I twin-engined a/c Damaged.

Captain Alfred claimed three Do 217s Destroyed and 2nd Lt. Collins one Me 410 Destroyed.

Major Montgomery observed a splash in the North Sea. Believing it to be a plane, he called in a Mayday.

Word was received that 1st Lt. Herbert Blanchfield, reported MIA on 9 May 44, is a POW, and that 1st Lt. Ralph Hofer, reported MIA 2 July 44, was killed in action.

22 Mar - Lt. Col. Woods leading "A" Group and Major Mc Kennon with "B" Group went to Ruhland on a bomber support. "A" Group chased a jet headed for Berlin and encountered FW 190s forming up over Furstenwalde. They bounced these Huns. Lt. Jahnke claimed a FW 190 Destroyed and Lt. Farrington claimed an FW 190 Destroyed. Woods got a total of five e/a, while Lts. Riedel, Hagan, and Robert Davis contributed four. In all, 11 e/a were Destroyed.

At a meeting in the Hanger of 334 Squadron, Capt. Jensen discussed the following:

1. Our last delinquency report was very good. He urged them to keep it that way. Hereafter, any EM reporting six or more hours late from pass will be tried by a Summary Court Martial except for extenuating circumstances.

2. Starting tonight, four men from 334 will be detailed to man the dispersal ack-ack guns from dusk to dawn in two-hour shifts with two hours off between shifts.

3. During alerts, NCOs will be responsible to disperse any Groups of EM.

4. Our Alert Detachment and Mobile Striking Force will pick up their rifles from Squadron Supply and keep them in the barracks.

5. All EM assigned to ack-ack duty will be required to pass an aircraft recognition test or take a course in aircraft recognition.

6. Starting 22 April, a few EM at a time, will be given a 48-hour pass to Paris, travel time excluded.

The film "Divide and Conquer" was shown this week.

24 Mar - Col. Stewart led "A" Group while Col. Woods led "B" Group on a morning area patrol to Munster, and then patrolled in the Rhine area, to cover the boys crossing the Rhine. No action was encountered.

At 1225 hours, Major Glover led "A" Group and Captain Alfred led "B" Group to patrol the same area as the morning mission. They, also, encountered no action but it made a long day "in the saddle" for the Pilots.

26 Mar - Major Mc Kennon took the group on a Fighter Sweep to the Worms, Weimar, Crailsheim area. They observed a heavy artillery duel north of Mannheim. No e/a were seen. Because of inclement weather and clouds, the three Squadrons became separated and each continued on the mission alone.

Lt. Bower's a/c was hit by 40mm, 20mm, and MG fire when he was NE of Erlangen. There was a five-inch hole in his right aileron and eight holes through the canopy. He sustained superficial flak wounds in the neck.

The 336 squadron lost two Pilots, Lts. Harry Davis and Earl Hustwit. Both were killed as the result of enemy fire.

Two separate TWXs were received from Headquarters Eighth Air Force congratulating all units for the support given the ground forces in securing the air over the Battle of the Rhine.

An e/a Destroyed Confirmation report was received Cofirming 26 planes Destroyed in the period from 12 Sept 45 through 25 Dec 45. The following Officers received credits:

Capt. Brown 3 Destroyed
Capt. Lang
Lt. Mc Fadden
Maj. Hively
F/O Harre each2 Destroyed
Lt. Cronin 1 3/4 Destroyed
Lt. Rentschler
Lt. Hoelscher
Lt. Dickmeyer each 1 1/2 Destroyed
Capt. Smith
Lt. Senecal
Capt. Howe
Lt. Werner
Maj. Montgomery
Maj. Ackerly
Lt. Payne
Lt. Clifton each 1 Destroyed
Major Mc Kennon 3/4 Destroyed

In addition, 27 e/a were also confirmed as Damaged.

All available Pilots were given a lecture by Lt. Guerra explaining the use of a new reflecting surface for radar that the Pilot is to unfold when in his dinghy. The device causes a "blip" that can be picked up by a radar equipped ASR a/c from a distance of 8 to 15 miles. It has been used with great success in the Pacific.

30 Mar - A Station Defense Practice Drill was held between 1330 and 1600 hours with all personnel reporting to stations previously assigned.

Major Norley led a Fighter Sweep to the Hamburg area.

The only excitement was encountered when five Me-262s crossed under the Group 6,000 feet below. The Group chased but was unable to catch the e/a.

Orders were received awarding **Air Medals or Oak Leaf Clusters to the Air Medal** to 21 Pilots.

1st Lt. Hugh Lindsay and 1st Lt. John Creamer, who have each completed 300 hours of operational time, have left to return to the States.

31 Mar - Lt. Col. Woods led "A" Group on an escort to Hassel where the bombers were after Ammunition Dumps. The Group was to make a maximum effort since this was an extremely important Depot, supplying front line troops. There was no action as 10/10ths clouds covered the area.

2nd Lt. Kenneth Foster is MIA. Lt. Jahnke reported: "I was Cobweb Black Leader when #3, Lt. Foster's engine quit at 17,000 feet. Efforts to restart were unsuccessful so I told him to steer 240 degrees as he lost altitude rapidly. Nuthouse was contacted for a fix which was finally obtained in spite of interference from other planes.

Lt. Foster crash-landed in the vicinity of Hengel, Holland. He called that he was OK. I told him I would pick him up but Horseback rescinded. I told him he was in Holland, not far from the Allied lines. I suggested that he take a 240 degree heading. He waved and smiled as we left." (He became a POW).

*****

Group "B" was led by Major Glover. After they left the bombers, they swept toward Hirchberg where they bounced three Russian P-39s. One turned on them and fired head-on at Lt. Payne's a/c, a 37 mm hitting his prop. Another P-39 then rocked his wings in recognition.

Lts. Spencer, Beeson, and Mabie and F/O Freeman took off to rendezvous with Steeple Morden A/C, and then with a Warwick over Yarmouth on an Air-Sea Rescue mission. F/O Freeman got lost in the dark and aborted. A motor launch was dropped to the crew of a Catalina off the Dutch coast. The Catalina had landed yesterday to pick up five of a Fort Crew and had been unable to take off. Our A/C guarded the Catalina until relieved. Later F/O Freeman went out to relieve the boys and reported that just before he had arrived on the scene, a Jet job dived in and strafed the Catalina but did not hurt anyone. A second boat was dropped but broke in half when it hit the water. A third boat was to be dropped because the Catalina was drifting rapidly in to close proximity to German territory.

Six new Officers were assigned to 334 Squadron: 2nd Lts. John Schnell, Thomas Seihl, Billy Skinner, Orville Slone, Milton Spencer, and Raymond Sylvester.

Monthly Consolidated Strength Report

334 Squadron	Officers 54	Enlisted Men 235
335 Squadron	Officers 52	Enlisted Men 240

1 April 1945 - April Fool's Day - Easter Sunday.

An early show was cancelled due to weather over the Continent so a truckload of the Pilots went to the Easter Service at the Station Chapel.

2 April - Double summer time went into effect at 0100 hours making our clocks two hours ahead of GMT from 2 April until 15 July.

There was a no-event trip to Aalberg West Jet A/D, led by Capt. Alfred. The most excitement was when the 448th Bomb Group luckily did not allow enough lead when they fired on us.

Capt. George Davis, shot down by flak on the Magdeburg show 3 Mar, returned to base today after being released from a German P/W Camp (Stalag Luft), which had been over-run by our front line troops. He's in fine shape with the exception of a fractured ankle, which he pranged on a stump when he bailed out of his Mustang at 700 feet into a forest. He's mighty proud of those "Kraut Crutches" which he used to hobble around the Dispersal.

2nd Lts. Olin Kiser and Charles Konsler completed their required 300 Operational hours on today's mission.

The 335 Squadron received eight new Pilots who are taking classes in ground school preparatory to OTU training in Mustangs. They are 2nd Lts. Paul Skogstad, Ralph Trietsch, Charles Thacker, John Smith, Almond Seymour, William Sparkman, Alston Stafford, and Richard Skerritt.

3 April - All line crews were rousted out this morning at 0415 hours only to be told an hour later to go back to bed since the mission had been scrubbed.

Donald Malmsten was promoted from 1st Lt. to Captain.

Seven Pilots of 334 Squadron were awarded the **Air Medal and/or Oak Leaf Clusters to the Air Medal**.

Our Group is still cooperating with A/SR to try to rescue the Catalina crew adrift north of the Frisian Islands. Another Walrus dropped a launch, but the crew was unable to reach it so Lt. Garcin strafed it, and set it on fire, and then left for base. Lt. O'Bryan took off to escort another Warwick to the scene.

4 April - Lt. Col. Woods led "A" Group and Col. Stewart lead "B" Group on a support to Parchim. As the bombers approached the target, they were attacked by eight Me 262s. Our Red, Blue, and Green Sections engaged these e/a. Capt. Kanaga and Lt. Dyer each Destroyed one, and Lt. Kennedy shared a kill with Lt. Fredericks, Ayers, and Bangh of 336. Lts. Harre and Jungling each Damaged one.

The Sections then rejoined the bombers. Three more 262s attacked but were chased away.

Last night at the Aeroclub, Tony Donadio, Tenor, former soloistof the Notre Dame Glee Club and Baltimore Symphony, gave a program of light semi-classics, sacred, and operatic music.

Tonight the 2d Air Division Band gave a concert in the Cinema. Then, the orchestra section furnished music for the weekly dance at the Aeroclub.

Captain George Davis 335-336 Squadron was shot down on 3 Mar 1945. He was still nursing a broken ankle when he was released one month later. His ankle was broken when he bailed out and landed on a stump. Weckbacher collection.

1st Lt. Charles E. Konsler (left) and Lt. Olin A. Kiser completed their tours on the same day, 2 April 1945. Both had a brief interlude while on DS to ferry P-51s to Sweden. On that mission, Konsler shot down his first e/a. Konsler collection.

The obviously expert butchers, Pilots from the 334 Squadron, prepare three pigs for the Squadron barbecue. Zigler collection.

Tommorow night, a play "Murder Without Crime" is scheduled for the Red Cross Aeroclub.

6 April - Lt. Young led an uneventful mission to Halle.

This was the first operational mission for Lt. Scanlon in a fighter plane, having finished a tour on Libs before transferring to this Group.

When the Group took off, the smell of woodsmoke penetrated the 334 Intelligence Office. A number of Pilots and crew members were digging a barbecue pit aided and abetted by liquid refreshment.

A few days ago, the Pilots each contributed four bob to a "Hog Fund" to pay for the party. The three pigs were slaughtered Thursday by Captains Howe and Malmsten and taken to the Officers' Mess cold-box.

At 1600 hours, the feast began with Barbecued pork, French fried potatoes, hot rolls, and beer. Hard liquor was served to the ample supply of visiting brass.

The PRO photographer took some remarkable candid shots.

An Order of the day was received from General Dwight D. Eisenhower:

"To every member of the AEF: The encirclement of the Ruhr by a wide pincer movement has cut off the whole of Army Group B and part of Army Group H, thus forming a large pocket of enemy troops whose fate is sealed and who are ripe for annihilation. The most vital industrial area is denied to the German war potential. The magnificent feat of arms will bring the war more rapidly to a close. It will long be remembered in history as an outstanding battle - The Battle of the Ruhr."

Lts. Ashcroft, Mabie, and Guerra were promoted to Captain.

A card was received, addressed to "The men of the 334th Fighter Squadron," dated 14 March 1945. The imprint on the top of the card read - "Just to let you know that along with many hundred thousands others in and around Philadelphia, I have today contributed to the Red Cross and have dedicated this donation to you." Eileen G. Ritz who sent the card, wrote as follows: "Dedicated to the memory of Lt. Morton Savage and his friends in the 334th Fighter Squadron, 4th Fighter Group. May God see you safely through till the end of the war sees you home again."

7 April - Major Glover led a Support mission to bombers attacking ammo dumps at Duneburg and Krummel. The Group had a spectacular form-up under the clouds, and they set course on the deck.

Near Steinhuder Lake, four jets made ineffective passes at the bombers who destroyed one of them. Two long-nosed FW 190s approached, intent on attacking the bombers. Major Norley climbed to attack one of the e/a which then dove straight through a B-17 formation, chopping off the tail of one of them. Later several Me-109s approached, and we attacked them. Six e/a were destroyed by Maj. Norley, and Lts. Buchanan, Hoelscher, Ayers, Riedel, and Davis.

Six P-51s, believed to be Jerry operated, were seen attacking B-17s.

A P-51 chasing an Me 109, was shot down by the bombers.

Major Norley started his third tour, having completed 553 1/2 hours on his first two tours.

Lt. Jahnke was taking off on a test flight when his engine cut out at about 100 feet. He crashed in a field off the east end of the runway. He completely destroyed the plane and suffered a bad cut on his forehead. He was taken to Braintree Hospital and given a transfusion and 15 stitches.

(l-r) 2nd Lt. Herman S. Rasmussen 335 Squadron was KIA when he bailed out at low altitude and his chute did not open in time. He was hit by flak while strafing the Munich-Brunnthal A/D on 9 April 1945. 1st Lt. Robert A. Cammer 335 Squadron became a POW when shot down by flak while strafing the Achmer A/D on 21 March 1945. Lt. Robert C. Buchholz 335 Squadron was KIA when hit by flak while strafing the Munich-Brunnthal A/D on 9 April 1945. Konsler collection.

8 April - Major Norley led again, this time to Bayreuth. After leaving the bombers, the Group split into three and went sweeping different areas with no action encountered. 2nd Lt. Homer Smith crashed and was killed on a local OTU flight.

PROGRAM - SALUTE THE GROUND MAN WEEK
Tuesday, 10 April 1945
1000 hours - Decoration Ceremony on Parade ground.

Wednesday, 11 April 1945
2000 hours - Dance at Red Cross Aeroclub.
2200 hours - Drawing for Plane ride at Dance.

Friday, 13 April 1945
1930 hours - Flying Eagles Orchestra in the Station Cinema.
2000 hours - Colonel Stewart in the Station Cinema.
2030 hours - Wattisham Glee Club in the Station Cinema.

9 April - Major Mc Kennon led to support attack on Neuberg A/D. The bombers scored very well.

The 335 Fighter Squadron found a parking area loaded with Me 410s, Ju 52s, and Ju 88s. They strafed, destroying 14 and damaging 15.

Lt. Buchholz got three UI, T/E, aircraft; Major Mc Kennon, three; and Lts. Elffner and Heaton, each two. Lts. Lee, Jennings, Burgess, and Hunter, each scored one.

Lt. Buchholz was hit by flak. He and Herman Rasmussen were both KIA.

The Station Soft Ball League got under way this afternoon. The 335 Raiders defeated the Ordinance Detonators by a score of 6-4.

10 April - The presentation ceremony and review of troops took place as scheduled, with all Squadrons participating. Brigadier General Jesse Auton of the 65th Fighter Wing presented the awards with Capt. Malmsten receiving the **Distinguished Flying Cross**.

Gen. Auton stressed the importance of the part played by the Ground Crews in the Air Force, regardless of rank. He praised the work of the men and urged them to keep up the fighting spirit of the Group until final victory is achieved.

Capt. Robert Evans sent a Letter of Commendation to all Personnel of 334 Squadron, praising them on the Presentation Ceremony and Review. It was accomplished with little or no practice. Gen. Auton commended the Squadron Personnel on their part in the activities.

Lt. Col. Woods took the Group (61 planes) on a support to Rechlin-Lars A/D. Again the group split up and Red Section of 334 Squadron, strafed Wittstock A/D with Major Montgomery claiming one Me 410; Lt. Mc Fadden, one Ju 88; Lt. Lowther, one Ju 52;

and Lt. Miller, one U/I T/E e/a Destroyed. Wilmer Collins shot down a 262.

Lt. Miller probably received machine gun slugs on one of the passes. He was heard being directed by MEW to B-78 (Kindhoven). He asked on the R/T for hospitalization.

Today, Lt. Wells completed his tour of operations.

Several Russian Generals paid a visit to Dispersal and were very much impressed.

12 April -

IN MEMORIAM

It is with deep regret and profound sorrow that we enter into these pages the announcement of the death of the Commander-in-Chief of the Armed Forces of the United States. President Franklin Delano Roosevelt passed away at Warm Springs, Georgia, 12 April 1945 at 1630 hours. He was 63 years of age.

14 April - Yesterday Col. Woods led the Group on a rather uneventful mission. Later 335 strafed an A/D with Capt. O'Donnel claiming one Ar-196 Destroyed, and 1st Lt. Loton Jennings, one He 115 Destroyed. Six others were damaged, but they did not burn. Possibly they had no gas in them.

Captain Thomas Bell completed his tour of Operations yesterday.

Lt. Jahnke, hospitalized after his accident on 7 April, returned to dispersal today. He gave this account of the accident: "I was running a test hop and immediately after take-off, the left bank cutout, smoking and on fire. As I turned port, the coolant popped and glycol streamed out fast. I decided to put it down in the field in front of me. Although I could not see due to the glycol, I made what I believe was a fair approach. I hit quite hard, knocking me about somewhat. The a/c was torn up completely. My seat tore loose along with the armour plate, throwing me against the gunsight. I did not reach 100 feet altitude during the hop."

*****

Major Norley presented the **Good Conduct Ribbon** to 50 Enlisted Men at a formation in the hangar.

15 April - On an escort to Ulm led by Captain Bell, the escort ended, and a Fighter Sweep was initiated. The 334 bounced two P-47s near Lake Constance. Two P-51s, carrying old type AAF markings, bounced our R/T Relay at 30,000 feet but broke off when Lt. James got on their tail.

Lt. Wozniak, the other R/T Relay, had engine trouble just after crossing-in, and he crash-landed 1 mile north of Wattau, Belgium. The Pilot was only slightly injured, but the plane was a total wreck.

16 April - "A" Group was led by Lt. Col. Woods while Major Norley led "B" Group on a support to Rosenheim and Prague. This was followed by a strafing mission in the Karlsbad-Salzburg and Prague Areas. Cobweb, 334 Squadron, strafed Gablingen A/D, near Augsburg. A P-51 fuselage was seen on the South end of the A/D. Many of the e/a were dug in holes or parked in craters on the A/D. In spite of this and the flak experienced, the Cobweb Squadron had a field day with 44 of various types destroyed and another 22 damaged.

Leading the list of Destroyed were:

Lts. Helfrecht and Antonides -	each 5
Lt. Denson and Maj. Norley -	each 4
Lts. Spencer, Ayers, Dyer, O'Bryan, and Bowers -	each 3
Lts. Harre, Dvorak, and Buchanan -	each 2

Lt. Arthur 1 1/2 Lts. Kennedy, Lowther, and Burnett - each 1

2nd Lt. Paul Burnett is MIA. He called on the R/T and said that he was hit while strafing the A/D. Lt. Bichanan and Lt. Mc Fadden saw a plane shooting at an e/a on the ground. The e/a exploded quite violently. The Pilot flew through the explosion. This may have been Lt. Burnett.

Five of the kites received minor damage from flak.

In the meantime, "B" Group was having a shootout at Prague, during which, Lt. Col. Woods was shot down. 2nd Lt. Edward McLoughlin did not return and was thought to have been hit by flak. Nine Caboose (335 Squadron) planes were slightly damaged by flak. Major Mc Kennon, who was leading Caboose, had a 20mm explode in the cockpit wounding him above the eye. He landed in France for medical attention.

The plan was for Becky Squadron, (336), to make the attack on the deck at Praha/Kbely A/D. Caboose would orbit to observe and knock out flak positions. The first pass disclosed no flak batteries; however, there was small arms and m/g fire.

Becky Squadron claimed 28 e/a Destroyed and 14 Damaged.

Lt. Pederson	8 Ju 52s Destroyed
F/O Baugh	5 Ju 88s Destroyed
Lt. Frederick	3 Destroyed
Lts. Collins, Brooker, Murchake, and Franklin -	each 2 Destroyed
Capt. Carpenter, Lts. Davis, Hastings and Meridith -	each 1 Destroyed

Caboose Squadron claimed 23 e/a Destroyed and 22 Damaged with the following scores:

Lts. Green, Halligan, and Jennings -	each 4 Destroyed
Maj. Mc Kennon, Lts. Hunter, Bucher, and Underwood -	each 3 Destroyed
Capt. O'Donnel, Lts. Couse and Miller -	each 2 Destroyed
Lts. Greenlese, Henderson, and F/O Freeman -	each 1 Destroyed

Lt. Harold H. Fredericks 336 Squadron was shot down by flak on 6 June 1944. He evaded and returned to the Group. On 29 May 1945 while ferrying surplus a/c to Speke Air Depot, he and Lt. Barnaby M. Wilhoit crashed in cloud covered terrain and became the last fatalities of the 4th Group in WWII. He is pictured with his Crew Chief "Moose" Mason. Zigler collection.

The total for the day was an unprecedented 105 e/a Destroyed.

Lt. Harold Fredericks reports that at the end of the third pass, Col. Woods called that his oil pressure was down to zero, and he was bailing out. He also heard Capt. Carpenter say he was bailing out. "I saw a ship going south of the A/D losing coolant. I followed it and identified it as Capt. Alfred's ship. In a turn, I lost sight of him for a few seconds, during which he could have bailed. I then saw his plane in a shallow dive, streaming coolant, go into the deck and explode on impact. Flying back to the A/D, I heard Lt. Ayer say he was bailing out. I could see 26 columns of smoke rising from the field, many columns fed by more than one plane. There were about 100 plus e/a on this A/D and 60 plus on Praha/Cakovice and Praha/Letnany A/Ds. There were Me 110s, Me 410s, Ju 87s, Ju 88s, and FW 190s parked on these Air Dromes. When I left, some of Caboose and Becky Squadrons were still strafing. Seven Pilots from Becky Squadron are MIA."

*****

1st Lt. Pederson states, "While attacking Praha/Kbely A/D, I was flying #3 to Col. Woods. After the first pass, I never saw the men in my Section again. They are all listed MIA. I made about 15 passes, Destroying four e/a and receiving flak hits. I then moved north to Praha/Letnany and Praha/Cakovice A/Ds and made six more passes, Destroying four more e/a. When my ammo was exhausted, I pulled up to 5,000 feet and orbited the fields. I counted at least 60 fires burning. I was one of the last to leave."

*****

F/O Donald Baugh recalled, "Flying #4 in Purple Section of Becky Squadron, we were the last to hit the A/D. There were already many fires burning. I made six passes, Destroying five e/a and then climbed to 3,000 feet. I counted 58 fires, but due to the congestion of the smoke and flame, I believe there were over 60 planes burning."

*****

Lt. Edward McLouchlin, 335 Squadron, was shot down and became a POW.

Combat Report: "I was flying #4 of Red Section of Caboose Squadron. We circled Praha/Kbely A/D while Horseback led the Group in to attack. We then made a pass, and I fired at a Ju 188 on the east end of the field. I got good strikes, and it burst into flames. I also hit another one, but it would not explode. I found myself alone and made another pass. I got good strikes on another JU 188 at the S/E corner of the field. I saw it burst into flame before I fired on the 4th JU 188 in the middle of the field. It would not burn. I then fired into a hangar with no apparent results. I pulled up to 5,500 feet and headed out when I got hit by flak, and my plane began to burn. I bailed and saw my kite explode on impact with the ground." - Edward McLoughlin, 2nd Lt. Air Corps

*****

Lt. Benjamin Griffin, 336 Squadron was shot down and became a POW. Upon return, he reported as follows: "Major Frederick Glover, Squadron CO, told me I was assigned as Wingman (#2) to Assistant Group Commander, Lt. Col. Sidney Woods. Major Glover said, 'Now, Ben, Col. Woods has not been on very many combat missions - so you stay with him - don't lose him!' I acknowledged the instructions and told Major Glover not to worry. However, I did not know at that time that fate had 40mm flak in store for both of us! We both got it, and so did our #4, Lt. Ayers. Three out of four, and we all ended up in the same jail on Praha-Kbely Airdrome. From there we journeyed to Stalag VII-A, our home for the dura-

tion. The bright side of this incident is that I Destroyed 6 e/a on that mission.

"I had been flying Lt. Pierini's former plane the 'Jersey Bounce II,' which I had inherited when Pierini returned to the States, and had then renamed 'Miss Marian.' The fifth e/a I Destroyed exploded violently as I flew over it. Flying debris cut the coolant line to the after cooler which sprayed coolant over my face. In spite of this, I made one more pass and Destroyed another plane. I then made a terrible error. I pulled up to 300 feet. This gave the flak gunners on the top of buildings an opportunity to zero in on me. Prior to this I had been so low, 'blowing their gun barrels off' that they could not see me until I had passed them. You know the rest!"

*****

The Group lost 8 Pilots and planes on this show. Alfred, and Carpenter (Leroy) were KIA, while Ayer, Griffin, Miller, Gimbel, McLoughlin, and Woods became POWs. All casualties were the result of flak.

17 April - Capt. Evans read the 83rd and 84th Articles of War to all personnel today.

The Group was off to an area support to the Karlsbad area under the leadership of Major Glover. The Squadron chased an Me 262 which crash-landed wheels up on Ruzyne A/D. The 336th Squadron tested for flak on an A/D and lost one Pilot, but claimed four e/a Destroyed. The Pilot, Robert Davis, was KIA as the result of flak. The destroyed were by Maj. Glover and Lts. Collins, Meredith, and Groshong.

Word was received that Lt. Wozniak, who crash-landed in Belgium 15 April, is now in the 65th General Hospital, Diss, England. He suffered a slight concussion and severe lacerations of the forehead. Prior to that mission, he needed only two hours to complete his tour.

19 April - Yesterday's uneventful mission to Passau gave Capt. Kanaga the operational hours necessary to complete his tour.

Word was received that Lt. Burnett, reported NYR 16 April, crash-landed near Kaiserlautern. He is believed safe and will be evacuated to Paris by the 12th TAC.

Lt. Michael Kennedy, reported NYR, 16 April, returned to base today. He said he lost the coin flip and had to stay at B-58 with Major Norley's kite until the radiator was repaired. It then blew a gasket so he scrounged a ride on a B-17 and C-47 back to England.

20 April - All personnel were required to report to the gas chamber to test gas masks.

Today's mission to Klatovny was led by Col. Stewart. It was uneventful with no e/a seen and no flak at all.

This was the first operational mission for 2nd Lts. Smith, Skerritt, Skogstad, and Stafford.

1st Lt. Paul Burnett, MIA 16 April, returned to base yesterday. He recounted an amazing experience: "While strafing e/a on Gablingen A/D, I made two unsuccessful passes, firing a short burst on the second one. On the third pass, I was lined up on two e/a on the field. I took a long burst on the first plane which then started to burn. I was raising my sight onto the second plane when the first one blew up with a terrific explosion.

I was unable to maneuver out of the blast and flew through the flames and flying debris. The flames and smoke turned my plane black and the exploding debris caused severe damage. The left wing was torn up on the leading edge and the left wing tank must have had a large hole in it, which dumped all the gas. The prop was bent out of line causing the engine to vibrate to the extent it felt like it would fall out. A stream of oil was leaking out over the left wing root next to the fuselage. Something had flown through the canopy leaving a large hole and splattering glass all over the cockpit. I jettisoned my canopy preparing to either set it down or jump if I could get some altitude. My wind screen was covered with black soot, and I couldn't see through it. I decided to get out of the area as far as I could and climb as high as I could. I flew for about 30 minutes on a 310 degree heading and managed to climb to 5,000 feet, where I felt I could bail safely.

In about five minutes, the oil pressure dropped to zero, and immediately white smoke streamed from the exhaust. I rolled the plane over on its back and attempted to bail out. I got about half way out and was thrown back against the armor-plating by the slipstream. I couldn't get out any further. I managed to fight my way back into the cockpit and righted the plane. I again rolled it over onto its back and attempted unsuccessfully to bail out. This time, I couldn't get back in.

After fighting desperately to get myself loose, something happened that caused me to be jerked out of the burning plane just as it hit the ground. Still concious, I found myself lying face down six feet away from the plane, which had gone straight in and was burning fiercely. I got out of my parachute and crawled to a ditch along a road a few feet away. I checked myself for injury and found that I was only shaken up a little.

Soon people were crowding around me, but since I couldn't speak German, I didn't understand what they were jabbering about. The Mayor was no help either, but I did understand there were American troops in Otterburg about 7 kilometers away. The people were very friendly, and the Mayor took me to his home and offered me something to eat and drink. Soon a German girl, who could speak English, came in and told me that American soldiers came in to patrol the town at night and would arrive soon. Two GIs in a jeep picked me up and took me to their command post in Otterberg. A Major in charge of the Aid Station checked me over, and I stayed there that night.

The next morning I was taken by an L-1 Observation Plane to Y-76 at Darmstadt. I was then flown by C-47 to another Station where I received travel orders and left by train to Paris, France. The next day, I received orders to leave by C-47 for London on Thursday. I arrived at base 19 April 1945."

*****

22 April - All available Pilots attended a lecture given by Capt. Godfrey concerning his experiences as a prisoner-of-war in the hands of the Wehrmacht, S.S. troops, and Luftwaffe personnel.

After being shot down, Godfrey was dazed and excited from cuts on his head and leg. He walked about 30 kilometers and had a few hours sleep. He then attempted a train ride but was captured by railway station guards whose job was to catch escapees.

Godfrey was taken to prison and shown a book with the complete history of the 4th Group enclosed. He was startled at the amazing accuracy of the Interrogating Officer's information. He was kept in solitary for one day and then moved to Sagan, a camp with three compounds with 2,000 men in each. While there, he saw every type of German aircraft being flown from Breslau to Central Germany - away from the Russian advance.

Godfrey escaped when they started to move the prisoners to Nurnberg but returned to Stalag Luft III in order to be treated for frozen feet. The POWs were then moved to Nurnberg and stayed there until this month. When he heard they were to be moved again, he cut throught the first of the 3 wire enclosures and hid in a manhole covering a cesspool. After three days, he walked away. He exchanged clothes with some French slave war-workers and met two GIs who also had escaped. He and the GIs walked to the lines but were caught by front-line troops and returned to Nurnberg. Again the POWs were to be moved but only 24 of the 50 captured could be found as they had hidden in latrines, barracks, etc. Capt, Godfrey was among the missing. When he left the Camp, he went to a farmhouse where he was aided by a German farmer, and then he walked to the American lines.

*****

23 April - This week, Lts. Trietsch and Seymour of 335 made their first operational flights.

A B-24 took off this morning with the first batch of EM who were granted a 48-hour pass to Paris. The 334 had three lucky winners on board - Cpls. Chervenak, Reyes, and Beu. They were chosen by a drawing from those eligible to go.

24 April - Lt. Gallant was airborne on a local flight. He was flying with Lt. Mummert and Lt. Hoelscher when they were jumped by a yellow-nosed Mustang. Gallant lost control at low altitude, and he crash-landed at Little Walden at 1530 hours. He miraculously escaped with only head injuries and a broken collar bone.

25 April - Col. Stewart led a Fighter Sweep to the Linz-Prague Area. Lt. Hoelscher sighted and attacked an Me 262. He got excellent strikes, but in following the jet, he was hit by flak over the Prague - Ruzyne A/D and is NYR. Hoelscher bailed out and was last seen talking to some farmers who appeared to be friendly. It was believed that he was on the edge of friendly territory. He was able to evade and to return. He probably destroyed the Me 262 before bailing out, this claiming to be the last e/a destroyed by the 4th Group in WWII.

26 April - Lt. Foster, reported MIA, 31 Mar 45, returned to Debden 21 April with this account: "I was flying Cobweb Green #3 on an escort to Hassel. On the return flight, my engine failed and I crash-landed near Ommen, Holland. Dutch people immediately welcomed me. A young English speaking chap told me to go to the nearby woods, and he would return later and help me.

At about noon, the young man returned with two boys and gave me food and some clothes. They said they would return later and move me. At three o'clock one of the boys returned with another man. They were all smiles, but soon the man surprised me by pointing a gun at me. He disarmed me. He turned me over to the Wehrmacht who then took me to Ommen. They searched me and relieved me of everything except my escape map, which they did not find. The next day, Easter Sunday, I was interrogated. I disclosed only my name, rank, and serial number.

Near my cell window was an air-raid shelter where Dutch boys and girls congregated. They rolled vile smelling cigarettes and handed them to me. An English speaking boy asked me to write a letter for him. I told him I was an American Pilot and asked him if he would help me to escape. He returned later and gave me a worn hacksaw blade and said that he would return again at nine o,clock and wait for me.

The next three days were spent in sawing bars in my cell. I was, again, interrogated and then placed in a room with two other chaps. One was Norwegian and the other was Dutch. They were both from the Royal Air Force. We all worked on the bars with the hack-saw blade. By evening, we were ready to go. We received our evening meal, a half loaf of bread and three chunks of meat. We made sandwiches of this and then broke out of the jail. We tramped cross country, crossing many irrigation ditches. At four o'clock in the morning, we finally found a farmer who took us in and hid us in a straw mow.

Two days later, the farmer made contact with the local underground. They provided us with civilian clothes and tobacco and paid the farmer 50 Guilders for hiding and feeding us. For a week, we remained hidden while war raged around us. On Friday the 13th, a girl came for us and took us to Meppel, which had just been liberated by the Canadians. Next morning, we hitch-hiked down the convoy route to Nijmegan and reported to a Canadian ex-POW camp. There they flew us to Paris. After three days, I returned to my Squadron on 21 April."

*****

27 April - Orders were received promoting Marvin Arthur, Clavin Beason, Arthur Bowers, and Paul Burnett from 2nd Lt. to 1st Lt.

The 334 Intelligence Officer, Capt. "Ben" Ezzel has been overseas 30 months today. This announcement caused a heated argument as to which of our Squadron Officers could claim the distinction of having the longest overseas service. It was unanimously agreed that "Ben" has.

All EM reported to sick quarters for a dental inspection.

The 335 Squadron received seven new Pilots today: Capt. Richard Tannerhill, 1st Lts. Robert Farmer and Richard Palmer, and 2nd Lts. Duanne Fowler, Carl Draughn, James Crine, and James Looney.

28 April - The Group awakened to about an inch of snow on the ground and snow showers off and on.

Two good films were shown at the Station Cinema. The first, "The Fighting Lady," depicted the life aboard a carrier and its splendid contribution to the war effort. The second, "Fury in the Pacific," gave us a view of the work being done by the Yanks on the other side of the world.

The Station Glee Club, organized and directed by Capt. Robert Evans, Squadron EO., "tried their wings" in their first performance in the Aeroclub.

On the 30th, the Discussion Topic will be "After V-E Day - What?"

The Assessed Enemy Casualty Report for the period 2 Jan 1945 to 27 Feb 1945 confirmed the following claims for 334 Squadron:

Capt. Malmsten	6 1/2 Destroyed
Capt. Bell	5 1/2 Destroyed
Lt. Payne	4 1/2 Destroyed
Lt. Ayers	4 Destroyed
Maj. Montgomery, Capt. Clifton, and Lt. Bowers -	each 3 Destroyed
Lts. Mc Fadden and Antonides -	each 2 Destroyed
Lts. Denson, Garcin, Harre, and Wells -	each 1 Destroyed
Lts. Senecal, Jahnke, Rentschler, Kennedy, Brown, O'Bryan, and Voyles -	each 1/2 Destroyed
	total 41

Monthly Consolidated Strength Report

334 Squadron	Officers 50	Enlisted Men 226
335 Squadron	Officers 55	Enlisted Men 240

12

We Pack Up and Head for Home

1 May 1945 - To provide all ground (non-rated) personnel with a chance to see the results of their contributions in the strategic air war against Germany and the capabilities of air power, those who so desired were to be taken on air tours (Operation "Trolley") of selected targets.

A daily Trolley with a crew of five was to take eight to ten passengers, depending on the number of visual positions on the B-24 aircraft.

Aircraft were to be dispatched in elements of three, with operational clearance filed from home bases for each Group. A minimum altitude of 1,000 feet was to be maintained over the terrain. Passengers and crews were especially briefed on the entire route, and they were given a background on the important targets and attacks to be seen. K reports were to be covered indicating assessed damage to the targets. As flight time was about seven hours, rations or box lunches were provided for crews and passengers. The proposed route was as follows: Base, Southwold, Ostend, Mannheim, Aschaffenberg, Frankfurt, Bingen, Koblenz, Bonn, Cologne, Dusseldorf, Ostend, Southwold, and Base.

3 May - Last night, Staff Sergeant Raymond Brown gave an hour and a half program of classical and semi-classical music in the upstairs lounge of the Aeroclub.

Major Henry Mills, reported MIA 6 Mar 1944, returned to Debden. He told us that most of our Pilots, who were taken into custody as prisoners-of-war and since liberated, were going directly to the States from the continent.

The following Memorandum was received from General Arnold to all Officers and Enlisted Men:

1. The war against Germany is drawing to a victorious conclusion. For the manner in which you have waged the air battle in that war, I extend my heartiest congratulations to each and every one of you. Concurrently, I should like to dwell a bit on what lies ahead.

2. Before the peace of the world is secure, it is essential that the full weight of our armed forces be directed against Japan. This is necessary in order that a quick and decisive termination of the struggle in the Pacific may be assured. It will require many of you to augment the increasing strength of the AAF personnel now engaged against Japan. Constant thought and study are being given to the numerous phases of your redeployment, prior to demobilization by all of us here in Washington. Completed plans are even now being implemented. You will be moved just as rapidly as available troop ships and air transports can ply the sea and air from your ports to the USA and back again.

3. When the demobilization phase begins, those of you who have served the longest in Europe and Africa, with minor exceptions, will return to your homes. However, we must first assure that all the Air Forces, together with their service elements, which will be required for an early decisive victory, are brought to bear on Japan. To do this, those of you having the least service overseas will be returned to the USA for leaves and furloughs at home, after

Major Henry L. "Hank" Mills 334 Squadron came to the 4th Group from 71ES. He had 6 e/a destroyed prior to "going down" near Berlin with engine trouble on 6 March 44. Ziegler collection.

which you will be reassembled and given a shakedown training before departing for the Pacific.

4. The problem of mastering new aircraft will confront many of you as you join the Japanese war. There are many differences in the techniques required for the operation and maintenance of the B-29s and other new types. You will find that it takes time to learn them. For this reason, your pretraining period in the USA may be extensive.

5. After the violence of the war against Germany, considerable time may be required for the readjustment to peace. A force sufficient to assure this readjustment must, therefore, remain in Europe. Those of you having served neither the longest nor the least will make up the occupational Air Force. Your return to the USA will be possible through rotation and replacement. This will be accomplished at the earliest date practicable, but probably not until the termination of the war in the Pacific.

6. The toughest part of the next several months will be the waiting period—waiting for your unit to begin its movement— waiting for transportation. I realize that full well, but we, assisted by your commanders, will do everything within our power not only to keep you usefully employed, but also to provide you with as wide a variety of recreation as it is possible to obtain.

7. In conclusion, I want you to understand clearly that I am as anxious to see you all go home as you are to get there. However, we must not lose sight of the fact that there is another job for us to do—in the Pacific. Some of you, but not all, will be needed for its accomplishment. This job will not be easy, but I am confident that the war against Japan will demonstrate once more the high morale and spirit which has been common to all the Army Air Force personnel throughout the world.

4 May - Orders were received to release from duty Capt. Robert Kanaga, 1st Lt. Charles Harre, and 1st Lt. Lewis Wells, for return to the ZI.

All EM reported to Station Sick Quarters for a physical profile examination.

There was a party at the Red Cross Club in Cambridge for American Service Men and their British wives.

5 May - Thirty-nine Air Medals and/or Oak Leaf Clusters to the Air Medal were awarded to various Pilots of 334 Squadron.

7 May - The **Purple Heart** was awarded to 1st Lt. Arthur Bowers for wounds received while on an operational mission over enemy occupied Continental Europe, 26 March 1945

The first Trolley left for the Ruhr today. Six EM from 334 Squadron went on this first trip. Upon returning, one fellow put it this way, "Words can't describe how much I enjoyed the trip." He urged all of us to take it if possible.

At 1515 hours this afternoon, a German broadcast announced that the remaining German Army had surrendered unconditionally.

Up until this time, no official announcement had been made by the Allies.

8 May -

GERMANY QUITS

"Today, May 8th, is VE-Day, officially proclaimed by the leaders of the Big Three in simultaneous declarations in Washington, London, and Moscow, ending the war five years, eight months, and seven days after the Nazis invaded Poland on September 1, 1939."

The capitulation to the Allies and Soviets had been signed yesterday in Rheims, France, at a schoolhouse serving as General Eisenhower's HQ.

All Officers and EM on the base stood formation on the Parade Ground at 1400 hours. Chaplain Brohm opened with a prayer, and then our CO, Col. Stewart, gave a short talk.

We made our last operational mission on 25 April 1945. There was no official announcement at that time, but we all knew the war was nearly over.

There was a formation in the hangar at 0900 hours. Capt. Evans informed us that Squadron activities were to be curtailed for a few days to enable us to celebrate the termination of hostilities. He outlined plans for today and then spoke of the upcoming Educational Program consisting of:

1. Classroom Procedure - bookkeeping, mathematics, etc.
2. Army Technical Schools - automechanics, radio, etc.
3. Correspondence Courses

Blackout regulations were terminated as of tonight.

A formation was held in Class "A" uniforms on the Parade Ground. After a victory prayer by our Chaplain, Col. Stewart praised the group's accomplishments and spoke of the continuing effort in the Pacific. He then told everyone to have a good time, after which the Station Band played the *"Star Spangled Banner."*

Lt. Millard Jenks, temporarily oblivious to his "duck farm" responsibilities, raises his glass for the first drink of the evening on V.E. Day. The Officers surrounding him obviously enjoy his toast. Zigler collection.

The Red Cross had refreshments available for the GIs and their guests, and there was plenty of free beer available at the Officers' Club and the Belly Tank.

At 2230 hours, there was a chemical bonfire on the Athletic Field (Due to salvage, paper, and wood were not used) followed by flares and fireworks.

After 30 months of complete blackout, it seemed strange seeing lights shining from all the windows in the barracks.

Nobody was arrested—this single item reflected the Group's morale better than any word picture.

Narrative: While Debden celebrated, as did all of England, a hospital ship slowly and silently pulled away from the dock in a harbor in Wales. Aboard the ship, an Ex-Kriegie sat at a table with a couple of doctors and a nurse. The four raised their glasses and toasted the end of the war. The Ex-POW was on his way to the States. His name was Frank Speer. Lt. Speer had flown with 334 Squadron and had been shot down while strafing on the mission to Poznan, Poland, on 29 May 1944. He was confined to the hospital ship to recover from scurvy, dysentery, and injuries while on his way to the States.

Lt. Speer had evaded capture when he crash-landed in Poland. He made his way across northern Germany to the edge of Denmark on foot. He had no food, no sleep, and no map. His escape map, instead of showing the territory over which he had been flying, had great details of southern France and the Pyrenees. He did have a compass, however, and with the compass and his memory of northern German geograpy, he was able to steer a course toward his desired destination. His plan to reach Denmark and stow away on a boat for Sweden was foiled when he passed out from exaustion after walking nearly 400 miles. He was awakened by the prodding of his head by a rifle barrel, on the other end of which stood a burly German soldier. There had been no opprtunity for discourse or negotiation—he had had it!

There followed a trip to an interrogation center, where the usual interrogation ended with eventual assignment to Stalag Luft III. There he met and became a close friend to Nelson Kennard. Lt. Kennard was a navigator. He had bailed out of his burning bomber over Hungary on 7 July 1945.

The two had shared much misery, starvation, disease, and pain as they endured the routine of captivity. There had been the dreadful winter "death march," and the smothering "forty and eight" trip to the filthy, flea and lice infested Stalag near Nurnberg. In the Spring, the Kriegies were again marched south, at which time Frank and Nelson managed to escape. They met up with some French forced laborers who sheltered them, and eventually the two managed to capture 24 German soldiers and turn them over to the liberating forces of Patton's Army. After a brief captivity by their liberating forces, Frank and Nelson had again escaped. They hitched rides on trucks, cars, and a plane as they made their way across Germany and France.

Lt. Frank Speer 334 Squadron, just returned from a mission, fills out his report as his Crew Chief (Bill Brong, center) nervously looks on. His concern is mirrored in the face of his assistant. Frank had 6 e/a to his credit when he was shot down by flak near Pozen on 29 May 1944. Speer collection.

Their odyssey ended at Camp Lucky Strike, where they were immediately deloused and hospitalized. Even with fresh new clothes and their strange (to them) new Eisenhower jackets, they could not talk their way out of this camp. They had been captured by the system! The only escape remaining was for them to work their way through "channels." The channels separated the two buddies; Nelson, who did not require additional hospitalization, left by one route, and Frank headed for the States in the hospital ship. (It was to be 45 years before they met again).

*****

10 May - Yesterday, there was a steady stream of customers all day at the snack bar, which was open extended hours.

There was a big dance at the Club last night, and the Cinema was open from 1500 hours to midnight.

At 1300 hours, an order was received to remove all the ammunition from all the aircraft.

Today, the Army's Point Discharge Plan was broadcast at 1800 hours. The main topic for the rest of the evening was "How many points do you have?"

12 May - At separate formations, the Enlisted Mens' training program was announced, and the Officers were informed that the Station was now to be run on a peace-time basis. The EM's program was to begin 14 May, while the Officers' Redeployment Training started yesterday with instruction in Engineering Maintenance (three hours) and Armament (four hours).

"Peace-Time flying rules are to be strictly followed: No flying over large cities and populated areas under 2,000 feet, and Air and Ground discipline are to be strictly enforced. If present wartime

Flight Commanders do not prove satisfactory in this respect, better qualified Pilots may be chosen."

Col. Stewart then said our one goal now is to train for a high peak of efficiency to beat the Japs.

The training program then continued with two hours of Maintenance training and an hour and three quarters of Formation Flying Training.

Lt. Hoelscher, reported MIA 25 April 1945, returned on the 9th and reported he had shot down a Me 262 over the Prague A/D, but picked up a 40 mm shell, tearing off his left elevator. He was able to reach Rakovnik, Czechoslovakia, where he bailed at 300 feet. He landed in the middle of some Czech Partisans who took care of him and hid him from the Germans. Then, by motorcycle, jeep, and various airplane rides, he hitched his way back to Debden.

*****

13 May - The Group participated in a 720 Fighter Victory Demonstration, saluting their former Commander James Doolittle by flying over his home on the Thames and then Eighth Air Force Hq. at High Wycombe. They flew at 2,000 feet except over London. The 700 Bombers, scheduled to participate, were grounded due to the low ceiling.

According to the "Daily Chronicle," some of the Fighters buzzed Gen. Doolittle's home.

Redeployment Formation Flying Training then continued.

Tommorow's scheduled training will include: Malaria Control, Gas Defense, Carbine, Military Courtesy, PT, and K-14 Gunsight.

15 May - 30 May - Redeployment Training continued. Possibly the busiest men in the ETO today were the Pilots. No poker playing now! The new Redeployment training Program kept them busy from 0800 hours until 1700 hours. Some of them took a dim view of this, but they were getting it just the same. One said, "This is Primary and Basic all over again." Another, with 217 Operational hours to his credit, said, *"War is Hell, but Peace is worse."*

In addition to the heavy schedule of Ground School, each Pilot was to participate in flying training, which consisted of Instrument Flying, Link Trainer, Night Flying, Dive Bombing, Rocket Firing, Range and Tracking, Navigation, and Formation Flying.

Eight Officers of 334 Squadron were awarded **Oak Leaf Clusters to the Air Medal**.

An order was received which immediately grounded all aircraft with less than 100 hours.

All aircraft are to be grounded until Squadron identifying letters have been painted in large black letters under the wings.

Jack McFadden was promoted from 1st Lt. to Captain.

Don Allen, talented artist, stands before one of his many "nose art" creations. He was kept busy with nose art requests for Pilots of 334 Squadron. George Anderson collection.

1st Lt. Frank M. Fink 335 Squadron, formerly 121ES was a talented caricature artist. He bailed out near Paris, due to engine failure, and became a POW 9 September 1943. Konsler Collection.

17 May -While flying formation with his Section at 30,000 feet, Capt. Richard Tannerhill spun in and crashed near Llanbedr, North Wales. It appeared from the action of the plane that Capt. Tannerhill was unconscious due to lack of oxygen. He was killed instantly.

1st Lt. Fink, shot down 9 Sept 1943, returned from POW camp back to Debden to renew old acquaintances.

S/Sgt Don Allen, noted for painting all the 334 insignias on all their planes since 1942, added another first to his long record by winning first prize for the "Ground Safety Contest."

Winners for the phrases in the contest were:

"Walk Awake" by Pfc William Burns.

"It's nice to cycle

Down country lanes

Eyes on the road

And not on the dames" by Cpl Woodrow Hebert.

With appropriate ceremony, in a formation in the Hangar, Major Norley presented **Air Medals** to 15 1st and 2nd Lts.

Tribute was paid to S/Sgt John DeKay and Sgt (Shippy) Shipkowski as they prepared to ship out for home. They had been in 334 Squadron since it was formed. "Thanks for your fellowship, and the best of luck to you both."

19 May - Another familiar face showed up in the Dispersal, 2nd Lt. Charles Poage. The past Christmas was one that he will remember for a long time to come. He not only flew a mission that day, but shot down two FW 190s before a third got him near Bonn. He was a POW until freed by the Red Army near Rostock. We knew nothing about the two e/a he had destroyed until he returned. He turned in claims for them.

Another POW returned today, Lt. Robert Cammer, who has been missing since the Achmer/Hesepe A/D strafing mission on 21 March 1945.

22 May - A very happy Lt. Willruth became a Captain, making everyone happy, especially him.

Letters written home could now have more color as the censorship has been lifted. EM could now write, seal, and drop their letters and parcels into the post box as though they were civilians once more. We were now able, for the first time, to tell the exact geographic location of our base in the U.K.

23 May - Sgt. Paul Grimm and Pvt. Edwin Spearry returned to the Squadron after being on DS in Sweden for over a month. They and Capt. Monroe were assigned, about the 1st of April, to a secret mission to Sweden. They went to Metfield A/D where they joined seven other EM from other Fighter Bases. For some unknown reason, they waited there for two weeks.

The Pilots also returned from Sweden where they had been since 13 April. On that day, Capt. Monroe, along with Lts. Olan Kiser and Charles Konsler from 335 and a number of Pilots from other bases, flew 50 Mustangs to Stockholm, Sweden. After a few days of sight seeing, Kiser and Konsler returned to Debden. Monroe, Grimm, and Spearry remained in Sweden to instruct Swedish personnel on the fine points of the P-51.

Although the Swedish Air Force had many types of planes, this was the first time they had P-51s. Capt. Monroe instructed on flying tactics, while Sgt. Grimm instructed on instruments and engineering, and Pvt. Spearry served as armament instructor.

After a short stay in Stockholm, they were moved to a fighter Base in Upsala, north of Stockholm. Since Upsala was a college town, many of the inhabitants could speak at least a little English. Pvt. Spearry noted that the Swedish cities were very modern and the country very beautiful. They found the people to be most hospitable, kind, and friendly.

Narration: Lt. "Chuck" Konsler explained his part in the mission. "Lt. Olin Kiser and I had finished our 300-hour tour of combat with the 4th on 2 April. We went to London for a few days R & R. After several days, we received a call from Debden Hq. asking if we wanted to volunteer for a real good deal of an assignment. We accepted and returned to Debden. We were sent to Station 336 at Metfield and arrived there with flying gear and a class-A uniform.

We joined thirty-some other Pilots, including Capt. Shelton Monroe from the 4th. We were each assigned a new P-51 and a list of inflight checks to perform on it prior to leaving on our as yet unknown mission. On the morning of 14 April, we were briefed on our mission, which was to deliver these P-51s to the Swedish Air Force at Stockholm, Sweden.

I was to fly in a flight of four in advance of the rest of the P-51s, which would be escorting a B-17 carrying our crews and our B-4 bags. We set course over the North Sea, and as we reached a point north of Denmark, we encountered a Me 109 and a FW 190. Lt. Bates, the flight leader took on the FW 190 and I tackled the Me 109. We each Destroyed our e/a, both of which plunged into the sea along with their Pilots.

I had completed a whole tour without ever having a chance to make a kill, and here, on a "volunteer" mission, I had my first opportunity and made good on it. I was overjoyed that I had volunteered.

When we arrived over Stockholm, we made our presence known in a manner that the Swedes had never before encountered; a couple of Pilots even flying under one of Stockholm's bridges. In spite of this raucous introduction, we were treated to a grand banquet and entertained graciously. The 15th was a Sunday, and it seemed that the most interesting thing to do was to go to see King Gustav V play tennis. Accordingly, Lt. Kiser and I went to the King's indoor court, where we received almost as much attention as the King.

After he was finished playing, I made it known that I would appreciate having the King's autograph. The King not only granted us the request, but said he wished to meet the two American Pilots. We met the King, who was very gracious, and just as I was shaking his hand, a nearby news photographer snapped a picture. The next morning, that picture was on the front page of every Stockholm newspaper.

After five memorable days, we embarked on a B-24 for the return trip to England and then on to Debden."

The "Station Glee Club" and the "Flying Eagles Dance Band" held a concert in the Station Cinema.

24 May - Flight Lt. Mahon, a member of the 121st Eagle Squadron, shot down by a FW 190 on the Dieppe Raid 19 Aug 1942, visited today. He had been a POW ever since and was just recently liberated. He was still wearing his RAF uniform with the famous "E.S." patch on the sleeve.

25 May - Our former CO, Major George Carpenter, returned to Debden. He was shot down on 18 April 1944 while returning from a Ramrod to Berlin. He said things got pretty rough when the Red Cross Parcels could no longer reach them. He, like all the others, was happy to be back in Debden and expected to be even happier when he reached "Dear Old Oil City, Pa." and saw all the folks once more.

26 May - The first square dance was held in the Aeroclub. It was new to the GIs and their girls, but they soon joined in and enjoyed it very much. The music was provided by the local "Hill Billy Band."

After 2 1/2 years of seven-day-a-week operations, the Group had converted back to a peace-time basis with Sundays off, with the exception of a small skeleton crew.

29 May - The Pilots were to deliver seven Mustangs from each Squadron to Speke A/D, near Liverpool. They ran into heavy low cloud. In letting down to find the field, only three were successful, Lts. Jungling, Moe, and Seymour. Two, Lts. Wilhoit and Fredericks, were killed as they crashed into a hillside. The rest returned to base.

Lt. Rabe returned to Debden from a POW Camp and told how he had hit a tree and crashed while strafing 21 Feb 1945.

1st Lt. Paul S. Riley 335 Squadron was an Ace with 9.5 e/a destroyed. He was in a major fight with 35 plus 190's. He shot down one and collided with a second. He was then hit by flak and bailed out to become a POW. Zigler.

Operations has become more like a reception area as more and more of the Pilots return from Prison camps. Fink and Rabe; two former RAF Pilots, Paul Riley, Robert Patterson, Hugh Ward, and Lt. Clifford Holske, all returned.

Lt. Patterson was shot down returning from a Ramrod to Oldenburg, 8 October 1943. He evaded in Belgium and Holland for two months before being picked up and incarcerated in Stalag Luft 3.

Lt. Riley, MIA since 24 April 1944, on a Free Lance to Ludwigshaven with 334 Squadron, had been jumped by 35 plus FW 190s. The Squadron destroyed ten of them. Lt. Riley claimed two Destroyed, which boosted that score to 12. He shot one down and had a mid-air collision with another, causing the Jerry to bail. The collision cut one-fourth of the left wing from Lt. Riley's plane, but he was able to keep it under control. He started for home at 4,000 feet, but was hit by flak, causing him to bail. He landed about 60 yards from the ack-ack battery that shot him down. It was fortunate because he was injured. They picked him up and immediately got him to a hospital.

1st Lt. Charles E. "Chuck" Konsler and Lt. Olin A. Kiser (back to camera) meet Gustav V, King of Sweden on 15 April 45 after delivering Mustangs to the Swedish Air Force. Konsler collection.

*****

Hugh Ward, missing since the first Berlin show, 4 March 1944, was thought killed. Megura of 334 had seen the wing, tail, and canopy fall off one of our kites after being attacked by 20 plus Me 109s and FW 190s near Berlin. No one ever dreamed he could live through this, let alone shoot down one of the e/a in the process. He looks forward to seeing all the home folks in Charleston, South Carolina.

*****

Lt. Holske failed to return from a Patrol mission during the D-Day invasion of Holland. We never heard anything from him until January this year when it was stated that he was a POW. He had been missing since 17 September 1944. His hands had been severely burned while attempting to get out, and he received no medical attention for two days. However, he received good treatment after that.

*****

During the month, Sgt."Sy" Koenig had accompanied several Pilots to Germany in a B-24. Their mission was to obtain a usable German fighter to inspect and to fly. Sy, being a crew chief and being able to read and write German, was enlisted to accompany the Pilots so he could change the cockpit data and instruments from German into English in order that the Pilots could safely fly the aircraft. After trying Bittburg, Weisbaden, and several other fields, the crew returned empty handed. Sy, however, enjoyed the ride in the B-24 and the opportunity to procure some German beer and Schnapps for himself and the Pilots.

Monthly Consolidated Status Report
335 Squadron   Officers 52   Enlisted Men 237

1 June 1945 - Redeployment Training continued -
The 335 Squadron began an intensive instrument flying program. The objective was to have the Pilots proficient in flying in heavy clouds. Every Pilot got instruction under a hood. They went to 9,000 feet; got under the hood; and flew on instruments. Meanwhile, an observer plane flew beside the instrument plane and observed his technical ability.

Capt. Kenneth Peterson, imprisoned at Barth on the Baltic for 14 months, gave an interesting talk on his PW experiences.

2 June - Two other Pilots returned from PW Camps, Capt. Don Ross and Lt. Edwin Mead. Ross was shot down on his second P-51 mission and Mead was shot down in a head-on pass with a Me 109 immediately after having shot down a Me 109. Both had been shot down in early 1944.

Copies of "*Lilly from Piccadilly,*" written by Cpl. Mickey Balsam, former Flying Eagle Band member, went on sale by Special Service at one Shilling each.

5 June - Two more Pilots returned, Capt. John Fitch and 2nd Lt. Edward McLoughlin, both shot down in early 1945.

6 June - General Eisenhower designated today a holiday marking the memory of Invasion Day, "*D-Day,*" and of those who gave their lives that we may live in peace.

7 June - All EM of 335 Squadron with 100 or more points reported to the orderly room. Thirty-two were told to pack and be ready to ship out at 0800 the next day. They were to be returned to the States and, presumably, discharged.

10 June - The 334 Fighter Squadron held its picnic party yesterday from 1500 hours to 2300 hours. In all probability, this would be the last complete gathering we were to enjoy since some were leaving for the States.

The picnic turned out wonderfully with nice weather conditions. There was plenty to eat as well as drink. The girls enjoyed playing volleyball with the men, and later they joined as partners in an egg-running contest.

Sgt. Baim, Capt. Ezzell, Major Norley, and countless others contributed their help in working wonders with the arrangements. Capt. Evans played the piano organ to the enjoyment of all.

11 June - Orders were received awarding the **Distinguished Flying Cross** to the following Pilots:

Capt. Thomas Bell	1st Lt. Charles Harre
Capt. Jack Mc Fadden	1st Lt. Kenneth Helfrecht
1st Lt. James Ayers	1st Lt. Raymond Dyer
1st Lt. Ralph Buchanan	1st Lt. Carl Payne
1st Lt. William Dvorak	Maj. Gerald Montgomery
1st Lt. William Hoelscher	1st Lt. Jerome Jahnke
Capt. David Howe	

The Training continues with subjects leading to the Pacific, such as: The Japanese, Survival in the Jungle, Protection from Parisites, etc., in addition to Aircraft Maintenance, Link Trainer, and air related activities.

The general scheme of the training was that half of the Pilots had classes in the morning and flight training in the afternoon. The other half had the program in reverse.

Jap plane recognition was being expedited by a contest, in which the winner in recognition picked up the daily deposited fines of a Shilling for anyone failing to take the daily test. The winner was top scorer for a two-week period.

At 1600 hours, all EM and Officers were summoned to the Hangar for a meeting. Capt. Patton explained the requirements and then asked for volunteers for the Occupational Air Force. Very little interest was generated.

18 June - All personnel were treated to a film, "On to Tokyo."

19 June - All 334 Personnel were treated to a five-mile hike. Not to be outdone, 335 took a nine-mile hike.

Special Service sponsored another tour, this time to Colchester, the oldest British town of record.

Squadron Supply started issuing the new O.D. Combat Jackets to the EM, causing much bitching, griping, and fussing because of the typical misfits.

22 June - Today was the annual Field Day. The activities were enhanced by the presence of a number of celebrities and many exhibitions.

A number of trucks left at 1000 hours for a golf tournament at Cambridge, featuring Chick Herbert and John Matthews, one of our own Station GIs. It was Herbert's game all the way, but it was enjoyed by all.

Another match featured Horton Smith, Chick Herbert, 1st Lt. William Henderson, and Cpl John Matthews.

At 1400 hours, there were several tennis sets played by Tom Falkenburg, one-time Jr. AA Champion; George Lott; Frank Guersey; Marie Hardwick, Women's Natl Tennis Champion; Lt. James Monroe; Capt. Kennedy; and Lt. Berney.

The following days were filled with more Redeployment Training.

28 June - Eighteen Pilots from 334 Squadron were awarded Oak Leaf Clusters to the Air Medal.

Later a meeting was held, and Capt. Evans discussed our return to the States, followed by Lt. Ingold, who told of the arrangements for the 4th of July program.

30 June - The day started with mixed emotions; fresh eggs in the Mess Hall caused great anticipation followed by an interminable queue ending in a delightfully delicious presentation of sunnyside up eggs.

Monthly Consolidated Strength Report

| 334 Squadron | Officers 52 | Enlisted Men 225 |
| 335 Squadron | Officers 49 | Enlisted Men 227 |

1 July 1945 - A letter was received from U.S. Strategic Air Forces in Europe concerning 1st Lt. Allen Bunte.

While strafing an airport near Berlin, 5 April 1944, Allen struck a high tension line. His plane began burning and he was too low to bail out. His cockpit was on fire as he jettisoned his canopy and headed for a small lake near Pottsdam.

He pushed the nose down and blacked out before he hit the water. When he came to a short time later, he was no longer on fire,

1st Lt. Allen F. Bunte 334 Squadron spent 18 months with the RCAF prior to joining the USAAF. He had 4 e/a to his credit when he crashed into a lake near Pottsdam and became a POW on 5 April 1944. Konsler.

but was sinking. He tried to unbuckle his parachute instead of his safety belt. Again he blacked out. His safety belt held him in the cockpit as the plane submerged.

"Next thing I knew I was free of the plane, floating towards the surface. How my safety belt loosened, I'll never know."

Bunte only had strength enough to inflate half of his Mae West, which barely kept him afloat. He alternated resting and paddling toward the shore a half mile away. After what seemed ages, he reached the branch of a tree overhanging the water and was able to pull himself out.

Exhausted, he began to crawl toward a small wooden shack in which he hoped to find shelter. There he thought he could rest and get up enough strength to find his morphine and take it. His scalp was slashed, and the blood running from the wound mixed with the mud on his body.

German civilians found him, wrapped him in a blanket, cleaned his wounds, hoisted him aboard a wagon, and took him to the Luftwaffe.

Then followed 13 months behind the barbed wire of a prisoner of war camp. When U.S. troops liberated the camp, he was flown to France. He hitched his way to Britain, where he visited his wife in Scotland.

He had three e/a to his credit when he went down and reported his fourth, a JU 52, on the last strafing mission. He had spent 18 months in the Royal Canadian Air Force before transferring to the AAF in October, 1942.

*****

We hosted the students and faculty of the Saffon Walden Training College, about 65 in all. Special Service picked them up, and they toured the Station and then witnessed their first game of real American baseball. They then had a concert by the Station Glee Club and were served refreshments in the Aeroclub before being transported to their Campus.

A very good USO show with real honest-to-goodness American girls played at the station Cinema for two shows.

An "On the Job Training Program" started with programs in Radio, Aviation Mechanics, Electrical Welding, Live Stock, Small Business, Bookkeeping and Typing, Amateur Photography, and others. Classes were to be held five days per week.

4 July - Independence Day - The entire field had a day off with breakfast served at the Aero Club. This was followed by sports events on the ball field. The 334 Squadron Enlisted Men beat the Officers very badly to the tune of 9-0.

At 1200 hours, the post was open to guests, and at the same time, all the bars on the post were opened.

Tea was served in the Aero Club at 1600 hours. At 1700 hours a very unusual event took place when any guests of the EM were invited to eat in the Mess Hall.

At 1900 hours, a Carnival was opened on the Parade Ground. There were booths for roulette, shooting gallery, weight guessing, etc. Prizes were cans of tomato or fruit juice.

In the evening, there was a dance at the Aero Club with music by the "Flying Eagles." More girls arrived for the dance. Refreshments were served during intermission. The dance was followed by an enjoyable fireworks display to end the festivities, prior to the girls leaving for home in the GI trucks.

5 July - Redeployment Training continued at a steady pace.

6 July - Mr. John Stoner gave an enjoyable concert of Piano Classics and Boogie-Woogie in the west lounge of the Aero Club.

So far, twelve of our 335 EM have been transferred out to be returned to the States.

10 July - Our crack 14 piece band "The Flying Eagles" left for a 30-day tour of the UK.

11 July - The 335 Squadron Pilots had a "Little Party" for the purpose of building and maintaining morale. Major McKennon's "White Baby Grand" was moved to the Dispersal, so plenty of "Boogie-Woogie" was available, as were several cases of Mild and Bitter.

Every Sunday, weather permitting, planes were available to take up base personnel. There was a long list of those waiting for a ride.

12 July - All 334 Squadron personnel and Hqs Detachment met in the Station Cinema where they were addressed by Lt. Ratcliff and Capt. Evans. The meeting concerned the move of the outfit to Steeple Morden. It covered the personal equipment to be taken and what activities would take place once they were established. More passes and furloughs would be granted, and the feeling was that it would not be long before we would be headed for the States.

Pending the move, all EM were to be restricted to the base as of 21 July 1945. Neither the Officers nor the EM were very excited about the move. They knew they would never find another Debden in England or the States. For most, it was to be like leaving home.

16 July - Orders were received promoting Carl Payne from 1st Lt. to Captain, and Gardon Denson, Marvin Moore, Leo Garcin, Billy Skinner, and Milton Spencer from 2nd Lt. to 1st Lt.

The 4th Fighter Group has been authorized Bronze Service Stars for the following campaigns, for those in service on the appropriate campaign dates: Air Offensive, Europe, Normandy, Northern France, Rhineland, Ardennes, and Central Europe.

18 July - To the end of the month - The Group was busy with the movement of planes, equipment, and personnel to Steeple Morden, after which everything had to be set up ready for future operations. The distance to the new base was about 25 miles, and with all the equipment involved in some departments, it took several days.

21 July - The Station Glee Club made a trip to London to sing at Kingsway Hall for the purpose of making a recording. Later they gave a concert at the Stage Door Canteen before a very large and appreciative audience. Thirteen of the Group were from 335 Squadron, more than from any other 4th organization.

23 July - Every available truck, trailer, and Jeep was pressed into service for the move. Some made as many as five trips. Even the Pilot's drove of 14 ducks, and the 335 Squadron dog, "Meatball," were moved in order to make Steeple as much like home as possible.

The Mess was opened at Steeple Morden and everyone, including the Officers, sweated out the chow line for about 45 minutes. The Officers' Mess was undergoing renovations and would not open for several days.

2nd Lt. William Spencer was named Squadron Intelligence Officer and Squadron Historian.

The 335 lost 16 Pilots as they shipped out for the States:

Pass was
ebrate thi:
the base.

A sm
of civiliar
pasture. T
ing old far
the GIs sa
next pub.
signs of "r
V-J D
Matthews
Orden
The I
1st Li
1st Li
Capt.
The r
other than

17 Au
tory Leave
ties among
GIs. The
EMs, was
the homev
Anotl
for home.
On th

28 Au
By th
cut to 36 (

**Staff Ser
Lackey wa
E.M. to b
335 Squad
duties in
Section an
mases wit
was insigh
tain perm
portion of
which he I
to burn. L**

Lt. William G. Spencer 334 Squadron, in late 1945 became a Jack-of-all-trades as he was fullfilling his duties as a combat Pilot. He was assigned additional duties as Intelligence Officer, Squadron Historian, and Director of the 4th Group mens' chorus. Thanks to Lt. Spencer's foresight, Squadron diaries were saved for future perusal. Spencer collection.

1st Lts. William Henderson and Oliver Bucher made Captain, and 2nd Lts. Underwood and Heaton were promoted to 1st Lt.

25 July - Our Last Day at Debden! Roll call was held at 0530 hours and everyone ate; packed their barracks bags; cleaned the barracks; and embarked by convoy at 0830 hours as scheduled. The Convoy arrived at 0930. The rest of the day was spent settling in.

The 335 moved into an area they immediately named "Shady Lane," since it was really a country setting. Tall trees and a thatched roof house were on two sides. A green field of "Spuds" and a huge thatched roof barn with cows and chickens were on the other two sides. "We country boys" really feel at home, or is it "home sick?"

Major McKennon and Major Norley spent the day as carpenters. They put up a ceiling in their hut using salvaged belly-tank crates.

30 July - The Officers' Mess opened to operate on a normal schedule. The barber shop, having been closed for over a week, opened to a long queue waiting outside. The PX also opened while the Red Cross, open since Saturday, seemed just like our old Aero Club with Ruby, Eileen, and Dore behind the snack-bar counter.

31 July - Col. Smith called a meeting of all personnel at which were discussed personal problems such as Insurance Policies, Income Tax, and other problems that have arisen.

Not only was it payday, but the Liberty Run to Cambridge, that great morale booster, opened on a Monday, Friday, and Sunday schedule. Also, a new Liberty Run was set up to Hitchin on Tuesday, Thursday, and Saturday nights of each week.

Monthly Consolidated Strength Report

334 Squadron	Officers 37	Enlisted Men 213
335 Squadron	Officers 36	Enlisted Men 218
336 Squadron	Officers 40	Enlisted Men 202

1 August - Today, brighter radiance than ever before, shown on the name of the prophet, General Billy Mitchel, the Wright Brothers, and other pioneer men of aviation as America quietly celebrated the 38th anniversary of the U.S. Army Air Forces. In 1907, a Division of the U.S. Signal Corps was commissioned to study the possible use of a flying machine for military purposes.

The original contract was won by the Wright Brothers. It specified an airplane capable of flying for sixty minutes and attaining a speed of 40 miles an hour while carrying two men with a combined weight not to exceed 350 lbs.

The first plane crashed during trial flights, injuring Orville and causing the AAF's first fatality—Lt. Thomas Selfridge, in whose honor the field near Detroit was named. The second plane was tested successfully on the same spot in June 1909.

Lt. Henry (Hap) Arnold was among the first Military Pilots trained. He later set an altitude record of 6,540 feet in June 1912.

Today was declared a holiday in honor of this 38th anniversary, with Group personnel taking off in all directions for the day.

The Aero Club held its first dance at this base. We sadly missed the familiar faces of the WAAFs from North Weald who had been attending our dances for over two years. However, there were plenty of new girls present to take their places. If they were a sample of what is to come, our guys would be a happy bunch. The very capable band was an RAF band from Bassingbourn.

The most recently assigned Pilot in the 335 Squadron is Lt. Robert G. Williams. Williams did his first combat flying with the RAF. Upon transferring to the USAAF, he had been assigned to the 334 Squadron where he flew 103 Combat Missions. He was shot down over Germany 21 Mar 1944, and he became a POW at Barth on the Baltic. He found many of his buddies there. He was liberated on 14 May 1945 and made his way back to Debden. He requested that he be assigned to Debden in order to stay in England a little longer rather than being returned to the States.

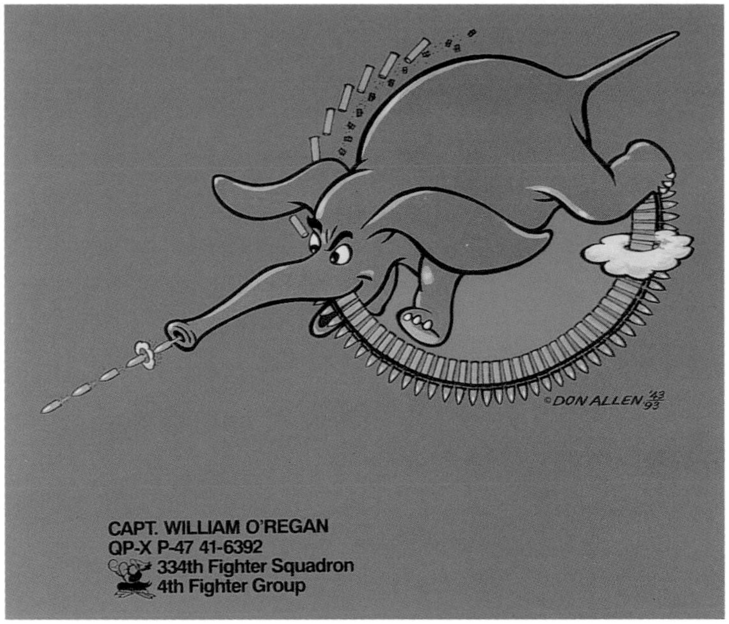
©DON ALLEN 43/93
CAPT. WILLIAM O'REGAN
QP-X P-47 41-6392
334th Fighter Squadron
4th Fighter Group

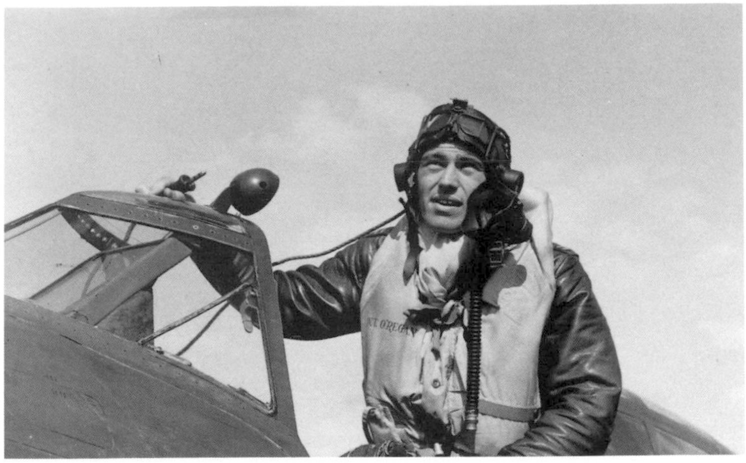

Captain William O'Regan's QP-X was a bullet spitting elephant. (*Above*) O'Regan sits in the cockpit of his P-47. He had been with 71ES and became Sq Ops Off of 334 Sq. (Konsler)

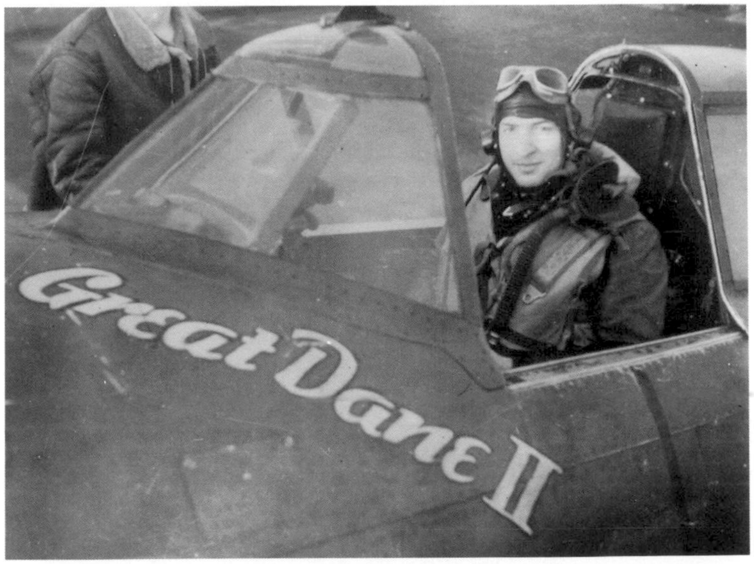
Great Dane II

Captain David Van Epps, 334 Sq., sits in P-47, QP-I, "Great Dane II." He was shot down by flak in April 44 and became a POW. (Weckbacher)

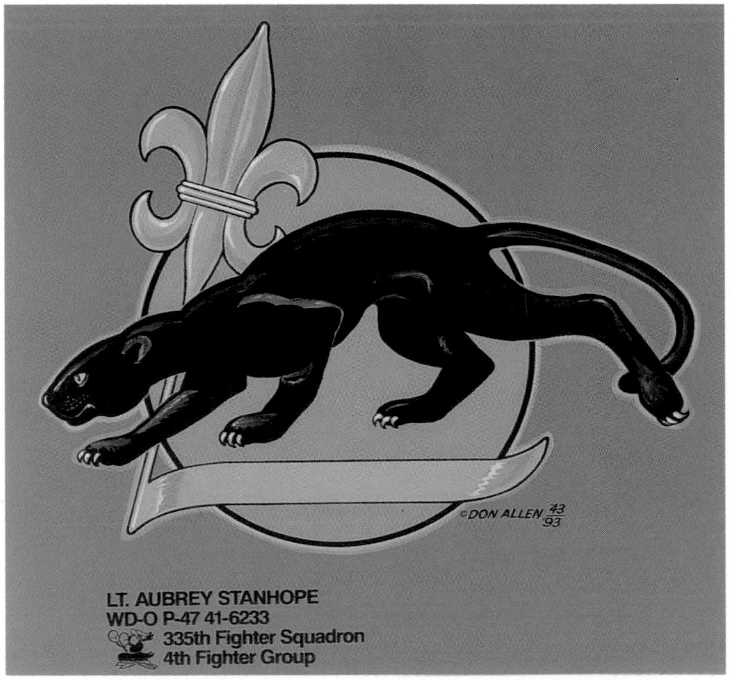
©DON ALLEN 43/93
LT. AUBREY STANHOPE
WD-O P-47 41-6233
335th Fighter Squadron
4th Fighter Group

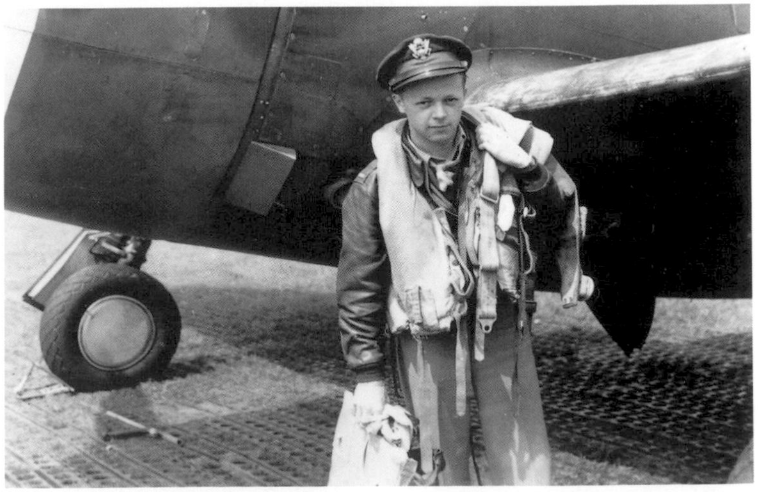

Lt. Aubrey Stanhope, 335 Sq., came to the Group from 121ES, and in Sept. 43 became a POW. His P-47, WD-O, sported a Black Panther on a *fleur de lis* background and was the first nose-art done by Don Allen. (Konsler)

(*Bottom, Right*) Capt. Robert Hobert 336 displays "Blue Goofis" VF-I. Capt. Hobert was downed in the North Sea and died of exposure on his return from a mission on 5 April 44. (Konsler) (*Bottom, Left*) Lt. Don Nee 336 SQ flew VF-N, "Sand Man" shown here by his crew chief J. Terrill. Nee was from 133ES. (George Anderson)

"Quack" was the fierce emblem of Capt. Robert Priser on his P-47 QP-L. Priser came from 71ES and became "A" Flight CO Sept 43. (Konsler)

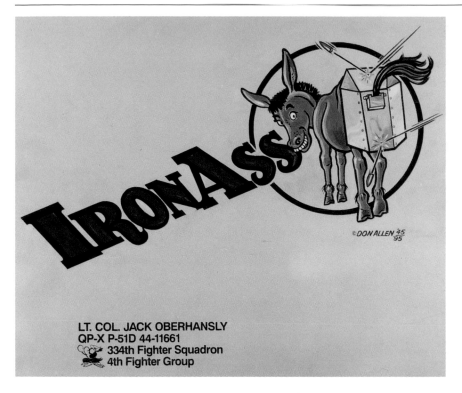

LT. COL. JACK OBERHANSLY
QP-X P-51D 44-11661
334th Fighter Squadron
4th Fighter Group

Jack Oberhansly's nose art, QP-X, "Iron Ass." Col. Oberhansly came to the 4th Group from the 78th Fighter Group where he was Deputy CO. He assumed the position of Deputy Group CO of the 4th and completed 150 combat missions by war's end. (Zigler)

CAPT. VERNON BOEHLE
QP-O P-47 41-6400
334th Fighter Squadron
4th Fighter Group

Capt. Vernon Boehle from 71ES flew P-47 "Indianapolis Indiana" prior to leaving in Nov, 43. (Konsler)